SOURCES OF INDIAN TRADITION

VOLUME II

INTRODUCTION TO
ORIENTAL CIVILIZATIONS

WM. THEODORE DE BARY, EDITOR

Sources of
Indian Tradition

VOLUME II

GENERAL EDITOR

Wm. Theodore de Bary

COMPILERS

Stephen N. Hay   I. H. Qureshi

COLUMBIA UNIVERSITY PRESS New York

The addition to the "Records of Civilization: Sources and Studies", of a group of translations of Oriental historical materials in a clothbound edition, from which this volume is taken, was made possible by funds granted by Carnegie Corporation of New York. That Corporation is not, however, the author, owner, publisher, or proprietor of this publication, and is not to be understood as approving by virtue of its grant any of the statements made or views expressed therein.

*Clothbound editions of Columbia University Press
books are Smyth-sewn and printed on
permanent and durable acid-free paper.*

PREFACE

The people of India and Pakistan, now numbering over 550 million, constitute more than one-sixth of the human race. Common sense alone makes us want to understand their ways of looking at life and their thinking on contemporary problems. Such an understanding is complicated by the fact that these people are heirs to a rich and complex set of cultural traditions, some reaching back more than three thousand years. The first volume of this work treated the genesis and efflorescence of these traditions—Hindu, Jain, Buddhist, and Islamic—in classical and medieval times. This volume deals principally with the transformation and enrichment which Hindu and Islamic traditions have undergone in a period of intensifying stimulation from, and reaction against, ideas and methods of thought and action emanating from the modern West.

The sources brought together here illustrate the main currents of thought developed by leaders of opinion on the Indian subcontinent in the nineteenth and twentieth centuries. Most of the men from whose writings selections have been chosen have contributed to clarifying and solving the contemporary problems of their society. The focus in these sources is thus neither on abstract ideas as such nor on particular events and issues, but on the middle ground where men confronting concrete situations enunciate general principles and policies as guides for action.

Of the thirty-six thinkers represented here, twenty-one can be identified as Hindus, nine as Muslims, four as Christians, one as Parsi, and one as both Hindu and Christian. The importance of religious affiliation decreases the closer we come to the present, however, and the chronological arrangement of the selections shows a gradual shift (evident also in modern Western thought) from religious to political and from political to economic preoccupations. While statements have been included from the writings of two influential British intellectuals who served in India, it would be manifestly impossible to do justice in this volume to all those Western intellectual traditions which Indians have assimilated through the use of the English language and a modern Western system of education. The sources of those traditions are already well-documented in other volumes of the *Records of Civilization* series. What the student should look for here are the many ways in which Western ideas—both ancient and modern—have been selected, reinterpreted, and combined with Indian traditions to form new syntheses, some of them (like nonviolent political action) having considerable relevance to the problems of other modernizing societies.

The reader of this anthology will readily perceive that traditions do not exist in a disembodied heaven of their own; they are created and transmitted by men, who frequently remold and restate them according to their individual likings and what they consider the needs of the times. "Hinduism" was for Gāndhi something quite different from what it was for Rāmmohun Roy in the nineteenth century or for Tilak or Nehru in the twentieth; nor was the "Islam" of Syed Ahmad identical with that of Iqbāl, Jinnāh, or Maudoodī. Indeed, the chief characteristic of Hindu and Islamic thought in modern South Asia has been the diversity of interpretations placed upon ancient traditions by a succession of leading thinkers, each of whom faced a different situation within his own community, within the India of his day, and with regard to the world outside India. A familiarity with these many views of tradition should deepen our insight into the further interpretations of their heritage which Indian and Pakistani intellectuals will formulate in the years to come.

STEPHEN N. HAY

Chicago
September 16, 1963

EXPLANATORY NOTE

In this reprinting, a number of minor changes have been made in the wording of introductory passages and a few errors have been corrected. In one case (the first selection from Vinobā Bhāve), a more accurate text of a document has been given; otherwise the sources remain as in previous printings. Full bibliographical data can be obtained from the list of sources in the clothbound edition.

As an aid to correct pronunciation of certain names and terms, long vowels have been marked with the superscribed macron in the essays or paragraphs introducing the sources. Pronounce "a" short as in but; "ā" long as in pot; "i" short as in pin; "ī" long as in bee; "u" short as in put; "ū" long as in boot. An easy way to memorize the sounds of these six vowels is to practice repeating them as a sequence of three pairs—a-ā, i-ī, u-ū. Some inconsistencies remain in the use of macrons; for example, "Gāndhi" appears in the text, rather than the more correct "Gāndhī."

Dr. Qureshi, now Vice Chancellor of the University of Karachi and formerly Visiting Professor at Columbia University, was largely responsible for the compilation of Chapters XXIV and XXVI. Dr. Hay, of the University of Chicago, was responsible for the other chapters and the editing.

The compilers wish to record here their thanks to all those who assisted them with criticisms and suggestions and especially the initiator and editor of this volume, Professor Wm. Theodore de Bary. Dr. Qureshi also wishes to thank Dr. S. M. Ikram, and Dr. Hay expresses his gratitude to Professors Amiya Chakravarty, Nirmal Kumar Bose, the late Sudhinranath Datta, Eloise Knapp Hay, R. C. Majumdar, Richard L. Park, Sibnarayan Ray, Percival Spear, and J. A. B. van Buitenen. Both compilers are indebted to Professor Eloise Knapp Hay for the chapter decorations.

Without the assistance of many publishers, a book of source readings such as this is not possible, and we are grateful for the cooperation of the following: Advaita Ashrama, Almora, India; Allen & Unwin, Ltd., London; All-Pakistan Political Science Association, Lahore; Mohammad Ashraf, Lahore; Asiatic Society of Mangal, Calcutta; Sri Aurobindo Ashram, Pondichéry, India; The Bodley Head, Ltd., London; Clarendon Press, Oxford; Current Book House, Bombay; Ganesh and Co., Ltd., Madras, India; S. P. Gokhale, Poona, India; Harvard University Press, Cambridge, Mass.; Hero Publications, Lahore; Indian Printing Works, Lahore; The India Press, Allahabad, India; Kitabistan, Allahabad, India; S. K. Lahin and Co., Calcutta; Luzac and Co., London; Macmillan & Co., Ltd., London and New York; al-Manar Academy, Lahore; Modern Review, Calcutta; John Murray, London, and the "Wisdom of the East" series; The Muslim World; G. A. Natesan and Co., Madras, India; The Navajivan Trust, Ahmedabad, India; P. M. Neogi, Calcutta; Orient Longmans Ltd., Calcutta; Oxford University Press, London; Pakistan Herald Press, Karachi; Panjab University Press, Lahore; People's Publishing House, Ltd., Bombay; Renaissance Publishers, Ltd., Calcutta; Roy and Son, Calcutta; A. W. Sahasvabuddhe, Sevagram, India; Sadharan Brahmo Samaj, Calcutta; Sarvodaya, Bombay; Theosophical Publishing Society, Banaras, India; Thomas and Co., Calcutta; Thompson and Co. Ltd., Madras, India; R. B. Tilak, Poona, India; The Vedanta Society, New York; Vedic Yantralaya, Ajmer, India; The Viking Press, Inc., New York; Visvabharati, Calcutta.

CONTENTS

[xii]

India and Pakistan

0   100   200   300 Miles

— — — — International Boundaries
— · — · — State Boundaries
★ National Capital
◉ Provincial Capital

AFGHANISTAN

Kabul ★

Islamabad ★

KASHMIR

Srinagar ◉

HIMACHAL PRADESH

WEST PAKISTAN

Lahore ◉   Amritsar ◉

Simla ◉

Chandigarh ◉

PUNJAB

NEPAL

SIKKIM

BHUTAN

NORTH EAST FRONTIER AGENCY

Delhi ◉

★ New Delhi

Kathmandu ◉
Bhadgaon ◉

ASSAM

NAGA

Shillong ◉

Karachi ◉

Jaipur ◉

RAJASTHAN

UTTAR PRADESH

Lucknow ◉

Allahabad ◉

Patna ◉
Banaras ◉

BIHAR

MANIPUR

EAST PAKISTAN

Dacca ◉

Arabian Sea

GUJARAT

Ahmadabad ◉

Baroda ·

Bhopal ◉

MADHYA PRADESH

Calcutta ◉

ORISSA

Bhubavaneshwar ◉
Puri ◉

MAHARASHTRA

Bombay ·

Poona ·

Hyderabad ◉

Bay of Bengal

MYSORE

ANDHRA PRADESH

GOA

Bangalore ◉

Madras ◉

Pondicherry ·

ANDAMAN and
NICOBAR ISLANDS

KERALA

MADRAS

Trivandrum ◉

CEYLON

Colombo ★

CHRONOLOGICAL TABLE

Modern India and Pakistan

1498	Vasco da Gama rounds the southernmost tip of Africa and lands on the Malabar coast.
1600	Queen Elizabeth grants charter to "certain adventurers for the trade of the East Indies."
1690	Calcutta founded by an agent of the English East India Company.
1742–1754	Dupleix Governor of Pondichéry for French East India Company.
1757	Clive's victory at Plassey gives English control of Bengal.
1784	Asiatick Society founded in Calcutta under Sir William Jones (1746–1794).
1799–1803	Abū-Tāleb (1752–1806?) visits England and Europe.
1815–1830	Rāmmohun Roy (1772–1833) active in religious controversy and social reform in Calcutta.
1818	Defeat of Marāthā Peshwa ends effective Indian resistance to British rule.
1827–1831	H.L.V. Derozio (1809–1831) teaches at Hindu College, Calcutta.
1828	Rāmmohun Roy founds Brāhmo Samāj.
1833	East India Company deprived by Parliament of all commercial functions.
1835	English system of education introduced, following Macaulay's recommendation.
1843	Debendranāth Tagore (1817–1905) re-establishes the Brāhmo Samāj.
1857–1858	Mutiny of Sepoy troops and widespread rebellion in Northern India.
1858	East India Company's rule replaced by that of a viceroy appointed by the British crown.
1865	Keshub Chunder Sen (1843–1884) secedes from the Brāhmo Samāj.
1875	Swami Dayānanda (1824–1883) founds the Ārya Samāj at Bombay. Syed Ahmad Khān (1817–1898) founds Muhammadan Anglo-Oriental College at Ālīgarh.
1877	Queen Victoria proclaimed Empress of India.
1879	Keshub Chunder Sen proclaims the New Dispensation.
1885	Indian National Congress inaugurated in Bombay.
1886	Death of Sri Rāmakrishna (born 1834).
1893	Mohandās K. Gāndhi (1869–1948) begins twenty year's work as lawyer in South Africa.
1894	Death of Bankim Chandra Chatterjee (born 1838).

1897	Swami Vivekānanda (1862–1902) receives triumphant welcome on return to India; founds Rāmakrishna Mission.
1901	Death of Justice M. G. Rānade (born 1842).
1905	Partition of Bengal arouses nationalist agitation, in which Surendranāth Banerjea (1848–1926), Bāl Gangādhar Tilak (1856–1920), Rabīndranāth Tagore (1861–1941), Brahmabāndhab Upādhyāy (1861–1907) and Aurobindo Ghose (1872–1950) take prominent part.
1906	Muslim League founded.
1907	Indian National Congress split by quarrel between Moderates and Extremists.
1909	Morley-Minto Reforms grant Muslim demand for separate electorates.
1911	Partition of Bengal annulled. Transfer of the Indian capital from Calcutta to Delhi announced.
1913	Rabīndranāth Tagore awarded Nobel Prize for his *Gītāñjali*.
1915	Death of G. K. Gokhale (born 1866).
1916	Moderate, Extremist and Muslim League leaders agree on demand for a national legislative assembly to be elected on a communal basis.
1919	Montagu-Chelmsford Reforms provide for legislative assembly to begin in 1921. Amritsar massacre.
1920	Death of Tilak. Gāndhi starts first nation-wide civil disobedience movement (suspended in 1922 after outbreaks of violence).
1920–1924	Khilāfat Movement, led by Muhammad Alī (1879–1930).
1930	Muhammad Iqbāl (1873–1938) proposes separate state for India's Muslims.
1930–1934	Second nation-wide civil disobedience movement.
1935	Government of India Act grants provincial self-government.
1940	Muslim League, under President Muhammad Alī Jinnāh, demands creation of sovereign Muslim state.
1941	Subhās Chandra Bose (1897–1945) escapes to join the Axis powers.
1942	Congress rejects Cripps' offer, demands British quit India.
1945–1947	Amid communal rioting and threats of mutiny, the British Labor government prepares to grant India complete self-government.
1947	India, under Prime Minister Jawaharlāl Nehru (1889–), and Pakistan, under Prime Minister Liāquat Ālī Khān (1895–1951) become independent dominions.
1948	Gāndhi assassinated in New Delhi. Death of Muhammad Ālī Jinnāh (born 1876).
1950	India becomes a republic within the Commonwealth.
1951–1952	Congress Party wins national elections. First Five-Year Plan begins.
1956	Pakistan adopts Islamic Constitution.

CHAPTER XX

THE OPENING OF INDIA TO THE WEST

The spreading of European power and civilization over the entire surface of the globe in recent centuries can be viewed as a continuing series of intrusions into the cultures of the non-European world. Nowhere in Asia have the effects of this penetration been more profoundly felt than in India. Because she was the first to receive the impact of European expansion, and the only major civilization on the continent to fall directly under foreign rule, the influence of the West on her life and thought has been deep and lasting.

The first Europeans to reach India by sea were the Portuguese. Their intrepid captain, Vasco da Gama, landed on the Malabar coast in 1498. Seventy-five years later we find them received at the Mughal court by the solicitous Emperor Akbar. In the words of Akbar's biographer: "They produced many of the rarities of their country, and the appreciative Khedive [the Emperor] received each one with special favor and made inquiries about the wonders of Portugal and the manners and customs of Europe. It seemed as if he did this from a desire of knowledge, for his sacred heart is a depot of spiritual and physical sciences. But his boding soul wished that these inquiries might be the means of civilizing (*istīnās,* i.e. familiarity or sociability) this savage [unsocial] race." [1] Akbar later summoned Jesuit missionaries from Goa to expound the principles of their religion, in which he was much interested, but he laughingly preferred his three hundred wives to the Christian ideal of monogamy.

When the French and British East India Companies first established their tiny trading settlements along the eastern and western coasts of India in the seventeenth century, the great empire of the Mughals still held sway. A century later it had collapsed, and various Muslim and Hindu chieftains were fighting among themselves for possession of its remnants.

[1] Abū'l Fazl, *Akbar-Nāma* (tr. by H. Beveridge), III, 37.

[1]

In protecting their commercial interests the sea-borne Europeans were drawn into the struggle. When in the early nineteenth century the British finally emerged victorious over both the local contenders and their French rivals, they found themselves masters of a population speaking fourteen different major languages, with two-ninths of them following Islam and most of the rest belonging to various Hindu castes and sub-castes, and with small minorities professing Sikhism, Jainism, Buddhism, Zoroastrianism, Nestorian Christianity and Judaism. Onto this cultural crazy-quilt the new rulers of India imposed a pattern of their own—not a religious but a secular one. Law and order, efficient government and free trade, were the new gods, and all Indians hoping for worldly success bowed down to them and worshiped them.

While some Indians opposed and the majority ignored the coming of the new order, others actively abetted the opening of their country to the West. Four representative men, each of whom played a notable part in the history of this period and left to posterity written records of his thinking, are considered in this chapter—one a Hindu merchant of the 1740s and 50s, the second a Muslim aristocrat of the early 1800s, the third a Christian of mixed European and Indian ancestry, and the fourth a brāhman scholar-reformer and founder of a new religious movement. The last two were active in Calcutta in the 1820s—just at the time the British were overcoming their earlier reluctance to interfere with established cultural patterns, and shortly before they took the decisive step of introducing English education.

Although these four men came from quite different religious and regional backgrounds, the question of what to do about the Westerner and his culture was in the forefront of their minds. All showed an inclination toward some aspects of the new culture and (except for the Christian) an aversion toward other aspects, but even in their likes and dislikes they differed noticeably. The attitudes which each reveals in his writings therefore give us unique insights into the complexity of Indian society in this crucial period, and furnish us with valuable clues to the later evolution of Indian thought as it responded to the incessant challenge of the West.

ĀNANDA RANGA PILLAI: HINDU AGENT FOR THE FRENCH

India in the eighteenth century was a land rife with internal dissensions and devoid of any central political power. Muslim governors and Hindu chieftains vied with each other for the remnants of the Mughal empire, while most of the population pursued their traditional occupations in relative indifference to the religious or regional origins of their rulers. Under these circumstances, the scattered seacoast settlements of the European trading companies attracted little attention, except from the Indian merchants who found it profitable to act as intermediaries between the foreign traders and the people of the hinterland.

The Hindu merchant Ānanda Ranga Pillai (1709–1761) rose to a position of great trust and influence as chief agent for the French colony of Pondichéry. Thanks to the diary which he kept faithfully for twenty-five years, we have an almost Pepysian record of the life of the tiny settlement and of its leading Indian citizen. Although most of the diary is a rather tedious chronicle of business transactions and political intrigue, we can find in it occasional glimpses of the attitude of an important Hindu toward his French masters and toward his own society.

One striking feature of *The Private Diary of Ananda Ranga Pillai* is the total absence in its author of national consciousness or sense of political loyalty to fellow Indians, as opposed to Europeans. Trade was his family's hereditary occupation and he therefore entered naturally into a symbiotic relation with the merchants from across the sea. He ardently supported the empire-building ambitions of his sponsor, François Dupleix, and identified the latter's fortunes with his own, regarding Dupleix not as a foreigner but simply as an individual with whom he enjoyed a mutually profitable connection. At the same time Ānanda Ranga remained a staunch and orthodox Hindu, never violating in the slightest the rules of his religion. In this respect he is representative of many generations of Indians from his day down to our own whose interest in things Western remained at the level of externals, and for whom European culture and thought seemed of little importance in comparison with the time-tested value of their traditional beliefs.

[3]

ĀNANDA RANGA PILLAI
On the Greatness of Dupleix

It is clear from his diary that Ānanda Ranga Pillai admired the brilliant French adventurer and preferred his rule to that of the Marāthā or Muslim potentates then contending for power in South India.

[From *The Private Diary of Ananda Ranga Pillai*, I, 299–301]

The English have captured the ships bound for Pondichéry, and have received a reinforcement of men-of-war from England and other places. This accounts for their activity; nevertheless they are much troubled owing to their leader, the governor, being a worthless fellow, and a man devoid of wisdom. Although Pondichéry receives no ships, her government lacks funds, the enemy has seized her vessels, she is feeble and wanting in strength, and her inhabitants are in misery; although she has all these disadvantages, no sooner is mention made of her than the nawabs [governors], and other magnates in the interior, become alarmed. When her name is uttered, her enemies tremble, and dare not stir. All this is owing to the ability, readiness, and luck of the present governor, M. Dupleix. His method of doing things is not known to any one, because none else is possessed of the quick mind with which he is gifted. In patience he has no equal. He has peculiar skill in carrying out his plans and designs; in the management of affairs, and in governing; in fitting his advice to times and persons; in maintaining at all times an even countenance; in doing things through proper agents; in addressing them in appropriate terms; and in assuming a bearing at once dignified and courteous towards all. . . .

Owing to these qualities, he has acquired such a reputation as to make all people say that he is the master, and that others are useless individuals. Because God has favored him with unswerving resolution, and because he is governing Pondichéry on an occasion when she is threatened with danger, her inhabitants are confident and fearless, and are even able to defy the people of towns opposed to them. This is due solely to the skill and administrative ability of the governor. If he did not occupy this position, and if the danger had occurred in the times of his predecessors, the inhabitants of this city would be a hundred times more disturbed and terrified than the followers of the invader: such is the general opinion regarding M. Dupleix. Besides this, if his courage, character, bearing, greatness of mind, and skill in the battlefield, were put to the test, he could be compared only with the Emperor Aurangzib, and Louis XIV; and not with any other monarch. But how am I to paint all his high and praiseworthy characteristics? I have described him only so far as my simple mind allows me. People of better capacity could do this more completely than I.

An Astrological Misfortune

Ānanda Ranga was a firm believer in astrology. It struck him as a calamity, explainable only by reference to the stars, that his brother should be so unusually devoid of worldly ambition.
[From *The Private Diary of Ananda Ranga Pillai*, III, 9–10]

Although my brother is thirty-four or thirty-five years old, he has no desire to acquire wealth, and no ambition to figure conspicuously in the service of the Company. He is, further, too retiring to hold any intercourse with Europeans. Far from accusing him, however, I can only worry myself with the thought that God has created him thus, and blame my own ill-luck. The young men of these days become, from their fifth year, thoroughly filled with aspirations. The great desire for employment, coupled, as it is, with a strong craving to acquire wealth, that is evinced by them is quite extraordinary, and is beyond one's comprehension and powers of expression. The very opposite to this, my brother—who is hard on thirty-five—although naturally possessed of the gifts of high culture, excellent parts, guarded temper, winning manners, handsome presence, and fortunate birth, is not blessed with the courage and spirit of enterprise which are indispensable to raising oneself to distinction. It is this defect that induces him to cast aside all aspirations to greatness, and to prefer to remain at home in obscurity. This warp in his mind I attribute to the weak and fruitless star which, according to my horoscope, will cast its shadow over me for some months to come. I cannot but impute to this circumstance his desire to resign his post in that city of Kubera [The God of Wealth], which has recently come under our rule, and to return empty-handed. This bears out the predictions of astrologers that my career, up to my thirty-eighth year, will not be marked by success. I entertain no doubt as to the truth of their statements, and shall, therefore, not lay any blame at his door.

[5]

An Improper Feast

When his arch-rival, a convert to Christianity, gave a public feast for Hindus and Christians alike, Ānanda Ranga's sense of propriety was offended. The firm maintenance of Hindu custom his attitude exemplifies was to be a major stumbling-block to social reformers of the succeeding centuries.

[From *The Private Diary of Ananda Ranga Pillai*, I, 293-95]

This day, there was an event worthy of record. In the village of Reddi-palaiyam, to the east of Ozhukarai, a church has been constructed by Kanakarāya Mudali, and he has placed some images therein. In honor of this, he invited, without distinction, all the Brāhmans, Vellāzhas, Kōmuttis, Chettis, goldsmiths, weavers, oil-mongers, and people of other castes; and all Europeans and Christians, and entertained them with a feast at Ozhukarai. Choultries [hostels] and gardens were allotted for the preparation of food by Brāhman cooks, and meals for Vellāzhas were cooked in the house of Agambadaiyans. All the arrangements were made in strict conformity with the religious scruples of each caste, and the people who attended received every attention. Meals for Europeans were prepared at Pondichéry, and brought over to Ozhukarai. Tables were procured for them to dine at, and every comfort was provided for them. The Governor M. Dupleix, and his consort, in company with all the members of Council, repaired thither, and partook of the banquet. He remained until five in the evening, and then returned to Mortāndi Chāvadi. All the people of Pondichéry who went to Ozhukarai enjoyed themselves, and proceeded homewards in the evening. Neither in the arrangements which Kanakarāya Mudali made, nor in the supplies which he procured, was there anything wanting. Nevertheless, despite the heavy cost of the entertainment, and the elaborate nature of the preparations, there was something which detracted from the splendor, grace, and excellence of the hospitalities. Persons of every persuasion should abide by the rules prescribed for them: their conduct so regulated would look consistent. Although of a different persuasion, he followed the practice of a Hindu; assembled people of that religion; and gave them a treat which afforded room for dispraise and derision, and every man gave vent to his criticisms as he saw fit. If he wished to conform to the rules of his church, and the commands of his scriptures, he should have entertained only the Euro-

[6]

peans, native Christians, pariahs,[1] and such others; whose associations brought them in touch with his religion. Even this would be considered derogatory to one of his position and reputation. However magnificent may be the style of any social act in which one indulges, if it be at variance with the established practice of the community concerned, it cannot redound to one's credit. If a man who has forsaken his religion, and joined another, reverts to the manners and customs of his former belief, he must inevitably draw upon himself contempt.

The Doctrine of Predestination

Commenting on Dupleix's ignominious departure from Pondichéry in 1754, Ānanda Ranga revealed his belief that all a man's thoughts and actions are preordained.

[From *The Private Diary of Ananda Ranga Pillai*, IX, 54]

This great man has been arrested and put with his property on board ship. Such is the fate of the man who seeks his own will without the fear of God; but he who acts with circumspection, and refrains from molesting the upright, escapes falling into sin. But a man's thoughts depend upon the times and seasons. Who then can be blamed? Such is the world. He who is destined to happiness will be wise; and he who is destined to misery will be foolish. Do not the Vedas say so? What was to be has come to pass.

The Collapse of the Old Order

Toward the end of French domination over South India, an inexperienced governor appointed a man of low caste to the position formerly held by Ānanda Ranga. Reflecting on the changes which the French had introduced into hierarchical Hindu society, the diarist commented bitterly.

[From *The Private Diary of Ananda Ranga Pillai*, XI, 318]

In times of decay, order disappears, giving place to disorder, and justice to injustice. Men no longer observe their caste rules, but transgress their bounds, so that the castes are confused and force governs. One man takes another man's wife and his property. Everyone kills or robs another. In short, there is anarchy. Who among the low is lower than a pariah beggar? And what worse can be imagined than for such a one to rule?

[1] A low caste of Hindus in South India.

[7]

Unless justice returns, the country will be ruined. This is what men say, and I have written it briefly.

ABŪ TĀLEB: MUSLIM TRAVELER TO THE WEST

Although Europeans had been visiting India since the days of Marco Polo, few Indians had the curiosity or the wherewithal to acquaint themselves at first hand with Europe and its culture. Hindus considered overseas travel to be defiling, and automatically outcast those who ventured abroad. Muslims, on the other hand, were not only free from such restrictions but had the example of Muhammad—a great traveler—and the duty of a pilgrimage to Mecca to encourage them in venturing overseas. It is, therefore, not surprising that one of the first educated Indians to travel to Europe should be a Muslim.

Mirza Abū Tāleb Khān was born in Lucknow in 1752 of Persian and Turkish descent. His mature life was spent in the service of the governors of Bengal and of Oudh, but a jealous prime minister retired him and cut off his pension. Abū Tāleb then sought employment with the British, whom he had assisted in putting down a rebellious Hindu prince. He moved his family to Calcutta and seems to have learned English fairly well, but his hopes of securing a good position were disappointed. He grew very despondent, and when a Scottish friend suggested they travel to England together at his expense, he reflected, ". . . that, as the journey was long and replete with danger, some accident might cause my death, by which I should be delivered from the anxieties of the world, and the ingratitude of mankind. I therefore accepted his friendly offer, and resolved to undertake the journey."

Despite his pessimistic frame of mind, Abū Tāleb seems by his own account to have greatly enjoyed his three years in Europe. No sooner had he arrived in London than he was presented to the king and queen, dubbed "the Persian prince," and lionized by the English aristocracy. He had ample opportunity to observe his hosts, and when writing his recollections did not hesitate to enumerate their national vices as well as their virtues.

The Travels of Mirza Abū Tāleb Khān, written in Persian on his return to Calcutta, gives us a unique insight into the reactions of an aristocratic Indian Muslim to English life. For the most part a careful account of the curiosities and customs he observed, the book is remarkably barren of reflections on the cultural and religious foundations of Western civilization, leaving the impression that as a Muslim he regarded them as unworthy of serious attention. On the other hand, the lighter side of London life greatly appealed to him, as it has to other Indians since his day. Abū Tāleb's comments on English characteristics, though superficial, are important as indicative of the major differences in outlook between the Indo-Persian culture created by the Mughals and the Indo-British culture which superseded it.

ABŪ TĀLEB
Muslim Indifference to Learning About the West

Abū Tāleb realized that his interest in Europe was exceptional and correctly predicted in the introduction to his book that his fellow-Muslims would continue to ignore Western learning out of "zeal for their religion."
[From *The Travels of Mirza Abū Tāleb Khān,* I, 1–6]

Glory be to God, the Lord of all worlds, who has conferred innumerable blessings on mankind, and accomplished all the laudable desires of his creatures. Praise be also to the Chosen of Mankind [Muhammad], the traveler over the whole expanse of the heavens, and benedictions without end on his descendants and companions.

The wanderer over the face of the earth, Abū Tāleb, the son of Mohammed of Ispahan, begs leave to inform the curious in biography, that, owing to several adverse circumstances, finding it inconvenient to remain at home, he was compelled to undertake many tedious journeys, during which he associated with men of all nations and beheld various wonders, both by sea and by land.

It therefore occurred to him, that if he were to write all the circumstances of his journey through Europe, to describe the curiosities and wonders which he saw, and to give some account of the manner and customs of the various nations he visited, all of which are little known to Asiatics, it would afford a gratifying banquet to his countrymen.

He was also of opinion, that many of the customs, inventions, sciences, and ordinances of Europe, the good effects of which are apparent

[9]

in those countries, might with great advantage be imitated by Mohammedans.

Impressed with these ideas, he, on his first setting out on his travels, commenced a journal, in which he daily inserted every event, and committed to writing such reflections as occurred to him at the moment: and on his return to Calcutta, in the year of the Hejira 1218 (A.D. 1803), having revised and abridged his notes, he arranged them in the present form.

[Here Abū Tāleb changes from the third to the first person, and laments:] I have named this work . . . "The Travels of Tāleb in the Regions of Europe"; but when I reflect on the want of energy and the indolent dispositions of my countrymen, and the many erroneous customs which exist in all Mohammedan countries and among all ranks of Mussulmans, I am fearful that my exertions will be thrown away. The great and the rich, intoxicated with pride and luxury, and puffed up with the vanity of their possessions, consider universal science as comprehended in the circle of their own scanty acquirements and limited knowledge; while the poor and common people, from the want of leisure, and overpowered by the difficulty of procuring a livelihood, have not time to attend to their personal concerns, much less to form desires for the acquirement of information on new discoveries and inventions; although such a passion has been implanted by nature in every human breast, as an honor and an ornament to the species. I therefore despair of their reaping any fruit from my labors, being convinced that they will consider this book of no greater value than the volumes of tales and romances which they peruse merely to pass away their time, or are attracted thereto by the easiness of the style. It may consequently be concluded, that as they will find no pleasure in reading a work which contains a number of foreign names, treats on uncommon subjects, and alludes to other matters which cannot be understood at the first glance, but require a little time for consideration, they will, under pretense of zeal for their religion, entirely abstain and refrain from perusing it.

Ode to London

Shortly after his arrival in London, Abū Tāleb composed a poem in praise of that city and its beauties. The following is a literal translation from the Persian.

[From *The Travels of Mirza Abū Tāleb Khān*, I, 218–20]

Henceforward we will devote our lives to London, and its heart-alluring
    Damsels:
Our hearts are satiated with viewing fields, gardens, rivers, and palaces.

We have no longing for the Toba, Sudreh, or other trees of Paradise:
We are content to rest under the shade of these terrestrial Cypresses.

If the Shaikh of Mecca is displeased at our conversion, who cares?
May the Temple which has conferred such blessings on us, and its Priests,
    flourish!

Fill the goblet with wine! If by this I am prevented from returning
To my old religion, I care not; nay, I am the better pleased.

If the prime of my life has been spent in the service of an Indian Cupid,
It matters not: I am now rewarded by the smiles of the British Fair.

Adorable creatures! whose flowing tresses, whether of flaxen or of jetty
    hue,
Or auburn gay, delight my soul, and ravish all my senses!

Whose ruby lips would animate the torpid clay, or marble statue!
Had I a renewal of life, I would, with rapture, devote it to your service!

These wounds of Cupid, on your heart, Tāleba, are not accidental:
They were engendered by Nature, like the streaks on the leaf of a tulip.

The Evil of Western Materialism

Abū Tāleb's catalogue of the vices of the English is one of the most interesting
parts of his book. In criticizing their irreligion, worldliness and love of luxury,
he anticipated the argument widely used by Indian nationalists a century later,
i.e., that Westerners were incurably materialistic and therefore unfit to rule a
religious country like India. In fairness to the English, he later added a shorter
list of their virtues.

    [From *The Travels of Mirza Abū Tāleb Khān*, II, 128–31]

The first and greatest defect I observed in the English is their want of
faith in religion, and their great inclination to philosophy [atheism]. The
effects of these principles, or rather want of principle, is very conspicuous
in the lower orders of people, who are totally devoid of honesty. They
are, indeed, cautious how they transgress against the laws, from fear of

punishment; but whenever an opportunity offers of purloining any thing without the risk of detection, they never pass it by. They are also ever on the watch to appropriate to themselves the property of the rich, who, on this account, are obliged constantly to keep their doors shut, and never to permit an unknown person to enter them. At present, owing to the vigilance of the magistrates, the severity of the laws, and the honor of the superior classes of people, no very bad consequences are to be apprehended; but if ever such nefarious practices should become prevalent and should creep in among the higher classes, inevitable ruin must ensue.

The second defect most conspicuous in the English character is pride, or insolence. Puffed up with their power and good fortune for the last fifty years, they are not apprehensive of adversity, and take no pains to avert it. Thus, when the people of London, some time ago, assembled in mobs on account of the great increase of taxes and high price of provisions, and were nearly in a state of insurrection—although the magistrates, by their vigilance in watching them, and by causing parties of soldiers to patrole the streets day and night, to disperse all persons whom they saw assembling together, succeeded in quieting the disturbance—yet no pains were afterwards taken to eradicate the evil. Some of the men in power said it had been merely a plan of the artificers to obtain higher wages (an attempt frequently made by the English tradesmen); others were of opinion that no remedy could be applied; therefore no further notice was taken of the affair. All this, I say, betrays a blind confidence, which, instead of meeting the danger and endeavoring to prevent it, waits till the misfortune arrives, and then attempts to remedy it. Such was the case with the late king of France, who took no step to oppose the Revolution till it was too late. This self-confidence is to be found, more or less, in every Englishman; it however differs much from the pride of the Indians and Persians.

Their third defect is a passion for acquiring money and their attachment to worldly affairs. Although these bad qualities are not so reprehensible in them as in countries more subject to the vicissitudes of fortune, (because, in England, property is so well protected by the laws that every person reaps the fruits of his industry, and, in his old age, enjoys the earnings or economy of his youth,) yet sordid and illiberal habits are generally found to accompany avarice and parsimony, and, consequently, render the possessor of them contemptible; on the contrary, generosity, if it does not launch into prodigality, but is guided by the hand of prudence, will render a man respected and esteemed.

The Strange Notion of Progress

Abū Tāleb's evident surprise at the modern Western belief in progress and the infinite perfectibility of human knowledge reflects the fact that before the advent of the British this idea had not occurred to Indian thinkers.

[From *The Travels of Mirza Abū Tāleb Khān*, II, 165–66]

The English have very peculiar opinions on the subject of *perfection*. They insist that it is merely an ideal quality, and depends entirely upon comparison; that mankind have risen, by degrees, from the state of savages to the exalted dignity of the great philosopher Newton; but that, so far from having yet attained *perfection*, it is possible that, in future ages, philosophers will look with as much contempt on the acquirements of Newton as we now do on the rude state of the arts among savages. If this axiom of theirs be correct, man has yet much to learn, and all his boasted knowledge is but vanity.

HENRY DEROZIO: POET AND EDUCATOR

One of the most brilliant figures in the intellectual world of Calcutta in the early nineteenth century was the Christian poet Henry Louis Vivian Derozio (1809–1831). His father, a successful merchant, was probably of mixed Portuguese and Indian descent, while both his mother and the stepmother who brought him up were English. He thus belonged to that tiny racial group accepted neither by the British ruling class, nor by Hindu and Muslim society—the so-called Anglo-Indians.

Derozio was raised in the Protestant faith and received the best English education available in Calcutta. Nevertheless, his part-Indian ancestry meant he could not hold a responsible government post. Finding office work for his father distasteful, he turned for a living to his uncle's indigo factory in the country. There, on the banks of the Ganges, he composed romantic poems whose publication made him the talk of Calcutta at seventeen. Two years later he was appointed assistant headmaster at the famous Hindu College, where the brightest young Bengalis were flocking to learn the new knowledge from the West. Here he found his true calling, and in two years achieved an ascendancy over the minds and hearts of his students that lasted long after his premature death.

Derozio's influence was as great outside the classroom as in. The discussion group he founded, the Academic Association, drew not only his pupils but some of the best minds in the city, both Indian and British. With keen intellect and unbounded fancy he expanded on such subjects as "free will . . . fate, faith, the sacredness of truth, the high duty of cultivating virtue and the meanness of vice, the nobility of patriotism, the attributes of God, and the arguments for and against the existence of the Deity . . . the hollowness of idolatry and the shams of the priesthood. . . ." According to his biographer, these themes ". . . stirred to their very depths the young, fearless, hopeful hearts of the leading Hindoo youths of Calcutta."[1]

Like Socrates in ancient Athens, Derozio soon found his influence on the young denounced by the orthodox as pernicious. Parents kept their sons from attending the Hindu College, and finally the board of managers demanded his resignation. His rejoinder, reproduced below, shows that deep love of intellectual freedom which is one of the best traditions of the modern West.

In another respect Derozio represents the first echo in India of Western ideas and attitudes. His verse carries the flavor of his contemporaries, the English romantic poets, and the sentiments he expresses remind us of theirs. His patriotism is an especially significant example. His poems to India are virtually the first expressions of Indian nationalist thought, and their appearance among other poetry whose inspiration is clearly derivative dramatizes the fact that modern nationalism is essentially an alien importation into the Indian world of ideas.

While battling the bonds of religious conservatism, he died of cholera at the age of twenty-two, leaving a generation of followers to carry on his work. One of his pupils, for example, was the Christian poet Michael Dutt, a pioneer in the creation of modern Bengali literature. His tremendous personal popularity with the youth of his time—despite his linguistic, racial, and religious affinity with the foreign rulers of the land—reflects the growing influence of Western thought among his countrymen. Symbol of the new India that was coming into being, Derozio was the first

[1] Thomas Edwards, *Biography of Henry Derozio*, in Bimanbehari Majumdar, *History of Political Thought from Rammohun to Dayananda*, I, 86–87.

and one of the finest flowers to spring from the implantation of European ideas in Indian soil.

HENRY DEROZIO
Letter Protesting His Dismissal

In 1831 the resistance of orthodox Hindus to Derozio's criticisms of their customs and beliefs culminated in his ouster from the Hindu College. One of the charges against Derozio was that he did not believe in the existence of God. To this he replied:
[From Bradley-Birt, *Poems of Henry Derozio*, pp. xlv–xlvii, li–lii]

I have never denied the existence of a God in the hearing of any human being. If it be wrong to speak at all upon such a subject, I am guilty, but I am neither afraid, nor ashamed to confess having stated the doubts of philosophers upon this head, because I have also stated the solution of these doubts. Is it forbidden anywhere to argue upon such a question? If so, it must be equally wrong to adduce an argument upon either side. Or is it consistent with an enlightened notion of truth to wed ourselves to only one view of so important a subject, resolving to close our eyes and ears against all impressions that oppose themselves to it?

How is any opinion to be strengthened but by completely comprehending the objections that are offered to it, and exposing their futility? And what have I done more than this? Entrusted as I was for some time with the education of youth peculiarly circumstanced, was it for me to have made them pert and ignorant dogmatists, by permitting them to know what could be said upon only one side of grave questions? Setting aside the narrowness of mind which such a course might have evinced, it would have been injurious to the mental energies and acquirements of the young men themselves. And (whatever may be said to the contrary), I can vindicate my procedure by quoting no less orthodox authority than Lord Bacon: "If a man," says this philosopher (and no one ever had a better right to pronounce an opinion upon such matters than Lord Bacon), "will begin with certainties he shall end in doubt." This, I need scarcely observe, is always the case with contented ignorance when it is roused too late to thought. One doubt suggests another, and universal scepticism is the consequence. I therefore thought it my duty to acquaint several of the College students with the substance of Hume's celebrated

dialogue between Cleanthes and Philo, in which the most subtle and refined arguments against theism are adduced. But I have also furnished
them with Dr. Reid's and Dugald Stewart's more acute replies to Hume
—replies which to this day continue unrefuted. This is the head and front
of my offending. If the religious opinions of the students have become
unhinged in consequence of the course I have pursued, the fault is not
mine. To produce convictions was not within my power; and if I am to
be condemned for the atheism of some, let me receive credit for the
theism of others. Believe me, my dear Sir, I am too thoroughly imbued
with a deep sense of human ignorance, and of the perpetual vicissitudes
of opinion, to speak with confidence even of the most unimportant matters. Doubt and uncertainty besiege us too closely to admit the boldness
of dogmatism to enter an enquiring mind; and far be it from me to say
"this is" and "that is not," when after the most extensive acquaintance
with the researches of science, and after the most daring flights of genius,
we must confess with sorrow and disappointment that humility becomes
the highest wisdom, for the highest wisdom assures man of his ignorance.

In explaining the decision of the managers to dismiss him, one of them wrote
that it ". . . was founded upon the expediency of yielding to popular clamor,
the justice of which it was not incumbent on them to investigate." At this,
Derozio hotly defended the principle of academic freedom, then virtually unknown in India.

Now that I have replied to your question, allow me to ask you, my
dear Sir, whether the expediency of yielding to popular clamor can be
offered in justification of the measures adopted by the Native [Indian]
Managers of the College towards me? Their proceedings certainly do not
record any condemnation of me, but does it not look very like condemnation of a man's conduct and character to dismiss him from office when
popular clamor is against him? Vague reports and unfounded rumors
went abroad concerning me; the Native Managers confirm them by acting
towards me as they have done. Excuse my saying it, but I believe there
was a determination on their part to get rid of me, not to satisfy popular
clamor, but their own bigotry. Had my religion and morals been investigated by them, they could have had no grounds to proceed against
me. They therefore thought it most expedient to make no enquiry, but
with anger and precipitation to remove me from the institution. The
slovenly manner in which they have done so is a sufficient indication of

the spirit by which they were moved; for in their rage they have forgotten what was due even to common decency. Every person who has heard of the way in which they have acted is indignant; but to complain of their injustice would be paying them a greater compliment than they deserve.

In concluding this letter allow me to apologize for its inordinate length, and to repeat my thanks for all that you have done for me in the unpleasant affair by which it has been occasioned.

I remain, etc.,

H. L. V. Derozio

India's Youth—The Hope of Her Future

That Derozio greatly enjoyed his work as an educator is clear from the following two sonnets. He placed his hopes on the young men then growing to maturity; where he failed to overcome the forces of orthodoxy, they would succeed. It is interesting to note the contradiction between his gloomy picture of India's past as a "tyrant's den" and his romantic picture of her former glories. In this respect Derozio foreshadows the mental conflict of later Indian nationalists who sought both to rid their country of the evils of the past and to bolster their claim to self-rule by glorifying an ancient and honorable national heritage.

[From Bradley-Birt, *Poems of Henry Derozio*, pp. 43, 120]

SONNET TO THE PUPILS OF THE HINDU COLLEGE

Expanding like the petals of young flowers
I watch the gentle opening of your minds,
And the sweet loosening of the spell that binds
Your intellectual energies and powers,
That stretch (like young birds in soft summer hours)
Their wings, to try their strength. O, how the winds
Of circumstances, and freshening April showers
Of early knowledge, and unnumbered kinds
Of new perceptions shed their influence;
And how you worship truth's omnipotence.
What joyance rains upon me, when I see
Fame in the mirror of futurity,
Weaving the chaplets you have yet to gain,
Ah! then I feel I have not lived in vain.

[17]

SONNET

Your hand is on the helm—guide on young men
The bark that's freighted with your country's doom.
Your glories are but budding; they shall bloom
Like fabled amaranths Elysian, when
The shore is won, even now within your ken,
And when your torch shall dissipate the gloom
That long has made your country but a tomb,
Or worse than tomb, the priest's, the tyrant's den.
Guide on, young men; your course is well begun;
Hearts that are tuned to holiest harmony
With all that e'en in thought is good, must be
Best formed for deeds like those which shall be done
But you hereafter till your guerdon's won
And that which now is hope becomes reality.

Poems to India

Taking his cue from the patriotism of the Irish and English romantic poets,
Derozio dedicated two sonnets to India. These poems are virtually the first
expression of the sentiment of Indian nationalism which in the twentieth century
was to force the British to grant independence to India and Pakistan.
[From Bradley-Birt, *Poems of Henry Derozio*, pp. 1, 2]

THE HARP OF INDIA

Why hang'st thou lonely on yon withered bough?
   Unstrung, forever, must thou there remain?
Thy music once was sweet—who hears it now?
   Why doth the breeze sigh over thee in vain?—
Silence hath bound thee with her fatal chain;
Neglected, mute and desolate art thou
   Like ruined monument on desert plain—
O! many a hand more worthy far than mine
   Once thy harmonious chords to sweetness gave,
And many a wreath for them did Fame entwine
   Of flowers still blooming on the minstrel's grave;
Those hands are cold—but if thy notes divine

[18]

May be by mortal wakened once again,
Harp of my country, let me strike the strain!

TO INDIA—MY NATIVE LAND
My country! in thy day of glory past
A beauteous halo circled round thy brow,
And worshiped as a deity thou wast.
Where is that glory, where that reverence now?
Thy eagle pinion is chained down at last,
And groveling in the lowly dust art thou:
Thy minstrel hath no wreath to weave for thee
Save the sad story of thy misery!
Well—let me dive into the depths of time,
And bring from out the ages that have rolled
A few small fragments of those wrecks sublime,
Which human eye may never more behold;
And let the guerdon of my labor be
My fallen country! one kind wish from thee!

RĀMMOHUN ROY: THE FATHER
OF MODERN INDIA

Born of devout brāhman parents in 1772, Rāmmohun Roy showed an
early interest in religious questions. An insatiable student, he mastered
Persian, as had his forefathers, in order to qualify for government service, and read Euclid, Aristotle, and the Qur'ān in Arabic. At his mother's
wish he next steeped himself in Sanskrit learning at Banaras, Hinduism's
major intellectual center. Between the ages of fifteen and twenty he
wandered through India in search of knowledge, going apparently as far
as Tibet, where he seems to have spent several years studying Buddhism.
  Eventually Rāmmohun entered the employ of the British, acquired a
remarkable fluency in the English language, and rose as high as a non-
Britisher could in the Bengal Civil Service. His success as an administrator
and an assured income from landed estates enabled him to retire at forty-
two and to settle permanently in Calcutta, then the political and intellectual
capital of India.

For the next sixteen years of his life, Rāmmohun threw himself with characteristic vigor into an extraordinary number of projects for the reform and enlightenment of his fellow-men. He was one of the first Indians to found and edit newspapers, publishing them in English, Bengali, and Persian. He started several secondary schools, led a successful campaign against widow-burning, and organized a religious society (the Brāhmo Samāj, or society of the worshipers of God), which was to exercise a deep influence on the social and religious life of modern India.

Rāmmohun carried on theological controversies with missionaries and orthodox brāhmans alike, and whether he was defending the precepts of Jesus or the teachings of the Vedas, his reasoning was always cogent and clear. So forceful were his arguments against the doctrine of the Trinity that he converted to Unitarianism the Scottish missionary with whom he was translating the New Testament into Bengali.

In the last years of his life he set a new precedent for Hindus by "crossing the black waters" to England, where he represented the powerless emperor of Delhi. While in London, he presented to a committee of Parliament recommendations on ways to improve the government of India, was given a dinner by the directors of the East India Company, and was everywhere honored as the unofficial ambassador of India to Britain. He died in Bristol in 1833, in the arms of his English Unitarian friends.

The first Indian whose ideas were profoundly affected by contact with modern Western culture, Rāmmohun Roy was also the first to give serious attention to the fundamental beliefs of the Christian religion. Although he rejected Christianity's doctrinal shell, he warmly welcomed its humanitarian message. At the same time, he singled out for attention those classical Hindu scriptures which came closest in content to an ethical monotheism, thereby offering to his fellow Hindus a means of reforming certain corrupt beliefs and practices without losing their self-respect. This strategic reinterpretation of Hinduism forestalled the impending conversion of numbers of educated Hindus who recognized as Rāmmohun did the merits of Christian ethics, for they now began to claim that these merits were also the property of their ancestral faith. For this and his other contributions to the regeneration of Hindu society and religion, Rāmmohun Roy well deserves the title given him by later generations— "The Father of Modern India."

RĀMMOHUN ROY
To the Believers of the Only True God

Rāmmohun Roy's great service to modern Hinduism has been to recover from obscurity the exalted religious ideas which centuries of neglect had overlaid with a hard caking of thoughtless custom and belief. In publicizing those portions of the Hindu scriptures which stress faith in one supreme Being, Rāmmohun attempted to demonstrate that idol-worship was an excrescence, not an essential part of his ancestral religion.

[From *Translation of an Abridgment of the Vedant*, pp. i–v, in *English Works*, pp. 3–5]

The greater part of Brahmuns, as well as of other sects of Hindoos, are quite incapable of justifying that idolatry which they continue to practice. When questioned on the subject, in place of adducing reasonable arguments in support of their conduct, they conceive it fully sufficient to quote their ancestors as positive authorities! And some of them are become very ill disposed towards me, because I have forsaken idolatry for the worship of the true and eternal God! In order, therefore, to vindicate my own faith, and that of our early forefathers, I have been endeavoring, for some time past, to convince my countrymen of the true meaning of our sacred books, and to prove that my aberration deserves not the opprobrium which some unreflecting persons have been so ready to throw upon me.

The whole body of the Hindoo theology, law, and literature is contained in the Veds [Vedas], which are affirmed to be coeval with the creation! These works are extremely voluminous; and being written in the most elevated and metaphorical style, are, as may be well supposed, in many passages seemingly confused and contradictory. Upwards of two thousand years ago, the great Byas [Vyāsa Bādarāyana], reflecting on the perpetual difficulty arising from these sources, composed with great discrimination a complete and compendious abstract of the whole, and also reconciled those texts, which appeared to stand at variance. This work he termed *The Vedant* [Vedanta], which, compounded of two Sungscrit [Sanskrit] words, signifies *The resolutions of all the Veds*. It has continued to be most highly revered by all the Hindoos, and, in place of the more diffuse arguments of the Veds, is always referred to as equal authority. But, from its being concealed within the dark curtain of the Sungscrit language, and the Brahmuns permitting themselves alone to interpret, or even to touch any book of the kind, the Vedant, although perpetually quoted, is little known to the Public; and the practice of few Hindoos indeed bears the least accordance with its precepts!

In pursuance of my vindication, I have, to the best of my abilities, translated this hitherto unknown work, as well as an abridgement thereof, into the Hindoostanee and Bengalee languages, and distributed them, free of cost, among my own countrymen as widely as circumstances have possibly allowed. The present is an endeavor to render an abridgment of the same into English, by which I expect to prove to my European friends that the superstitious practices which deform the Hindoo religion have nothing to do with the pure spirit of its dictates!

I have observed, that, both in their writings and conversation, many Europeans feel a wish to palliate and soften the features of Hindoo idolatry, and are inclined to inculcate that all objects of worship are considered by their votaries as emblematical representations of the Supreme Divinity! If this were indeed the case, I might perhaps be led into some examination of the subject, but the truth is, the Hindoos of the present day have no such views of the subject, but firmly believe in the real existence of innumerable gods and goddesses, who possess, in their own departments, full and independent power; and to propitiate them, and not the true *God,* are Temples erected, and ceremonies performed. There can be no doubt, however, and it is my whole design to prove, that every rite has its derivation from the allegorical adoration of the true Deity; but, at the present day, all this is forgotten; and among many it is even heresy to mention it!

I hope it will not be presumed, that I intend to establish the preference of my faith over that of other men. The result of controversy on such a subject, however multiplied, must be ever unsatisfactory. For the reasoning faculty which leads men to certainty in things within its reach produces no effect on questions beyond its comprehension. I do no more than assert that if correct reasoning and the dictates of common sense induce the belief of a wise, uncreated Being who is the supporter and ruler of the boundless universe, we should also consider him, the most powerful and supreme existence,—far surpassing our powers of comprehension or description. And although men of uncultivated minds and even some learned individuals (but in this one point blinded by prejudice) readily choose as the object of their adoration any thing which they can always see and which they pretend to feed, the absurdity of such conduct is not, thereby, in the least degree diminished.

My constant reflections on the inconvenient or, rather, injurious rites introduced by the peculiar practice of Hindoo idolatry, which, more than any other pagan worship destroys the texture of society, together with compassion for my countrymen, have compelled me to use every possible effort to awaken them from their dream of error; and by making them acquainted with their scriptures, enable them to contemplate, with true devotion, the unity and omnipresence of nature's God.

By taking the path which conscience and sincerity direct, I, born a Brahmun, have exposed myself to the complainings and reproaches, even of some of my relations, whose prejudices are strong, and whose temporal advantage depends upon the present system. But, these, however accumulated, I can tranquilly bear, trusting that a day will arrive when my humble endeavors will be viewed with justice—perhaps acknowledged with gratitude. At any rate, whatever men may say, I cannot be deprived of this consolation: my motives are acceptable to that Being, who beholds in secret, and compensates openly!

The Superiority of the Christian Ethic

As the most learned and progressive Hindu of his time, Rāmmohun Roy was deeply interested in the new religious teachings being disseminated by the Christian missionaries. On reading the New Testament he formed the idea of bringing together only the ethical teachings it contains, leaving out the doctrinal passages (an idea which had already occurred to Jefferson, who did not publish his selections). He opened the volume with the following introduction.

[From *The Precepts of Jesus, the Guide to Peace and Happiness,* pp. xxi-xxiv; *English Works,* pp. 483–85]

A conviction in the mind of its total ignorance of the nature and of the specific attributes of the Godhead, and a sense of doubt respecting the real essence of the soul, give rise to feelings of great dissatisfaction with our limited powers, as well as with all human acquirements which fail to inform us on these interesting points. On the other hand, a notion of the existence of a supreme superintending power, the author and preserver of this harmonious system, who has organized and who regulates such an infinity of celestial and terrestrial objects, and a due estimation of that law which teaches that man should do unto others as he would wish to be done by, reconcile us to human nature, and tend to render our existence agreeable to ourselves and profitable to the rest of mankind. The former of these sources of satisfaction, namely, a belief in God, prevails generally, being derived either from tradition and instruction, or from an attentive survey of the wonderful skill and contrivance displayed in the works of nature. The latter, although it is partially taught also in every system of religion with which I am acquainted, is principally inculcated by Christianity. This essential characteristic of the Christian religion I was for a long time unable to distinguish as such, amidst the various doctrines I found insisted upon in the writings of Christian authors, and in the conversation of those teachers of Christianity with whom I have had the honor of holding communication. Amongst those opinions, the most prevalent seems to be that no one is justly entitled to the appellation of Christian who does not believe in the divinity of Christ, and of the Holy Ghost, as well as in the divine nature of God, the Father of all created beings. Many allow a much greater latitude to the term Christian, and consider it as comprehending all who acknowledge the Bible to contain the revealed will of God, however they may differ from others in their interpretations of particular passages of scripture; whilst some require from him who claims the title of Christian only an adherence to the doctrines of Christ, as taught by himself, without insisting on implicit confidence in those of the Apostles, as being, except when speaking from inspiration, like other men, liable to mistake and error. That they were so is obvious from the several instances of differences of opinion amongst the Apostles recorded in the Acts and Epistles.[1]

Voluminous works, written by learned men of particular sects for the purpose of establishing the truth, consistency, rationality, and priority of their own peculiar doctrines, contain such a variety of arguments, that I cannot hope to be able to adduce here any new reasonings of sufficient novelty and force to attract the notice of my readers. Besides, in matters of religion particularly, men in general, through prejudice and partiality to the opinions which they once form, pay little or no attention to opposite sentiments (however reasonable they may be) and often turn a

---

[1] See Acts 11.2, 3; 15.2, 7; 1 Corinthians 1.12; Galatians 2.11–13. [Roy's footnote]

deaf ear to what is most consistent with the laws of nature, and conformable to the dictates of human reason and divine revelation. At the same time, to those who are not biased by prejudice, and who are, by the grace of God, open to conviction, a simple enumeration and statement of the respective tenets of different sects may be a sufficient guide to direct their inquiries in ascertaining which of them is the most consistent with the sacred traditions, and most acceptable to common sense. For these reasons, I decline entering into any discussion on these points, and confine my attention at present to the task of laying before my fellow-creatures the words of Christ, with a translation from the English into Sungskrit, and the language of Bengal. I feel persuaded that by separating from the other matters contained in the New Testament, the moral precepts found in that book, these will be more likely to produce the desirable effect of improving the hearts and minds of men of different persuasions and degrees of understanding. For historical and some other passages are liable to the doubts and disputes of free-thinkers and anti-Christians, especially miraculous relations, which are much less wonderful than the fabricated tales handed down to the natives of Asia, and consequently would be apt at best to carry little weight with them. On the contrary, moral doctrines, tending evidently to the maintenance of the peace and harmony of mankind at large, are beyond the reach of metaphysical perversion, and intelligible alike to the learned and to the unlearned. This simple code of religion and morality is so admirably calculated to elevate men's ideas to high and liberal notions of one God, who has equally subjected all living creatures, without distinction of cast, rank, or wealth, to change, disappointment, pain, and death, and has equally admitted all to be partakers of the bountiful mercies which he has lavished over nature, and is also so well fitted to regulate the conduct of the human race in the discharge of their various duties to God, to themselves, and to society, that I cannot but hope the best effects from its promulgation in the present form.

A Counterattack Against the Missionaries

The Precepts of Jesus caused an uproar among the Protestant missionaries in Calcutta, and, because he rejected the divinity of Christ, Rāmmohun Roy found himself entangled in a theological controversy with Joshua Marshman, one of their leaders, for over three years. In defense of his position, Roy pub-

[25]

lished three *Appeals to the Christian Public*, the last of which ran to 303 pages and was replete with citations in Greek and Hebrew. But this long controversy seems to have embittered Rāmmohun Roy, for in 1823 he started, under a pseudonym, *The Brahmunical Magazine; or, the Missionary and the Brahmun*, with the subtitle, "Being a Vindication of the Hindoo Religion Against the Attacks of Christian Missionaries."

[From *The Brahmunical Magazine* (1823), pp. 1–4; *English Works*, pp. 145–47]

For a period of upwards of fifty years, this country [Bengal] has been in exclusive possession of the English nation, during the first thirty years of which from their word and deed it was universally believed that they would not interfere with the religion of their subjects, and that they truly wished every man to act in such matters according to the dictates of his own conscience. Their possessions in Hindoostan and their political strength have, through the grace of God, gradually increased. But during the last twenty years, a body of English Gentlemen who are called missionaries have been publicly endeavoring, in several ways, to convert Hindoos and Mussulmans of this country into Christianity. The first way is that of publishing and distributing among the natives various books, large and small, reviling both religions, and abusing and ridiculing the gods and saints of the former; the second way is that of standing in front of the doors of the natives or in the public roads to preach the excellency of that of others; the third way is that if any natives of low origin become Christians from the desire of gain or from any other motives, these Gentlemen employ and maintain them as a necessary encouragement to others to follow their example.

It is true that the apostles of Jesus Christ used to preach the superiority of the Christian religion to the natives of different countries. But we must recollect that they were not the rulers of those countries where they preached. Were the missionaries likewise to preach the Gospel and distribute books in countries not conquered by the English, such as Turkey, Persia, &c. which are much nearer England, they would be esteemed a body of men truly zealous in propagating religion and in following the example of the founders of Christianity. In Bengal, where the English are the sole rulers, and where the mere name of Englishman is sufficient to frighten people, an encroachment upon the rights of her poor timid and humble inhabitants and upon their religion cannot be

[26]

viewed in the eyes of God or the public as a justifiable act. For wise and good men always feel disinclined to hurt those that are of much less strength than themselves, and if such weak creatures be dependent on them and subject to their authority, they can never attempt, even in thought, to mortify their feelings.

We have been subjected to such insults for about nine centuries, and the cause of such degradation has been our excess in civilization and abstinence from the slaughter even of animals, as well as our division into castes which has been the source of want of unity among us.

It seems almost natural that when one nation succeeds in conquering another, the former, tho' their religion may be quite ridiculous, laugh at and despise the religion and manners of those that are fallen into their power. For example, Mussulmans, upon their conquest of India, proved highly inimical to the religious exercises of Hindoos. When the generals of Chungezkhan [Chingis Khan], who denied God and were like wild beasts in their manners, invaded the western part of Hindoostan, they universally mocked at the profession of God and of futurity expressed to them by the natives of India. The savages of Arracan on their invasion of the eastern part of Bengal always attempted to degrade the religion of Hindoos. In ancient days, the Greeks and the Romans, who were gross idolators and immoral in their lives, used to laugh at the religion and conduct of their Jewish subjects—a sect who were devoted to the belief of one God. It is therefore not uncommon if the English missionaries, who are of the conquerors of this country, revile and mock at the religion of its natives. But as the English are celebrated for the manifestation of humanity and for administering justice, and as a great many Gentlemen among them are noticed to have had an aversion to violate equity, it would tend to destroy their acknowledged character if they follow the example of the former savage conquerors in disturbing the established religion of the country; because to introduce religion by means of abuse and insult, or by affording the hope of worldly gain, is inconsistent with reason and justice. If by the force of argument they can prove the truth of their own religion and the falsity of that of Hindoos, many would of course embrace their doctrines, and in case they fail to prove this, they should not undergo such useless trouble, nor tease Hindoos any longer by their attempts at conversion. In consideration of the small huts in which Brahmuns of learning generally reside, and the simple food, such as vegetables &c. which they are accustomed to eat, and the poverty which obliges them to live upon charity, the missionary Gentlemen may not, I hope, abstain from controversy from contempt of them; for truth & true religion do not always belong to wealth and power, high names, or lofty palaces.

Hinduism Is Not Inferior to Christianity

Although he urged his countrymen to feel no resentment toward the missionaries, but only "compassion, on account of their blindness to the errors into which they themselves have fallen," Rāmmohun Roy was less than compassionate in his reply to a public letter charging him with having insulted the Christian religion. In this, his most extreme statement in defense of Hindu culture and religion, he advanced arguments which are still widely used in India today.

> [From a letter to the editor of the *Bengal Hurkaru* (May 23, 1823); *English Works,* pp. 906, 908]

If by the "ray of intelligence" for which the Christian says we are indebted to the English, he means the introduction of useful mechanical arts, I am ready to express my assent and also my gratitude; but with respect to *science, literature,* or *religion,* I do not acknowledge that we are placed under any obligation. For by a reference to History it may be proved that the world was indebted to *our ancestors* for the first dawn of knowledge, which sprang up in the East, and thanks to the Goddess of Wisdom, we have still a philosophical and copious language of our own which distinguishes us from other nations who cannot express scientific or abstract ideas without borrowing the language of foreigners. . . .

Before "A Christian" indulged in a tirade about persons being "degraded by *Asiatic* effeminacy" he should have recollected that almost all the ancient prophets and patriarchs venerated by Christians, nay even Jesus Christ himself, a Divine Incarnation and the *founder* of the Christian Faith, were Asiatics. So that if a Christian thinks it degrading to be born or to reside in Asia, he directly reflects upon them. . . .

It is unjust in the Christian to quarrel with Hindoos because (he says) they cannot comprehend the sublime mystery of his religion [the Doctrine of the Trinity]; since he is equally unable to comprehend the sublime mysteries of ours, and since both these mysteries equally transcend the human understanding, one cannot be preferred to the other.

In Defense of Hindu Women

In a letter to an American friend, Rāmmohun Roy stated his willingness to support the moral principles preached by Jesus "even at the risk of my own life." Roy actually did risk his life while conducting his arduous campaign against the Hindu practice of suttee (*satī*) by which widows were encouraged to burn themselves to death on their husbands' funeral pyres. The threats of ultraconservative Hindus notwithstanding, Rāmmohun carried his campaign to a successful conclusion by helping the British to overcome their doubts about proscribing the custom. Having devastated his imaginary opponent by references to the highest Sanskrit authorities, he concluded his *Second Conference Between an Advocate for and an Opponent of the Practice of Burning Widows Alive* with an appeal to humanitarian standards of justice and mercy, and a passionate defense of the rights of women.

[From *English Works*, pp. 359–63]

Advocate. I alluded in page 18, line 18, to the real reason for our anxiety to persuade widows to follow their husbands, and for our endeavors to burn them pressed down with ropes: namely, that women are by nature of inferior understanding, without resolution, unworthy of trust, subject to passions, and void of virtuous knowledge; they according to the precepts of the Shastru [shāstra] are not allowed to marry again after the demise of their husbands, and consequently despair at once of all worldly pleasure; hence it is evident that death to these unfortunate widows is preferable to existence, for the great difficulty which a widow may experience by living a purely ascetic life as prescribed by the Shastrus is obvious; therefore if she do not perform concremation, it is probable that she may be guilty of such acts as may bring disgrace upon her paternal and maternal relations, and those that may be connected with her husband. Under these circumstances we instruct them from their early life in the idea of concremation, holding out to them heavenly enjoyments in company with their husbands, as well as the beatitude of their relations, both by birth and marriage, and their reputation in this world. From this many of them, on the death of their husbands, become desirous of accompanying them; but to remove every chance of their trying to escape from the blazing fire, in burning them we first tie them down to the pile.

Opponent. The reason you have now assigned for burning widows alive is indeed your true motive, as we are well aware; but the faults which you have imputed to women are not planted in their constitution by nature. It would be therefore grossly criminal to condemn that sex to death merely from precaution. By ascribing to them all sorts of improper conduct, you have indeed successfully persuaded the Hindoo community to look down upon them as contemptible and mischievous creatures, whence they have been subjected to constant miseries. I have therefore to offer a few remarks on this head. Women are in general inferior to men in bodily strength and energy; consequently the male part of the community, taking advantage of their corporeal weakness, have denied to them those excellent merits that they are entitled to by nature, and afterwards they are apt to say that women are naturally incapable of acquiring those merits. But if we give the subject consideration, we may easily ascertain whether or not your accusation against them is consistent with justice. As to their inferiority in point of understanding, when did you ever afford them a fair opportunity of exhibiting their natural capacity? How then can you accuse them of want of understanding? If after instruction in knowledge and wisdom a person cannot comprehend or retain what has been taught him, we may consider him as deficient; but as you keep women generally void of education and acquirements, you cannot therefore in justice pronounce on their inferiority. On the contrary, Leelavutee, Bhanoomutee (the wife of the Prince of Kurnat) and that of Kalidas, are celebrated for their thorough knowledge of the Shastrus: moreover in the Vrihudarunyuk Oopunishad [*Bṛihad Āraṇyaka Upaniṣad*] of the Ujoor Ved [Yajur Veda] it is clearly stated, that Yagnuvulkyu [Yājnavalkya] imparted divine knowledge of the most difficult nature to his wife Muitreyee, who was able to follow and completely attain it!

Secondly. You charge them with want of resolution, at which I feel exceedingly surprised. For we constantly perceive in a country where the name of death makes the male shudder, that the female from her firmness of mind offers to burn with the corpse of her deceased husband; and yet you accuse those women of deficiency in point of resolution.

Thirdly. With regard to their trustworthiness, let us look minutely into the conduct of both sexes, and we may be enabled to ascertain which of them is the most frequently guilty of betraying friends. If we enumerate such women in each village or town as have been deceived by men, and such men as have been betrayed by women, I presume that the number of deceived women would be found ten times greater than that of the betrayed men. Men are in general able to read and write and manage public affairs, by which means they easily promulgate such faults as women occasionally commit, but never consider as criminal the misconduct of men towards women. One fault they have, it must be acknowledged; which is, by considering others equally void of duplicity as themselves to give their confidence too readily, from which they suffer much misery, even so far that some of them are misled to suffer themselves to be burnt to death.

In the fourth place, with respect to their subjection to the passions, this may be judged of by the custom of marriage as to the respective sexes; for one man may marry two or three, sometimes even ten wives and upwards; while a woman, who marries but one husband, desires at his death to follow him, forsaking all worldly enjoyments, or to remain leading the austere life of an ascetic.

Fifthly. The accusation of their want of virtuous knowledge is an injustice. Observe what pain, what slighting, what contempt, and what afflictions their virtue enables them to support! How many Kooleen [1] Brahmuns are there who marry ten or fifteen wives for the sake of money, that never see the greater number of them after the day of marriage, and visit others only three or four times in the course of their life. Still amongst those women, most, even without seeing or receiving any support from their husbands, living dependent on their fathers or brothers, and suffering much distress, continue to preserve their virtue. And when Brahmuns or those of other tribes bring their wives to live with them, what misery do the women not suffer? At marriage the wife is recognized as half of her husband, but in after conduct they are treated worse than inferior animals. For the woman is employed to do the work of a slave in the house, such as in her turn to clean the place very early in the morning, whether cold or wet, to scour the dishes, to wash the floor, to cook night and day, to prepare and serve food for her husband, father, and mother-in-law, sisters-in-law, brothers-in-law, and friends and connections! (For amongst Hindoos more than in other tribes relations long reside together, and on this account quarrels are more common amongst brothers respecting their worldly affairs.) If in the preparation

---

[1] Or Kūlin. An elite group found among certain Bengal brāhman and kāyastha subcastes. Their men were much sought after as husbands.

or serving up of the victuals they commit the smallest fault, what insult do they not receive from their husband, their mother-in-law, and the younger brothers of their husband? After all the male part of the family have satisfied themselves, the women content themselves with what may be left, whether sufficient in quantity or not. Where Brahmuns or Kayustus [2] are not wealthy, their women are obliged to attend to their cows, and to prepare the cow-dung for firing. In the afternoon they fetch water from the river or tank, and at night perform the office of menial servants in making the beds. In case of any fault or omission in the performance of those labors, they receive injurious treatment. Should the husband acquire wealth, he indulges in criminal amours to her perfect knowledge and almost under her eyes, and does not see her perhaps once a month. As long as the husband is poor she suffers every kind of trouble, and when he becomes rich she is altogether heartbroken. All this pain and affliction their virtue alone enables them to support. Where a husband takes two or three wives to live with him, they are subjected to mental miseries and constant quarrels. Even this distressed situation they virtuously endure. Sometimes it happens that the husband, from a preference for one of his wives, behaves cruelly to another. Amongst the lower classes, and those even of the better class who have not associated with good company, the wife on the slightest fault, or even on bare suspicion of her misconduct, is chastised as a thief. Respect to virtue and their reputation generally makes them forgive even this treatment. If, unable to bear such cruel usage, a wife leaves her husband's house to live separately from him, then the influence of the husband with the magisterial authority is generally sufficient to place her again in his hands; when, in revenge for her quitting him, he seizes every pretext to torment her in various ways, and sometimes even puts her privately to death. These are facts occurring every day, and not to be denied. What I lament is, that seeing the women thus dependent and exposed to every misery, you feel for them no compassion, that might exempt them from being tied down and burnt to death.

For Freedom of the Press

In 1823 the East India Company promulgated an ordinance restricting the freedom of the press by requiring all newspapers to be licensed under terms

[2] Kāyasthas, the caste of scribes, second to brāhmans in importance in Bengal.

laid down by the government. Rāmmohun Roy responded by drawing up a memorial to the governor-general on behalf of the Indian community, in which he contended that their loyalty depended on the continuing enjoyment of those civil liberties which had reconciled them to British rule—an argument echoed later by many an Indian nationalist.

[From *English Works,* pp. 441–43]

After this Rule and Ordinance shall have been carried into execution, your Memorialists are therefore extremely sorry to observe that a complete stop will be put to the diffusion of knowledge and the consequent mental improvement now going on, either by translations into the popular dialect of this country from the learned languages of the East, or by the circulation of literary intelligence drawn from foreign publications. And the same cause will also prevent those natives who are better versed in the laws and customs of the British nation from communicating to their fellow-subjects a knowledge of the admirable system of government established by the British, and the peculiar excellencies of the means they have adopted for the strict and impartial administration of justice. Another evil of equal importance in the eyes of a just ruler is that it will also preclude the natives from making the government readily acquainted with the errors and injustice that may be committed by its executive officers in the various parts of this extensive country; and it will also preclude the natives from communicating frankly and honestly to their Gracious Sovereign in England and his Council the real condition of His Majesty's faithful subjects in this distant part of his dominions and the treatment they experience from the local government; since such information cannot in future be conveyed to England, as it has heretofore been, either by the translations from the native publications inserted in the English newspapers printed here and sent to Europe, or by the English publications which the natives themselves had in contemplation to establish before this Rule and Ordinance was proposed.

After this sudden deprivation of one of the most precious of their rights, which has been freely allowed them since the establishment of the British power, a right which they are not, and cannot, be charged with having ever abused, the inhabitants of Calcutta would be no longer justified in boasting that they are fortunately placed by Providence under the protection of the whole British nation, or that the king of England

and his Lords and Commons are their legislators, and that they are secured in the enjoyment of the same civil and religious privileges that every Briton is entitled to in England.

Your Memorialists are persuaded that the British government is not disposed to adopt the political maxim so often acted upon by Asiatic princes that the more a people are kept in darkness, their rulers will derive the greater advantages from them; since, by reference to history, it is found that this was but a short-sighted policy which did not ultimately answer the purpose of its authors. On the contrary, it rather proved disadvantageous to them; for we find that as often as an ignorant people, when an opportunity offered, have revolted against their rulers, all sorts of barbarous excesses and cruelties have been the consequence; whereas a people naturally disposed to peace and ease, when placed under a good government from which they experience just and liberal treatment, must become the more attached to it, in proportion as they become enlightened and the great body of the people are taught to appreciate the value of the blessings they enjoy under its rule.

Every good ruler, who is convinced of the imperfection of human nature, and reverences the Eternal Governor of the world, must be conscious of the great liability to error in managing the affairs of a vast empire; and therefore he will be anxious to afford every individual the readiest means of bringing to his notice whatever may require his interference. To secure this important object, the unrestrained liberty of publication is the only effectual means that can be employed. And should it ever be abused, the established Law of the Land is very properly armed with sufficient powers to punish those who may be found guilty of misrepresenting the conduct or character of government, which are effectually guarded by the same laws to which individuals must look for protection of their reputation and good name.

Your Memorialists conclude by humbly entreating your Lordship to take this Memorial into your gracious consideration; and that you will be pleased by not registering the above Rule and Ordinance, to permit the natives of this country to continue in possession of the civil rights and privileges which they and their fathers have so long enjoyed under the auspices of the British nation, whose kindness and confidence they are not aware of having done anything to forfeit.

With remarkable accuracy, Rāmmohun Roy predicted the rise of Indian nationalism in a letter of 1828 to an English friend. At the same time he indicated
that by enlightened and democratic government the connection between India
and Britain might be prolonged to their mutual advantage.

[From *English Works,* p. xxiii]

Supposing that one hundred years hence the native character becomes
elevated from constant intercourse with Europeans and the acquirement
of general and political knowledge as well as of modern arts and sciences,
is it possible that they will not have the spirit as well as the inclination
to resist effectually any unjust and oppressive measures serving to degrade them in the scale of society? It should not be lost sight of that
the position of India is very different from that of Ireland, to any
quarter of which an English fleet may suddenly convey a body of
troops that may force its way in the requisite direction and succeed in
suppressing every effort of a refractory spirit. Were India to share one-
fourth of the knowledge and energy of that country, she would prove
from her remote situation, her riches and her vast population, either
useful and profitable as a willing province, an ally of the British empire,
or troublesome and annoying as a determined enemy.

In common with those who seem partial to the British rule from the
expectation of future benefits arising out of the connection, I necessarily
feel extremely grieved in often witnessing acts and regulations passed
by government without consulting or seeming to understand the feelings
of its Indian subjects and without considering that this people have had
for more than half a century the advantage of being ruled by and associated with an enlightened nation, advocates of liberty and promoters of
knowledge.

THE DECISION TO INTRODUCE
ENGLISH EDUCATION

No single act of British policy has had a more lasting influence on the
evolution of modern Indian thought than the decision in 1835 to use

governmental funds to support education in the English language and to adopt the curriculum prevalent in English schools. The introduction of this system of education had two main results. On the one hand it greatly accelerated the diffusion of Western ideas and the Western outlook on life among Indian intellectuals. On the other hand, both the rapid penetration of foreign ways and attitudes and the publication of the Hindu classics in English translation stimulated movements defending Hinduism or demanding greater political opportunities for Indians—movements whose leaders often wrote, spoke, and thought in English.

The East India Company, in its initial caution to leave undamaged the traditional bases of Indian society and culture, had decided to sponsor Persian, Arabic, and Sanskrit studies as early as the 1770s. Later when the Company became the paramount power in India, many Indians realized that to get jobs with the new government they would have to learn English, even though Persian continued to be used for official purposes well into the nineteenth century. The more enlightened among them, men like Rāmmohun Roy, saw that tremendous advantages could be gained by direct contact with the whole corpus of Western learning which English education would make possible, and they therefore raised their voices against the antiquarian policy.

The Committee on Public Instruction was slow to react to the growing demand for a new educational system. When Thomas Babington Macaulay (fresh from England and thirty-four years old) was made its president in 1834, the Committee was hopelessly divided between the "Anglicists" and the "Orientalists." The former saw the need to train a host of loyal government servants able to conduct the routine clerical work of the Company. The latter feared that a Westernizing policy would offend the sensibilities of the Indian upper classes and possibly lead to their general rebellion. Seeing that a decision was needed, Macaulay ended the stalemate by supporting the Anglicists with all the weight of his influence and all the power of his pen. As soon as his recommendations were accepted he threw himself into the work of setting up the new system.

The introduction of English education in India has had profound social and political effects. The older elite were gradually replaced by a new class of Indians trained in a foreign language and a foreign culture, able to act as intermediaries between the British and the bulk of the people. Influenced by the secular spirit of English education, the members of this class gradually dropped their exclusive attachment to the religious traditions in which their ancestors had been raised. Breaking out of the mold of caste and custom they embraced Western ideas and standards of behavior. As Macaulay predicted, these men, "Indian in blood and color, but English in taste, in opinions, in morals, and in intellect," led their countrymen in reinvigorating India's regional languages and literatures. At the same time, wherever they went they helped to spread Western ways and ideas into the interior of the country.

English education produced another drastic change in the Indian environment. By providing a common language and a common cultural background for men in all parts of India previously separated by linguistic, regional, and cultural differences, it offered Indians the opportunity of creating a common, modern culture of their own. It was only a question of time until these new conditions of all-Indian unity gave birth to political self-consciousness and to Indian nationalism itself.

A more ominous result was the effect of the new system on the relations between Hindus and Muslims. The substitution of English for Persian as the paramount language of government, diplomacy, and culture throughout the Indian subcontinent was naturally a bitter pill for Muslims to swallow. Resentful of the new order, Muslims tended to ignore it, "sulking in their tents," while Hindus flocked to the government and missionary schools in greater numbers than could be admitted. As time passed, the cultural gap between the two communities widened, until intelligent Muslims realized that English-educated Hindus were dominating the scene, both politically and economically. Long before the Muslims bestirred themselves to catch up, however, their Hindu rivals had begun the task of adjusting age-old beliefs and customs to the impact of European learning, and had moreover acquired a new pride in their own culture which made reconciliation with the Muslims increasingly difficult.

For thinking men in both communities, the introduction of English education ultimately revolutionized their traditional modes of thought and opened up to them a brave new world of almost limitless dimensions. Henceforth they might reject Western culture, they might recklessly embrace it, or they might respond to its challenge by revivifying and reinterpreting the legacy of the past—but, however they reacted, they could not escape from its compelling presence.

SIR WILLIAM JONES
The Orientalist Viewpoint

The suspension of government support for the study of Persian, Arabic, and Sanskrit was stubbornly resisted by members of the Committee on Public Instruction who had studied these languages and discovered the riches contained in their literatures. These Orientalists owed much to the example of Sir William Jones (1746–1794), a brilliant pioneer of Asian studies whose arrival in Calcutta in 1784 gave the decisive impulse to the founding of the Asiatick Society (now the Asiatic Society of Bengal).

Jones' preface to his *Grammar of the Persian Language* of 1771 eloquently stated the cultural and practical reasons why Englishmen should apply themselves to mastering this tongue. He later had occasion also to praise Sanskrit for its ". . . wonderful structure; more perfect than the *Greek,* more copious than the *Latin,* and more exquisitely refined than either." [1]

Although the Orientalists were defeated on the question of educational policy, their high evaluation of India's classical heritage helped eventually to foster in English-educated Indians a pride in their own past which was of cardinal importance in the nineteenth-century renaissance of Hinduism and the rise of Hindu nationalism.

[From *The Works of Sir William Jones,* V, 165–66, 172–74]

The Persian language is rich, melodious, and elegant; it has been spoken for many ages by the greatest princes in the politest courts of Asia; and a number of admirable works have been written in it by historians, philosophers, and poets, who found it capable of expressing with equal advantage the most beautiful and the most elevated sentiments.

It must seem strange, therefore, that the study of this language should be so little cultivated at a time when a taste for general and diffusive learning seems universally to prevail; and that the fine productions of a celebrated nation should remain in manuscript upon the shelves of our public libraries, without a single admirer who might open their treasures to his countrymen, and display their beauties to the light; but if we consider the subject with a proper attention, we shall discover a variety of causes which have concurred to obstruct the progress of Eastern literature.

[1] *The Works of Sir William Jones,* III, 34.

Some men never heard of the Asiatick writings, and others will not be convinced that there is any thing valuable in them; some pretend to be busy, and others are really idle; some detest the Persians, because they believe in Mahomed, and others despise their language, because they do not understand it: we all love to excuse, or to conceal, our ignorance, and are seldom willing to allow any excellence beyond the limits of our own attainments: like the savages, who thought that the sun rose and set for them alone, and could not imagine that the waves, which surrounded their island, left coral and pearls upon any other shore.

Another obvious reason for the neglect of the Persian language is the great scarcity of books, which are necessary to be read before it can be perfectly learned: the greater part of them are preserved in the different museums and libraries of Europe, where they are shown more as objects of curiosity than as sources of information; and are admired, like the characters on a Chinese screen more for their gay colors than for their meaning. . . .

Since the literature of Asia was so much neglected, and the causes of that neglect were so various, we could not have expected that any slight power would rouse the nations of Europe from their inattention to it; and they would, perhaps, have persisted in despising it, if they had not been animated by the most powerful incentive that can influence the mind of man: interest was the magick wand which brought them all within one circle; interest was the charm which gave the languages of the East a real and solid importance. By one of those revolutions, which no human prudence could have foreseen, the Persian language found its way into India; that rich and celebrated empire, which, by the flourishing state of our commerce, has been the source of incredible wealth to the merchants of Europe. A variety of causes, which need not be mentioned here, gave the English nation a most extensive power in that kingdom: our India Company began to take under their protection the princes of the country, by whose protection they gained their first settlement; a number of important affairs were to be transacted in peace and war between nations equally jealous of one another, who had not the common instruments of conveying their sentiments; the servants of the company received letters which they could not read, and were ambitious of gaining titles of which they could not comprehend the meaning; it was found highly dangerous to employ the natives as interpreters, upon whose fidelity they could not depend; and it was at last discovered, that they must apply themselves to the study of the Persian language, in which all the letters from the Indian princes were written. A few men of parts and taste, who resided in Bengal, have since amused themselves with the literature of the East, and have spent their leisure in reading the poems and histories of Persia; but they found a reason in every page to regret their ignorance of the Arabick language, without which their knowledge must be very circumscribed and imperfect. The languages of Asia will now, perhaps, be studied with uncommon ardor; they are known to be useful, and will soon be found instructive and entertaining; the valuable manuscripts that enrich our publick libraries will be in a few years elegantly printed; the manners and sentiments of the Eastern nations will be perfectly known; and the limits of our knowledge will be no less extended than the bounds of our empire.

RĀMMOHUN ROY

Letter on Education

Having established several schools at his own expense, at which the young men of Bengal could acquire through the medium of English the best and most modern European education, Rāmmohun Roy was sincerely shocked when the government decided in 1823 to found and support a new college for Sanskrit studies. His letter protesting against the plan shows how warmly he welcomed the introduction of Western learning among his countrymen. The superb English in which he couched his appeal, and the fact that Roy represented the more advanced section of the Hindu community, provided the Anglicists on the Committee on Public Instruction with powerful ammunition in their struggle against the Orientalists.

[From *English Works*, pp. 471–74]

To His Excellency the Right Honorable Lord Amherst,
    Governor-General in Council
My Lord,
    Humbly reluctant as the natives of India are to obtrude upon the notice of government the sentiments they entertain on any public measure, there are circumstances when silence would be carrying this respectful feeling to culpable excess. The present rulers of India, coming from a distance of many thousand miles to govern a people whose language, literature, manners, customs, and ideas, are almost entirely new and strange to them, cannot easily become so intimately acquainted with their

real circumstances as the natives of the country are themselves. We should therefore be guilty of a gross dereliction of duty to ourselves and afford our rulers just grounds of complaint at our apathy did we omit, on occasions of importance like the present, to supply them with such accurate information as might enable them to devise and adopt measures calculated to be beneficial to the country, and thus second by our local knowledge and experience their declared benevolent intentions for its improvement.

The establishment of a new Sanscrit School in Calcutta evinces the laudable desire of government to improve the natives of India by education—a blessing for which they must ever be grateful, and every well-wisher of the human race must be desirous that the efforts made to promote it should be guided by the most enlightened principles, so that the stream of intelligence may flow in the most useful channels.

When this seminary of learning was proposed, we understood that the government in England had ordered a considerable sum of money to be annually devoted to the instruction of its Indian subjects. We were filled with sanguine hopes that this sum would be laid out in employing European gentlemen of talent and education to instruct the natives of India in mathematics, natural philosophy, chemistry, anatomy, and other useful sciences, which the natives of Europe have carried to a degree of perfection that has raised them above the inhabitants of other parts of the world.

While we looked forward with pleasing hope to the dawn of knowledge thus promised to the rising generation, our hearts were filled with mingled feelings of delight and gratitude, we already offered up thanks to Providence for inspiring the most generous and enlightened nations of the West with the glorious ambition of planting in Asia the arts and sciences of modern Europe.

We find that the government are establishing a Sanscrit school under Hindu pandits to impart such knowledge as is already current in India. This seminary (similar in character to those which existed in Europe before the time of Lord Bacon) can only be expected to load the minds of youth with grammatical niceties and metaphysical distinctions of little or no practical use to the possessors or to society. The pupils will there acquire what was known two thousand years ago with the addition of vain and empty subtleties since then produced by speculative men such as is already commonly taught in all parts of India.

The Sanscrit language, so difficult that almost a lifetime is necessary for its acquisition, is well known to have been for ages a lamentable check to the diffusion of knowledge, and the learning concealed under this almost impervious veil is far from sufficient to reward the labor of acquiring it. But if it were thought necessary to perpetuate this language for the sake of the portion of valuable information it contains, this might be much more easily accomplished by other means than the establishment of a new Sanscrit College; for there have been always and are now numerous professors of Sanscrit in the different parts of the country engaged in teaching this language, as well as the other branches of literature which are to be the object of the new seminary. Therefore their more diligent cultivation, if desirable, would be effectually promoted, by holding out premiums and granting certain allowances to their most eminent professors, who have already undertaken on their own account to teach them, and would by such rewards be stimulated to still greater exertion.

From these considerations, as the sum set apart for the instruction of the natives of India was intended by the government in England for the improvement of its Indian subjects, I beg leave to state, with due deference to your Lordship's exalted situation, that if the plan now adopted be followed, it will completely defeat the object proposed, since no improvement can be expected from inducing young men to consume a dozen years of the most valuable period of their lives in acquiring the niceties of Vyakaran or Sanscrit Grammar, for instance, in learning to discuss such points as the following: *khada,* signifying to eat, *khadati* he or she eats, query, whether does *khadati* taken as a whole convey the meaning he, she, or it eats, or are separate parts of this meaning conveyed by distinctions of the words, as if in the English language it were asked how much meaning is there in the *eat* and how much in the *s,* and is the whole meaning of the word conveyed by these two portions of it distinctly or by them taken jointly?

Neither can much improvement arise from such speculations as the following which are the themes suggested by the Vedanta: In what manner is the soul absorbed in the Deity? What relation does it bear to the Divine Essence? Nor will youths be fitted to be better members of society by the Vedantic doctrines which teach them to believe that all visible things have no real existence, that as father, brother, etc. have no real

[42]

entity, they consequently deserve no real affection, and therefore the sooner we escape from them and leave the world the better.

Again, no essential benefit can be derived by the student of the *Mimamsa* from knowing what it is that makes the killer of a goat sinless by pronouncing certain passages of the Vedanta and what is the real nature and operative influence of passages of the Vedas, &c.

The student of the Nyaya Shastra cannot be said to have improved his mind after he has learned from it into how many ideal classes the objects in the universe are divided, and what speculative relation the soul bears to the body, the body to the soul, the eye to the ear, &c.

In order to enable your Lordship to appreciate the utility of encouraging such imaginary learning as above characterized, I beg your Lordship will be pleased to compare the state of science and literature in Europe before the time of Lord Bacon with the progress of knowledge made since he wrote.

If it had been intended to keep the British nation in ignorance of real knowledge, the Baconian philosophy would not have been allowed to displace the system of the schoolmen which was the best calculated to perpetuate ignorance. In the same manner the Sanscrit system of education would be the best calculated to keep this country in darkness, if such had been the policy of the British legislature. But as the improvement of the native population is the object of the government, it will consequently promote a more liberal and enlightened system of instruction, embracing mathematics, natural philosophy, chemistry, anatomy, with other useful sciences, which may be accomplished with the sums proposed by employing a few gentlemen of talent and learning educated in Europe and providing a college furnished with necessary books, instruments, and other apparatus.

In presenting this subject to your Lordship, I conceive myself discharging a solemn duty which I owe to my countrymen, and also to that enlightened sovereign and legislature which have extended their benevolent care to this distant land, actuated by a desire to improve the inhabitants, and therefore humbly trust you will excuse the liberty I have taken in thus expressing my sentiments to your Lordship.

I have the honor, etc.,

Rammohun Roy

[43]

THOMAS BABINGTON MACAULAY

Minute on Education

Following Rāmmohun Roy's letter on education by twelve years, Macaulay, in his famous "Minute on Education," used many of the arguments and even some of the phraseology of his predecessor. His exaggeratedly low opinion of classical Sanskrit and Arabic literature was born of his almost total ignorance in this realm of knowledge. His judgment was nevertheless basically well-intended, for his purpose was not the eradication of non-Western learning in India, but its regeneration through contact with the best learning produced by the modern West.

After citing and giving his interpretation of the Act of Parliament providing for ". . . the revival and promotion of literature . . . and for the introduction and promotion of a knowledge of the sciences" in India, Macaulay continued his argument.

[Macaulay, *Prose and Poetry*, pp. 721–24, 725, 728–29]

We now come to the gist of the matter. We have a fund to be employed as government shall direct for the intellectual improvement of the people of this country. The simple question is, what is the most useful way of employing it?

All parties seem to be agreed on one point, that the dialects commonly spoken among the natives of this part of India contain neither literary nor scientific information, and are, moreover, so poor and rude that, until they are enriched from some other quarter, it will not be easy to translate any valuable work into them. It seems to be admitted on all sides that the intellectual improvement of those classes of the people who have the means of pursuing higher studies can at present be effected only by means of some language not vernacular amongst them.

What then shall that language be? One-half of the committee maintain that it should be the English. The other half strongly recommend the Arabic and Sanscrit. The whole question seems to me to be, which language is the best worth knowing?

I have no knowledge of either Sanscrit or Arabic. But I have done what I could to form a correct estimate of their value. I have read translations of the most celebrated Arabic and Sanscrit works. I have conversed both here and at home with men distinguished by their proficiency in the Eastern tongues. I am quite ready to take the Oriental learning at the

[44]

valuation of the Orientalists themselves. I have never found one among them who could deny that a single shelf of a good European library was worth the whole native literature of India and Arabia. The intrinsic superiority of the Western literature is, indeed, fully admitted by those members of the committee who support the Oriental plan of education.

It will hardly be disputed, I suppose, that the department of literature in which the Eastern writers stand highest is poetry. And I certainly never met with any Orientalist who ventured to maintain that the Arabic and Sanscrit poetry could be compared to that of the great European nations. But when we pass from works of imagination to works in which facts are recorded, and general principles investigated, the superiority of the Europeans becomes absolutely immeasurable. It is, I believe, no exaggeration to say, that all the historical information which has been collected from all the books written in the Sanscrit language is less valuable than what may be found in the most paltry abridgments used at preparatory schools in England. In every branch of physical or moral philosophy, the relative position of the two nations is nearly the same.

How, then, stands the case? We have to educate a people who cannot at present be educated by means of their mother-tongue. We must teach them some foreign language. The claims of our own language it is hardly necessary to recapitulate. It stands preeminent even among the languages of the West. It abounds with works of imagination not inferior to the noblest which Greece has bequeathed to us; with models of every species of eloquence; with historical compositions, which, considered merely as narratives, have seldom been surpassed, and which, considered as vehicles of ethical and political instruction, have never been equaled; with just and lively representations of human life and human nature; with the most profound speculations on metaphysics, morals, government, jurisprudence, and trade; with full and correct information respecting every experimental science which tends to preserve the health, to increase the comfort, or to expand the intellect of man. Whoever knows that language has ready access to all the vast intellectual wealth, which all the wisest nations of the earth have created and hoarded in the course of ninety generations. It may safely be said that the literature now extant in that language is of far greater value than all the literature which three hundred years ago was extant in all the languages of the world together. Nor is this all. In India, English is the language spoken by the ruling class. It is spoken by the higher class of natives at the seats of government. It is likely to become the language of commerce throughout the seas of the East. It is the language of two great European communities which are rising, the one in the south of Africa, the other in Australasia, communities which are every year becoming more important and more closely connected with our Indian empire. Whether we look at the intrinsic value of our literature, or at the particular situation of this country, we shall see the strongest reason to think that, of all foreign tongues, the English tongue is that which would be the most useful to our native subjects.

The question now before us is simply whether, when it is in our power to teach this language, we shall teach languages in which, by universal confession, there are no books on any subject which deserve to be compared to our own; whether, when we can teach European science, we shall teach systems which, by universal confession, whenever they differ from those of Europe, differ for the worse; and whether, when we can patronize sound philosophy and true history, we shall countenance, at the public expense, medical doctrines which would disgrace an English farrier, astronomy which would move laughter in girls at an English boarding school, history abounding with kings thirty feet high and reigns thirty thousand years long, and geography, made up of seas of treacle and seas of butter.

We are not without experience to guide us. History furnishes several analogous cases, and they all teach the same lesson. There are in modern times, to go no further, two memorable instances of a great impulse given to the mind of a whole society—of prejudices overthrown, of knowledge diffused, of taste purified, of arts and sciences planted in countries which had recently been ignorant and barbarous.

The first instance to which I refer is the great revival of letters among the Western nations at the close of the fifteenth and beginning of the sixteenth century. At that time almost every thing that was worth reading was contained in the writings of the ancient Greeks and Romans. Had our ancestors acted as the Committee of Public Instruction has hitherto acted; had they neglected the language of Cicero and Tacitus; had they confined their attention to the old dialects of our own island; had they printed nothing and taught nothing at the universities but chronicles in Anglo-Saxon, and romances in Norman-French, would England have been what she now is? What the Greek and Latin were to the contemporaries of More and Ascham, our tongue is to the people of India. The literature of England is now more valuable than that of classical antiquity. I doubt whether the Sanscrit literature be as valuable as that of our Saxon and Norman progenitors. In some departments, in history, for example, I am certain that it is much less so.

Another instance may be said to be still before our eyes. Within the last hundred and twenty years, a nation which has previously been in a state as barbarous as that in which our ancestors were before the Crusades, has gradually emerged from the ignorance in which it was sunk, and has taken its place among civilized communities. I speak of Russia. There is now in that country a large educated class, abounding with persons fit to serve the state in the highest functions, and in no wise inferior to the most accomplished men who adorn the best circles of Paris and London. There is reason to hope that this vast empire, which in the time of our grandfathers was probably behind the Punjab, may, in the time of our grandchildren, be pressing close on France and Britain in the career of improvement. And how was this change effected? Not by flattering national prejudices, not by feeding the mind of the young Muscovite with old women's stories which his rude fathers had believed, not by filling his head with lying legends about St. Nicholas, not by encouraging him to study the great question—whether the world was or was not created on the 13th of September, not by calling him "a learned native" when he has mastered all these points of knowledge, but by teaching him those foreign languages in which the greatest mass of information had been laid up, and thus putting all that information within his reach. The languages of Western Europe civilized Russia. I cannot doubt that they will do for the Hindoo what they have done for the Tartar.

Macaulay next showed that the demand for English education was far greater than that for Sanskrit and Arabic.

All the declamations in the world about the love and reverence of the natives for their sacred dialects will never, in the mind of any impartial person, outweigh the undisputed fact that we cannot find, in all our vast empire, a single student who will let us teach him those dialects unless we will pay him. . . . Why then is it necessary to pay people to learn Sanscrit and Arabic? Evidently because it is universally felt that the Sanscrit and Arabic are languages, the knowledge of which does not compensate for the trouble of acquiring them. On all such subjects the state of the market is the decisive test.

[Answering the claims of the Orientalists, he asserted:] But there is yet another argument which seems even more untenable. It is said that the Sanscrit and Arabic are the languages in which the sacred books of a hundred millions of people are written, and that they are, on that account, entitled to peculiar encouragement. Assuredly it is the duty of the British government in India to be not only tolerant, but neutral on all religious questions. But to encourage the study of a literature admitted to be of small intrinsic value, only because that literature inculcates the most serious errors on the most important subjects, is a course hardly reconcilable with reason, with morality, or even with that very neutrality which ought, as we all agree, to be sacredly preserved. It is confessed that a language is barren of useful knowledge. We are to teach it because it is fruitful of monstrous superstitions. We are to teach false history, false astronomy, false medicine, because we find them in company with a false religion. We abstain, and I trust shall always abstain, from giving any public encouragement to those who are engaged in the work of converting natives to Christianity. And while we act thus, can we reasonably and decently bribe men out of the revenues of the state to waste their youth in learning how they are to purify themselves after touching an ass, or what text of the Vedas they are to repeat to expiate the crime of killing a goat?

It is taken for granted by the advocates of Oriental learning that no native of this country can possibly attain more than a mere smattering of English. They do not attempt to prove this; but they perpetually insinuate it. They designate the education which their opponents recommend as a mere spelling book education. They assume it as undeniable, that the question is between a profound knowledge of Hindoo and Arabian literature and science on the one side, and a superficial knowledge of the rudiments of English on the other. This is not merely an assumption, but an assumption contrary to all reason and experience. We know that foreigners of all nations do learn our language sufficiently to have access to all the most abstruse knowledge which it contains, sufficiently to relish even the more delicate graces of our most idiomatic writers. There are in this very town natives who are quite competent to discuss political or scientific questions with fluency and precision in the English language. I have heard the very question on which I am now writing discussed by native gentlemen with a liberality and an intelligence which would do credit to any member of the Committee of Public Instruction. Indeed it is unusual to find, even in the literary circles of the continent, any foreigner who can express himself in English with so much facility and correctness as we find in many Hindoos. Nobody, I suppose, will contend that English is so difficult to a Hindoo as Greek to an Englishman. Yet an intelligent English youth, in a much smaller number of years than our unfortunate pupils pass at the Sanscrit College, becomes able to read, to enjoy, and even to imitate, not unhappily, the compositions of the best Greek authors. Less than half the time which enables an English youth to read Herodotus and Sophocles ought to enable a Hindoo to read Hume and Milton.

To sum up what I have said, I think it clear that we are not fettered by the Act of Parliament of 1813; that we are not fettered by any pledge expressed or implied; that we are free to employ our funds as we choose; that we ought to employ them in teaching what is best worth knowing; that English is better worth knowing than Sanscrit or Arabic; that the natives are desirous to be taught English, and are not desirous to be taught Sanscrit or Arabic; that neither as the languages of law, nor as the languages of religion, have the Sanscrit and Arabic any peculiar claim to our engagement; that it is possible to make natives of this country thoroughly good English scholars; and that to this end our efforts ought to be directed.

In one point I fully agree with the gentlemen to whose general views I am opposed. I feel with them, that it is impossible for us, with our limited means, to attempt to educate the body of the people. We must at present do our best to form a class who may be interpreters between us and the millions whom we govern; a class of persons, Indian in blood and color, but English in taste, in opinions, in morals, and in intellect. To that class we may leave it to refine the vernacular dialects of the country, to enrich those dialects with terms of science borrowed from the Western nomenclature, and to render them by degrees fit vehicles for conveying knowledge to the great mass of the population.

CHAPTER XXI

THE RENASCENCE OF
HINDUISM

Just as the Muslim conquest had injected a fresh stream of religious thought into the veins of Hindu society, so the British conquest brought with it new views of the world, man, and God. Confronted with the message of Islam that all believers are equal in the sight of their Maker, religious leaders like Kabīr and Nānak had come forth in the fifteenth and sixteenth centuries to translate this teaching into traditional Hindu terms. Similarly in the nineteenth century a series of creative individuals emerged from the ranks of Hindu society to respond to the combined challenge of Christian religious ideas and of modern Western rationalist and utilitarian thought.

The renascence of Hinduism grew out of the favorable conditions created by the new rulers of India. The establishment of law and order under British administration provided Hindus with an unprecedented opportunity to improve their position vis-à-vis their former rulers, the Muslims. While the latter remained resentful of (and to a certain extent distrusted by) the new conquerors, educated Hindus entered the service of the Christian power in growing numbers. They studied English, read enthusiastically the classics of English literature, and became virtually the Anglicized Indians Macaulay had intended them to become.

A few Hindus became Christians, most clung stubbornly to orthodoxy, while a third group tried to combine the best features of both religions. Rāmmohun Roy carefully distinguished between English virtues and English errors, and defended Hinduism against the criticisms of the missionaries as vigorously as he challenged the orthodox to abandon its excrescences. Rāmmohun's policy of war on two fronts set the keynote for later champions of Hinduism against Christianity. The more deeply they were imbued by English education with a humanitarian outlook, the more keenly sensitive they became when faced with the missionaries' charge that Hinduism was a pagan and idolatrous religion, laden with barbarous customs. In order to defend Hinduism, therefore, they first had to reform it.

The Brāhmo Samāj remained for two generations after Rāmmohun Roy's death the focus of efforts to purify Hinduism and to immunize it against the Christian virus by a partial incorporation of Christian ideas and practices. Debendranāth Tagore first strengthened the Samāj's corporate worship and noble monotheism. Next Keshub Chunder Sen used revivalist sermons and Brāhmo missionaries to spread a gospel which became so close to Christian in its content that his conversion was thought imminent. The initiative then passed to Swāmī Dayānanda, who based his radical social reforms entirely on the authority of the Vedas.

Amid the hubbub of these self-conscious efforts to check the advance of Christian influence, Hindu society suddenly discovered in its midst a genuine saint and mystic. In the end, Sri Rāmakrishna's simple devotion to the traditional concepts and deities of his faith proved a more effective force than all the oratory of his predecessors. As Jesus was followed by Saint Paul, Rāmakrishna had dynamic Swāmī Vivekānanda to preach his "Gospel" to India and to the world.

The Hindu response to the Christian challenge had now come full circle from resistance, through defense by imitation, to proud self-confidence. In large part, the mounting pressure of Western secular institutions and missionary activity on Hindu society was responsible for solidifying the Hindu stand as the nineteenth century progressed. At the same time, the attention and praise which classical Indian thought was receiving from a host of European scholars added considerably to the momentum of the Hindu revival. Many Westernized Indians first took interest in the *Bhagavad Gītā* and the story of the Buddha on making their acquaintance in Sir Edwin Arnold's poetic English translations. Their self-confidence turned to pride when they read the dictum of Professor Max Müller, England's foremost Sanskritist, that in India ". . . the human mind has most fully developed some of its choicest gifts, has most deeply pondered on the greatest problems of life." [1]

Even more encouraging were the growing numbers of Europeans who rejected Western civilization and became rabid partisans of Indian culture. In 1875 the Russian Madame Blavatsky and the American Colonel

[1] F. Max Müller: *India, What Can It Teach Us?*, p. 6.

Olcott founded the Theosophical Society, which held reincarnation, karma, and other Hindu or Buddhist conceptions as central doctrines. In 1882 they moved the headquarters of the Society to Adyar, Madras. Mrs. Annie Besant, the Society's next leader, made India her permanent home from 1893 onward, and took such a prominent part in Indian politics that in 1917 she became President of the Indian National Congress—the fifth and last Britisher to receive this honor. Next came Irish-born Margaret Noble, Vivekānanda's most fervent disciple, who settled in Calcutta, took the name of Sister Niveditā (i.e., the dedicated one), and made a deep impression on Bengali thought and culture in the first decade of this century.

In the last analysis, however, European influences—whether friendly or hostile—of necessity played but a secondary role in the renascence of Hinduism. It was primarily through the efforts of a series of devout and devoted men that this ancient religion was able to recover in such a remarkable manner the deepest sources of its original inspiration. Even though their efforts primarily affected only the Western-educated (a tiny fraction of the total mass of Hindu society), this minority nevertheless possessed an influence far greater than its numbers would indicate. For they provided the leaders of the future—the Tagores and the Gāndhis—whose understanding of their Hindu heritage was decisively shaped by that galaxy of religious thinkers who had preceded them in the nineteenth century.

DEBENDRANĀTH TAGORE: RE-CREATOR OF THE BRĀHMO SAMĀJ

The influence of Rāmmohun Roy on succeeding generations was kept alive by the Brāhmo Samāj (the society of the worshipers of God) he had founded in 1828–30. After Roy's death in England, his close friend Dwārkanāth Tagore, one of India's first entrepreneurial capitalists, gave the little group his financial support, but its numbers dwindled steadily. Meanwhile, Dwārkanāth's eldest son Debendranāth (1817–1905), who used to play in Rāmmohun's yard as a boy in Calcutta, had started a small association of his own which met monthly to discuss religious questions.

In 1843 Debendranāth merged his group with the remnant of Rāmmohun Roy's, preserving the original name but injecting a new spirit into the older organization.

Under Debendranāth's devoted leadership, the Brāhmo Samāj attracted numbers of Bengal's ablest young men, many of them belonging like himself to the brāhman caste. Their spiritual center was the common worship of the one true God. Like Rāmmohun Roy, the Brāhmos (as they came to be called) opposed both the idolatry of popular Hinduism and the tactics of the Christian missionaries. Debendranāth recounts in his *Autobiography* an incident which illustrates his zeal in defense of purified Hinduism. Hearing that graduates of mission schools were becoming converts to Christianity, he called a mass meeting of the leading Hindu citizens of Calcutta and raised sufficient funds to start a free school for their children. "Thenceforward the tide of Christian conversion was stemmed," he wrote, "and the designs of the missionaries were knocked on the head." [1]

At heart, Debendranāth's nature was more devotional than combative. When his fiery young disciple, Keshub Chunder Sen, split the Samāj by insisting that Brāhmos discontinue wearing the sacred thread used by high-caste Hindus, Debendranāth withdrew from active leadership of his remaining followers and spent many months traveling to places of pilgrimage or meditating in the Himalayas. His piety throughout his long life earned him the honorific title of *Maharshi*, "the great sage."

In addition to his work in strengthening the Brāhmo Samāj Debendranāth continued the work, started by Rāmmohun Roy, of rediscovering and reviving Hindu monotheism. To find an authoritative scriptural canon for the Samāj he sent four students to Banaras, each assigned to learn one of the four Vedas. The results of their researches being inconclusive, Debendranāth came increasingly to rely on personal intuition as his authority and even composed a creed and a sacred book for the use of Brāhmos. The lofty theism and deeply devotional spirit of these documents seem to spring from the same blend of Upanishadic and Christian inspirations we find in the writings of Rāmmohun Roy. Debendranāth Tagore's contribution to the revitalization of Hinduism was therefore a happy combination of preserving and of adding creatively to its best traditions.

[1] Debendranāth Tagore, *Autobiography*, p. 39.

DEBENDRANĀTH TAGORE

The Conflict Between Sanskritic and Western Education

Debendranāth tells in his *Autobiography* the story of his search for religious certainty. The following passage describes the way he resolved the conflict between the two intellectual traditions in which he was educated.

[From Debendranāth Tagore, *Autobiography,* pp. 9–10]

As on the one hand there were my Sanskrit studies in the search after truth, so on the other hand there was English. I had read numerous English works on philosophy. But with all this, the sense of emptiness of mind remained just the same, nothing could heal it, my heart was being oppressed by that gloom of sadness and feeling of unrest. Did subjection to nature comprise the whole of man's existence? I asked. Then indeed are we undone. The might of this monster is indomitable. Fire, at a touch, reduces everything to ashes. Put out to sea in a vessel, whirlpools will drag you down to the bottom, gales will throw you into dire distress. There is no escape from the clutches of this Nature-fiend. If bowing down to her decree be our end and aim, then indeed are we undone. What can we hope for, whom can we trust? Again I thought, as things are reflected on a photographic plate by the rays of the sun, so are material objects manifested to the mind by the senses, this is what is called knowledge. Is there any other way but this of obtaining knowledge? These were the suggestions that Western philosophy had brought to my mind. To an atheist this is enough, he does not want anything beyond nature. But how could I rest fully satisfied with this? My endeavor was to obtain God, not through blind faith but by the light of knowledge. And being unsuccessful in this, my mental struggles increased from day to day. Sometimes I thought I could live no longer.

Suddenly, as I thought and thought, a flash as of lightning broke through this darkness of despondency. I saw that knowledge of the material world is born of the senses and the objects of sight, sound, smell, touch, and taste. But together with this knowledge, I am also enabled to know that I am the knower. Simultaneously with the facts of seeing, touching, smelling, and thinking, I also come to know that it is I who see, touch, smell, and think. With the knowledge of objects comes the knowledge of the subject, with the knowledge of the body comes the knowledge of the spirit within. It was after a prolonged search for truth that I found this bit of light, as if a ray of sunshine had fallen on a place full of extreme darkness. I now realized that with the knowledge of the outer world we come to know our inner self. After this, the more I thought over it, the more did I recognize the sway of wisdom operating throughout the whole world. For us the sun and moon rise and set at regular intervals, for us the wind and rain are set in motion in the proper seasons. All these combine to fulfil the one design of preserving our life. Whose design is this? It cannot be the design of matter, it must be the design of mind. Therefore this universe is propelled by the power of an intelligent being.

I saw that the child, as soon as born, drinks at its mother's breast. Who taught it to do this? He alone, who gave it life. Again who put love into the mother's heart? Who but He that put milk into her breast. He is that God who knows all our wants, whose rule the universe obeys. When my mind's eye had opened thus far, the clouds of grief were in a great measure dispelled. I felt somewhat consoled.

One day, while thinking of these things I suddenly recalled how, long ago, in my early youth, I had once realized the Infinite as manifested in the infinite heavens. Again I turned my gaze towards this infinite sky, studded with innumerable stars and planets, and saw the eternal God, and felt that this glory was His. He is infinite wisdom. He from whom we have derived this limited knowledge of ours, and this body, its receptacle, is Himself without form. He is without body or senses. He did not shape this universe with his hands. By His will alone did He bring it into existence. He is neither the Kali [1] or Kalighat,[2] nor the family *Shalgram*.[3] Thus was laid the axe at the root of idolatry.

The Call to Renunciation

Had he followed in his father's footsteps, Debendranāth could have become one of India's wealthiest men. But his innermost desire was to seek salvation through the traditional path of renunciation.

[From Debendranāth Tagore, *Autobiography*, p. 41]

My father was in England. The task of managing his various affairs devolved upon me. But I was not able to attend to any business matters

---

[1] Kālī—the Great Goddess.   [2] The temple of Kālī in Calcutta.   [3] The family idol.

properly. My subordinates used to do all the work, I was only concerned with the Vedas, the Vedanta, religion, God, and the ultimate goal of life. I was not even able to stay quietly in the house. My spirit of renunciation became deeper under all this stress of work. I felt no inclination to become the owner of all this wealth. To renounce everything and wander about alone, this was the desire that reigned in my heart. Imbued with His love I would roam in such lonely places that none would know; I would see His glory on land and water, would witness His mercy in different climes, would feel His protective power in foreign countries, in danger and peril; in this enthusiastic frame of mind I could no longer stay at home.

A Decisive Dream

When his father died, Debendranāth was faced with the choice of performing the customary Hindu funeral rites, in which offerings are made to various gods, or of remaining true to his vow to renounce idolatry. The decision came to him in this dream, whose conclusion gives us a good insight into the Hindu conceptions of religion and filial piety.
[From Debendranāth Tagore, *Autobiography*, pp. 48–49]

Which would triumph, the world or religion?—one could not tell—this was what worried me. My constant prayer to God was "Vouchsafe strength unto my weak heart, be Thou my refuge." All these anxieties and troubles would not let me sleep at night, my head felt dazed on the pillow. I would now doze off and again wake up. It was as if I was sleeping on the borderland between waking and sleeping. At such a time some one came to me in the dark and said "Get up," and I at once sat up. He said "Get out of bed" and I got up; he said "follow me" and I followed. He went down the steps leading out of the inner apartments, I did the same and came out into the courtyard with him. We stood before the front door. The durwans [4] were sleeping. My guide touched the door, and the two wings flew open at once. I went out with him into the street in front of the house. He seemed to be a shadowlike form. I could not see him clearly, but felt myself constrained to do immediately whatever he bade me. From thence he mounted up upwards to the sky, I also followed him. Clusters of stars and planets were shedding a bright

---

[4] Doorkeepers.

lustre, right and left and in front of me, and I was passing through them. On the way I entered a sea of mist, where the stars and planets were no longer visible. After traversing the mist for some distance I came upon a still full moon, like a small island in that vaporous ocean. The nearer I came the larger grew that moon. It no longer appeared round, but flat like our earth. The apparition went and stood on that earth, and I did likewise. The ground was all of white marble. Not a single blade of grass was there—no flowers, no fruit. Only that bare white plain stretched all around. The moonlight there was not derived from the sun. It shone by virtue of its own light. The rays of the sun could not penetrate the surrounding mist. Its own light was very soft, like the shade we have in the daytime. The air was pleasing to the senses. In the course of my journey across this plain I entered one of its cities. All the houses and all the streets were of white marble, not a single soul was to be seen in the clean and bright and polished streets. No noise was to be heard, everything was calm and peaceful. My guide entered a house by the road and went up to the second floor, I also went with him. I found myself in a spacious room, in which there were a table and some chairs of white marble. He told me to sit down, and I sat down in one of the chairs. The phantom then vanished. Nobody else was there. I sat silent in that silent room; shortly afterwards the curtain of one of the doors in front of the room was drawn aside and my mother appeared. Her hair was down, just as I had seen it on the day of her death. When she died, I never thought that she was dead. Even when I came back from the burning ground after performing her funeral ceremonies, I could not believe that she was dead. I felt sure that she was still alive. Now I saw that living mother of mine before me. She said "I wanted to see thee, so I sent for thee. Hast thou really become one who has known Brahma? Sanctified is the family, fulfilled is the mother's desire." On seeing her, and hearing these sweet words of hers my slumber gave way before a flood of joy. I found myself still tossing on my bed.

The Brāhmo Samāj and Its Relation to Orthodox Hinduism

After Keshub Chunder Sen had seceded from the Samāj, taking the majority of Brāhmos with him, Debendranāth pronounced in 1867 the following message on "gradualism" in matters of social reform.

[From Debendranāth Tagore, *Autobiography*, pp. 152–53]

We are worshipers of Brahma, the Supreme Being. In this we are at one with Orthodox Hinduism, for all our shastras declare with one voice the supremacy of the worship of Brahma, enjoining image worship for the help of those who are incapable of grasping the highest Truth.

Our first point of distinction is in the positive aspect of our creed wherein worship is defined as consisting in "Loving Him and doing the works He loveth"—this at once differentiates us from all religions and creeds which postulate a special or verbal revelation or wherein definite forms, rites, or ceremonials are deemed essential one way or the other.

The negative aspect of our creed which prohibits the worship of any created being or thing as the Creator further distinguishes us from all who are addicted to the worship of avatars or incarnations or who believe in the necessity of mediators, symbols, or idols of any description.

We base our faith on the fundamental truths of religion, attested by reason and conscience and refuse to permit man, book, or image to stand in the way of the direct communion of our soul with the Supreme Spirit.

This message of the Brāhmo Samāj in the abstract does not materially differ from the doctrines of the pure theistic bodies all the world over. Viewed historically and socially, however, the Brāhmo Samāj has the further distinction of being the bearer of this message to the Hindu people. This was the idea of its founder Ram Mohun Roy, this points to the duty incumbent upon all Brahmos of today, and will serve as the guiding principle in the selection of texts, forms, and ceremonials as aids to the religious life.

We are in and of the great Hindu community and it devolves upon us by example and precept to hold up as a beacon the highest truths of the Hindu shastras. In their light must we purify our heritage of customs, usages, rites, and ceremonies and adapt them to the needs of our conscience and our community. But we must beware of proceeding too fast in matters of social change, lest we be separated from the greater body whom we would guide and uplift.

While we should on no account allow any consideration of country, caste, or kinship to prevent our actions being consistent with our faith, we must make every allowance for, and abstain from, persecuting or alienating those who think differently from us. Why should we needlessly wound the feelings of our parents and elders by desecrating an image which they regard with the highest reverence, when all that our conscience can demand of us is to refrain from its adoration?

[58]

The steering of this middle course is by no means an easy task, but during my long experience I have been led greatly to hope for a brighter future by the sympathetic response of our orthodox brethren to the ideal held up before them. The amount of conformity nowadays expected by even the most orthodox, demands so little of us that a little tact and common sense will in most cases be sufficient to obviate all friction.

Nevertheless, great as are the claims of our land and our people, we must never forget that we are Brahmos first, and Indians or Hindus afterwards. We must on no account depart from our vow of renouncing the worship of images and incarnations, which is of the essence of our religion. It is a sound policy on our part to sink our minor differences, but on matters of principle no compromise is possible. Our Motherland is dear to us, but Religion is dearer, Brahma is dearest of all, dearer than son, dearer than riches, supreme over everything else.

A Farewell Message to His Followers

In 1889, thinking that he was about to die, Debendranāth set down eighteen principles for his followers. Combined in this document we find both the Christian emphasis on brotherly love and the Hindu conception of the relationship between ātman and Brahman. (The Sanskrit texts of passages in quotation marks have been omitted.)

[From Debendranāth Tagore, *Autobiography*, pp. 191–95.]

Dearly Beloved Brethren,

"Be ye united together; speak ye in unity; united know ye each the heart of the other. As the gods of old with one mind received each his offering due, even so be ye of one mind!"

"Harmonious may your efforts be, and harmonious your thoughts and heart, so that beauteous Peace may dwell in your midst!" "Live ye all one in heart and speech." This loving blessing and benediction which I have just expressed in Vedic words, it is meet ye should keep well in view, in the midst of the world's wranglings and jars. If to this end ye follow the way, then shall ye become gainers of your end. This way is the way of unity. If ye follow this way, all contentions shall depart from amongst you. Peace shall reign, and the Brāhmo religion shall have triumph.

1. The Brāhmo religion is a spiritual religion. Its seed-truth is this: By the soul shalt thou know the Supreme Soul. When God is seen in the soul, then, indeed, is He seen everywhere. The dearest dwelling-place

of Him who is the root of all this complexity, the One Sovereign of all this universe, is the soul of man. If ye know not the soul, then all is empty. The soul is of the knowledge of God.

2. In this body dwells the soul, and within it, in the pure refulgence of spiritual consciousness, the pure, bodiless Supreme Soul is to be seen. With mind and body subdued, unattached to all outward things, even-minded in sorrow and joy, self-contained, the Supreme Soul is to be viewed. This is spiritual union. When with love ye are united in this spiritual union, ye shall be delivered from all sin and shall attain the steps of salvation. After death, the body will be left here, but, united in this spiritual union, the soul shall dwell with the Soul Supreme for ever.

3. As for the health of the body ye partake of your regular daily meals, so for the soul's health the worship of God must be performed every day. The worship of God is the soul's sustenance.

4. "Loving Him and the doing of deeds pleasant in His sight, this, indeed, is His worship." That Brahma, who is beyond Time and Space, and who yet pervades Time and Space, the Witness of all, Truth, Wisdom, and Infinity—knowing Him to be the Soul's Ruler, and the Heart's Lord—adore Him every day with love, and, for the good of the world, be engaged in the performance of works of righteousness which are pleasing in His sight. Never dissever these two ever-united limbs of God's worship.

5. Let only that be done which promoteth well-being. Do no evil to an evil-doer. If any should work unrighteousness, it should not be requited by unrighteousness. Always be righteous. Evil should be overcome by good, and unrighteousness by righteousness.

6. Contend with no one. Restrain anger; and, imbued with love and charity, behave justly to all. Let love be thy rule of conduct with regard to others.

7. By day and night instruct yourselves—govern yourselves—and accept righteousness as the end of existence. For him who can subdue his heart and senses, there remains no cause for sorrow and suffering. For him who cannot restrain himself there is suffering on every side.

8. He who desireth the good of mankind must look on others as he looks on himself. It behoves thee to love thy neighbor, since it pleases thee to be loved by him, and to avoid giving pain by hatred, since it causes thee pain to be hated by another. Thus in all things shalt thou deal with others by comparing them with thyself; for as pleasure and pain affect

thee, so do they affect all creatures. Such conduct alone is the means of attaining well-being.

9. He who adores God and loves man is a saint. Such a man never rejoices in finding fault with men, for man is beloved of him. He is pained by the sight of a fault in others, and lovingly does he labor for its correction. He loves man as man; and owing to that love, is pleased by the sight of good, and grieved by the sight of evil in man. Therefore he is unable to proclaim the faults of others with rejoicing.

10. The satisfaction of the inner spirit, or, in other words, a good conscience, is the unfailing fruit of the practice of righteousness. In this favor of conscience is felt the favor of God. If the inner spirit is satisfied, all sufferings cease. Without the practice of righteousness, the inner spirit is never satisfied. The mind may find enjoyment in the pleasures of the world, but if the conscience is diseased, then even the height of worldly bliss becomes valueless. Therefore, by the practice of righteousness, ye shall preserve a clear conscience, and ye shall abandon all things whereby the satisfaction of the spirit may be marred.

11. Ye shall seek the practice of righteousness to the utmost of your power. If, after the exercise of all your power, ye fail to attain the end, yet ye shall acquire merit thereby. God does not reckon what portion of His infinite work is performed by individuals. Let every one use the powers given him, without reservation; this is God's ordinance.

12. Ye shall abjure sinful thoughts, sinful speech, and sinful acts. Those who do not sin in thought, word, deed, or judgment—such saints truly practice austerity; not those who mortify the flesh. Therefore, abstaining from sin, engage in good works. Persevering on the road of righteousness, ye shall earn your livelihood.

13. If, by perseverence on the road of righteousness, ye are completely cast down, even then ye shall not turn your thoughts to unrighteous means. Protect dharma with your lives, and dharma will protect you.

14. Not father or mother, nor wife or child, nor friend or relation, remains as our stay in the next world. Righteousness alone remains. Alone a man is born, alone he dies, alone he enjoys the good fruits of his righteous acts, and alone he suffers the evil consequences of his bad deeds. Friends, leaving on the earth his body like a stock or stone, turn away from him; but righteousness follows him whither he goeth. Therefore, ye shall, step by step, acquire righteousness, which shall be your stay.

Dharma is our friend in this world, and dharma is the guide to the next. "Dharma is as honey unto all creatures."

15. "Not by wealth, nor by children, nor by works, but by renunciation alone, is immortality attained." Renunciation is not the renunciation of the world by becoming an anchorite, dwelling in the wilderness, but dwelling at home, and living in the world, all lusts of the heart should be cast out.

"When all lusts that dwell in the heart of man are cast out, then the mortal becomes immortal, and even on earth attains God."

16. With all diligence shall ye cherish your wives and children and relations; but, being yourselves free from desire, remain unattached to the fruit of your acts, and then ye shall be able to mount the steps of salvation. God's own love furnishes the most perfect example. See how mindful He is of the interests of the world. He never forgets to give food even to a single worm or insect. Even in the bowels of arid mountains, He supplies nourishment to living creatures. Yet He keeps nothing for Himself. He is always giving to all, and never receives. By the light of this example, ye, too, forgetting yourselves, shall be vowed to work for the good of the world. Being united to Him, ye shall perform the duties of life. That which ye shall know to be His command, ye must obey with your lives. That which ye shall know to be against His will, ye shall shun like poison. If thus, forgetful of self, ye perform His work, then be sure He will not forget you, with gratitude receive it as plenty. In whatever condition He may place you, with that be contented. In seasons of prosperity, live in obedience to Him; and, in seasons of adversity, take refuge in Him; and ye shall not be perplexed. At the time of action, act resting in Him; at the time of rest, rest even in Him. This body will move about on earth, but your souls will be united with Him. Even in death there is no dissolution of this union.

17. Blessed is that soul which, self-subdued, freed from sin and impurity like the moon from the shadow of eclipse, and casting off the pride of flesh, can rest in the Supreme Soul. That soul is not cast down by disease, is not frightened by death; it sees from here the abode of God; to it the door of the infinitude of progress is opened, and before it millions on millions of heavens shine forth. On this side is the billowy world of change, on the other side the Peaceful Abode of God; in the middle God

Himself, like a bridge, preserves the position of both. Neither day nor night, nor death, disease, or sorrow, nor good or evil deed, is able to cross this bridge. All kinds of sin fall back from there. Sin has no power in the Sinless Abode of Brahma. The liberated soul, leaving behind him the sin and sorrow of this world, attains the Abode of Brahma, beyond this world. There the blind cease to be blind; the sin-stricken become free from sin; for the Abode of Brahma is for ever resplendent; to that splendor there is no end.

18. Following the previous teachings of Brahma-dharma, I make you this offering of my last words. May ye realize it in your lives and attain to everlasting salvation—this is my prayer!

Om—Peace, Peace, Peace.

KESHUB CHUNDER SEN AND THE INDIANIZATION OF CHRISTIANITY

The stormy career of Keshub Chunder Sen [1] encompassed both the peak and the later decline of the influence of the Brāhmo Samāj on Indian intellectual life. With his great energy and oratorical skill he brought to fulfillment the openness to Christian inspiration of Rāmmohun Roy and the intuitionist doctrine of Debendranāth Tagore. Yet his very enthusiasm was his undoing, for by the time of his death he had shattered the Samāj into three separate organizations and damaged its prestige irrevocably.

Keshub's grandfather was a contemporary and friend of Rāmmohun Roy, but did not share the great reformer's ideas on religion. The Sen family was one of the most Westernized in Bengal, and young Keshub grew up speaking English more fluently than Bengali. His career as a student at the Hindu College was marred by his failure in mathematics, but he took great interest in philosophy and ethics. At nineteen his religious spirit found its natural orbit in the Brāhmo Samāj. Within a short time Keshub had become Debendranāth's most beloved disciple. When he was excommunicated by his own family for having taken his wife to

[1] Or Keshab Chandra Sen.

[63]

a Brāhmo ceremony, Keshub found shelter in the home of his religious teacher.

With unquenchable energy, Keshub threw himself into the activities of the Brāhmo Samāj, founding discussion groups and schools, organizing famine relief, advocating remarriage for widows and education for young women, writing religious tracts, and giving sermons. His fiery oratory in fluent English stirred educated audiences in many parts of India, especially in Bombay, and branches of the Samāj sprang up in cities beyond the borders of Bengal.

Keshub's zeal for social reform carried him far beyond the moderate position taken by Debendranāth. The two finally parted in 1865 over the wearing of the sacred thread and Keshub set up an independent organization which he named the Brāhmo Samāj of India. From this point on, his faith in inspiration as the guide to action grew more pronounced. In 1878 another and more fatal fission took place within his own movement. Despite his prolonged advocacy of a minimum age for Brāhmo marriages, and his opposition to idolatry, he was persuaded to marry his thirteen-year-old daughter to a Hindu prince, feeling that such was the will of God. Scandalized by this betrayal of his previous principles, most of his followers abandoned him and set up a third group, the Sādhāran (General) Brāhmo Samāj.

In the last years of his life Keshub experimented in synthesizing elements from the world's major religions. Although he borrowed devotional and yogic practices from Hinduism, he drew even more heavily on Christian teachings and practices. The New Dispensation which he proclaimed in 1879 appropriated much from the Christian church which it claimed to supplant, including among other things a direct revelation from God, apostles, missionaries, monastic orders, and the doctrines of sin, salvation, and the divinity of Christ.

Of Keshub's work little remained after his death in 1884 at the age of forty-five. The flaming enthusiasm which had launched him on so many enterprises, and the eloquent oratory which electrified so many audiences, left surprisingly few monuments. But the force of his example was felt in Bengal for decades, and his methods—particularly his oratorical conquests and his synthesizing of Indian and Western ideas—have been imitated by later religious leaders and nationalist politicians alike.

[64]

KESHUB CHUNDER SEN

Enthusiasm

Two years before his death Keshub penetratingly summed up his nature and the activities into which it had plunged him.

[From Mozoomdar, *Life and Teachings of Keshub Chunder Sen,* pp. 15–16]

If I ask thee, O Self, in what creed wast thou baptized in early life? The self answers in the baptism of fire. I am a worshiper of the religion of fire, I am partial to the doctrine of enthusiasm. To me a state of being on fire is the state of salvation. My heart palpitates as soon as I perceive any coldness in my life. When the body becomes cold, it is death, when religion becomes cold, it is death also. It may take time to know whether I am a sinner or not, but it is easy to know whether I am alive or dead; I at once decide this by finding whether I am warm or cold. I live in the midst of fire, I love, embrace, and exalt fire. Every sign of heat fills me with joy, hope, zeal. As soon as I feel the fire is losing its heat, I feel as if I would jump into the sea and drown myself. When I find that a man after five years of enthusiasm is getting to be lukewarm, I at once conclude he is on the highway of a sinful life, that before long death will tread on his neck. I have always felt a cold condition to be a state of impurity. Coldness and hell have always been the same to my mind. Around my own life, around the society in which I lived, I always kept burning the flame of enthusiasm. When I succeeded in serving one body of men, I always sought another body whom I might serve. When I successfully worked in one department of life, I always sighed to work in other departments also. When I gathered truths from one set of scriptures, I have longed for others, and before finishing these I have looked out for others again, lest anything should become old or cold to me. This is my life that I am continually after new ideas, new acquirements, new enjoyments.

Loyalty to the British Nation

Keshub was only voicing the sentiments of his time when he declared British rule providential for India. His conviction that India had a reciprocal contribution to make to England was a relatively new idea, and one which was to take on increasing importance in the nationalist era. This speech was delivered in Calcutta in 1877, shortly after Queen Victoria had assumed the title of Empress of India.

[From "Philosophy and Madness in Religion," in *Keshub Chunder Sen's Lectures in India,* pp. 322–26]

Loyalty shuns an impersonal abstraction. It demands a person, and that person is the sovereign, or the head of the state, in whom law and constitutionalism are visibly typified and represented. We are right then if our loyalty means not only respect for law and the Parliament, but personal attachment to Victoria, Queen of England and Empress of India. [Applause.] What makes loyalty so enthusiastic is not, however, the presence of purely secular feelings, but of a strong religious sentiment. By loyalty I mean faith in Providence. It is this faith which gives loyalty all its sanctity and solidity, and establishes it in the individual heart and in society as a holy passion. Do you not believe that there is God in history? Do you not recognize the finger of special providence in the progress of nations? Assuredly the record of British rule in India is not a chapter of profane history, but of ecclesiastical history. [Cheers.] The book which treats of the moral, social, and religious advancement of our great country with the help of Western science, under the paternal rule of the British nation, is indeed a sacred book. There we see clearly that it is Providence that rules India through England. [Applause.] Were you present at the magnificent spectacle at Delhi, on the day of the assumption of the imperial title by our sovereign? Some men have complained that no religious ceremony was observed on the occasion, and indeed opinion is divided on this point. None, however, can gainsay the fact that the whole affair, from beginning to end was a most solemn religious ceremony, and I rejoice I am privileged to say this in the presence of our noble-hearted Viceroy. Was any devout believer in Providence there? To him I appeal. Let him say whether the imperial assemblage was not a spectacle of deep moral and religious significance. Did not the eye of the faithful believer see that God Himself stretched His right hand and placed the Empress' crown upon Victoria's head? [Loud cheers.] And did he not hear the Lord God say unto her: "Rule thy subjects with justice and truth and mercy, according to the light given unto thee and thy advisers, and let righteousness and peace and prosperity dwell in the Empire"? [Applause.]

Would you characterize this sight and this sound as a visionary dream?

Is there no truth in the picture? Who can deny that Victoria is an instrument in the hands of Providence to elevate this degraded country in the scale of nations, and that in her hands the solemn trust has lately been most solemnly reposed? Glory then to Empress Victoria! [Applause.] Educated countrymen, you are bound to be loyal to your Divinely-appointed sovereign. Not to be loyal argues base ingratitude and absence of faith in Providence. You are bound to be loyal to the British government, that came to your rescue, as God's ambassador, when your country was sunk in ignorance and superstition and hopeless jejuneness, and has since lifted you to your present high position. This work is not of man, but of God, and He has done it, and is doing it, through the British nation. As His chosen instruments, then, honor your sovereign and the entire ruling body with fervent loyalty. The more loyal we are, the more we shall advance with the aid of our rulers in the path of moral, social, and political reformation. India in her present fallen condition seems destined to sit at the feet of England for many long years, to learn Western art and science. And, on the other hand, behold England sits at the feet of hoary-headed India to study the ancient literature of this country. [Applause.] All Europe seems to be turning her attention in these days towards Indian antiquities, to gather the priceless treasures which lie buried in the literature of Vedism and Buddhism. Thus while we learn modern science from England, England learns ancient wisdom from India. Gentlemen, in the advent of the English nation in India we see a reunion of parted cousins, the descendants of two different families of the ancient Aryan race. Here they have met together, under an overruling Providence, to serve most important purposes in the Divine economy. The mutual intercourse between England and India, political as well as social, is destined to promote the true interests and lasting glory of both nations. We were rejoiced to see the rajahs and maharajahs of India offering their united homage to Empress Victoria and her representative at the imperial assemblage. Far greater will be our rejoicing when all the chiefs and people of India shall be united with the English nation, in a vast international assemblage, before the throne of the King of Kings and the Lord of Lords! [Loud cheers.] May England help us to draw near to that consummation, by giving us as much of the light of the West as lies in her power! That is her mission in India. May she fulfill it nobly and honorably. Let England give us her industry and arts, her exact sciences and

[67]

her practical philosophy, so much needed in a land where superstition and prejudices prevail to an alarming extent. But we shall not forget our ancient sages and Rishis. Ye venerable devotees of ancient India! teach us meditation and asceticism and loving communion. Let England baptize us with the spirit of true philosophy. Let the sages of Aryan India baptize us with the spirit of heavenly madness. Let modern England teach hard science and fact; let ancient India teach sweet poetry and sentiment. Let modern England give us her fabrics; but let the gorgeous East lend her charming colors. Come then, fellow countrymen and friends, and accept this divine creed, in which you will find all that is goodliest, fairest, and sweetest, based upon a foundation scientific, strong and sound—a creed in which truth and love are harmonized. Let us have only fifty young men from our universities, trained in science and philosophy, and baptized with the spirit of madness, and let these men go forth as missionary-soldiers of God, conquering and to conquer, and in the fullness of time the banners of truth shall be planted throughout the length and breadth of the country. [Loud cheers.]

The Asiatic Christ

Whereas Rāmmohun Roy welcomed only the moral influence of Jesus, Keshub embraced Christ as the fulfillment of India's devotional striving. He also took Roy's assertion that Jesus was an Asian by birth and used it as an argument for better understanding between the rulers and the ruled in India.

[From "Jesus Christ: Europe and Asia," in *Keshub Chunder Sen's Lectures in India,* pp. 33–34]

Europeans and natives are both the children of God, and the ties of brotherhood should bind them together. Extend, then, to us, O ye Europeans in India! the right hand of fellowship, to which we are fairly entitled. If, however, our Christian friends persist in traducing our nationality and national character, and in distrusting and hating Orientalism, let me assure them that I do not in the least feel dishonored by such imputations. On the contrary, I rejoice, yea, I am proud, that I am an Asiatic. And was not Jesus Christ an Asiatic? [Deafening applause.] Yes, and his disciples were Asiatics, and all the agencies primarily employed for the propagation of the Gospel were Asiatic. In fact, Christianity was founded and developed by Asiatics, and in Asia.

When I reflect on this, my love for Jesus becomes a hundredfold intensified; I feel him nearer my heart, and deeper in my national sympathies. Why should I then feel ashamed to acknowledge that nationality which he acknowledged? Shall I not rather say he is more congenial and akin to my Oriental nature, more agreeable to my Oriental habits of thought and feeling? And is it not true that an Asiatic can read the imageries and allegories of the Gospel, and its descriptions of natural sceneries, of customs, and manners, with greater interest, and a fuller perception of their force and beauty, than Europeans? [Cheers.] In Christ we see not only the exaltedness of humanity, but also the grandeur of which Asiatic nature is susceptible. To us Asiatics, therefore, Christ is doubly interesting, and his religion is entitled to our peculiar regard as an altogether Oriental affair. The more this great fact is pondered, the less I hope will be the antipathy and hatred of European Christians against Oriental nationalities, and the greater the interest of the Asiatics in the teachings of Christ. And thus in Christ, Europe and Asia, the East and the West, may learn to find harmony and unity. [Deafening applause.]

An Indian National Church

With characteristic enthusiasm, Keshub saw in the simple theism of the Brāhmo Samāj a platform on which the major religious traditions of India—Hindu, Muslim, Christian—could unite. The resulting faith, he thought, would sustain not only the future church of India, but would qualify India to take part in a world-wide religious brotherhood. Keshub's expectation that Hindus and Muslims would willingly merge into this national church is but one more example of his supreme optimism.

[From "The Future Church," in *Keshub Chunder Sen's Lectures in India,* pp. 155–60]

I have briefly described the general features of the church of the future—its worship, creed, and gospel. Before I conclude I must say a few words with special reference to this country. There are some among us who denounce Mahomedanism as wholly false, while others contend that Hinduism is altogether false. Such opinions are far from being correct; they only indicate the spirit of sectarian antipathy. Do you think that millions of men would to this day attach themselves so devotedly to these systems of faith unless there was something really valuable and true in them? This cannot be. There is, no doubt, in each of these

[69]

creeds, much to excite to ridicule, and perhaps indignation—a large amount of superstition, prejudice, and even corruption. But I must emphatically say it is wrong to set down Hinduism or Mahomedanism as nothing but a mass of lies and abominations, and worthy of being trampled under foot. Proscribe and eliminate all that is false therein: there remains a residue of truth and purity which you are bound to honor. You will find certain central truths in these systems, though surrounded by errors, which constitute their vitality, and which have preserved them for centuries in spite of opposition, and in which hundreds of good men have always found the bread of life. It is these which form even now the mighty pillars of Hinduism and Mahomedanism, and challenge universal admiration and respect. It is idle to suppose that such gigantic systems of faith will be swept away by the fervor of youthful excitement, or the violent fulminations of sectarian bigotry, so long as there is real power in them. All the onslaughts which are being leveled against them in this age of free inquiry and bold criticism will tend, not to destroy them, but to purify them and develop their true principles. The signs of the times already indicate this process of purification and development; and I believe this process will gradually bring Hinduism and Mahomedanism, hitherto so hostile to each other, into closer union, till the two ultimately harmonize to form the future church of India.

The Hindu's notion of God is sublime. In the earliest Hindu scriptures God is represented as the Infinite Spirit dwelling in His own glory, and pervading all space, full of peace and joy. On the other hand, the Mahomedans describe their God as infinite in power, governing the universe with supreme authority as the Lord of all. Hence the principal feature of the religion of the Hindu is quiet contemplation, while that of the religion of the Mahomedan is constant excitement and active service. The one lives in a state of quiet communion with his God of peace; the other lives as a soldier, ever serving the Almighty Ruler, and crusading against evil. These are the primary and essential elements of the two creeds, and, if blended together, would form a beautiful picture of true theology, which will be realized in the future church of this country. As the two creeds undergo development, their errors and differences will disappear, and they will harmoniously coalesce in their fundamental and vital principles. The future creed of India will be a composite faith, resulting from the union of the true and divine elements of

Hinduism and Mahomedanism, and showing the profound devotion of the one and the heroic enthusiasm of the other. The future sons and daughters of this vast country will thus inherit precious legacies from Hinduism and Mahomedanism, and, while enjoying the blessings of the highest and sweetest communion with the God of love, will serve Him in the battlefield of life with fidelity to truth and unyielding opposition to untruth and sin. As regards Christianity and its relation to the future church of India, I have no doubt in my mind that it will exercise great influence on the growth and formation of that church. The spirit of Christianity has already pervaded the whole atmosphere of Indian society, and we breathe, think, feel, and move in a Christian atmosphere. Native society is being roused, enlightened, and reformed under the influence of Christian education. If it is true that the future of a nation is determined by all the circumstances and agencies which today influence its nascent growth, surely the future church of this country will be the result of the purer elements of the leading creeds of the day, harmonized, developed, and shaped under the influence of Christianity.

But the future church of India must be thoroughly national; it must be an essentially Indian church. The future religion of the world I have described will be the common religion of all nations, but in each nation it will have an indigenous growth, and assume a distinctive and peculiar character. All mankind will unite in a universal church; at the same time, it will be adapted to the peculiar circumstances of each nation, and assume a national form. No country will borrow or mechanically imitate the religion of another country; but from the depths of the life of each nation its future church will naturally grow up. And shall not India have its own national church? Dr. Norman McLeod, in expounding last year, in this very hall, his ideas of the future church of this country, said emphatically that it would be a purely Indian church, and not a reproduction of any of the established churches of the West. Though I differ from that learned and liberal-minded gentleman in regard to the doctrines and tenets of that church as set forth by him, I fully agree with him that that church must have a strictly national growth and a national organization. Neither will Germany adopt the religious life of China, nor will India accept blindly that of England or of any other European country. India has religious traditions and associations, tastes and customs, peculiarly sacred and dear to her, just as every other country has, and it is idle to expect that she will forego these; nay, she cannot do so, as they are interwoven with her very life. In common with all other nations and communities, we shall embrace the theistic worship, creed, and gospel of the future church—we shall acknowledge and adore the Holy One, accept the love and service of God and man as our creed, and put our firm faith in God's almighty grace as the only means of our redemption. But we shall do all this in a strictly national and Indian style. We shall see that the future church is not thrust upon us, but that we independently and naturally grow into it; that it does not come to us as a foreign plant, but that it strikes its roots deep in the national heart of India, draws its sap from our national resources, and develops itself with all the freshness and vigor of indigenous growth. One religion shall be acknowledged by all men, One God shall be worshiped throughout the length and breadth of the world; the same spirit of faith and love shall pervade all hearts; all nations shall dwell together in the Father's house—yet each shall have its own peculiar and free mode of action. There shall, in short, be unity of spirit, but diversity of forms; one body, but different limbs; one vast community, with members laboring, in different ways and according to their respective resources and peculiar tastes, to advance their common cause. Thus India shall sing the glory of the Supreme Lord with Indian voice and with Indian accompaniments, and so shall England and America, and the various races and tribes and nations of the world, with their own peculiar voice and music, sing His glory; but all their different voices and peculiar modes of chanting shall commingle in one sweet and swelling chorus—one universal anthem proclaiming in solemn and stirring notes, in the world below and the heavens above, "the Fatherhood of God and the brotherhood of man." May the Merciful Lord hasten the advent of the true church, and establish peace and harmony among His children! And as His name has been solemnly chanted tonight in this splendid hall by an immense concourse of worshipers of various races and tribes, so may all His children assemble in His holy mansions, and blending their million voices in one grand chorus, glorify Him time without end.

The New Dispensation

The central idea of Keshub's New Dispensation was that the new faith constituted a direct continuation of the Old and New Testament revelations. Implicit in his bold claims lay the assumption that the Hindu religious genius was able to reconcile and harmonize all conflicting creeds. This daring concept of India's spiritual mission to the world has been voiced by many of her thinkers since Keshub's time.

[From "We Apostles of the New Dispensation," in *Keshub Chunder Sen's Lectures in India*, pp. 464–68, 484–85]

Admit, then, that Paul was a necessary logical adjunct and consequent of Christ, as Moses was, indeed, his antecedent. Does the continuity stop here? No. If the New Testament follows the Old in the line of logical sequence, the new dispensation follows as necessarily all the old dispensations which have gone before it. If you cannot separate Paul from Christ, surely you cannot separate us from Paul. Are we not servants of Paul and apostles of Jesus? Yes. You cannot regard us otherwise. When I say the New Dispensation is a sequence of the Christian dispensation you will no doubt admit a chronological succession. You will perhaps go further, and trace a theological connection. But you have yet to discover a logical succession. Students of logic will yet recognize in the present movement a deduction and a sequence resulting from the Christian dispensation. You cannot deny us. We are the fulfillment of Moses. He was simply the incarnation of Divine conscience. But there was no science in his teachings, that science which in modern times is so greatly honored. Let Moses grow into modern science, and you have the new dispensation, which may be characterized as the union of the conscience and science. As for Christ, we are surely among his honored ambassadors. We are a deduction and corollary from his teachings. The new dispensation is Christ's prophecy fulfilled. Did not Jesus predict and foreshadow a fuller dispensation of light and grace? Did he not say the Comforter would come after him, and guide the world "into all truth"? Do you not remember those prophetic words?: "I have yet many things to say unto you, but ye cannot bear them now. Howbeit when he, the spirit of truth, is come, he will guide you into all truth." And touching the subject of synthetic unity, one can hardly conceive a clearer foreboding than is to be found in those words of Paul: "That in the dispensation of the fullness of time he might gather together in one all things in Christ, both which are in heaven and which are in earth, even in him." Inasmuch as the present dispensation sums up all things in a divine synthesis unifying all in God, and seeks new light in the direct inspiration of the Comforter or Holy Spirit, one cannot fail to recognize

[73]

in it the fulfillment of an ancient prophecy, the realization of Christian and Pauline anticipations. What do we see before us in India today but the fruit of that tree, whose seed Jesus planted, and Paul watered, centuries ago? The unbeliever may hold that Christ wholly denies us, and is far away from us. But faith points to his spirit in us, and maintains an unbroken continuity of dispensation. Wherever a dozen disciples are gathered in his name, he is there. We in India are imbued with his spirit. If it be true that the faith of our ancient Aryan ancestors has permeated us, it is equally true that Christ has leavened us and Christianized us. The Acts of his Hindu Apostles will form a fresh chapter in his universal gospel. Can he deny us, his logical succession? Surely he cannot. And so Paul too. Wilt thou reject us, Saint Paul? Revered Brother, wilt thou cast us away as thine enemies? Is not thy spirit in us? Let our lives testify. Gentlemen, what was Paul's great mission? To obliterate the distinction between Jew and Gentile. "I speak to you Gentiles," said he; "inasmuch as I am the apostle of Gentiles, I magnify mine office." "There is no difference between the Jew and the Greek: for the same Lord over all is rich unto all that call upon him." Again, in his Epistle to the Corinthians, "By one Spirit are we all baptized into one body, whether we be Jews or Gentiles." Paul was raised by God to break caste, and level the distinctions of race and nationality; and nobly did he fulfill his mission. The Jew and the Gentile he made into one body. The modern Pauls of the new dispensation are carrying on a similar crusade against caste in India. The obnoxious distinctions between Brahmin and Sudra, between Hindu and Yavana, between Asiatic and European, the new gospel of love thoroughly proscribes.

In the kingdom of God there is no invidious distinction, and therefore this dispensation gathers all men and nations, all races and tribes, the high and the low, and seeks to establish one vast brotherhood among the children of the great God, who hath made of one blood all nations of men. Let them that have eyes see that in the midst of the great spiritual revolution and revival going on in this land, Moses and Christ and Paul are gathering through us the many tribes of Israel, and uniting all in the name of the kingdom of heaven. . . .

In all ages devout and godly men have eaten the flesh of saints and been in turn eaten by others. Divinity went into the flesh of Christ.

Then Christ was eaten by Paul and Peter. They were eaten by the fathers and the martyrs and all the saints in Christendom, and all these have we of modern times eaten, assimilated, and absorbed, making their ideas and character our own. Thus one nation may swallow another, and be identified with it. Thus one generation may draw into itself the character and faith of another generation. And we too may enter into each other and dwell in each other. We Hindus are specially endowed with, and distinguished for, the yoga faculty, which is nothing but this power of spiritual communion and absorption. This faculty, which we have inherited from our forefathers, enables us to annihilate space and time, and bring home to our minds an external Deity and an external humanity. Waving the magic wand of yoga, we say to the Ural mountains and the river Ural, Vanish, and lo! they disappear. And we command Europe to enter into the heart of Asia, and Asia to enter into the mind of Europe, and they obey us, and we instantly realize within ourselves an European Asia and an Asiatic Europe, a commingling of oriental and occidental ideas and principles. We say to the Pacific, Pour thy waters into the Atlantic; and we say to the West, Roll back to the East. We summon ancient India to come into modern India with all her rishis and saints, her asceticism and communion and simplicity of character, and behold a transfiguration! The educated modern Hindu cast in Vedic mold! How by yoga one nation becomes another! How Asia eats the flesh and drinks the blood of Europe! How the Hindu absorbs the Christian; how the Christian assimilates the Hindu! Cultivate this communion, my brethren, and continually absorb all that is good and noble in each other. Do not hate, do not exclude others, as the sectarians do, but include and absorb all humanity and all truth. Let there be no antagonism, no exclusion. Let the embankment which each sect, each nation, has raised, be swept away by the flood of cosmopolitan truth, and let all the barriers and partitions which separate man from man be pulled down, so that truth and love and purity may flow freely through millions of hearts and through hundreds of successive generations, from country to country, from age to age. Thus shall the deficiencies of individual and national character be complemented, and humanity shall attain a fuller and more perfect standard of religious and moral life.

DAYĀNANDA SARASWATĪ: VEDIC REFORMER

While Keshub Chunder Sen was preaching an Indianized version of Christianity in Bengal, a stern ascetic arose in northern India who vigorously rejected Western ideas and undertook instead to revive the ancient religion of the Aryans. Swāmī Dayānanda Saraswatī (1824–1883) was even more ardent a reformer than Keshub, yet he drew his strength from purely indigenous sources. Standing foursquare on the authority of the Vedas, he fearlessly denounced the evils of post-Vedic Hinduism.

Dayānanda was born into a brāhman family in a princely state of Gujarat, a section of western India relatively untouched by British cultural influence. His well-to-do father instructed him in Sanskrit and Shaivism from the age of five, but Dayānanda revolted against idol-worship at fourteen, and to avoid being married ran away from home at nineteen to become a sannyāsī (religious mendicant) of the *Sarasvatī* order. He spent the next fifteen years as a wandering ascetic, living in jungles, in Himalayan retreats, and at places of pilgrimage throughout northern India. A tough, blind old teacher completed his education by literally beating into him a reverence for the four Vedas and a disdain for all later scriptures.

For the rest of his life Dayānanda lectured in all parts of India on the exclusive authority of the Vedas. Time after time he challenged all comers to religious debates, but few could withstand his forceful forensic attack. Idol-worship is not sanctioned by the Vedas, he pointed out, nor is untouchability, nor child marriage, nor the subjection of women to unequal status with men. The study of the Vedas should be open to all, not just to brāhmans, and a man's caste should be in accordance with his merits. Such revolutionary teachings evoked the wrath of the orthodox and numerous attempts were made on Dayānanda's life. His great physical strength saved him from swordsmen, thugs, and cobras, but the last of many attempts to poison him succeeded. Like John the Baptist, he accused a princely ruler of loose living, and the woman in question instigated his death by having ground glass put in his milk.

Dayānanda's energetic and sometimes acrimonious method of preaching epitomized the change among Hindu religious leaders from a passive or defensive attitude to an active and aggressive one. His claims were sometimes extravagant, however, as with his assertion that firearms and electricity were described in the Vedas. His followers dubbed him "the Luther of India," and considering the fervor of his reforms and the great importance which he attached to the Vedas as a holy "book," the analogy is quite apt. The Ārya Samāj (the Society of the Āryas, or "noble men") which he established at Bombay in 1875 has since reflected the militant character of its founder, and from its stronghold in the Punjab has contributed to the rise of Hindu nationalism.

DAYĀNANDA SARASWATĪ
Of Mice and Idols

A major turning point in Dayānanda's life came at fourteen, when he observed for the first time a special all-night fast and vigil in honor of the god Shiva. What other Hindu boys accepted unthinkingly caused in him such revulsion that he waged war on idolatry for the rest of his days.

[From Har Bilas Sarda, *Life of Dayanand Saraswati*, pp. 5-6]

Wherever the *Siva Purāna*[1] was to be read and explained, there my father was sure to take me along with him. Finally unmindful of my mother's remonstrances, he imperatively demanded that I should begin practicing Parthiva Puja.[2] When the great day of gloom and fasting— called Shivaratri—arrived, this day falling on the 13th of Vadya of Magh,[3] my father regardless of the protest of my mother that my strength might fail, commanded me to keep a fast adding that I had to be initiated on that night into the sacred legend and participate in that night's long vigil in the temple of Shiva. Accordingly, I followed him along with other young men, who accompanied their parents. This vigil is divided into four parts called *paharas,* consisting of three hours each. Having completed my task, namely, having sat up for the first two paharas till the hour of midnight, I remarked that the pujaris, or temple servants and some of the lay devotees, after having left the inner temple, had fallen asleep outside. Having been taught for years that by sleeping on that particular night, the worshiper loses all the good effect of his devotion, I tried to refrain from drowsiness by bathing my eyes now

---

[1] Didactic tale of Shiva.   [2] The worship of the clay emblem of Shiva.
[3] Vadya, the dark, or second fortnight of the lunar month. Māgha, the eleventh month of the Hindu calendar.

and then with cold water. But my father was less fortunate. Unable to resist fatigue, he was the first to fall asleep, leaving me to watch alone.

Thoughts upon thoughts crowded upon me, and one question arose after another in my disturbed mind. Is it possible, I asked myself, that this semblance of man, the idol of a Personal God that I see bestriding his bull before me, and who, according to all religious accounts, walks about, eats, sleeps, and drinks; who can hold a trident in his hand, beat upon his dumroo [drum], and pronounce curses upon men—is it possible that he can be the Mahadeva, the great Deity, the same that is invoked as the Lord of Kailas,[4] the supreme being and the Divine hero of all the stories we read of in the Puranas? Unable to resist such thoughts any longer, I awoke my father abruptly asking him to enlighten me and tell me whether this hideous emblem of Shiva in the temple was identical with the Mahadeva (Great God) of the scriptures, or something else. "Why do you ask it?" said my father. Because, I answered, I feel it impossible to reconcile the idea of an omnipotent, living God, with this idol, which allows the mice to run upon its body, and thus suffers its image to be polluted without the slightest protest. Then my father tried to explain to me that this stone representation of the Mahadeva of Kailasa, having been consecrated with the Veda mantras in the most solemn way by the holy Brahmins, became in consequence the God himself, and is worshiped as such, adding that as Shiva cannot be perceived personally in this Kali Yug—the age of mental darkness—we have the idol in which the Mahadeva of Kailasa is worshiped by his votaries; this kind of worship is pleasing to the great Deity as much as if, instead of the emblem, he were there himself. But the explanation fell short of satisfying me. I could not, young as I was, help suspecting misinterpretation and sophistry in all this. Feeling faint with hunger and fatigue, I begged to be allowed to go home. My father consented to it, and sent me away with a sepoy, only reiterating once more his command that I should not eat. But when once home, I told my mother of my hunger and she fed me with sweetmeats, and I fell into profound sleep.

In the morning, when my father returned and learnt that I had broken my fast, he felt very angry. He tried to impress me with the enormity of sin; but do what he could I could not bring myself to believe that that idol and Mahadeva were one and the same God, and therefore, could

[4] A mountain peak of the Himalayas where Shiva's Heaven is believed to be situated.

[78]

not comprehend why I should be made to fast for the worship of the former. I had, however, to conceal my lack of faith, and bring forward as an excuse for abstaining from regular worship my ordinary studies, which really left me little or rather no time for anything else. In this I was strongly supported by my mother and even my uncle who pleaded my cause so well that my father had to yield at last and allowed me to devote my whole attention to my studies.

A Debate with a Christian and a Muslim

Dayānanda loved to engage in religious debates, usually with orthodox Hindus, but occasionally with representatives of other faiths. The following summary of his debate with a Christian minister and a Muslim *maulvi* [5] gives a good picture of his harshly critical attitude toward their respective religions—an attitude which led his later followers into intermittent friction with India's Muslims.

[From Har Bilas Sarda, *Life of Dayanand Saraswati*, pp. 170-72]

As time was short, after some talk it was decided that the question "What is salvation and how to attain it," should be discussed. As both the Christians and the Muslims declined to open the debate, Swamiji opened it. He said:

"Mukti or salvation means deliverance, in other words, to get rid of all suffering, and to realize God, to remain happy and free from rebirth. Of the means to attain it, the first is to practice truth, that is truth which is approved both by one's conscience and God. That is truth, in uttering which, one gets encouragement, happiness, and fearlessness. In uttering untruth, fear, doubt, and shame are experienced. As the third mantra of the fortieth chapter of Yajurveda says, those who violate God's teachings, that is, those who speak, act, or believe against one's conscience are called Asur, Rakkhshas, wicked and sinful. The second means to attain salvation is to acquire knowledge of the Vedas and follow truth. The third means is to associate with men of truth and knowledge. The fourth is by practicing Yoga, to eliminate untruth from the mind and the soul, and to fix it in truth. The fifth is to recite the qualities of God and meditate on them. The sixth is to pray to God to keep one steadfast in truth (gyana), realization of the reality and dharma, to keep one away from

[5] A term denoting a Muslim learned in Islamic law and theology.

[79]

untruth, ignorance and adharma, and to free one from the woes of birth and death and obtain mukti. When a man worships God wholeheartedly and sincerely, the merciful God gives him happiness. Salvation, dharma, material gain and fulfillment of desires, and attainment of truth are the results of one's efforts, and not otherwise. To act according to the teaching of God is dharma and violation of it is adharma. Only rightful means should be adopted to attain success and prosperity. Injustice, untruth and unrighteous means should not be made use of to gain happiness.

Rev. Scott said:

"Salvation does not mean deliverance from woes. Salvation only means to be saved from sins and to obtain Heaven. God had created Adam pure, but he was misled by Satan and committed sin which made all his descendants sinful. Man commits sin of his own accord as the clock works by itself, that is to say, one cannot avoid committing sin by one's own effort and so cannot get salvation. One can obtain salvation only by believing in Christ. Wherever Christianity spreads, people are saved from sin. I have attained salvation by believing in Christ."

Maulvi Muhammad Hasim said:

"God does what he wishes to do; whom He wishes He gives salvation, just as a judge acquits those with whom he is pleased and punishes those with whom he is displeased. God does what He likes. He is beyond our control. We must trust whoever is the ruler for the time being. Our Prophet is the ruler of the present time. We can get salvation by putting our trust in Him. With knowledge we can do good work, but moksha or salvation lies in His hands."

Swamiji replied that:

"Suffering is the necessary result of sin; whoever avoids sin will be saved from suffering. The Christians believe God to be powerful; but to believe that Satan misled Adam to commit sin is to believe that God is not All powerful; for, if God had been All powerful, Satan could not have misled Adam, who had been created pure by God. No sensible man can believe that Adam committed sin and all his descendants became sinful. *He alone undergoes suffering who commits sin; no one else.* You say that Satan misleads everyone, I therefore ask you who misled Satan. If you say no one misled him, then as Satan misled himself, so must Adam have done it. Why believe in Satan then? If you say, somebody else must have misled Satan, then the only one who could have done it was God. In that case when God himself misleads and gets others to commit sin, then how can He save people from sin. Satan disturbs and spoils God's creation, but God neither punishes him nor imprisons him, nor puts him to death. This proves that God is powerless to do so. Those who believe in Satan cannot avoid committing sins, for they believe that Satan gets them to commit sin and they themselves are not sinful. Again, when God's only son suffered crucifixion for the sins of all people, then the people need not be afraid of being punished for their sins and they can go on committing sins with impunity. The illustration of the clock given by the Padree sahib is also inappropriate. "The clock works only as its *maker has given it the power* to do. The clock cannot alter it. Then again how can you continue to live in Paradise. Adam was misled there by Satan into eating wheat. Will you not eat wheat and be expelled from Paradise? You gentlemen believe God to be like a man. Man has limited knowledge and does not know everything, he therefore stands in need of recommendation of someone who possesses knowledge. But God is All-knowing and All-powerful. He does not stand in need of any recommendation or help from any prophet or anyone else; otherwise, where would be the difference between God and man? Nor does He according to you remain just, for He does not do justice, if he pardons the culprit on the recommendations of anybody. If God is present everywhere, He cannot have a body; for if he has a body, He will be subject to limitation and will not be infinite, and then he must be subject to birth and death. Is God incapable of saving his worshipers without Christ's intervention? Nor has God any need of a prophet. It is true that where there are good people in a country, people improve because of good men's teachings. As regards the Maulvi sahib, he is wrong in saying that God does what He likes, because then He does not remain just. As a fact, he gives salvation only to those whose works deserve it. Without sin and righteousness there can be no suffering and no happiness. God is the ruler for all time. If God gives salvation on the recommendation of others, he becomes dependent. God is All-powerful. It is a matter of surprise that though the Mussalmans believe God to be one and without a second, yet they made the prophet take part with God in bestowing salvation."

[81]

The Virtues of Europeans

For all his disdain for the Christian religion, Swāmī Dayānanda was not oblivious to the good qualities of India's British rulers, particularly those virtues (such as marrying the person of one's choice) for which he found support in the Vedas.

[From *The Light of Truth*, pp. 443-44]

Q. Look at the Europeans! They wear boots, jackets, and trousers, live in hotels, and eat of the hands of all. These are the causes of their advancement.

A. This is your mistake, since the Muhammadans and low-caste people eat of the hands of every one and yet they are so backward. The causes of their advancement are:

1. The custom of child-marriage does not prevail among them.

2. They give their boys and girls sound training and education.

3. They *choose* their own life-partners. Such marriages are called *Swyamvara*,[1] because a maid chooses her own consort.

4. They do not allow their children to associate with bad people. Being well educated, they do not fall into the snares of any unprincipled person.

5. Whatever they do, they do after discussing it thoroughly among themselves and referring it to their representative assembly.

6. They sacrifice everything, their wealth, their hearts, aye, their very lives, for the good of their nation.

7. They are not indolent, on the contrary, live active lives.

8. They allow boots and shoes made in their country (or those made after their pattern in this country) to be taken into courts, and offices, but never Indian shoes. This must suffice to convince you that they value their boots much more than the natives of this country.

9. They have been in this country for more than one hundred years, and yet they wear thick clothing, as they used to do at home, up to this day. They have not changed the fashion of their country, but many among you have copied their dress. This shows that you are foolish, while they are wise. No wise man will ever imitate others.

10. Every one among them does his duty most faithfully.

11. They always obey orders (of their superiors).

[1] One's own choosing.

[82]

12. They help their countrymen in trade, etc.

It is the possession of such sterling qualities and the doing of such noble deeds that have contributed to the advancement of the Europeans. They have not become great by wearing boots, shoes, and eating in hotels and doing such other ordinary things or by doing evil things.

A Statement of My Beliefs

In an appendix to *The Light of Truth*, Swāmī Dayānanda summed up his credo, of which the essence is that God is one, and the Vedas are His word.
  [From *The Light of Truth*, pp. 677–78]

I believe in a religion based on universal and all-embracing principles which have always been accepted as true by mankind, and will continue to command the allegiance of mankind in the ages to come. Hence it is that the religion in question is called the *primeval eternal religion*, which means that it is above the hostility of all human creeds whatsoever. Whatever is believed in by those who are steeped in ignorance or have been led astray by sectaries is not worthy of being accepted by the wise. That faith alone is really true and worthy of acceptance which is followed by *Aptas,* i.e., those who are true in word, deed and thought, promote public good and are impartial and learned; but all that is discarded by such men must be considered as unworthy of belief and false.

My conception of God and all other objects in the universe is founded on the teachings of the Veda and other true Shastras, and is in conformity with the beliefs of all the sages, from Brahma [2] down to Jaimini.[3] I offer a statement of these beliefs for the acceptance of all good men. That alone I hold to be acceptable which is worthy of being believed by all men in all ages. I do not entertain the least idea of founding a new religion or sect. My sole aim is to believe in truth and help others to believe in it, to reject falsehood and help others to do the same. Had I been biased, I would have championed any one of the religions prevailing in India. But I have not done so. On the contrary, I do not approve of what is objectionable and false in the institutions of this or any other country, nor do I reject what is good and in harmony with the dictates of true religion, nor have I any desire to do so, since a contrary conduct is wholly unworthy of man. He alone is entitled to be called a man who

[2] The first promulgator of the Vedas.   [3] The author of the Pūrva Mīmāmsā Sūtras.

possesses a thoughtful nature and feels for others in the same way as he does for his own self, does not fear the unjust, however powerful, but fears the truly virtuous, however weak. Moreover, he should always exert himself to his utmost to protect the righteous, and advance their good, and conduct himself worthily towards them even though they be extremely poor and weak and destitute of material resources. On the other hand, he should constantly strive to destroy, humble, and oppose the wicked, sovereign rulers of the whole earth and men of great influence and power though they be. In other words, a man should, as far as it lies in his power, constantly endeavor to undermine the power of the unjust and to strengthen that of the just, he may have to bear any amount of terrible suffering, he may have even to quaff the bitter cup of death in the performance of this duty, which devolves on him on account of being a man, but he should not shirk it.

Now I give below a brief summary of my beliefs. Their detailed exposition has been given in this book in its proper place.

1. He, Who is called *Brahma* or the Most High; who is *Paramātmā*, or the Supreme Spirit Who permeates the whole universe; Who is a true personification of Existence, Consciousness, and Bliss; Whose nature, attributes, and characteristics are Holy; Who is Omniscient, Formless, All-pervading, Unborn, Infinite, Almighty, Just, and Merciful; Who is the author of the universe, sustains and dissolves it; Who awards all souls the fruits of their deeds in strict accordance with the requirements of absolute justice and is possessed of the like attributes—even *Him* I believe to be the Great God.

2. I hold that the four Vedas—the repository of Knowledge and Religious Truths—are the Word of God. They comprise what is known as the *Sanhita—Mantra* [4] portion only. They are absolutely free from error, and are an authority unto themselves. In other words, they do not stand in need of any other book to uphold their authority. Just as the sun (or a lamp) by his light, reveals his own nature as well as that of other objects of the universe, such as the earth—even so are the *Vedas*.

[4] The collections of hymns which make up the first part of each of the four Vedas.

SHRI RĀMAKRISHNA: MYSTIC AND SPIRITUAL TEACHER

Shri Rāmakrishna (1836–1886) was among the most saintly of the many religious leaders to whom modern India has given birth. A son of Bengal, like Debendranāth and Keshub, he was, unlike them, a child of the soil and never lost his rustic simplicity. Like Dayānanda, he personified the rebirth of an ancient tradition in the midst of an era of increasing Westernization and modernization. But unlike that militant Gujarātī, he practiced and preached a gentle faith of selfless devotion to God and of ultimate absorption in Him.

Rāmakrishna imbibed from his boyhood days as the son of a village priest the spirit of devotion to Kālī, the Divine Mother, which the songs of Rāmprasād had made popular in rural Bengal in the eighteenth century. Ecstatic communion with the Divine, an aspect of this tradition, came naturally to the attractive young brāhman, and at the age of seven he experienced his first mystical trance. He received no formal education in Sanskrit or English, and could read and write Bengali only moderately well. Yet this "God-intoxicated" man attained to a wisdom that was the envy of many of his enlightened, English-educated contemporaries.

His elder brother took him at sixteen to Calcutta, where they were eventually installed as priests of a new temple on the Hooghly River, a branch of the Ganges. For the next twelve years Rāmakrishna put himself through every known type of spiritual discipline in an agonized search for God. Finally his efforts were rewarded with a series of mystical experiences during which he saw God in a variety of manifestations—as a Divine Mother, as Sītā, as Rāma, as Krishna, as Muhammad, as Jesus Christ, and worshiped Him in the manner of Muslims, Jains, and Buddhists—in each case suiting his dress, food and meditation to the particular religious tradition concerned.

Through the aid of Keshub Chunder Sen, who greatly admired him, Rāmakrishna began to attract disciples from among the Westernized middle class of Calcutta. His keen insight into the hearts of men made him an excellent teacher, and his natural simplicity and purity made a profound impression on these young men. From him they learned to draw strength from the living traditions of popular Hinduism; through them his teachings became known to all India and the world at large.

RĀMAKRISHNA
The World As Seen by a Mystic

Rāmakrishna lived in a state of consciousness so close to continual meditation that he was able to see great meaning in the smallest incidents. One of his disciples collected his sayings and anecdotes as he related them. They show us the world as he saw it—a world permeated by the presence of the Divine.

[From *The Gospel of Rāmakrishna*, pp. 207–14]

I practiced austerities for a long time. I cared very little for the body. My longing for the Divine Mother was so great that I would not eat or sleep. I would lie on the bare ground, placing my head on a lump of earth, and cry out loudly: "Mother, Mother, why dost Thou not come to me?" I did not know how the days and nights passed away. I used to have ecstasy all the time. I saw my disciples as my own people, like children and relations, long before they came to me. I used to cry before my Mother, saying: "O Mother! I am dying for my beloved ones (Bhaktas); do Thou bring them to me as quickly as possible."

At that time whatever I desired came to pass. Once I desired to build a small hut in the Panchavati [1] for meditation and to put a fence around it. Immediately after I saw a huge bundle of bamboo sticks, rope, strings, and even a knife, all brought by the tide in front of the Panchavati. A servant of the Temple, seeing these things, ran to me with great delight and told me of them. There was the exact quantity of material necessary for the hut and the fence. When they were built, nothing remained over. Everyone was amazed to see this wonderful sight.

When I reached the state of continuous ecstasy, I gave up all external forms of worship; I could no longer perform them. Then I prayed to my Divine Mother: "Mother, who will now take care of me? I have no power to take care of myself. I like to hear Thy name and feed Thy Bhaktas and help the poor. Who will make it possible for me to do these things? Send me someone who will be able to do these for me." As the answer to this prayer came Mathura Bābu, [2] who served me so long

---

[1] Five sacred trees planted together to form a grove used for contemplation.
[2] A wealthy disciple. Bābu is a respectful Bengali form of address.

and with such intense devotion and faith! Again at another time I said to the Mother: "I shall have no child of my own, but I wish to have as my child a pure Bhakta, who will stay with me all the time. Send me such an one." Then came Rākhāl (Brahmānanda).

Those who are my own are parts of my very Self.

ii

In referring to the time of joyous illumination which immediately followed His enlightenment, He exclaimed:

What a state it was! The slightest cause aroused in me the thought of the Divine Ideal. One day I went to the Zoological Garden in Calcutta. I desired especially to see the lion, but when I beheld him, I lost all sense-consciousness and went into samādhi. Those who were with me wished to show me the other animals, but I replied: "I saw everything when I saw the king of beasts. Take me home." The strength of the lion had aroused in me the consciousness of the omnipotence of God and had lifted me above the world of phenomena.

Another day I went to the parade ground to see the ascension of a balloon. Suddenly my eyes fell upon a young English boy leaning against a tree. The very posture of his body brought before me the vision of the form of Krishna and I went into samādhi.

Again I saw a woman wearing a blue garment under a tree. She was a harlot. As I looked at her, instantly the ideal of Sītā [3] appeared before me! I forgot the existence of the harlot, but saw before me pure and spotless Sītā, approached Rāma, the Incarnation of Divinity, and for a long time I remained motionless. I worshiped all women as representatives of the Divine Mother. I realized the Mother of the universe in every woman's form.

Mathura Bābu, the son-in-law of Rāshmoni, invited me to stay in his house for a few days. At that time I felt so strongly that I was the maid-servant of my Divine Mother that I thought of myself as a woman. The ladies of the house had the same feeling; they did not look upon me as a man. As women are free before a young girl, so were they before me. My mind was above the consciousness of sex.

What a Divine state it was! I could not eat here in the Temple. I would

[3] The consort of Rāma, hero of the *Rāmāyaṇa*. She exemplifies the Hindu ideal of womanhood.

[87]

walk from place to place and enter into the house of strangers after their meal hour. I would sit there quietly, without uttering a word. When questioned, I would say: "I wish to eat here." Immediately they would feed me with the best things they had.

iii

Once I heard of a poor Brāhmin who was a true devotee and who lived in a small hut in Bāghbāzār. I desired to see him, so I asked Mathura Bābu to take me to him. He consented, immediately ordered a large carriage, and drove me there. The Brāhmin's house was so small that he scarcely had room to receive us, and he was much surprised to see me coming with such a rich man in such a carriage!

At another time I wished to meet [Debendranāth] Tagore. He is a very rich man, but in spite of his enormous wealth he is devoted to God and repeats His Holy Name. For this reason I desired to know him. I spoke about him to Mathura Bābu. He replied: "Very well, Bābā,[4] I will take Thee to him; he was my classmate." So he took me and introduced me to him, saying: "This holy man has come to see you. He is mad after God." I saw in him a little pride and egotism. It is natural for a man who has so much wealth, culture, fame, and social position. I said to Mathura Bābu: "Tell me, does pride spring from true wisdom or from ignorance? He who has attained to the highest knowledge of Brāhman cannot possess pride or egotism, such as 'I am learned,' 'I am wise,' 'I am rich,' and so on." While I was speaking with [Debendranāth] Tagore, I went into a state from where I could see the true character of every individual. In this state the most learned pandits and scholars appear to me like blades of grass. When I see that scholars have neither true discrimination nor dispassion, then I feel that they are like straws; or they seem like vultures who soar high in the heavens, but keep their minds on the charnel-pits below on the earth. In [Debendranāth] I found both spiritual knowledge and worldly desire. He has a number of children, some of whom are quite young. A doctor was present. I said: "When you have so much spiritual knowledge, how can you live constantly in the midst of so much worldliness? You are like Rājā Janaka;[5] you can keep your mind on God, remaining amid worldly pleasures and luxury. Therefore I have come to see you. Tell me something of the Divine Be-

---

[4] An affectionate form of address.   [5] King Janaka, the father of Sītā.

[88]

ing." [Debendranāth] then read some passages from the Vedas and said: "This world is like a chandelier, and each Jiva (individual soul) is like a light in it." Long ago, when I spent nearly all my time meditating at the Panchavati, I saw the same thing. When [Debendranāth's] words harmonized with my experience, I knew that he must have attained to some true knowledge. I asked him to explain. He said: "Who would have known this world? God has created man to manifest His glory. If there were no light in the chandelier, it would be all dark. The chandelier itself would not be visible." After a long conversation [Debendranāth] Tagore begged me to come to the anniversary of the Brāhmo-Samāj. I answered: "If it be the will of the Lord. I go wherever He takes me."

Fix Your Mind on God

During one of his visits with Keshub Chunder Sen and his disciples, Rāmakrishna advised the Brāhmos to cultivate the liberating powers of the mind.
    [From *The Gospel of Rāmakrishna*, pp. 158–60]

A Brāhmo: Revered Sir, is it true that God cannot be realized without giving up the world?

The Bhagavān,[6] smiling: Oh no! You do not have to give up everything. You are better off where you are. By living in the world you are enjoying the taste of both the pure crystallized sugar and of the molasses with all its impurities. You are indeed better off. Verily I say unto you, you are living in the world, there is no harm in that; but you will have to fix your mind on God, otherwise you cannot realize Him. Work with one hand and hold the Feet of the Lord with the other. When you have finished your work, fold His feet to your heart with both your hands.

Everything is in the mind. Bondage and freedom are in the mind. You can dye the mind with any color you wish. It is like a piece of clean white linen: dip it in red and it will be red, in blue it will be blue, in green it will be green, or any other color. Do you not see that if you study English, English words will come readily to you? Again, if a pandit studies Sanskrit, he will readily quote verse from Sacred Books. If you keep your mind in evil company, your thoughts, ideas, and words will be colored with evil; but keep in the company of Bhaktas, then your thoughts, ideas and words will be of God. The mind is everything. On

[6] Blessed One.

[89]

one side is the wife, on the other side is the child; it loves the wife in one way and the child in another way, yet the mind is the same.

By the mind one is bound; by the mind one is freed. If I think I am absolutely free, whether I live in the world or in the forest, where is my bondage? I am the child of God, the son of the King of kings; who can bind me? When bitten by a snake, if you assert with firmness: "There is no venom in me," you will be cured. In the same way, he who asserts with strong conviction: "I am not bound, I am free," becomes free.

Some one gave me a book of the Christians. I asked him to read it to me. In it there was only one theme—sin and sin, from the beginning to the end. (To Keshub) In your Brāhmo-Samāj the main topic is also sin. The fool who repeats again and again: "I am bound. I am bound," remains in bondage. He who repeats day and night: "I am a sinner, I am a sinner," becomes a sinner indeed.

Beware of the Wicked

Rāmakrishna's advice to his disciples was often of a very practical nature, as this example shows.
[From *The Gospel of Rāmakrishna*, pp. 42–44]

One of the devotees present said: But when a person is annoyed with me, Bhagavān, I feel unhappy. I feel that I have not been able to love everyone equally.

Rāmakrishna: When you feel that way, you should have a talk with that person and try to make peace with him. If you fail after such attempts, then you need not give it further thought. Take refuge with the Lord. Think upon Him. Do not let your mind be disturbed by any other thing.

Devotee: Christ and Chaitanya have both taught us to love all mankind.

Rāmakrishna: You should love everyone because God dwells in all beings. But to wicked people you should bow down at a distance. (To Bijoy, smiling): Is it true that people blame you because you mix with those who believe in a Personal God with form? A true devotee of God should possess absolute calmness and never be disturbed by the opinions of others. Like a blacksmith's anvil, he will endure all blows and persecutions and yet remain firm in his faith and always the same. Wicked people may say many things about you and blame you; but if you long for God, you should endure with patience. One can think on God even dwelling in the midst of wicked people. The sages of ancient times, who lived in forests, could meditate on God although surrounded by tigers, bears, and other wild beasts. The nature of the wicked is like that of a tiger or bear. They attack the innocent and injure them. You should be especially cautious in coming in contact with the following: First, the wealthy. A person who possesses wealth and many attendants can easily do harm to another if he so desires. You should be very guarded in speaking with him; sometimes it may even be necessary to agree with him in his opinion. Second, a dog. When a dog barks at you, you must not run, but talk to him and quiet him. Third, a bull. When a bull chases you, you should always pacify him by talking to him. Fourth, a drunkard. If you make him angry, he will call you names and swear at you. You should address him as a dear relative, then he will be happy and obliging.

When wicked people come to see me, I am very careful. The character of some of them is like that of a snake. They may bite you unawares. It may take a long time and much discrimination to recover from the effects of that bite. Or you may get so angry at them that you will wish to take revenge. It is necessary, however, to keep occasionally the company of holy men. Through such association right discrimination will come.

Parables and Sayings

There is much in Rāmakrishna's homely yet charming wisdom that reminds the reader of the teachings of Jesus. Both men took experiences from everyday life and used them to illustrate profound moral and religious truths. But despite the many similarities in the sayings and parables of the two teachers, it is clear that there remains a basic difference between the Hindu and the Judeo-Christian conception of the nature and means of salvation.

[From *Teachings of Sri Rāmakrishna,* pp. 31–94, 351]
The vegetables in the cooking pot move and leap till the children think they are living beings. But the grown-ups explain that they are not moving of themselves; if the fire be taken away they will soon cease to stir. So it is ignorance that thinks "I am the doer." All our strength is the strength of God. All is silent if the fire be removed. A marionette dances well, while the wires are pulled; but when the master's hand is gone, it falls inert. [p. 31]

. . . .

The guru said: "Everything that exists is God," and the disciple understood this literally. Passing along the road, he met an elephant. The driver shouted from his high place: "Move away, move away!" But the disciple thought: "Why should I move away? I am God and so is the elephant. What fear can God have of himself?" Thinking thus he did not move. At last the elephant took him by his trunk and dashed him aside. He was severely hurt, and going back to his guru, he told his story. The guru said: "It is quite true that you are God. It is true that the elephant is God too, but God was also in the form of the elephant-driver. Why did you not listen to the God on top?" [p. 46]

. . . .

At a game of chess the onlookers can tell what is the correct move better than the players themselves. Men of the world think they are very clever; but they are attached to things of this world—money, honors, pleasure, etc. Being actually engaged in the play it is hard for them to hit upon the right move. Holy men who have given up the world are not attached to it. They are like the onlookers at a game of chess. They see things in their true light and can judge better than the men of the world. [p. 68]

. . . .

As a nail cannot be driven into a stone, yet it enters easily into the earth, so the advice of the pious does not affect the soul of a worldly man, while it pierces deep into the heart of a believer. [p. 94]

. . . .

A man woke up at midnight and desired to smoke. He wanted a light, so he went to a neighbor's house and knocked at the door. Someone opened the door and asked him what he wanted. The man said: "I wish to smoke. Can you give me a light?" The neighbor replied: "Bah! What is the matter with you? You have taken so much trouble to come and [awaken] us at this hour, when in your hand you have a lighted lantern!" What a man wants is already within him; but he still wanders here and there in search of it. [p. 351]

[From Müller, *Rāmakrishna, His Life and Sayings*, pp. 134–80]
A disciple, having firm faith in the infinite power of his guru, walked over a river even by pronouncing his name. The guru, seeing this, thought

within himself: "Well, is there such a power even in my name? Then I must be very great and powerful, no doubt!" The next day he also tried to walk over the river pronouncing "I, I, I," but no sooner had he stepped into the waters than he sank and was drowned. Faith can achieve miracles, while vanity or egoism is the death of man. [p. 134]

. . . .

A man after fourteen years of hard asceticism in a lonely forest obtained at last the power of walking over the waters. Overjoyed at this acquisition, he went to his guru, and told him of his grand feat. At this the master replied: "My poor boy, what thou hast accomplished after fourteen years' arduous labor, ordinary men do the same by paying a penny to the boatman." [p. 154]

. . . .

When a wound is perfectly healed, the slough falls off it itself; but if the slough be taken off earlier, it bleeds. Similarly, when the perfection of knowledge is reached by a man, the distinctions of caste fall off from him, but it is wrong for the ignorant to break such distinctions. [p. 147]

. . . .

The light of the gas illumines various localities with various intensities. But the life of the light, namely, the gas, comes from one common reservoir. So the religious teachers of all climes and ages are but as many lampposts through which is emitted the light of the spirit flowing constantly from one source, the Lord Almighty. [p. 148]

. . . .

The difference between the modern Brāhmaism [of the Brāhmo Samāj] and Hinduism is like the difference between the single note of music and the whole music. The modern Brahmas are content with the single note of Brahman, while the Hindu religion is made up of several notes producing a sweet and melodious harmony. [p. 153]

. . . .

As it is very difficult to gather together the mustard-seeds that escape out of a torn package, and are scattered in all directions; so, when the human

[93]

mind runs in diverse directions and is occupied with many things in the world, it is not a very easy affair to collect and concentrate it. [p. 167]

. . . .

He who would learn to swim must attempt swimming for some days. No one can venture to swim in the sea after a single day's practice. So if you want to swim in the sea of Brahman, you must make many ineffectual attempts at first, before you can successfully swim therein. [p. 175]

. . . .

As the village maidens carry four or five pots of water placed one over the other upon their heads, talking all the way with one another about their own joys and sorrows, and yet do not allow one drop of water to be spilt, so must the traveler in the path of virtue walk along. In whatever circumstances he may be placed, let him always take heed that his heart does not swerve from the true path. [p. 177]

. . . .

When an elephant is let loose, it goes about uprooting trees and shrubs, but as soon as the driver pricks him on the head with the goad he becomes quiet; so the mind when unrestrained wantons in the luxuriance of idle thoughts, but becomes calm at once when struck with the goad of discrimination. [p. 180]

. . . .

Know thyself, and thou shalt then know the non-self and the Lord of all. What is my ego? Is it my hand, or foot, or flesh, or blood, or muscle, or tendon? Ponder deep, and thou shalt know that there is no such thing as I. As by continually peeling off the skin of the onion, so by analyzing the ego it will be found that there is not any real entity corresponding to the ego. The ultimate result of all such analysis is God. When egoism drops away, Divinity manifests itself. [p. 180]

SWĀMĪ VIVEKĀNANDA: HINDU MISSIONARY TO THE WEST

Among Sri Rāmakrishna's disciples was a young Calcutta-born student on whom he showered special attention and praise. This boy Narendranāth Datta (1863–1902) came from a Kāyastha family of lawyers and received a good Western-style education. When he first visited Rāmakrishna he was planning to study law in England and then follow the profession which was the high road to success in British India. Within a year's time his interviews with the master mystic had changed the course of his life. He resolved to give up worldly pursuits and adopt the life of a sannyāsī. After twelve years of ascetic discipline he became famous as Swāmī Vivekānanda, the apostle to the world of his master's philosophy of God-realization.

Vivekānanda's meteoric career as missionary of Vedantic Hinduism to the West began in 1893 when he addressed the First World Parliament of Religions at Chicago. After four years of lecturing in America and England he returned to India a national hero and took up the task of regenerating his fellow-countrymen. He literally burned himself out in their service, dedicating the Rāmakrishna Mission to both social work and religious education, and rousing young men with his fiery speeches to devote themselves to uplifting the poor and starving millions of India.

Although he died at thirty-nine, Vivekānanda's example had a powerful impact on the thinking of his own and later generations. Despite his scorn for politics, his success in preaching to the world the greatness of Hinduism gave his countrymen an added sense of dignity and pride in their own culture. His zeal to serve the downtrodden masses opened a new dimension of activity to Indian nationalist leaders, whose Western outlook had heretofore isolated them from the vast majority of their countrymen. Gāndhi, the greatest to work in this new field, acknowledged his debt to the Swāmī in this respect.

Vivekānanda called India to become great by realizing her own possibilities and by living up to her own highest ideals. The heart and soul of his teaching was the message of his beloved master, Rāmakrishna: That each man was potentially divine, and so should both work to unleash the infinite power within himself, and should help other men to do the same.

VIVEKĀNANDA
Man Is God

In his series of lectures entitled "Practical Vedanta," delivered in London in 1896, Vivekānanda set forth the teachings of his master, Rāmakrishna. The central point of his message was that God is within man, that in his inmost being, man is God.

[From *The Complete Works of the Swami Vivekananda*, II, 324–25]

Do you not remember what the Bible says: "If you cannot love your brother whom you have seen, how can you love God whom you have not seen?" If you cannot see God in the human face, how can you see Him in the clouds, or in images made of dull, dead matter, or in mere fictitious stores of your brain? I shall call you religious from the day you begin to see God in men and women and then you will understand what is meant by turning the left cheek to the man who strikes you on the right. When you see man as God, everything, even the tiger, will be welcome. Whatever comes to you is but the Lord, the Eternal, the Blessed One, appearing to us in various forms, as our father, and mother, and friend, and child; they are our own soul playing with us.

As our human relationships can thus be made divine so our relationship with God may take any of these forms and we can look upon Him as our father or mother or friend or beloved. Calling God Mother is a higher idea than calling Him Father, and to call Him Friend is still higher, but the highest is to regard Him as the Beloved. The highest point of all is to see no difference between lover and beloved. You may remember, perhaps, the old Persian story, of how a lover came and knocked at the door of the beloved and was asked: "Who are you?" He answered: "It is I," and there was no response. A second time he came, and exclaimed: "I am here," but the door was not opened. The third time he came, and the voice asked from inside: "Who is there?" He replied: "I am thyself, my beloved," and the door opened. So is the relation between God and ourselves. He is in everything, He is everything. Every man and woman is the palpable, blissful, living God. Who says God is unknown? Who says He is to be searched after? We have found God eternally. We have been living in Him eternally. He is eternally known, eternally worshiped.

The Rationale of Caste and Idol-Worship

In contrast with the Brāhmo reformers and Dayānanda, Vivekānanda justified the caste system as good, and the worship of idols as useful for those who need them. Yet he interpreted these ancient practices in a way that brought them into harmony with the western ideals of social and religious equality.

[From *The Complete Works of the Swami Vivekananda*, III, 245–46, 460]

Caste is a natural order. I can perform one duty in social life, and you another; you can govern a country, and I can mend a pair of old shoes, but there is no reason why you are greater than I, for can you mend my shoes? Can I govern the country? I am clever in mending shoes, you are clever in reading Vedas, but there is no reason why you should trample on my head; why if one commits murder should he be praised, and if another steals an apple why should he be hanged! This will have to go. Caste is good. That is the only natural way of solving life. Men must form themselves into groups, and you cannot get rid of that. Wherever you go there will be caste. But that does not mean that there should be these privileges. They should be knocked on the head. If you teach Vedanta to the fisherman, he will say, I am as good a man as you, I am a fisherman, you are a philosopher, but I have the same God in me as you have in you. And that is what we want, no privileges for any one, equal chances for all; let every one be taught that the Divine is within, and every one will work out his own salvation. [pp. 245-46]

. . . .

This external worship of images has, however, been described in all our Shastras as the lowest of all the low forms of worship. But that does not mean that it is a wrong thing to do. Despite the many iniquities that have found entrance into the practices of image-worship as it is in vogue now, I do not condemn it. Aye, where would I have been, if I had not been blessed with the dust of the holy feet of that orthodox, image-worshiping Brahmana [Rāmakrishna]!

Those reformers who preach against image-worship, or what they denounce as idolatry—to them I say: "Brothers! If you are fit to worship God-without-Form discarding any external help, do so, but why do you condemn others who cannot do the same? A beautiful large edifice, the glorious relic of a hoary antiquity has, out of neglect or disuse, fallen into a dilapidated condition; accumulations of dirt and dust may be lying everywhere within it; may be, some portions are tumbling down to the ground. What will you do to it? Will you take in hand the necessary cleansing and repairs and thus restore the old, or will you pull the whole edifice down to the ground and seek to build another in its place, after a sordid modern plan whose permanence has yet to be established? We have to reform it, which truly means to make ready or perfect by necessary cleansing and repairs, not by demolishing the whole thing. There the function of reform ends." [p. 460]

Vivekānanda developed the idea, put forth by Keshub, that India should take practical knowledge from Europe, and in exchange should teach religious wisdom to the world. In a speech about Rāmakrishna delivered in New York he stated most emphatically his claim that the Orient (by which he primarily meant India) was superior to the West in spiritual matters.

[From *The Complete Works of the Swami Vivekananda,* IV, 150–52]

"Whenever virtue subsides and vice prevails, I come down to help mankind," declares Krishna, in the *Bhagavad-Gita.* Whenever this world of ours, on account of growth, on account of added circumstances, requires a new adjustment, a wave of power comes, and as man is acting on two planes, the spiritual and the material, waves of adjustment come on both planes. On the one side, of the adjustment on the material plane, Europe has mainly been the basis during modern times, and of the adjustment on the other, the spiritual plane, Asia has been the basis throughout the history of the world. Today, man requires one more adjustment on the spiritual plane; today when material ideas are at the height of their glory and power, today when man is likely to forget his divine nature, through his growing dependence on matter, and is likely to be reduced to a mere money-making machine, an adjustment is necessary; the voice has spoken, and the power is coming to drive away the clouds of gathering materialism. The power has been set in motion which, at no distant date, will bring unto mankind once more the memory of its real nature, and again the place from which this power will start will be Asia. This world of ours is on the plan of the division of labor. It is vain to say that one man shall possess everything. Yet how childish we are! The baby in its ignorance thinks that its doll is the only possession that is to be coveted in this whole universe. So a nation which is great in the possession of material power thinks that that is all that is to be coveted, that that is all that is meant by progress, that that is all that is meant by civilization, and if there are other nations which do not care for possession, and do not possess that power, they are not fit to live, their whole existence is useless! On the other hand, another nation may think that mere material civilization is utterly useless. From the Orient came the voice which once told the world, that if a man possesses everything that is under the sun

[98]

and does not possess spirituality, what avails it? This is the Oriental type; the other is the Occidental type.

Each of these types has its grandeur, each has its glory. The present adjustment will be the harmonizing, the mingling of these two ideals. To the Oriental, the world of spirit is as real as to the Occidental is the world of senses. In the spiritual, the Oriental finds everything he wants or hopes for; in it he finds all that makes life real to him. To the Occidental he is a dreamer; to the Oriental, the Occidental is a dreamer, playing with ephemeral toys, and he laughs to think that grown-up men and women should make so much of a handful of matter which they will have to leave sooner or later. Each calls the other a dreamer. But the Oriental ideal is as necessary for the progress of the human race as is the Occidental, and I think it is more necessary. Machines never made mankind happy, and never will make. He who is trying to make us believe this, will claim that happiness is in the machine, but it is always in the mind. The man alone who is the lord of his mind can become happy, and none else. And what, after all, is power of machinery? Why should a man who can send a current of electricity through a wire be called a very great man, and very intelligent man? Does not Nature do a million times more than that every moment? Why not then fall down and worship Nature? What avails it if you have power over the whole of the world, if you have mastered every atom in the universe? That will not make you happy unless you have the power of happiness in yourself, until you have conquered yourself. Man is born to conquer Nature, it is true, but the Occidental means by "Nature" only the physical or external Nature. It is true that external Nature is majestic, with its mountains, and oceans, and rivers, and with the infinite powers and varieties. Yet there is a more majestic internal Nature of man, higher than the sun, moon, and the stars, higher than this earth of ours, higher than the physical universe, transcending these little lives of ours; and it affords another field of study. There the Orientals excel, just as the Occidentals excel in the other. Therefore it is fitting that, whenever there is a spiritual adjustment, it should come from the Orient. It is also fitting that when the Oriental wants to learn about machine-making, he should sit at the feet of the Occidental and learn from him. When the Occident wants to learn about the spirit, about God, about the soul, about the meaning and the mystery of this universe, he must sit at the feet of the Orient to learn.

Indian Thought to Conquer the World

In a lecture in Madras Swāmī Vivekānanda challenged his audience to conquer the West with India's spirituality. Through such speeches as this he instilled a feeling of self-confidence in the youth of the country, thus contributing to the later movement for national independence.

[From *The Complete Works of the Swami Vivekananda*, III, 276–77]

This is the great ideal before us, and every one must be ready for it— the conquest of the whole world by India—nothing less than that, and we must all get ready for it, strain every nerve for it. Let foreigners come and flood the land with their armies, never mind. Up, India, and conquer the world with your spirituality! Aye, as has been declared on this soil first, love must conquer hatred, hatred cannot conquer itself. Materialism and all its miseries can never be conquered by materialism. Armies when they attempt to conquer armies only multiply and make brutes of humanity. Spirituality must conquer the West. Slowly they are finding out that what they want is spirituality to preserve them as nations. They are waiting for it, they are eager for it. Where is the supply to come from? Where are the men ready to go out to every country in the world with the messages of the great sages of India? Where are the men who are ready to sacrifice everything, so that this message shall reach every corner of the world? Such heroic souls are wanted to help the spread of truth. Such heroic workers are wanted to go abroad and help to disseminate the great truths of the Vedanta. The world wants it; without it the world will be destroyed. The whole of the Western world is on a volcano which may burst tomorrow, go to pieces tomorrow. They have searched every corner of the world and have found no respite. They have drunk deep of the cup of pleasure and found it vanity. Now is the time to work so that India's spiritual ideas may penetrate deep into the West. Therefore, young men of Madras, I specially ask you to remember this. We must go out, we must conquer the world through our spirituality and philosophy. There is no other alternative, we must do it or die. The only condition of national life, of awakened and vigorous national life, is the conquest of the world by Indian thought.

America and India's Poor

While he was preaching the philosophy of the Vedanta to the people of the West, Vivekānanda was worrying about the poverty of his own countrymen. In 1894 he wrote from Chicago to the Mahārāja of Mysore, one of India's most enlightened princes, giving his opinion of American materialism, and asking for help in his new-found ambition to educate their nation's poor.

[From *The Complete Works of the Swami Vivekananda*, IV, 307–9]

Sri Narayana bless you and yours. Through your Highness' kind help it has been possible for me to come to this country. Since then I have become well-known here, and the hospitable people of this country have supplied all my wants. It is a wonderful country and this is a wonderful nation in many respects. No other nation applies so much machinery in their everyday work as do the people of this country. Everything is machine. Then again, they are only one-twentieth of the whole population of the world. Yet they have fully one-sixth of all the wealth of the world. There is no limit to their wealth and luxuries. Yet everything here is so dear. The wages of labor are the highest in the world; yet the fight between labor and capital is constant.

Nowhere on earth have women so many privileges as in America. They are slowly taking everything into their hands and, strange to say, the number of cultured women is much greater than that of cultured men. Of course, the higher geniuses are mostly from the rank of males. With all the criticism of the Westerners against our caste, they have a worse one —that of money. The almighty dollar, as the Americans say, can do anything here.

No country on earth has so many laws, and in no country are they so little regarded. On the whole our poor Hindu people are infinitely more moral than any of the Westerners. In religion they practice here either hypocrisy or fanaticism. Sober-minded men have become disgusted with their superstitious religions and are looking forward to India for new light. Your Highness cannot realize without seeing, how eagerly they take in any little bit of the grand thoughts of the holy Vedas, which resist and are unharmed by the terrible onslaughts of modern science. The theories of creation out of nothing, of a created soul, and of the big tyrant of a God sitting on a throne in a place called heaven, and of the eternal hell-fires, have disgusted all the educated; and the noble thoughts of the Vedas about the eternity of creation and of the soul, and about the God in our own soul, they are imbibing fast in one shape or other. Within fifty years the educated of the world will come to believe in the eternity of both soul and creation, and in God as our highest and perfect nature, as taught in our holy Vedas. Even now their learned priests are interpreting the Bible in that way. My conclusion is that they require more spiritual civilization, and we, more material.

The one thing that is at the root of all evils in India is the condition of the poor. The poor in the West are devils; compared to them ours are angels, and it is therefore so much the easier to raise our poor. The only service to be done for our lower classes is, to give them education, *to develop their lost individuality*. That is the great task between our people and princes. Up to now nothing has been done in that direction. Priest-power and foreign conquest have trodden them down for centuries, and at last the poor of India have forgotten that they are human beings. They are to be given ideas; their eyes are to be opened to what is going on in the world around them, and then they will work out their own salvation. Every nation, every man, and every woman must work out their own salvation. Give them ideas—that is the only help they require, and then the rest must follow as the effect. Ours is to put the chemicals together, the crystallization comes in the law of nature. Our duty is to put ideas into their heads, they will do the rest. This is what is to be done in India. It is this idea that has been in my mind for a long time. I could not accomplish it in India, and that was the reason of my coming to this country. The great difficulty in the way of educating the poor is this. Supposing even your Highness opens a free school in every village, still it would do no good, for the poverty in India is such, that poor boys would rather go to help their fathers in the fields, or otherwise try to make a living, than come to the school. Now if the mountain does not come to Mahomet, Mahomet must go to the mountain. If the poor boy cannot come to education, education must go to him. There are thousands of single-minded, self-sacrificing Sannyasins in our own country, going from village to village, teaching religion. If some of them can be organized as teachers of secular things also, they will go from place to place, from door to door, not only preaching but teaching also. Suppose two of these men go to a village in the evening with a camera, a globe, some maps, etc. They can teach a great deal of astronomy and geography to the ignorant. By telling stories about different nations, they can give the poor a hundred times more information through the ear than they can get in a lifetime through books. This requires an organization, which again means money. Men enough there are in India to work out this plan, but alas! they have no money. It is very difficult to set a wheel in motion, but when once set, it goes on with increasing velocity. After seeking help in my own country and failing to get any sympathy from the rich, I came over to this country through your Highness' aid. The Americans do not care a bit whether the poor of India die or live. And why should they, when our own people never think of anything but their own selfish ends?

My noble prince, this life is short, the vanities of the world are transient, but they alone live who live for others, the rest are more dead than alive. One such high, noble-minded, and royal son of India as your Highness can do much towards raising India on her feet again, and thus leave a name to posterity which shall be worshiped.

That the Lord may make your noble heart feel intensely for the suffering millions of India sunk in ignorance, is the prayer of—

Vivekananda

Modern India

In one of his last essays, written in Bengali in 1899, Vivekānanda declared India's independence of Western standards. Scouting blind imitation of foreign models as unmanly, he called on his compatriots to take pride in their past and to unite rich and poor, high and low castes, in order to make their nation strong.

[From *The Complete Works of the Swami Vivekananda*, IV, 408–13]

It has been said before that India is slowly awakening through her friction with the outside nations, and, as the result of this little awakening is the appearance, to a certain extent, of free and independent thought in modern India. On one side is modern Western science, dazzling the eyes with the brilliance of myriad suns, and driving in the chariot of hard and fast facts collected by the application of tangible powers direct in their incision; on the other are the hopeful and strengthening traditions of her ancient forefathers, in the days when she was at the zenith of her glory—traditions that have been brought out of the pages of her history by the great sages of her own land and outside, that run for numberless years and centuries through her every vein with the quickening of life drawn from universal love, traditions that reveal unsurpassed valor, superhuman genius, and supreme spirituality, which are the envy of the gods—these inspire her with future hopes. On one side, rank materialism, plenitude of fortune, accumulation of gigantic power, and intense sense-pursuits, have through foreign literature caused a tremendous stir; on the other, through the confounding din of all these discordant sounds, she hears, in low yet unmistakable accents, the heart-rending cries of her ancient gods, cutting her to the quick. There lie before her various strange luxuries introduced from the West—celestial drinks, costly well-served food, splendid apparel, magnificent palaces, new modes of conveyance—new manners, new fashions, dressed in which moves about the well-educated girl in shameless freedom; all these are arousing unfelt desires in her; again, the scene changes and in its place appear, with stern presence, Sītā, Sāvitrī,[1] austere religious vows, fastings, the forest retreat, the matted locks and orange garb of the semi-naked Sannyasin, Samadhi, and the search after the Self. On one side, is the independence of Western societies based on self-interest; on the other, is the extreme self-sacrifice of the Aryan society. In this violent conflict, is it strange that Indian society should be tossed up and down? Of the West, the goal is—individual independence, the language—money-making education, the means—politics; of India, the goal is—Mukti, the language—the Veda, the means—renunciation. For a time, modern India thinks, as it were: I am running this worldly life of mine in vain expectation of uncertain spiritual welfare hereafter, which has spread its fascination over me; and again, lo! spellbound she listens: "Here, in this world of death and change, O man, where is thy happiness?"

On one side, New India is saying: "We should have full freedom in the selection of husband and wife; because, the marriage in which are involved the happiness and misery of all our future life, we must have the right to determine, according to our own free will." On the other, Old India is dictating: "Marriage is not for sense enjoyment, but to perpetuate the race. This is the Indian conception of marriage. By the producing of children, you are contributing to, and are responsible for, the future good or evil of the society. Hence, society has the right to dictate whom

[1] Sāvitrī, famed in Indian legend for having saved her doomed husband from the God of Death.

you shall marry and whom you shall not. That form of marriage obtains in society, which is conducive most to its well-being; do you give up your desire of individual pleasure for the good of the many."

On one side New India is saying: "If we only adopt Western ideas, Western language, Western food, Western dress and Western manners, we shall be as strong and powerful as the Western nations"; on the other, Old India is saying: "Fools! By imitation, other's ideas never become one's own—nothing, unless earned, is your own. Does the ass in the lion's skin become the lion?"

On one side, New India is saying: "What the Western nations do are surely good, otherwise how did they become so great?" On the other side, Old India is saying: "The flash of lightning is intensely bright, but only for a moment; look out, boys, it is dazzling your eyes. Beware!"

Have we not then to learn anything from the West? Must we not needs try and exert ourselves for better things? Are we perfect? Is our society entirely spotless, without any flaw? There are many things to learn, we must struggle for new and higher things till we die—struggle is the end of human life. Sri Rāmakrishna used to say: "As long as I live, so long I learn." That man or that society which has nothing to learn is already in the jaws of death. Yes, learn we must many things from the West, but there are fears as well.

A certain young man of little understanding used always to blame Hindu Shastras before Sri Rāmakrishna. One day he praised the *Bhagavad-Gītā*, on which Sri Rāmakrishna said: "Methinks some European pandit has praised the *Gītā*, and so he has also followed suit."

O India, this is your terrible danger. The spell of imitating the West is getting such a strong hold upon you, that what is good or what is bad is no longer decided by reason, judgment, discrimination, or reference to the Shastras. Whatever ideas, whatever manners the white men praise or like, are good; whatever things they dislike or censure are bad! Alas! What can be a more tangible proof of foolishness than this?

The Western ladies move freely everywhere—therefore, that is good; they choose for themselves their husbands—therefore, that is the highest step of advancement; the Westerners disapprove of our dress, decorations, food, and ways of living—therefore, they must be very bad; the Westerners condemn image-worship as sinful—surely then, image-worship is the greatest sin, there is no doubt of it!

[105]

The Westerners say that worshiping a single Deity is fruitful of the highest spiritual good—therefore, let us throw our Gods and Goddesses into the river Ganges! The Westerners hold caste distinctions to be obnoxious—therefore, let all the different castes be jumbled into one! The Westerners say that child-marriage is the root of all evils—therefore, that is also very bad, of a certainty it is!

We are not discussing here whether these customs deserve countenance or rejection; but if the mere disapproval of the Westerners be the measure of the abominableness of our manners and customs, then it is our duty to raise our emphatic protest against it.

The present writer has, to some extent, personal experience of Western society. His conviction resulting from such experience has been that there is such a wide divergence between the Western society and the Indian as regards the primal course and goal of each, that any sect in India, framed after the Western model, will miss the aim. We have not the least sympathy with those who, never having lived in Western society and, therefore, utterly ignorant of the rules and prohibitions regarding the association of men and women that obtain there, and which act as safeguards to preserve the purity of the Western women, allow a free rein to the unrestricted intermingling of men and women in our society.

I observed in the West also, that the children of weaker nations, if born in England, give themselves out as Englishmen, instead of Greek, Portuguese, Spaniard, etc., as the case may be. All drift towards the strong, that the light of glory which shines in the glorious may anyhow fall and reflect on one's own body; i.e., to shine in the borrowed light of the great is the one desire of the weak. When I see Indians dressed in European apparel and costumes, the thought comes to my mind—perhaps they feel ashamed to own their nationality and kinship with the ignorant, poor, illiterate, downtrodden people of India! Nourished by the blood of the Hindu for the last fourteen centuries, the Parsee is no longer a "Native"! Before the arrogance of the casteless, who pretend to be and glorify themselves in being Brāhmans, the true nobility of the old, heroic, high-class Brāhman melts into nothingness! Again, the Westerners have now taught us that those stupid, ignorant, low-caste millions of India clad only in loin cloths are non-Aryans! They are therefore no more our kith and kin!

Oh India! With this mere echoing of others, with this base imitation of others, with this dependence on others, this slavish weakness, this vile detestable cruelty, wouldst thou, with these provisions only, scale the highest pinnacle of civilization and greatness? Wouldst thou attain, by means of thy disgraceful cowardice, that freedom deserved only by the brave and the heroic? Oh India! Forget not that the ideal of thy womanhood is Sītā, Sāvitrī, Damayanti;[2] forget not that the God thou worshippest is the great Ascetic of ascetics, the all-renouncing Shankara, the Lord of Uma;[3] forget not that thy marriage, thy wealth, thy life are not for sense-pleasure, are not for thy individual personal happiness; forget not that thou art born as a sacrifice to the *Mother's* altar; forget not that thy social order is but the reflex of the Infinite Universal Motherhood; forget not that the lower classes, the ignorant, the poor, the illiterate, the cobbler, the sweeper, are thy flesh and blood, thy brothers. Thou brave one, be bold, take courage, be proud that thou art an Indian, and proudly proclaim: "I am an Indian, every Indian is my brother." Say: "The ignorant Indian, the poor and destitute Indian, the Brāhman Indian, the Pariah Indian, is my brother." Thou too clad with but a rag round thy loins proudly proclaim at the top of thy voice: "The Indian is my brother, the Indian is my life, India's gods and goddesses are my God, India's society is the cradle of my infancy, the pleasure-garden of my youth, the sacred heaven, the *Vārānasi,*[4] of my old age." Say, brother: "The soil of India is my highest heaven, the good of India is my good," and repeat and pray day and night: "O Thou Lord of Gauri,[5] O Thou Mother of the Universe, vouchsafe manliness unto me! O Thou Mother of Strength, take away my weakness, take away my unmanliness, and—*Make me a Man!*"

[2] Damayantī, celebrated in Indian legend for her devotion to her husband Nala.
[3] Umā, a name of the wife of Shiva or Shankara (the Gracious One).
[4] Banaras.   [5] A name for the wife of Shiva.

CHAPTER XXII

NATIONALISM TAKES ROOT:
THE MODERATES

Before the British conquest, the concept of membership in a permanent political order embracing and involving them all seems to have been unknown to the inhabitants of India. Dynasties rather than nations were the centers of political power and the foci of personal loyalties. Powerful rulers like Ashoka, Samudragupta, and Harsha had indeed succeeded in bringing large parts of the subcontinent under their sway, but their empires dissolved with the death of the last strong ruler in each reigning line. Thanks largely to the genius of Akbar (1542–1605), the Mughal empire created a somewhat more durable administrative order, but internal dissensions and Persian-Afghan invasions led to the empire's dismemberment after the passing of the militant Aurangzeb (1619–1707). For a time the Mārāthas gave promise of re-establishing Hindu dominion, but again their rule could not even unite all of Hindudom around their standard, let alone bridge the gap between India's two major religious traditions.

A new chapter opened when British arms and diplomacy placed the whole of the subcontinent under one paramount power for the first time in history. They imposed not only peace and unity on India, but a relatively efficient administrative machinery as well. Gradually the sinews of a new nation were strengthened by the introduction of printing and journalism, railroads, a postal and telegraph system, and by the growth of an all-India economy centering in large modern cities accessible to ocean-going ships.

The new political and economic order attracted able Indians anxious to improve their status and increase their wealth by entering its service. A new class emerged to mediate between the foreign rulers or traders and the mass of the people. Using their knowledge of English as the key to advancement, Indian clerks and functionaries found employment in government posts; Indian lawyers pleaded in British-style courts; Indian businessmen dealt with foreign firms; and Indian teachers imparted to their countrymen the language and culture of the conquerors. This rising middle class demonstrated a loyalty to the British which outweighed the angry discontent of the old elite—both Muslim and Hindu. The supression of the latter in the Mutiny and Rebellion of 1857–58 only confirmed the entrenched position of their parvenu successors.

But the English education which provided so many willing collaborators for the British in India eventually proved the undoing of their empire. For one thing, the members of the new middle class—whether from the South or the North, from Bengal or from Mahārāshtra—could all communicate with each other through the medium of a common language. Equally important, their reading of the English classics instilled in them the Western ideals of justice, freedom, and love of country. As their numbers grew they found the good government jobs too few, with the best ones reserved for Europeans. To economic frustration was added the bitter sting of racial discrimination, for "the Mutiny" of 1857 had sharpened British suspicions of Indian loyalty, while the late nineteenth-century doctrines of social Darwinism and aggressive imperialism compounded to increase the white man's feeling of inherent superiority over his darker-skinned subjects. Ignoring the sympathetic statements made in Parliament and the conciliatory proclamation of Queen Victoria in 1858, Britishers in India saw little reason to grant Indians a greater measure of control over their own affairs.

Under these circumstances, it was not long before the seed-idea of nationalism implanted by their reading of Western books began to take root in the minds of intelligent and energetic Indians. A. O. Hume, a Scotsman sympathetic to their aspirations, made possible the first meeting (in 1885) of the Indian National Congress, which was intended to serve as a forum for the discussion of political reforms and patriotic projects. From this beginning as a safety-valve through which the upper classes could air their grievances, the Congress quickly transformed itself into an all-India nationalist organization.

The Moderates, the first men to come forward as leaders of the nationalist movement, shared a great many assumptions with those liberal Englishmen who advised and encouraged them. They believed in the providential character of British rule and in the gradual evolution of

India toward enlightenment and self-government under that rule. They regretted the backwardness of Hindu society and worked to bring about the reform of its grosser evils. The poverty of the people depressed them, and they therefore concerned themselves with plans for India's economic improvement. Although they were not men devoid of religious faith, they accepted the divorce of religion from government and maintained a secular view of politics which contrasted markedly with the religious outlook of the Extremists, who later posed a serious challenge to their leadership.

Having become, as Macaulay proposed, "English in taste, in opinions, in morals, and in intellect," the Indian Moderates gained certain advantages but at the same time ran certain risks in guiding the nationalist movement. Their familiarity with British culture enabled them to appeal to the best instincts of their rulers, from whom they demanded the same rights and liberties which all Britons took for granted. Their knowledge of the gradual rise of democratic government in English history furnished them with useful ammunition, and they repeatedly harked back to the assurances given by Parliament and Queen Victoria that Indians would be allowed to compete freely with Europeans for positions in the Indian Civil Service.

In relation to their rivals the Extremists, however, the position of the Moderates was bound to be somewhat vulnerable for several reasons. Their heavy reliance on British good faith embarrassed them whenever the concessions they asked for were refused or postponed. Moreover, the more anglicized they became in their thinking, the further they removed themselves from emotional rapport with the bulk of the population—the illiterate, poverty-stricken, and religious-minded peasantry.

In one respect the Moderates did yeoman's service in tending to the needs of the peasantry. Unwilling to attack British rule for the political and social reforms it had introduced, they focused their attention on the obvious disparity between Britain's prosperity and India's poverty. Dādābhāi Naoroji, an Indian businessman resident in London, placed the blame for his country's plight on foreign rule, and in doing so was seconded by English socialist theoreticians. The Bengali leader Surendranāth Banerjea accepted Dādābhāi's thesis, while M. G. Rānade (pronounced Rānadé) sought a constructive solution in rapid industrialization under government auspices. Rānade's disciple G. K. Gokhale (pronounced Gokhalé) left the theorizing to others, and bent his efforts to reducing the load of taxation burdening the Indian people.

These four men were probably the most outstanding moderate leaders in the opening decades of the nationalist movement. It is significant that all were scholarly in temperament, and spent part of their early careers as teachers in colleges imparting English education to Indian students. Each possessed a flawless command of the English language and was able to hold his own in debates with Englishmen. Three of them—Naoroji, Banerjea, and Gokhale—made speaking tours in Great Britain to impress the British electorate with the importance of greater self-government for India. The same three were also elected presidents of the Congress, and all four were deeply involved in its work.

Although the Extremist leaders could muster far greater support by appealing to popular Hindu symbols and traditions, it is doubtful that they could have succeeded in freeing India without the patient, more diplomatic efforts of the Moderates. Their greater willingness to cooperate with the British in instituting administrative reforms kept the nationalist movement from "going off the rails" into senseless violence, which could only lead to severe reprisals and political deadlock. Their contribution to the achievement of self-government has largely been forgotten by subsequent generations, but independent India's dedication to parliamentary democracy, economic development, and social progress stands as mute testimony to their farsighted wisdom.

DĀDĀBHĀI NAOROJI: ARCHITECT OF INDIAN NATIONALISM

Inevitable as the rise of Indian nationalism may seem in retrospect to have been under the conditions created by British rule, its emergence would have been impossible without the strenuous efforts of devoted national leaders. The first of a long series of such men, Dādābhāi Naoroji drew the plans and laid the foundations for India's self-government.

This architect of Indian nationalism was neither Hindu nor Muslim, but a descendant of the followers of Zoroaster who had fled Persia after the Muslim conquest of that country. Settling as refugees along the western coast of India the Zoroastrians became known as Parsīs (Persians). When the British came to trade they emerged as the group most willing to do business, for they were bound neither by caste rules nor by prejudice against taking interest on loans, and as a minority group they had little to lose and much to gain by dealing with the Europeans. As a result of their trading contacts, the Parsīs became the most Westernized and the wealthiest single community in India.

Dādābhāi Naoroji was born in Bombay in 1825, the son of a Zoroastrian priest. His family name, Dordi, was little used; but the original meaning of the word (twisted rope made of coconut husk) had a symbolic significance for Dādābhāi, who was absolutely inflexible once he had made up his mind. "You may burn a *dordi*," he once said, "but you can never take the twist out of it. So it is with me. When once I form a decision, nothing will dislodge me from it." [1]

Tenacity of purpose was indeed his chief characteristic. He so distinguished himself in his studies at the Elphinstone Institution (Bombay's leading college) that he became at twenty-seven its Professor of Mathematics—the first Indian to attain such an academic rank. At thirty he left India to become a partner in the first Indian firm to do business in England. His aim in moving permanently to London, the heart of the empire, was not to gain wealth, but to enable himself to appeal directly to the British public for a better understanding of India's problems. For fifty years Dādābhāi delivered papers on Indian subjects to numerous learned societies, submitted memoranda and petitions to British officials concerned with India, and agitated both privately and publicly—all in the service of one cause: that Indians should be granted the same rights and privileges as other British subjects.

With his famous theory of "the drain" of India's wealth to Britain, Dādābhāi Naoroji sounded the keynote of Indian economic nationalism. But for all his bitter condemnation of the costliness of foreign government to his country, he never advocated violent action as a solution. His loyalty to the parliamentary system of government was rewarded in 1892 with his election to the British House of Commons on the Liberal ticket. The first Indian member of Parliament, he served both his London constituency and the interests of India for three years, succeeding in his attempt

[1] R. P. Masani, *Dadabhai Naoroji: The Grand Old Man of India*, p. 25.

to have a parliamentary commission investigate the financial administration of British India.

Dādābhāi punctuated his long residence in England with frequent visits to India. In 1873–74 he served as chief minister to the Indian state of Baroda to prevent it from being annexed by the British crown (the usual penalty for misgovernment in the princely states). He took a prominent part in the first session of the Indian National Congress in 1885, and was thrice elected its president—in 1886, 1893, and 1906. The younger generation of nationalist leaders all looked up to the patriarchal patriot for advice, and Gāndhi especially revered him. He died in Bombay in 1917, but to this day the affectionate title "the Grand Old Man of India" is associated with his name.

DĀDĀBHĀI NAOROJI
The Pros and Cons of British Rule

In the discussion following the presentation of a paper on India to a learned society in London in 1871, Dādābhāi drew up an impromptu account of the advantages and disadvantages of British rule to India. It shows both his fairness in recognizing the good the British had done, and his persistent criticism of the crushing cost to India of their rule.

[From *Essays, Speeches, Addresses, and Writings . . . of the Hon'ble Dadabhai Naoroji*, pp. 131–36]

Credit—*In the Cause of Humanity*: Abolition of suttee and infanticide.

Destruction of Dacoits, Thugs, Pindarees,[1] and other such pests of Indian society.

Remarriage of Hindoo widows, and charitable aid in time of famine.

Glorious work all this, of which any nation may well be proud, and such as has not fallen to the lot of any people in the history of mankind.

In the Cause of Civilization: Education, both male and female. Though yet only partial, an inestimable blessing as far as it has gone, and leading gradually to the destruction of superstition, and many moral and social evils. Resuscitation of India's own noble literature, modified and refined by the enlightment of the West.

The only pity is that as much has not been done as might have been in this noble work; but still India must be, and is, deeply grateful.

[1] Armed thieves, highway murderers, robber bands.

[113]

Politically: Peace and order. Freedom of speech and liberty of the press. Higher political knowledge and aspirations. Improvement of government in the native States. Security of life and property. Freedom from oppression caused by the caprice or avarice of despotic rulers, and from devastation by war. Equal justice between man and man (sometimes vitiated by partiality to Europeans). Services of highly educated administrators, who have achieved the above-mentioned good results.

Materially: Loans for railways and irrigation. (I have been particularly charged with ignoring this, but I consider it one of the greatest benefits you have conferred upon India, inasmuch as it has enabled us to produce more than we could before, though there is not yet enough for all India's ordinary wants, and I have said this in my paper.) I cannot ascertain the exact amount of investments in irrigation works, but I take them to be about £10,000,000, making the total £110,000,000. The development of a few valuable products, such as indigo, tea, coffee, silk, &c. Increase of exports. Telegraphs.

Generally: A slowly growing desire of late to treat India equitably, and as a country held in trust. Good intentions.

No nation on the face of the earth has ever had the opportunity of achieving such a glorious work as this. I hope in this credit side of the account I have done no injustice, and if I have omitted any item which anyone may think of importance, I shall have the greatest pleasure in inserting it. I appreciate, and so do my countrymen, what England has done for India, and I know that it is only in British hands that her regeneration can be accomplished. Now for the debit side.

Debit—In the Cause of Humanity: Nothing. Everything, therefore, is in your favor under this head.

In the Cause of Civilization: As I have said already, there has been a failure to do as much as might have been done, but I put nothing to the debit. Much has been done, or I should not be standing here this evening.

Politically: Repeated breach of pledges to give the natives a fair and reasonable share in the higher administration of their own country, which has much shaken confidence in the good faith of the British word. Political aspirations and the legitimate claim to have a reasonable voice in the legislation and the imposition and disbursement of taxes, met to a very slight degree, thus treating the natives of India not as British subjects, to whom representation is a birthright.

(I stop here a moment to say a word as to a mistake into which my friend, Mr. Hyde Clarke, fell, in supposing that I desired the government of India to be at once transferred to the natives. In my belief a greater calamity could not befall India than for England to go away and leave her to herself.)

Consequent on the above, an utter disregard of the feelings and views of the natives. The great moral evil of the drain of the wisdom and practical administration and statesmanship, leaving none to guide the rising generation. (Here, again, have I been misunderstood. I complain not of Englishmen returning to their own country, but of the whole administration being kept entirely in English hands, so that none of the natives are brought up to and taught the responsibilities and duties of office, so that we have none amongst ourselves to guide us as our elders and to teach us our duties as citizens and as moral beings. A foster mother or nurse will never supply the place of the real mother, and the natives will therefore naturally follow their own leaders, unless you prove more kind, humane, and considerate. Draw these leaders on your side.) The indifference to India, even of a large portion of those who have had an Indian career, and who are living on Indian pensions. The culpable indifference of a large portion of the people, the public press, and Parliament of this country to the interests of India; therefore, periodical committees of inquiry are absolutely necessary, for the knowledge that such will take place would be a check on careless administration. With regard to the native states, though their system is improving, it is most unjust that their cases should be decided in secret. The frequent change of officials is a constant source of disturbance in policy, and though it may be unavoidable, it is none the less hard upon India.

Financially: All attention is engrossed in devising new modes of taxation, without any adequate effort to increase the means of the people to pay; and the consequent vexation and oppressiveness of the taxes imposed, imperial and local. Inequitable financial relations between England and India, i.e. the political debt of £100,000,000 clapped on India's shoulders, and all home charges also, though the British exchequer contributes nearly £3,000,000 to the expenses of the colonies. The crushing and economically rude and unintelligent policy of making the present generation pay the whole cost of public works for the benefit of the future, instead of making the political like all other machinery, and distributing the weight so as to make a small power lift a large weight by the aid of time. The results of trying to produce something out of nothing, of the want of intelligent adaptation of financial machinery, and of much reckless expenditure; in financial embarrassments, and deep discontent of the people.

Materially: The political drain,[2] up to this time, from India to England, of above £500,000,000, at the lowest computation, in principal alone, which with interest would be some thousands of millions. The further continuation of this drain at the rate, at present, of above £12,000,000, with a tendency to increase. (I do not mean this as a complaint; you must have a return for the services rendered to India, but let us have the means of paying. If I have a manager to whom I pay £1,000 a year, and he only makes the business produce £400, so that £600 a year must be paid him out of capital, any man of business can see what will be the result. Peace and order will soon be completely established by the closing of the concern.)

The consequent continuous impoverishment and exhaustion of the country, except so far as it has been very partially relieved and replenished by the railway and irrigation loans, and the windfall of the consequences of the American war, since 1850. Even with this relief, the material condition of India is such that the great mass of the poor people have hardly 2*d* a day and a few rags, or a scanty subsistence.

The famines that were in their power to prevent, if they had done their duty, as a good and intelligent government. The policy adopted during the last fifteen years of building railways, irrigation works, etc., is hopeful, has already resulted in much good to your credit, and if persevered in, gratitude and contentment will follow.

[An] increase of exports [without adequate compensation]; [a] loss of manufacturing industry and skill. Here I end the debit side. . . .

To sum up the whole, the British rule has been—morally, a great blessing; politically peace and order on one hand, blunders on the other; materially, impoverishment (relieved as far as the railway and other loans go). The natives call the British system "Sakar ki Churi," the knife of sugar. That is to say there is no oppression, it is all smooth and sweet, but it is the knife, notwithstanding. I mention this that you should

---

[2] Dādābhāi refers to the export from India of the savings and pensions of British officials and to other costs of British rule such as supplies and military expenditures.

know these feelings. Our great misfortune is that you do not know our wants. When you will know our real wishes, I have not the least doubt that you would do justice. The genius and spirit of the British people is fair play and justice. The great problems before the English statesmen are two: 1) To make the foreign rule self-supporting, either by returning to India, in some shape or other, the wealth that has been, and is being, drawn from it, or by stopping that drain in some way till India is so far improved in its material condition as to be able to produce enough for its own ordinary wants and the extraordinary ones of a costly distant rule. If you cannot feel yourself actuated by the high and noble ambition of the amelioration of 200,000,000 of human beings, let your self-interest suggest to you to take care of the bird that gives the golden egg of £12,000,000 a year to your nation, and provisions to thousands of your people of all classes. In the name of humanity, I implore our rulers to make up their minds not to prevent the restoration of the equilibrium, after the continuous exhaustion by drain and by horrible famines. I do not in the least grudge any legitimate benefit England may derive for its rule in India. On the contrary, I am thankful for its invaluable moral benefits; but it is the further duty of England to give us such a government, and all the benefit of its power and credit, as to enable us to pay, without starving or dying by famine, the tribute or price for the rule; 2) How to satisfy reasonably the growing political aspirations and just rights of a people called British subjects to have a fair share in the administration and legislation of their own country. If the Select Committee solve these two problems, before which all other difficulties, financial or others, are as nothing, they will deserve the blessings of 200,000,000 of the human race.

The Blessings of British Rule

Dādābhāi's presidential address at the second session of the Congress in 1886 rings with protestations of loyalty and gratitude to British rule for the unity, peace, civil liberties and education it brought to the Indian people.
[From *Essays, Speeches, Addresses, and Writings . . . of the Hon'ble Dadabhai Naoroji*, pp. 332–33]

The assemblage of such a Congress is an event of the utmost importance in Indian history. I ask whether in the most glorious days of Hindu

[117]

rule, in the days of Rajahs like the great Vikram,[3] you could imagine the possibility of a meeting of this kind, where even Hindus of all different provinces of the kingdom could have collected and spoken as one nation. Coming down to the later empire of our friends, the Mahomedans, who probably ruled over a larger territory at one time than any Hindu monarch, would it have been, even in the days of the great Akbar himself, possible for a meeting like this to assemble composed of all classes and communities, all speaking one language, and all having uniform and high aspirations of their own?

Well, then, what is it for which we are now met on this occasion? We have assembled to consider questions upon which depend our future, whether glorious or inglorious. It is our good fortune that we are under a rule which makes it possible for us to meet in this manner. [Cheers.] It is under the civilizing rule of the Queen and people of England that we meet here together, hindered by none, and are freely allowed to speak our minds without the least fear and without the least hesitation. Such a thing is possible under British rule and British rule only. [Loud cheers.] Then I put the *question* plainly: Is this Congress a nursery for sedition and rebellion against the British Government [cries of "no, no"]; or is it another stone in the foundation of the stability of that Government [cries of "yes, yes"]? There could be but one answer, and that you have already given, because we are thoroughly sensible of the numberless blessings conferred upon us, of which the very existence of this Congress is a proof in a nutshell. [Cheers.] Were it not for these blessings of British rule I could not have come here, as I have done, without the least hesitation and without the least fear that my children might be robbed and killed in my absence; nor could you have come from every corner of the land, having performed, within a few days, journeys which in former days would have occupied as many months. [Cheers.] These simple facts bring home to all of us at once some of those great and numberless blessings which British rule has conferred upon us. But there remain even greater blessings for which we have to be grateful. It is to British rule that we owe the education we possess; the people of England were sincere in the declarations made more than half a century ago that India was a sacred charge entrusted to their care by Providence, and that they were bound to administer it for the good of India, to the

[3] Vikramāditya, a great and good king in Indian legend.

glory of their own name, and the satisfaction of God. [Prolonged cheering.] When we have to acknowledge so many blessings as flowing from British rule—and I could descant on them for hours, because it would simply be recounting to you the history of the British empire in India— is it possible that an assembly like this, every one of whose members is fully impressed with the knowledge of these blessings, could meet for any purpose inimical to that rule to which we owe so much? [Cheers.] The thing is absurd. Let us speak out like men and proclaim that we are loyal to the backbone [cheers]; that we understand the benefits English rule has conferred upon us; that we thoroughly appreciate the education that has been given to us, the new light which has been poured upon us, turning us from darkness into light and teaching us the new lesson that kings are made for the people, not people for their kings; and this new lesson we have learned amidst the darkness of Asiatic despotism only by the light of free English civilization. [Loud cheers.]

The Moral Impoverishment of India

The frustration felt by the swelling ranks of educated Indians who were excluded from government positions is well expressed in Dādābhāi's memorandum of 1880. Note the veiled threat with which this selection concludes.

[From *Essays, Speeches, Addresses, and Writings . . . of the Hon'ble Dadabhai Naoroji,* pp. 465–67]

In this Memorandum I desire to submit for the kind and generous consideration of His Lordship the Secretary of State for India, that from the same cause of the deplorable drain, besides the material exhaustion of India, the moral loss to her is no less sad and lamentable.

With the material wealth go also the wisdom and experience of the country. Europeans occupy almost all the higher places in every department of government, directly or indirectly under its control. While *in* India they acquire India's money, experience, and wisdom, and when they go, they carry both away with them, leaving India so much poorer in material and moral wealth. Thus India is left without, and cannot have, those elders in wisdom and experience, who in every country are the natural guides of the rising generations in their national and social conduct, and of the destinies of their country—and a sad, sad loss this is!

Every European is isolated from the people around him. He is not their mental, moral or social leader, or companion. For any mental or moral influence or guidance or sympathy with the people, he might just as well be living in the moon. The people know not him, and he knows not, nor cares for the people. Some honorable exceptions do, now and then, make an effort to do some good they can, but in the very nature of things, these efforts are always feeble, exotic, and of little permanent effect. These men are not always in the place, and their works die away when they go.

The Europeans are not the natural leaders of the people. They do not belong to the people. They cannot enter into their thoughts and feelings; they cannot join or sympathize with their joys or griefs. On the contrary, every day the estrangement is increasing. Europeans deliberately and openly widen it more and more. There may be very few social institutions started by Europeans in which natives, however fit and desirous to join, are not deliberately and insultingly excluded. The Europeans are and make themselves strangers in every way. All they effectually do is to eat the substance of India, material and moral, while living there, and when they go, they carry away all they have acquired, and their pensions and future usefulness besides.

This most deplorable moral loss to India needs most serious consideration, as much in its political as in its national aspect. Nationally disastrous as it is, it carries politically with it its own nemesis. Without the guidance of elderly wisdom and experience of their own natural leaders, the education which the rising generations are now receiving is naturally leading them (or call it misleading them, if you will) into directions which bode no good to the rulers, and which, instead of being the strength of the rulers as it ought to and can be, will turn out to be their great weakness. The fault will be of the rulers themselves for such a result. The power that is now being raised by the spread of education, though yet slow and small, is one that in time must, for weal or woe, exercise great influence. In fact it has already begun to do so. However strangely the English rulers, forgetting their English manliness and moral courage, may, like the ostrich, shut their eyes by gagging acts or otherwise, to the good or bad influences they are raising around them, this good or evil is rising nevertheless. The thousands that are being sent out by the universities every year find themselves in a most anomalous position. There is no place for them in their motherland. They may beg in the streets or break stones on the roads, for aught the rulers seem to care for their natural rights, position, and duties in their own country. They may perish or do what they like or can, but scores of Europeans must go from this country to take up what belongs to them, and that, in spite of every profession for years and years past and up to the present day, of English statesmen, that they must govern India for India's good, by solemn acts and declarations of Parliament, and above all, by the words of the August Sovereign Herself. For all practical purposes all these high promises have been hitherto, almost wholly, the purest romance, the reality being quite different.

The educated find themselves simply so many dummies, ornamented with the tinsel of school education, and then their whole end and aim of life is ended. What must be the inevitable consequence? A wild, spirited horse, without curb or reins, will run away wild, and kill and trample upon every one that came in his way. A misdirected force will hit anywhere and destroy anything. The power that the rulers are, so far to their credit, raising, will, as a nemesis recoil against themselves, if with this blessing of education they do not do their whole duty to the country which trusts to their righteousness, and thus turn this good power to their own side. The nemesis is as clear from the present violence to nature, as disease and death arise from uncleanliness and rottenness. The voice of the power of the rising education is, no doubt, feeble at present. Like the infant, the present dissatisfaction is only crying at the pains it is suffering. Its notions have not taken any form or shape or course yet, but it is growing. Heaven only knows what it will grow to! He who runs may see, that if the present material and moral destruction of India continued, a great convulsion must inevitably arise, by which either India will be more and more crushed under the iron heel of despotism and destruction, or may succeed in shattering the destroying hand and power. Far, far is it from my earnest prayer and hope that such should be the result of the British rule.

"SURRENDER-NOT" BANERJEA: BENGALI MODERATE

The Hindu renascence in nineteenth-century Bengal was accompanied by a gradual political awakening in that province. Politics, however, unlike religion, came as a comparatively new category of thought to Bengali Hindus after centuries of domination by Muslim rulers. Following the example set by Rāmmohun Roy, a growing number of men emerged from the English-speaking middle class infused by their Western-style education with new ideals of patriotism and public service.

To this group Allan Octavian Hume, the retired civil servant who fathered the organization of the Indian National Congress, appealed with his letter of 1883, addressing the graduates of Calcutta University. "You are the salt of the land," he wrote. "And if amongst even you, the elite, fifty men cannot be found with sufficient power of self-sacrifice, sufficient love for and pride in their country, sufficient genuine and unselfish heart-felt patriotism to take the initiative, and if needs be, devote the rest of their lives to the Cause—then there is no hope for India." [1]

To one Calcutta University graduate Hume's appeal was entirely superfluous, for Surendranāth Banerjea (1848–1926) had already cast himself into the stormy sea of national service. A brāhman and the son of a doctor, Surendranāth had been one of the first Indians to be admitted to the select Indian Civil Service, the so-called "steel frame" of British administration; but his failure to correct a false report prepared in his name by a subordinate had caused him to be dismissed—a punishment far more severe than English members of the I.C.S. received for similar oversights. Undismayed, Surendranāth journeyed to London to appeal his case. When the appeal was denied, he appeared for bar examinations, only to be refused again. With the two swiftest roads to success—the civil service and the law—closed to him, Surendranāth returned to Calcutta, convinced that "the personal wrong done to me was an illustration of the impotency of our people," and determined to spend his life "redressing our wrongs and protecting our rights, personal and collective." [2]

The rest of his long life was only the acting out of this resolve. Starting as a teacher, he soon founded a patriotic association, then a newspaper, then a college. As Keshub Chunder Sen had captivated audiences in many parts of the land with his revivalist sermons, so Surendranāth used his oratorical gifts to rouse Indians from Bengal to the Punjab to a greater sense of loyalty to their country. When he was jailed for

---

[1] William Wedderburn, *Allan Octavian Hume, C.B.*, pp. 51–52.

[2] Surendranāth Banerjea, *A Nation in Making, Being the Reminiscences of Fifty Years in Public Life*, p. 33.

criticizing a British judge, he started the tradition (still popular in India) of welcoming imprisonment in order to demonstrate the injustice of a governmental law or policy.

Surendranāth's career dramatizes the change of heart in countless educated Indians from blind loyalty to British rule to stubborn resistance against its evils. Despite his sufferings at the hands of the authorities, Surendranāth insisted that only constitutional means be used in the struggle for self-government. When the Extremists cried for more drastic measures against the foreigner, he opposed them as firmly as he opposed the British. Twice president of the Congress, he left it in 1918 to head the All-India Liberal Federation when the younger Congress leaders threatened to obstruct the introduction of the important Montagu-Chelmsford Reforms. His persistence in his chosen course earned him the respect of Indians and British alike and won him the aptly coined nickname of "Surrender-not" Banerjea.

SURENDRANĀTH BANERJEA
The Need for Indian Unity

Understanding between Hindus and Muslims formed a major plank in the Moderates' platform. In one of Surendranāth's earliest speeches (in 1878) he exhorted the young men of the country to strive for unity as a patriotic duty.

[From *Speeches and Writings of Hon. Surendranath Banerjea*, pp. 227–31]

Young men, whom I see around me in such large numbers, you are the hopes of your families. May I not also say, you are the hopes of your country? Your country expects great things from you. Now I ask, how many of you are prepared, when you have finished your studies at the college, to devote your lives, to consecrate your energies to the good of your country? I repeat the question and I pause for a reply. [Here the speaker paused for a few seconds. Cries of "all, all" from all sides of the gallery]. The response is in every way worthy of yourselves and of the education which you are receiving. May you prove true to your resolve, and carry out in life the high purposes which animate your bosoms.

Gentlemen, I have a strong conviction and an assured belief that there comes a time in the history of a nation's progress, when every man may verily be said to have a mission of his own to accomplish. Such a time has now arrived for India. The fiat has gone forth. The celestial mandate has been issued that every Indian must now do his duty, or stand condemned before God and man. There was such a time of stirring activity in the glorious annals of England, when Hampden offered up his life for the deliverance of his own country, when Algernon Sydney laid down his head on the block to rid his country of a hated tyrant, when English bishops did not hesitate in the discharge of their duty to their Fatherland to descend from the performance of their ecclesiastical functions and appear as traitors before the bar of a Criminal Court. These are glorious reminiscences in England's immortal history, which Englishmen to this day look back upon with pride and satisfaction. It is not indeed necessary for us to have recourse to violence in order to obtain the redress of our grievances. Constitutional agitation will secure for us those rights, the privileges which in less favoured countries are obtained by sterner means. But peaceful as are the means to be enforced, there is a stern duty to be performed by every Indian. And he who fails in that duty is a traitor before God and man.

In holding up for your acceptance the great principle of Indian unity, I do not lay claims to originality. Three hundred years ago, in the Punjab, the immortal founder of Sikhism, the meek, the gentle, the blessed Nānak preached the great doctrine of Indian unity and endeavored to knit together Hindus and Musulmans under the banner of a common faith. That attempt was eminently successful. Nānak became the spiritual founder of the Sikh empire. He preached the great doctrine of peace and good will between Hindus and Musulmans. And standing in the presence of his great example, we too must preach the great doctrine of peace and good will between Hindus and Musulmans, Christians and Parsees, aye between all sections of the great Indian community. Let us raise aloft the banner of our country's progress. Let the word "Unity" be inscribed there in characters of glittering gold. We have had enough of past jealousies, past dissensions, past animosities. The spirits of the dead at Paniput [1] will testify to our bloody strifes. The spirits of the dead in other battlefields will testify to the same fact. There may be religious differences between us. There may be social differences

---

[1] Pānīpat, the site of numerous pitched battles in Indian history. It lies about fifty miles north of Delhi.

between us. But there is a common platform where we may all meet, the platform of our country's welfare. There is a common cause which may blind [bind] us together, the cause of Indian progress. There is a common Divinity, to whom we may uplift our voices in adoration, the Divinity who presides over the destinies of our country. In the name then of a common country, let us all, Hindus, Musulmans, Christians, Parsees, members of the great Indian community, throw the pall of oblivion over jealousies and dissensions of bygone times and embracing one another in fraternal love and affection, live and work for the benefit of a beloved Fatherland. Under English auspices there is indeed a great future for India. I am confident of the great destinies that are in store for us. You and I may not live to see that day. These eyes of ours may not witness that spectacle of ineffable beauty. It may not be permitted to us to exclaim Simeonlike, "Now Lord, lettest thou thy servant depart in peace." It may not be permitted to us to exclaim like the Welsh Bard on the heights of Snowdon, "Visions of glory, spare my aching sight." But is it nothing to know when you are dying, when you are about to take leave of this world, of its joys and sorrows, when the past of your life is unfurled before you, when eternity opens wide its portals, is it nothing to know at that last awful, supreme moment of your lives, that you have not lived in vain, that you have lived for the benefit of others, that you have lived to help in the cause of your country's regeneration? Let us all lead worthy, honorable, and patriotic lives, that we may all live and die happily and that India may be great. This is my earnest and prayerful request. May it find a response in your sympathetic hearts.

Faith in England

The backbone of the Moderates' creed was faith that the British would grant self-government to India when she was prepared for it. Surendranāth enunciated this creed in the peroration of his presidential address to the Congress in 1895.

[From *Speeches and Writings of the Hon. Surendranath Banerjea*, pp. 93–96]

We feel that in this great struggle in which we are engaged, the moral sympathies of civilized humanity are with us. The prayers of the good and the true in all parts of the world follow us. They will welcome as glad tidings of great joy the birth of an emancipated people on the banks of the Ganges. For, have they not all read about our ancient civilization; how, in the morning of the world, before the Eternal City had been built upon the Seven Hills, before Alexander had marched his army to the banks of the Tigris, before Babylonian astronomers had learnt to gaze upon the starry world, our ancestors had developed a great civilization, and how that civilization has profoundly influenced the course of modern thought in the highest concerns of man? Above all, we rely with unbounded confidence on the justice and generosity of the British people and of their representatives in Parliament.

It is not that we mistrust the authorities here. But the higher we mount, the purer is the atmosphere. The impurities generated by local causes cannot touch those who, removed from local influences, represent in a loftier sphere of responsibility the majesty and the greatness of the English nation. Let us freely acknowledge the tribute we owe to the British government in India. What government could have accorded a speedier recognition to Congress claims than the government of India has done? Within the lifetime of a generation we have achieved changes —beneficent changes of far-reaching moment—which it would have taken many generations to accomplish elsewhere, which in less fortunately situated countries could not have been accomplished except, perhaps, after bloodshed and tumult. All this we freely acknowledge. For all this we are truly grateful. All this fills [us] with hope for the future.

Nevertheless we feel that much yet remains to be done, and the impetus must come from England. To England we look for inspiration and guidance. To England we look for sympathy in the struggle. From England must come the crowning mandate which will enfranchise our peoples. England is our political guide and our moral preceptor in the exalted sphere of political duty. English history has taught us those principles of freedom which we cherish with our lifeblood. We have been fed upon the strong food of English constitutional freedom. We have been taught to admire the eloquence and genius of the great masters of English political philosophy. We have been brought face to face with the struggles and the triumphs of the English people in their stately march towards constitutional freedom. Where will you find better models of courage, devotion, and sacrifice; not in Rome, not in Greece, not even in France in the stormy days of the Revolution—courage tempered by caution, enthusiasm leavened by sobriety, partisanship softened by a large-hearted charity—all subordinated to the one predominating sense of love of country and love of God.

We should be unworthy of ourselves and of our preceptors—we should, indeed, be something less than human—if, with our souls stirred to their inmost depths, our warm Oriental sensibilities roused to an unwanted pitch of enthusiasm by the contemplation of these great ideals of public duty, we did not seek to transplant into our own country the spirit of those free institutions which have made England what she is. In the words of Lord Lansdowne, a wave of unrest is passing through this country. But it is not the unrest of discontent or disloyalty to the British government—it is the unrest which is the first visible sign of the awakening of a new national life. It is the work of Englishmen—it is the noblest monument of their rule—it is the visible embodiment of the vast moral influence which they are exercising over the minds of the people of India. Never in the history of the world have the inheritors of an ancient civilization been so profoundly influenced by the influx of modern ideas. In this Congress from year to year we ask England to accomplish her glorious work. The course of civilization following the path of the sun has traveled from East to West. The West owes a heavy debt to the East. We look forward to the day when that debt will be repaid, not only by the moral regeneration, but by the political enfranchisement of our people.

Faith in Social Progress

In concluding his memoirs in his old age, Surendranāth looked back at the changes that had taken place in Hindu society during his lifetime, and summed up that faith in gradual reform which is one of the hallmarks of a Moderate.

[From *A Nation in Making*, pp. 397–98]

I feel that if we have to advance in social matters, we must, so far as practicable, take the community with us by a process of steady and gradual uplift, so that there may be no sudden disturbance or dislocation, the new being adapted to the old, and the old assimilated to the new. That has been the normal path of progress in Hindu society through the long centuries. It would be idle to contend that Hindu society is today where it was two hundred years ago. It moves slowly, perhaps more slowly than many would wish, but in the words of Galileo "it does move," more or less according to the lines of adaptation that I have indicated. The question of sea-voyage, or child-marriage, or even enforced widowhood, is not today where it was in the latter part of the last century. Fifty years ago I was an outcaste (being an England-returned Brahmin) in the village where I live. Today I am an honored member of the community. My public services have, perhaps, partly contributed to the result. But they would have been impotent, as in the case Ram Mohun Roy for many long years after his death, if they were not backed by the slow, the silent, the majestic forces of progress, working noiselessly but irresistibly in the bosom of society, helping on the fruition of those ideas which have been sown in the public mind. Remarkable indeed have been, in many respects, the relaxations and the removal of restrictions of caste. Dining with non-Hindus, which was an abomination not many years ago, is now connived at, if not openly countenanced. A still more forward step towards loosening the bonds of caste has been taken within the last few years. The barriers of marriage between some sub-castes have been relaxed, and marriages between hitherto prohibited sub-castes of Brahmins and Kayasthas are not infrequent, and I have had some personal share in this reform. Beneficent are the activities of the Brāhmo Samāj, but behind them is the slower but larger movement of the general community, all making towards progress.

M. G. RĀNADE: PIONEER MAHĀRĀSHTRIAN REFORMER

Western cultural influence, like British rule itself, came to different parts of India at different times. The coastal ports founded in the sixteenth and seventeenth centuries—Madras, Bombay, Calcutta—became and remain today the centers of the new order of life and thought. The spread of this order into the hinterland, however, was a slow and irregular process. Bengal, the home of a number of thinkers considered thus far, was the first province to fall entirely under British sway and therefore the first to react to the impact of Western ways and ideas.

On the opposite side of the Indian subcontinent, protected by their mountain fortresses in the Western Ghats, the proud kingdoms of

Mahārāshtra were among the last to surrender to foreign rule. The leadership which made this prolonged resistance possible came notably from two caste groups. The fighting Marāthā-Kunbi castes under Shivaji (1630?–1680) and his descendants, provided most of the military force, while the small but influential Chitpāvan brāhman caste provided the peshwas (prime ministers) and intellectual leaders of later times. Even after the final defeat of the Peshwa's government in 1818 the city of Poona remained the center of Mahārāshtrian intellectual life. In the closing decades of the nineteenth century the Chitpāvan brāhman caste produced three leaders whose names were to be inscribed in Indian nationalism's hall of fame—Rānade, Gokhale, and Tilak.

Mahādev Govind Rānade, the eldest of three children, was born in 1842 in a strictly orthodox household. An extremely serious student, he begged his father to send him to school in Bombay to complete his English education. At fourteen he entered the Elphinstone Institution, and at seventeen took his place in the first class to enroll in the new Bombay University. He distinguished himself by his diligence and originality of thought, and became a teacher of economics and later of history and literature at his alma mater. But he chose to make his career in the law, and before he was thirty received his first appointment as a subordinate judge in the government courts at Poona.

During his thirty years as a judge, Rānade gently but firmly worked for the reform of such social evils as child marriage, the non-remarriage of widows, and the seclusion of women. In many ways his efforts resembled those of Rāmmohun Roy, whom he admired as a patriot and as a godly man. Rānade was one of the early members of the Prārthanā Samāj (Prayer Society, modeled after the Brāhmo Samāj), whose founding in 1867 was sparked by Keshub Chunder Sen's earlier visits to Bombay. Under Rānade's judicious guidance, the Prārthanā Samāj did not cut itself off from the rest of Hindu society, but strove gradually to bring the orthodox around to its position. Despite the vociferous and sometimes violent opposition of Tilak and his school, Rānade's policy of moderation in social reform met with increasing success.

Disqualified from entering active politics by his judgeship, Rānade's contribution to the nationalist movement was largely in the realm of social and economic reform. In 1887, he founded the Indian National Social Conference as a separate organization which met concurrently with the annual Congress sessions, and in 1890 inaugurated the Industrial Association of Western India. Rānade's views on economics grew out of his long and patient study of Indian problems. He concluded that their constructive solution lay in a vigorous policy of Industrial and commercial development under British government auspices.

Rānade's infinite capacity for taking pains, his saintly disposition, and his devotion to the welfare of India inspired to greater patriotic endeavor the hundreds of younger men with whom he maintained contact in person or through correspondence. He was a Moderate in the best sense of the term—scholarly, patient, practical, constructive, never wasting his time in denouncing those who held other views. After his death in 1901 his memory continued to inspire the leaders of Western India—Gokhale, and after him Gāndhi, carrying on the tradition he initiated of social and economic reform as an integral part of selfless public service.

MAHĀDEV GOVIND RĀNADE
Revivalism versus Reform

The ludicrous impracticability of reviving ancient traditions merely because they were ancient was tellingly demonstrated by Rānade in one of his Social Conference addresses. Having explained why he rejected the suggestion of the Brāhmo and Ārya Samājists that all social reformers should convert to those faiths, he went on to analyze the four basic causes of the degeneration of Indian society.

[From Chintamini, *Indian Social Reform*, Part II, pp. 89–95]

While the new religious sects condemn us for being too orthodox, the extreme orthodox section denounce us for being too revolutionary in our methods. According to these last, our efforts should be directed to revive, and not to reform. I have many friends in this camp of extreme orthodoxy, and their watchword is that revival, and not reform, should be our motto. They advocate a return to the old ways, and appeal to the old authorities and the old sanction. Here also, as in the instance quoted above, people speak without realizing the full significance of their own words. When we are asked to revive our institutions and customs, people seem to be very much at sea as to what it is they seem to revive. What particular period of our history is to be taken as the old? Whether the period of the Vedas, of the Smritis, of the Puranas or of the Mahomedan or modern Hindu times? Our usages have been changed from time to time by a slow process of growth, and in some cases of decay and corruption, and we cannot stop at a particular period without breaking the continuity of the whole. When my revivalist friend presses his argument upon me, he has to seek recourse in some subterfuge which really furnishes no reply to the question—what shall we revive? Shall we revive the old habits of our people when the most sacred of our caste indulged in all the abominations as we now understand them of animal food and drink which exhausted every section of our country's zoology and botany? The men and the gods of those old days ate and drank forbidden things to excess in a way no revivalist will now venture to recommend. Shall we revive the twelve forms of sons, or eight forms of marriage, which included capture, and recognized mixed and illegitimate intercourse? Shall we revive the Niyoga system of procreating sons on our brother's wives when widowed? Shall we revive the old liberties taken by the Rishis and by the wives of the Rishis with the marital tie? Shall we revive the hecatombs of animals sacrificed from year's end to year's end, and in which human beings were not spared as propitiatory offerings? Shall we revive the Shakti worship of the left hand with its indecencies and practical debaucheries? Shall we revive the sati and infanticide customs, or the flinging of living men into the rivers, or over rocks, or hookswinging, or the crushing beneath Jagannath car?[1] Shall we revive the internecine wars of the Brahmins and Kshatriyas, or the cruel persecution and degradation of the aboriginal population? Shall we revive the custom of many husbands to one wife or of many wives to one husband? Shall we require our Brahmins to cease to be landlords and gentlemen, and turn into beggars and dependants upon the king as in olden times? These instances will suffice to show that the plan of reviving the ancient usages and customs will not work our salvation, and is not practicable. If these usages were good and beneficial, why were they altered by our wise ancestors? If they were bad and injurious, how can any claim be put forward for their restoration after so many ages? Besides, it seems to be forgotten that in a living organism,

[1] A huge wagon used to carry the idol of Jagannāth, "the Lord of the Universe," in the city of Puri. In fits of frenzy devotees would hurl themselves in front of its wheels. The word "juggernaut" derives from this source.

as society is, no revival is possible. The dead and the buried or burnt are dead, buried, and burnt once for all, and the dead past cannot therefore be revived except by a reformation of the old materials into new organized beings. If revival is impossible, reformation is the only alternative open to sensible people, and now it may be asked what is the principle on which this reformation must be based? People have very hazy ideas on this subject. It seems to many that it is the outward form which has to be changed, and if this change can be made, they think that all the difficulties in our way will vanish. If we change our outward manners and customs, sit in a particular way, or walk in a particular fashion, our work according to them is accomplished. I cannot but think that much of the prejudice against the reformers is due to this misunderstanding. It is not the outward form, but the inward form, the thought and the idea which determines the outward form, that has to be changed if real reformation is desired.

Now what have been the inward forms or ideas which have been hastening our decline during the past three thousand years? These ideas may be briefly set forth as isolation, submission to outward force or power more than to the voice of the inward conscience, perception of fictitious differences between men and men due to heredity and birth, passive acquiescence in evil or wrong doing, and a general indifference to secular well-being, almost bordering upon fatalism. These have been the root ideas of our ancient social system. They have as their natural result led to the existing family arrangements where the woman is entirely subordinated to the man and the lower castes to the higher castes, to the length of depriving men of their natural respect for humanity. All the evils we seek to combat result from the prevalence of these ideas. They are mere corollaries to these axiomatic assumptions. They prevent some of our people from realizing what they really are in all conscience, neither better nor worse than their fellows, and that whatever garb men may put on, they are the worse for assuming dignities and powers which do not in fact belong to them. As long as these ideas remain operative on our minds, we may change our outward forms and institutions, and be none the better for the change. These ideas have produced in the long course of ages their results on our character, and we must judge their good or bad quality, as Saint Paul says, by the fruits they have borne. Now that these results have been disastrous, nobody disputes or doubts, and the lesson to be drawn for our guidance in the future from this fact is that the current of these ideas must be changed, and in the place of the old worship we paid to them, we must accustom ourselves and others to worship and reverence new ideals. In place of isolation, we must cultivate the spirit of fraternity or elastic expansiveness. At present it is everybody's ambition to pride himself upon being a member of the smallest community that can be conceived, and the smaller the number of those with whom you can dine, or marry, or associate, the higher is your perfection and purity, the purest person is he who cooks his own food, and does not allow the shadow of even his nearest friend to fall upon his cooked food. Every caste and every sect has thus a tendency to split itself into smaller castes and smaller sects in practical life. Even in philosophy and religion, it is a received maxim that knowledge is for the few, and that salvation is only possible for the esoteric elect with whom only are the virtues of sanctity and wisdom, and that for the rest of mankind, they must be left to wander in the wilderness, and grovel in superstition and even vice, with only a coloring of so-called religion to make them respectable. Now all this must be changed. The new mold of thought on this head must be, as stated above, cast on the lines of fraternity, a capacity to expand outwards, and to make more cohesive inwards the bonds of fellowship. Increase the circle of your friends and associates, slowly and cautiously if you will, but the tendency must be towards a general recognition of the essential equality between man and man. It will beget sympathy and power. It will strengthen your own hands, by the sense that you have numbers with you, and not against you, or as you foolishly imagine, below you.

The next idea which lies at the root of our helplessness is the sense that we are always intended to remain children, to be subject to outside control and never to rise to the dignity of self-control by making our conscience and our reason the supreme, if not the sole, guide to our conduct. All past history has been a terrible witness to the havoc committed by this misconception. We are children, no doubt but the children of God, and not of man, and the voice of God is the only voice [to] which we are bound to listen. Of course, all of us cannot listen to this voice when we desire it, because from long neglect and dependence upon outside help, we have benumbed this faculty of conscience in us. With too many of us, a thing is true or false, righteous or sinful, simply because

[133]

somebody in the past has said that it is so. Duties and obligations are duties and obligations, not because we feel them to be so, but because somebody reputed to be wise has laid it down that they are so. In small matters of manners and courtesies, this outside dictation is not without its use. But when we abandon ourselves entirely to this helpless dependence on other wills, it is no wonder that we become helpless as children in all departments of life. Now the new idea which should take up the place of this helplessness and dependence is not the idea of a rebellious overthrow of all authority, but that of freedom responsible to the voice of God in us. Great and wise men in the past, as in the present, have a claim upon our regards, but they must not come between us and our God— the Divine principle enthroned in the heart of every one of us high or low. It is this sense of self-respect, or rather respect for the God in us, which has to be cultivated. It is a very tender plant which takes years and years to make it grow. But there is the capacity and the power, and we owe it as a duty to ourselves to undertake the task. Revere all human authority, pay your respects to all prophets and all revelations, but never let this reverence and respect come in the way of the dictates of conscience, the Divine command in us.

Similarly there is no doubt that men differ from men in natural capacities, and aptitudes, and that heredity and birth are factors of considerable importance in our development. But it is at the same time true they are not the only factors that determine the whole course of our life for good or for evil, under a law of necessity. Heredity and birth explain many things, but this Law of Karma does not explain all things! What is worse, it does not explain the mystery that makes man and woman what they really are, the reflection and the image of God. Our passions and our feelings, our pride and our ambition, lend strength to these agencies, and with their help the Law of Karma completes our conquest, and in too many cases enforces our surrender. The new idea that should come in here is that this Law of Karma can be controlled and set back by a properly trained will, when it is made subservient to a higher will than ours. This we see in our everyday life, and Necessity, or the Fates are, as our own texts tell us, faint obstacles in the way of our advancement if we devote ourselves to the Law of Duty. I admit that this misconception is very hard to remove, perhaps the hardest of the old ideas. But removed it must be, if not in this life or generation, in many lives and generations, if we are ever to rise to our full stature.

The fourth old form or idea to which I will allude here is our acquiescence in wrong or evil doing as an inevitable condition of human life, about which we need not be very particular. All human life is a vanity and a dream, and we are not much concerned with it. This view of life is in fact atheism in its worst form. No man or woman really ceases to be animal who does not perceive or realize that wrong or evil-doing, impurity and vice, crime and misery, and sin of all kinds, is really our animal existence prolonged. It is the beast in us which blinds us to impurity and vice, and makes them even attractive. There must be nautches [2] in our temples, say our priests, because even the Gods cannot do without these impure fairies. This is only a typical instance of our acquiescence in impurity. There must be drunkenness in the world, there must be poverty and wretchedness and tyranny, there must be fraud and force, there must be thieves and the law to punish them. No doubt these are facts, and there is no use denying their existence, but in the name of all that is sacred and true, do not acquiesce in them, do not hug these evils to your bosom, and cherish them. Their contact is poisonous, not the less deadly because it does not kill, but it corrupts men. A healthy sense of the true dignity of our nature, and of man's high destiny, is the best corrective and antidote to this poison. I think I have said more than enough to suggest to your reflecting minds what it is that we have to reform. All admit that we have been deformed. We have lost our stature, we are bent in a hundred places, our eyes lust after forbidden things, our ears desire to hear scandals about our neighbors, our tongues lust to taste forbidden fruit, our hands itch for another man's property, our bowels are deranged with indigestible food. We cannot walk on our feet, but require stilts or crutches. This is our present social polity, and now we want this deformity to be removed; and the only way to remove it is to place ourselves under the discipline of better ideas and forms such as those I have briefly touched above. Now this is the work of the Reformer. Reforms in the matter of infant marriage and enforced widowhood, in the matter of temperance and purity, inter-marriage between castes, the elevation of the low castes, and the re-admission of converts, and the regulation of our endowments and charities, are reforms only so far and no further as they check the influence of the old ideas and promote the growth of the new tendencies. The Reformer has to infuse in himself the light and warmth of nature,

[2] Women attached to temples as dancers (and sometimes as prostitutes).

and he can only do it by purifying and improving himself and his surroundings. He must have his family, village, tribe, and nation recast in other and new molds, and that is the reason why Social Reform becomes our obligatory duty, and not a mere pastime which might be given up at pleasure. Revival is, as I have said, impossible; as impossible as mass-conversion into other faiths. But even if it were possible, its only use to us would be if the reforms elevated us and our surroundings, if they made us stronger, braver, truer men with all our faculties of endurance and work developed, with all our sympathies fully awakened and refined, and if with our heads and hearts acting in union with a purified and holy will, they made us feel the dignity of our being and the high destiny of our existence, taught us to love all, work with all, and feel for all.

Hindu-Muslim Cooperation

In his speech to the Indian Social Conference of 1899, Rānade stressed the importance of religious toleration, suggesting that the members of each community avoid mutual recrimination, and cooperate instead in the work of social reform.

[From Chintamini, *Indian Social Reform,* Part II, pp. 122–25]

If the lessons of the past have any value, one thing is quite clear, namely, that in this vast country no progress is possible unless both Hindus and Mahomedans join hands together, and are determined to follow the lead of the men who flourished in Akbar's time and were his chief advisers and councillors, and sedulously avoid the mistakes which were committed by his greatgrandson Aurangzib. Joint action from a sense of common interest, and a common desire to bring about the fusion of the thoughts and feelings of men so as to tolerate small differences and bring about concord—these were the chief aims kept in view by Akbar and formed the principle of the new divine faith formulated in the Din-i-ilahi.[3] Every effort on the part of either Hindus or Mahomedans to regard their interests as separated and distinct, and every attempt made by the two communities to create separate schools and interests among themselves, and not to heal up the wounds inflicted by mutual hatred

---

[3] "Divine Faith," the synthesis of religious ideas proclaimed by the Mughal Emperor Akbar.

of caste and creed, must be deprecated on all hands. It is to be feared that this lesson has not been sufficiently kept in mind by the leaders of both communities in their struggle for existence and in the acquisition of power and predominance during recent years. There is at times a great danger of the work of Akbar being undone by losing sight of this great lesson which the history of his reign and that of his two successors is so well calculated to teach. The Conference which brings us together is especially intended for the propagation of this "din"[4] or "dharma," and it is in connection with that message chiefly that I have ventured to speak to you today on this important subject. The ills that we are suffering from are most of them, self-inflicted evils, the cure of which is to a large extent in our own hands. Looking at the series of measures which Akbar adopted in his time to cure these evils, one feels how correct was his vision when he and his advisers put their hand on those very defects in our national character which need to be remedied first before we venture on higher enterprises. Pursuit of high ideas, mutual sympathy and cooperation, perfect tolerance, a correct understanding of the diseases from which the body politic is suffering, and an earnest desire to apply suitable remedies—this is the work cut out for the present generation. The awakening has commenced, as is witnessed by the fact that we are met in this place from such distances for joint consultation and action. All that is needed is that we must put our hands to the plow, and face the strife and the struggle. The success already achieved warrants the expectation that if we persevere on right lines, the goal we have in view may be attained. That goal is not any particular advantage to be gained in power and wealth. It is represented by the efforts to attain it, the expansion and the evolution of the heart and the mind, which will make us stronger and braver, purer and truer men. This is at least the lesson I draw from our more recent history of the past thousand years, and if those centuries have rolled away to no purpose over our heads, our cause is no doubt hopeless beyond cure. That is however not the faith in me; and I feel sure it is not the faith that moves you in this great struggle against our own weak selves, than which nothing is more fatal to our individual and collective growth. Both Hindus and Mahomedans have their work cut out in this struggle. In the backwardness of female education, in the disposition to overleap the bounds of their own religion, in

[4] Arabic term for which the English word "religion" is only an approximate translation.

matters of temperance, in their internal dissensions between castes and creeds, in the indulgence of impure speech, thought, and action on occasions when they are disposed to enjoy themselves, in the abuses of many customs in regard to unequal and polygamous marriages, in the desire to be extravagant in their expenditure on such occasions, in the neglect of regulated charity, in the decay of public spirit in insisting on the proper management of endowments—in these and other matters both communities are equal sinners, and there is thus much ground for improvement on common lines. Of course the Hindus, being by far the majority of the population, have other difficulties of their own to combat with; and they are trying in their gatherings of separate castes and communities to remedy them each in their own way. But without cooperation and conjoint action of all communities, success is not possible, and it is on that account that the general Conference is held in different places each year to rouse local interest, and help people in their separate efforts by a knowledge of what their friends similarly situated are doing in other parts. This is the reason of our meeting here, and I trust that this message I have attempted to deliver to you on this occasion will satisfy you that we cannot conceive a nobler work than the one for which we have met here today.

India's Need: State Guidance of Economic Development

Rānade's essay of 1892 on "Indian Political Economy" may be regarded as the cornerstone of the economic theory which underlies the present Five Year Plans. He first showed that English *laissez faire* doctrines were being challenged by more recent theories of the science of economics and were not necessarily relevant to India's problems, then continued with a diagnosis of the Indian economy.

[From Rānade, *Essays on Indian Economics*, pp. 22–25, 33–36]

This resumé of the past and contemporary history of the growth of economic Sciences in England, France, Germany, Italy, and America will satisfy the student that modern European thought does not at all countenance the view of the English writers of the Ricardian School, that the principles of the science, as they have enunciated them in their textbooks, are universally and necessarily true for all times and places, and for all stages of advancement. Modern thought is veering to the conclusion that the individual and his interests are not the center round which the theory should revolve, that the true center is the body politic of which that individual is a member, and that collective defense and well-being, social education and discipline, and the duties, and not merely the interests, of men, must be taken into account, if the theory is not to be merely utopian. The method to be followed is not the deductive but the historical method, which takes account of the past in its forecast of the future; and relativity, and not absoluteness, characterizes the conclusions of economical science. There are those who seek to get over this difficulty by differentiating the science from what they are disposed to call the art of economy. This divorce of theory and practice is, however, a mischievous error, which relegates the science to the sterility of an ideal dream or a puzzle, and condemns the art to the position of a rule of the thumb. Theory is only enlarged practice, practice is theory studied in its relation to proximate causes. The practice is predetermined by the theory which tests its truth, and adapts it to different conditions by reason of its grasp of the deep-seated, permanent, and varied basal truths. I hope thus to have shown that the nature of the subject itself as a branch of social science, which is best studied historically and not deductively, the actual practice of the most civilized nations and the history of the growth of its theory given above alike establish the doctrine of relativity, and the predominant claim of collective welfare over individual interests, as the principal features in which the highest minds of the present day chiefly differ from the economical writers of the old school, with their *a priori* conclusions based on individual self-interest and unrestricted competition.

We have next to consider the bearings of this enlarged view of the science in its Indian aspects. The characteristics of our social life are the prevalence of status over contract, of combination over competition. Our habits of mind are conservative to a fault. The aptitudes of climate and soil facilitate the production of raw materials. Labor is cheap and plentiful, but unsteady, unthrifty, and unskilled. Capital is scarce, immobile, and unenterprising. Cooperation on a large scale of either capital or labor is unknown. Agriculture is the chief support of nearly the whole population, and this agriculture is carried on under conditions of uncertain rainfall. Commerce and manufactures on a large scale are but recent importations, and all industry is carried on, on the system of petty farming, retail dealing, and job working by poor people on borrowed capital. There is an almost complete absence of a landed gentry or wealthy middle class. The land is a monopoly of the State. The desire for accumulation is very weak, peace and security having been almost unknown over large areas for any length of time till within the last century. Our laws and institutions favour a low standard of life, and encourage subdivision and not concentration of wealth. The religious ideals of life condemn the ardent pursuit of wealth as a mistake to be avoided as far as possible. These are old legacies and inherited weaknesses. Stagnation and dependence, depression and poverty—these are written in broad characters on the face of the land and its people. To these must be added the economical drain of wealth and talents, which foreign subjection has entailed on the country. As a compensation against all these depressing influences, we have to set off the advantage of a free contact with a race which has opened the country to the commerce of the world, and by its superior skill and resources has developed communications in a way previously unknown. If we wish to realize our situation fully, we may not overlook this factor, because, it represents the beam of light which alone illumines the prevailing darkness. It cannot well be a mere accident that the destinies of this country have been entrusted to the guidance of a nation whose characteristic strength is opposed to all our weaknesses, whose enterprise, chiefly in commerce and manufactures, knows no bounds, whose capital overflows the world, among whom contract has largely superseded status, and competition and cooperation play a predominant part, whose view of life is full of hope, and whose powers of organization have never been surpassed.

Rānade next advanced several reasons why industrial enterprise should be encouraged, and urged government action to populate untilled lands, protect peasants against excessive taxation, and prevent exploitation by landlords or money-lenders. In his conclusion he argued that the state should play a more active role in the economic development of the country.

Lastly comes the great department of governmental interference. The meddlesomeness of the mercantile system provoked a reaction against state control and guidance towards the end of the last century in favor of natural liberty. The doctrines of this negative school have now in their turn been abused by a too logical extension of its principles. There is a decided reaction in Europe against the *laissez faire* system. Even in England, the recent factory legislation, the qualified recognition by law of Trades-Unionism, the poor law system, and the Irish Land Settlement, are all instances which indicate the same change of view. Speaking roughly, the province of state interference and control is practically being extended so as to restore the good points of the mercantile system without its absurdities. The State is now more and more recognized as the national organ for taking care of national needs in all matters in which individual and cooperative efforts are not likely to be so effective and economic as national effort. This is the correct view to take of the true functions of a state. To relegate them to the simple duty of maintaining peace and order is really to deprive the community of many of the advantages of the social union. Education, both liberal and technical, post and telegraphs, railway and canal communications, the pioneering of new enterprise, the insurance of risky undertakings—all these functions are usefully discharged by the State. The question is one of time, fitness, and expediency, not one of liberty and rights. In our own country the State has similarly enlarged its functions with advantage. The very fact that the rulers belong to a race with superior advantages imposes this duty on them of attempting things which no native rulers, past or present, could as well achieve, or possibly even think of. This obligation is made more peremptory by the fact that the State claims to be the sole landlord, and is certainly the largest capitalist in the country. While the State in India has done much in this way in the working of iron and coal fields, and in the experiments made about cotton and tobacco, and in tea and coffee and cinchona Plantations, it must be admitted that, as compared with its resources and the needs of the country, these attempts are as nothing by the side of what has been attempted with success in France, Germany, and other countries, but which, unhappily, has not been attempted in this country. Even if political considerations forbid independent action in the matter of differential duties, the pioneering of new enterprises is a duty which the government might more systematically undertake with advantage. In truth, there is no difference of principle between lending such support and guidance, by the free use of its credit and superior organization, in pioneering industrial undertaking or subsidizing private cooperative effort, and its guaranteeing minimum interest to railway companies. The building up of national, not merely state, credit on broad foundations by helping people to acquire confidence in a free and largely ramified banking system, so advantageously worked in Europe under different forms, has also not been attempted here. There is, lastly, the duty cast on it of utilizing indigenous resources, and organizing them in a way to produce in India in state factories all products of skill which the state departments require in the way of stores. These are only a few of the many directions in which, far more than exchange and frontier difficulties, the highest statesmanship will have a field all its own for consideration and action. They will, no doubt, receive such consideration if only the minds of the rulers were once thoroughly freed from the fear of offending the so-called maxims of rigid economical science. It is time that a new departure should take place in this connection, and it is with a view to drawing public attention to this necessity that I have ventured to place before you the results of modern economic thought. In this, as in other matters, the conditions of Indian life are more faithfully reproduced in some of the continental countries and in America than in happy England, proud of its position, strong in its insularity, and the home of the richest and busiest community in the modern industrial world. If the attempt I have made leads to a healthy and full discussion of the change of policy I advocate, I shall regard myself amply repaid for my trouble.

G. K. GOKHALE: SERVANT OF INDIA

The work of reform begun by Rānade was ably shouldered by his younger friend and colleague G. K. Gokhale. So close was the personal relationship between the two men during Rānade's lifetime—for years they met weekly to discuss their ideas and projects—that Gokhale's excursions into active politics can be regarded as the logical extension of his teacher's endeavors. Sprung from the same proud Mahārāshtrian stock, both leaders nevertheless clung to the policy of cooperation with the government and of moderate opposition to its evils. Gokhale, however, had to endure the merciless attacks of the Extremists during the stormiest decade in Indian politics up to that time.

Gopāl Krishna Gokhale (1866–1915) dedicated his life to public service at the age of nineteen, on his graduation from Elphinstone College, by joining the Deccan Education Society in Poona. Members of the Society took a vow of poverty for twenty years in order to devote their time exclusively to educating their fellow-countrymen. For his part, Gokhale became a teacher of English and mathematics in the Fergusson College which the Society founded in 1885. He soon met Justice Rānade and began his long and fruitful apprenticeship under him—examining documents, weighing evidence, analyzing fiscal data, and preparing comprehensive memoranda on public questions.

Gokhale attracted public attention with the sagacity of his carefully prepared speeches, and in 1899 was elected a member of the recently formed Legislative Council for the state of Bombay. When only thirty-six, he became the Indian representative of this state on the Imperial Legislative Council, despite its limited powers the highest law-making body in India. For the last thirteen years of his life he wore himself out with his efforts to secure government cooperation in granting much needed financial and administrative reforms for India. "No taxation without representation," was the essence of his demand, and his annual speeches on the imperial budget effected many concessions from harassed ministers of finance.

In 1905 Gokhale founded the Servants of India Society in Poona, modeling it after the lay and monastic orders of the Catholic Church. Famine relief, education, Hindu-Muslim unity, and the elevation of the lowest castes were among the fields in which it carried on the work begun by its founder. Gokhale also took great interest in the problems of Indian emigrants to South Africa, giving freely of his advice and encouragement to their leader, M. K. Gāndhi. Although bitterly reviled by Tilak and other supporters of violent action to end foreign rule, Gokhale's readiness to cooperate with the British in introducing gradual reforms helped to pave the way for the eventual peaceful transfer of power to an independent India.

GOPĀL KRISHNA GOKHALE
Taxation Without Representation

Soon after taking his place in the Imperial Legislative Council, Gokhale made the first of his annual budget speeches. His attacks on the government's taxation policy are representative of the Moderates' preoccupation with the economic shortcomings of British rule.

[From *Speeches of the Honourable Mr. G. K. Gokhale,* pp. 1-2, 8-11]

Your Excellency, I fear I cannot conscientiously join in the congratulations which have been offered to the Hon'ble Finance Member on the huge surplus which the revised estimates show for the last year. A surplus of seven crores [1] of rupees is perfectly unprecedented in the history of Indian finance, and coming as it does on the top of a series of similar surpluses realized when the country has been admittedly passing through very trying times, it illustrates to my mind in a painfully clear manner the utter absence of a due correspondence between the condition of the people and the condition of the finances of the country. Indeed, my Lord, the more I think about this matter the more I feel—and I trust Your Lordship will pardon me for speaking somewhat bluntly—that these surpluses constitute a double wrong to the community. They are a wrong in the first instance in that they exist at all—that government should take so much more from the people than is needed in times of serious depression and suffering; and they are also a wrong, because they lend themselves to easy misinterpretation and, among other things, render possible the phenomenal optimism of the Secretary of State for India, who seems to imagine that all is for the best in this best of lands. A slight examination of these surpluses suffices to show that they are mainly, almost entirely, currency surpluses, resulting from the fact that government still maintain the same high level of taxation which they considered to be necessary to secure financial equilibrium when the rupee stood at its lowest. . . .

A taxation so forced as not only to maintain a budgetary equilibrium but to yield as well "large, continuous, progressive surpluses"—even in years of trial and suffering—is, I submit, against all accepted canons of finance. In European countries, extraordinary charges are usually met out of borrowings, the object being to avoid, even in times of pressure, impeding the even, normal development of trade and industry by any sudden or large additions to the weight of public burdens. In India, where the economic side of such questions finds such scant recognition, and the principle of meeting the charges of the year with the resources of the year is carried to a logical extreme, the anxiety of the Financial Administration is not only to make both ends meet in good and bad years alike, but to present large surpluses year after year. The Hon'ble Finance Member remarks in his Budget Statement under "Army Services": "It must be remembered that India is defraying from revenues the cost of undertaking both rearmament and the reform of military reorganization in important departments. I believe that this is an undertaking which has not been

[1] One crore equals ten millions.

[144]

attempted by other countries without the assistance of loans in some form or other. Even in England, extraordinary military requirements for fortifications and barracks have been met by loans for short terms of years repayable by installments out of revenues. If profiting by a period of political tranquillity we can accomplish this task without the raising of a loan and the imposition of a permanent burden on future generations, I think that we shall be able to congratulate ourselves on having done that which even the richest nations of Europe have not considered it advisable to attempt."

Every word of this citation invites comment. How comes it that India is doing in regard to these extraordinary charges that which even the richest nations of Europe have not considered it advisable to attempt? The obvious answer is that in those countries it is the popular assemblies that control taxation and expenditure; in India the tax-payer has no constitutional voice in the shaping of these things. If we had any votes to give, and the government of the country had been carried on by an alternation of power between two parties, both alike anxious to conciliate us and bid for our support, the Hon'ble Member would assuredly have told a different tale. But I venture to submit, my Lord, that the consideration which the people of Western countries receive in consequence of their voting power should be available to us, in matters of finance at any rate, through an "intelligent anticipation"—to use a phrase of Your Lordship's —of our reasonable wishes on the part of government.

But even thus—after doing what the richest nations of Europe shrink from attempting—meeting all sorts of extraordinary charges, amounting to about 70 crores in sixteen years, out of current revenues—we have "large, continuous, progressive surpluses," and this only shows, as Colonel Chesney points out in the March number of the *Nineteenth Century and After,* that more money is being taken from the people than is right, necessary, or advisable, or, in other words, the weight of public taxation has been fixed and maintained at an unjustifiably high level. Taxation for financial equilibrium is what we all can understand, but taxation kept up in the face of the difficulties and misfortunes of a period of excessive depression and for "large, continuous and progressive surpluses" is evidently a matter which requires justification. At all events, those who have followed the course of the financial history of the period will admit that the fact viewed *per se* that "such large, continuous, and progressive surpluses" have occurred during the period—as a result not of a normal expansion of fiscal resources but of a forced up and heavy taxation—does not connote, as Lord George Hamilton contends, an advancing material prosperity of the country or argue any marvelous recuperative power on the part of the masses—as the Hon'ble Sir Edward Law urged last year. To them, at any rate, the apparent paradox of a suffering country and an overflowing treasury stands easily explained and is a clear proof of the fact that the level of national taxation is kept unjustifiably high, even when government are in a position to lower that level.

Improving the Lot of Low-Caste Hindus

One of Gokhale's chief concerns in the realm of social reform was the lot of the so-called "untouchables." The appeal launched in this speech to a social conference in 1903 was answered after his death by Gāndhi's devotion to their cause.

[From *Speeches of the Honourable Mr. G. K. Gokhale*, pp. 740–47]

Mr. President and Gentlemen: The proposition which has been entrusted to me runs thus—"That this Conference holds that the present degraded condition of the low castes is, in itself and from the national point of view, unsatisfactory, and is of opinion that every well-wisher of the country should consider it his duty to do all he can to raise their moral and social condition by trying to rouse self-respect in these classes and placing facilities for education and employment within their reach."

Gentlemen, I hope I am not given to the use of unnecessarily strong language and yet I must say that this resolution is not as strongly worded as it should have been. The condition of the low castes—it is painful to call them low castes—is not only unsatisfactory as this resolution says, it is so deeply deplorable that it constitutes a grave blot on our social arrangements; and, further, the attitude of our educated men towards this class is profoundly painful and humiliating. I do not propose to deal with this subject as an antiquarian; I only want to make a few general observations from the standpoint of justice, humanity, and national self-interest. I think all fair-minded persons will have to admit that it is absolutely monstrous that a class of human beings, with bodies similar to our own, with brains that can think and with hearts that can feel, should be perpetually condemned to a low life of utter wretchedness, servitude, and mental and moral degradation, and that permanent barriers should be placed in their way so that it should be impossible for them ever to overcome them and improve their lot. This is deeply revolting to our sense of justice. I believe one has only to put oneself mentally into their place to realize how grievous this injustice is. We may touch a cat, we may touch a dog, we may touch any other animal, but the touch of these human beings is pollution! And so complete is now the mental degradation of these people that they themselves see nothing in such treatment to resent, that they acquiesce in it as though nothing better than that was their due.

I remember a speech delivered seven or eight years ago by the late Mr. Ranade in Bombay, under the auspices of the Hindu Union Club. That was a time when public feeling ran high in India on the subject of the treatment which our people were receiving in South Africa. Our friend, Mr. Gandhi, had come here on a brief visit from South Africa and he was telling us how our people were treated in Natal and Cape Colony and the Transvaal—how they were not allowed to walk on footpaths or travel in first-class carriages on the railway, how they were not admitted into hotels, and so forth. Public feeling, in consequence, was deeply stirred, and we all felt that it was a mockery that we should be called British subjects, when we were treated like this in Great Britain's colonies. Mr. Ranade felt this just as keenly as any one else. He had been a never-failing adviser of Mr. Gandhi, and had carried on a regular correspondence with him. But it was Mr. Ranade's peculiar greatness that he always utilized occasions of excitement to give a proper turn to the national mind and cultivate its sense of proportion. And so, when every one was expressing himself in indignant terms about the treatment which our countrymen were receiving in South Africa, Mr. Ranade came forward to ask if we had no sins of our own to answer for in that direction. I do not exactly remember the title of his address. I think it was "Turn the searchlight inwards," or some such thing. But I remember that it was a great speech—one of the greatest that I have ever been privileged to hear. He began in characteristic fashion, expressing deep sympathy with the Indians in South Africa in the struggle they were manfully carrying on. He rejoiced that the people of India had awakened to a sense of the position of their countrymen abroad, and he felt convinced that this awakening was a sign of the fact that the dead bones in the valley were once again becoming instinct with life. But he proceeded to ask: "Was this sympathy with the oppressed and downtrodden Indians to be confined to those of our countrymen only who had gone out of India? Or was it to be general and to be extended to all cases where there was oppression and injustice?" It was easy, he said, to denounce foreigners, but those who did so were bound in common fairness to look into themselves and see if they were absolutely blameless in the matter. He then described the manner in which members of low caste were treated by our own community in different parts of India. It was a description which filled the audience with feelings of deep shame and pain and indignation. And Mr. Ranade very justly asked whether it was for those who tolerated such disgraceful oppression and injustice in their own country to indulge in all that denunciation of the people of South Africa. This question, therefore, is, in the first place, a question of sheer justice.

Next, as I have already said, it is a question of humanity. It is sometimes urged that if we have our castes, the people in the West have their classes, and after all, there is not much difference between the two. A little reflection will, however, show that the analogy is quite fallacious. The classes of the West are a perfectly elastic institution, and not rigid or cast-iron like our castes. Mr. Chamberlain, who is the most masterful personage in the British empire today, was at one time a shoemaker and then a screwmaker. Of course, he did not make shoes himself, but that was the trade by which he made money. Mr. Chamberlain today dines with royalty, and mixes with the highest in the land on terms of absolute equality. Will a shoemaker ever be able to rise in India in the social scale in a similar fashion, no matter how gifted by nature he might be? A great writer has said that castes are eminently useful for the preservation of society, but that they are utterly unsuited for purposes of progress. And this I think is perfectly true. If you want to stand where you were a thousand years ago, the system of castes need not be modified in any material degree. If, however, you want to emerge out of the slough in which you have long remained sunk, it will not do for you to insist on a rigid adherence to caste. Modern civilization has accepted greater equality for all as its watchword, as against privilege and exclusiveness, which were the root-ideas of the old world. And the larger humanity of these days requires that we should acknowledge its claims by seeking the amelioration of the helpless condition of our downtrodden countrymen.

Finally, gentlemen, this is a question of national self-interest. How can we possibly realize our national aspirations, how can our country ever hope to take her place among the nations of the world, if we allow large numbers of our countrymen to remain sunk in ignorance, barbarism, and degradation? Unless these men are gradually raised to a higher level, morally and intellectually, how can they possibly understand our thoughts or share our hopes or cooperate with us in our efforts? Can you not realize that so far as the work of national elevation is concerned, the energy, which these classes might be expected to represent, is simply unavailable to us? I understand that that great thinker and observer—Swami Vivekananda—held this view very strongly. I think that there is not much hope for us as a nation unless the help of all classes, including those that are known as low castes, is forthcoming for the work that lies before us. Moreover, is it, I may ask, consistent with our own self-respect that these men should be kept out of our houses and shut out from all social intercourse as long as they remain within the pale of Hinduism, whereas the moment they put on a coat and a hat and a pair of trousers and call themselves Christians, we are prepared to shake hands with them and look upon them as quite respectable? No sensible man will say that this is a satisfactory state of things. Of course, no one expects that these classes will be lifted up at once morally and intellectually to a position of equality with their more-favored countrymen.

This work is bound to be slow and can only be achieved by strenuous exertions for giving them education and finding for them honourable employment in life. And, gentlemen, it seems to me that, in the present state of India, no work can be higher or holier than this. I think if there is one question of social reform more than another that should stir the enthusiasm of our educated young men and inspire them with an unselfish purpose, it is this question of the degraded condition of our low castes. Cannot a few men—five percent, four percent, three, two, even one percent—of the hundreds and hundreds of graduates that the university turns out every year, take it upon themselves to dedicate their lives to this sacred work of the elevation of low castes? My appeal is not to the old or the middle-aged—the grooves of their lives are fixed—but I think I may well address such an appeal to the young members of our community—to those who have not yet decided upon their future course and who entertain the noble aspiration of devoting to a worthy cause the education which they have received. What the country needs most at the present moment is a spirit of self-sacrifice on the part of our educated young men, and they may take it from me that they cannot spend their lives in a better cause than raising the moral and intellectual level of these unhappy low castes and promoting their general well-being.

The Servants of India Society

The charter of the Servants of India Society embodies Gokhale's most cherished aims for the uplift of his country.

[From *Speeches of the Honourable Mr. G. K. Gokhale,* Appendix, pp. 182–83, 184]

For some time past, the conviction has been forcing itself on many earnest and thoughtful minds that a stage has been reached in the political education and national advancement of the Indian people, when, for further progress, the devoted labors of a specially trained agency, applying itself to the task in a true missionary spirit, are required. The work that has so far been done has indeed been of the highest value. The growth, during the last fifty years, of a feeling of common nationality, based upon common tradition, common disabilities, and common hopes and aspirations, has been most striking. The fact that we are Indians first, and Hindoos, Mahomedans, Parsees, or Christians afterwards, is being realized in a steadily increasing measure, and the idea of a united and renovated India, marching onwards to a place among the nations of the world worthy of her great past, is no longer a mere idle dream of a few imaginative minds, but is the definitely accepted creed of those who form the brain of the community—the educated classes of the country. A creditable beginning has already been made in matters of education and of local self-government; and all classes of the people are slowly but steadily coming under the influence of liberal ideas. The claims of public life are every day receiving wider recognition, and attachment to the land of our birth is growing into a strong and deeply cherished passion of the heart. The annual meetings of the National Congress and of provincial and other conferences, the work of political associations, the writings in the columns of the Indian press—all bear witness to the new life that is coursing in the veins of the people. The results achieved so far are undoubtedly most gratifying, but they only mean that the jungle has been

[150]

cleared and the foundations laid. The great work of rearing the super-structure has yet to be taken in hand, and the situation demands, on the part of workers, devotion and sacrifices proportionate to the magnitude of the task.

The Servants of India Society has been established to meet in some measure these requirements of the situation. Its members frankly accept the British connection, as ordained, in the inscrutable dispensation of Providence, for India's good. Self-government on the lines of English colonies is their goal. This goal, they recognize, cannot be attained without years of earnest and patient work and sacrifices worthy of the cause. Moreover, the path is beset with great difficulties—there are constant temptations to turn back—bitter disappointments will repeatedly try the faith of those who have put their hand to the work. But the weary toil can have but one end, if only the workers grow not fainthearted on the way. One essential condition of success is that a sufficient number of our countrymen must now come forward to devote themselves to the cause in the spirit in which religious work is undertaken. Public life must be spiritualized. Love of country must so fill the heart that all else shall appear as of little moment by its side. A fervent patriotism which rejoices at every opportunity of sacrifice for the motherland, a dauntless heart which refuses to be turned back from its object by difficulty or danger, a deep faith in the purpose of Providence that nothing can shake —equipped with these, the worker must start on his mission and reverently seek the joy which comes of spending oneself in the service of one's country.

The Servants of India Society will train men, prepared to devote their lives to the cause of the country in a religious spirit, and will seek to promote, by all constitutional means, the national interests of the Indian people. Its members will direct their efforts principally towards: 1) creating among the people, by example and by precept, a deep and passionate love of the motherland, seeking its highest fulfillment in service and sacrifice; 2) organizing the work of political education and agitation and strengthening the public life of the country; 3) promoting relations of cordial goodwill and cooperation among the different communities; 4) assisting educational movements, especially those for the education of women, the education of backward classes and industrial and scientific education; and 5) the elevation of the depressed classes. The headquarters of the Society will be at Poona, where it will maintain a Home for its members, and attached to it, a library for the study of political questions. The following constitution has been adopted for the Society.

1. The Society shall be called "The Servants of India Society."

2. The objects of the Society are to train men to devote themselves to the service of India as national missionaries and to promote by all constitutional means the national interests of the Indian people. . . .

[Items 3 to 8 and 10 onward deal with organizational questions.]

9. Every member, at the time of admission, shall take the following seven vows:

(*a*) That the country will always be the first in his thoughts and he will give to her service the best that is in him.

(*b*) That in serving the country he will seek no personal advantage for himself.

(*c*) That he will regard all Indians as brothers, and will work for the advancement of all, without distinction of caste or creed.

(*d*) That he will be content with such provision for himself and his family, if he has any, as the Society may be able to make. He will devote no part of his energies to earning money for himself.

(*e*) That he will lead a pure personal life.

(*f*) That he will engage in no personal quarrel with any one.

(*g*) That he will always keep in view the aims of the Society and watch over its interests with the utmost zeal, doing all he can to advance its work. He will never do anything which is inconsistent with the objects of the Society.

CHAPTER XXIII

THE MARRIAGE OF POLITICS AND RELIGION: THE EXTREMISTS

In much the same way as the opening of India to Western cultural influence stimulated the renascence of Hinduism, so the imposition of foreign rule inevitably evoked powerful indigenous reactions in the political sphere. The militant xenophobia which had found expression in scattered attempts at die-hard resistance to British conquest, and in the unorganized uprisings of 1857-58, finally crystallized in the late nineteenth century in the group of zealous nationalists known as the Extremists. This group possessed two weapons which were unavailable to previous opponents of British rule. Firstly, they shared with their Moderate rivals the use of a common "national" language, English, and through it enjoyed the opportunities for political agitation provided by the press, the schools, and the Indian National Congress. Secondly, they were able to draw on the newly formulated ideals of renascent Hinduism and to create a potent ideology out of the marriage between these ideals and the imported concepts of patriotism and national unity.

Being impatient to throw off the foreign yoke, the Extremists concentrated on building up mass support for the nationalist movement. To create this support and to unify the Westernized elite with the illiterate peasantry they appealed to three principal ties common to both the educated and the uneducated—language, history, and religion. Casting off the use of English wherever possible, they wrote and spoke in the regional languages understood by the common people. As a means of heightening patriotic fervor they fostered pride in a glorious past, when Hindu kings and warriors ruled the land. Most effective of all because it had the broadest appeal was the use of religious symbolism and terminology to instill in all Hindus a fervent devotion to the Motherland.

In contrast to the Moderates, the Extremists regarded such tasks as social reform and Hindu-Muslim cooperation as merely side issues draining energies from the political struggle and weakening Hindu solidarity. At times their anger at Muslim collaboration with the British spurred them to engage openly in anti-Muslim activity, heedless of the fact that in so doing they were ruining the chances of creating an independent but undivided India. The 1905 Partition of Bengal into Hindu and Muslim majority areas drove a further wedge between the two religious communities, for it encouraged prominent Muslims to enter into a tacit alliance with the British against Hindu ambitions (the Muslim League was founded in 1906, and its demand for separate electorates was granted in 1909). The danger that the more numerous and better-educated Hindu community would preempt the positions of power and influence in a self-governing India gave many Muslims a pressing reason to convert to friendship their traditional hostility to the British.

Both Moderates and Extremists insisted that divided Bengal be reunited, but the latter urged that radical measures be taken to coerce the ruling power. In essence, their program was much like the one Gāndhi introduced fifteen years later, being based on the principle of reducing Indian dependence on the British in every possible way. Its principal aims were the boycott of foreign goods, the use of Indian-made articles (or Swadeshi—"one's own country"), the strengthening of an indigenous system of education, and in time the creation of a parallel government of, by, and for the Indian people.

Such a bold stand, coupled with the religious ideology that motivated it, captured the imagination of younger men more readily than did the cautious policies of the Moderates, and the following of the Extremists increased rapidly in numbers after 1905. Their abortive attempt to gain control of the Congress led to a schism in that body at the 1907 session. For the next decade most of the Extremist leaders were either in jail, in exile, or in retirement, but the continuance of terrorist activity—climaxing in an attempt on the Viceroy's life in 1912—showed that their memory was still honored in their absence. The rescinding of the Partition of Bengal in 1911 and the altered situation produced by the First World War made it possible for the Moderates and the Extremists to patch up their quarrel in 1916. The death of the Extremists' greatest leader, Tilak, in 1920 marked the end of an era, for in that same year the Congress came under Gāndhi's uniquely effective control.

Although the heyday of the Extremists was short-lived, their chief contribution to modern Indian thought—the creation of Hindu nationalism through the union of religious and political ideals—is likely to endure for some time to come. It is entirely possible that as the influence of English culture (by which most Extremists were deeply affected, but against which all reacted in one way or another) diminishes in independent India, a more virulent and violent form of this nationalism may yet emerge.

BANKIM CHANDRA CHATTERJEE: NATIONALIST AUTHOR

Gokhale's saying, "What Bengal thinks today, all India thinks tomorrow," is nowhere more applicable than in the case of the Bengali writer Bankim Chandra Chatterjee. Bankim, although he took no part in politics, first employed the triple appeal of language, history, and religion which enabled Hindu nationalism to win such widespread support in the opening decade of the twentieth century. His historical novels in Bengali reminded his readers that their glorious past should inspire them to achieve an equally glorious future, and demonstrated the power of the pen as an instrument for stirring up patriotic emotions in times when overt political action was impossible.

Bankim was born near Calcutta in 1838, the son of a brāhman landlord and local deputy collector of revenue. A brilliant student, he passed through the anglicized educational system with distinction and was in 1858 one of two in Calcutta University's first graduating class. He was immediately offered a position as deputy magistrate in the Bengal civil service, and for all but one year held this same rank until his retirement in 1891—a mute comment on the opportunities for advancement given to Indians in government service. Fortunately he found an outlet for his natural talent in another direction, and throughout his career as an official used his spare time to write stories and novels which captured the imagination of literate Bengal. Bankim employed a new prose style which combined the virtues of Sanskritized Bengali and the vigor of the common speech, and for the first time since the introduction of English education made it respectable for Bengalis to write in their own mother tongue.

Nationalism in all parts of the world has often been associated with attachment to a common language and its accompanying literary heritage. Bankim could thus be credited with quickening Bengali, as distinct from an all-Indian, nationalism. But this distinction was rendered largely superfluous after 1905, when the agitation against the Partition of Bengal took on a nation-wide character. By the same token, the poem *Bande Mātaram* (*Hail to the Mother*) which first appeared in one of his novels soon became the *Marseillaise* of the nationalist movement throughout the country.

Bankim's original concept, "the Mother" of *Bande Mātaram,* referred at the same time to the land of Bengal and to the female aspect of the Hindu deity. From this fusion of the hitherto separate objects of patriotic and religious devotion sprang the central concept of modern Hindu nationalism. The concept of the divine Motherland, equating as it did love of country with love of God, made an instinctive appeal to the devout Hindu peasantry, for whom the secular reformism and Westernized nationalism of the Moderate leaders remained beyond comprehension.

For all the strength of dedication and mass appeal it generated, Hindu nationalism acted as a regressive force both in hindering social reform and in exacerbating the latent hostility between Hindus and Muslims. Bankim's novels faithfully reflect these two shortcomings, for with rare exceptions they picture well-meaning reformers as fools and Muslims as knaves. Nevertheless, his magic blend of religious sentiment, glorification of the Hindu past, and a beautiful style assured Bankim of lasting popularity among Bengalis, and exerted a far-reaching influence on the rise of extremist Hindu nationalism throughout India.

BANKIM CHANDRA CHATTERJEE
The Language of the Masses

In a letter to the editor of a new English-language periodical, Bankim explained why he, too, was founding a review—in Bengali. His concluding remarks illustrate the linguistic complexity of India as a whole, and remain almost as true today as when they were written.

[From "Letter from Bankim Chandra Chatterjee," in *Bengal: Past and Present*, Vol. VIII, Part 2 (April–June, 1914), pp. 273–74]

I wish you every success in your project. I have myself projected a Bengali magazine with the object of making it the medium of communication and sympathy between the educated and the uneducated classes. You rightly say that the English for good or evil has become our vernacular; and this tends daily to widen the gulf between the higher and the lower ranks of Bengali society. This I think is not exactly what it ought to be; I think that we ought to *disanglicize* ourselves, so to speak, to a certain extent, and to speak to the masses in the language which they understand. I therefore project a Bengali magazine. But this is only half the work we have to do. No purely vernacular organ can completely represent the Bengali culture of the day. Just as we ought to address ourselves to the masses of our own race and country, we have also to make ourselves intelligible to the other Indian races, and to the governing race. There is no hope for India until the Bengali and the Panjabi understand and influence each other, and can bring their joint influence to bear upon the Englishman. This can be done only through the medium of the English, and I gladly welcome your projected periodical.

Hail to the Mother

In *Ānandamath* (*The Abbey of Bliss*), his most famous novel, Bankim took as his theme the Sannyāsī Rebellion in Bengal of the 1770s, attributing to these raiding ascetics a sort of religious nationalism whose focus was God in the form of the Mother. He neatly avoided the charge of disloyalty to British rule by making the Muslims (still the titular rulers of Bengal) the villains of the piece. In this excerpt, Bhavānanda, one of the sannyāsīs, reveals to a new disciple the group's mission and the *mystique* which sustains it.

[From *Abbey of Bliss*, pp. 31–37; *Bande Mātaram* translation in Ghose, *Collected Poems and Plays*, II, 227–28]

In that smiling moonlit night, the two silently walked across the plain. Mahendra [the disciple] was silent, sad, careless, and a little curious.

Bhavananda suddenly changed his looks. He was no more the steady and mild anchorite, nor wore any more the warlike hero's face—the face of the slayer of a captain of forces. Not even was there in his mien the proud disdain with which he had scolded Mahendra even now. It seemed as if his heart was filled with joy at the beauteous sight of the earth, lulled in peace and beaming under the silvery moon, and of the glory in her wilds and woods and hills and streams, and grew cheery like the ocean smiling with the rise of the moon. Bhavananda grew chatty, cheerful, cordial, and very eager to talk. He made many an attempt to open a conversation with his companion but Mahendra would not speak. Having no option left, he then began to sing to himself:

> Mother, I bow to thee!
> Rich with thy hurrying streams,
> Bright with thy orchard gleams,
> Cool with thy winds of delight,
> Dark fields waving, Mother of might,
> Mother free.

Mahendra was a little puzzled to hear the song; he could not grasp anything. Who could be the mother, he thought.

> Rich with thy hurrying streams,
> Bright with orchard gleams.
> Cool with thy winds of delight,
> Dark fields waving, Mother of might,
> Mother free.

He asked, "Who is the mother?" Bhavananda did not answer but sang on:

> Glory of moonlight dreams
> Over the branches and lordly streams,
> Clad in thy blossoming trees,
> Mother, giver of ease,
> Laughing low and sweet!
> Mother, I kiss thy feet,
> Speaker sweet and low!
> Mother, to thee I bow.

"It is the country and no mortal mother," cried Mahendra. "We own no other mother," retorted Bhavananda; "they say, 'the mother and the land of birth are higher than heaven.' We think the land of birth to be no other than our mother herself. We have no mother, no father, no brother, no wife, no child, no hearth or home, we have only got the mother—

Rich with hurrying streams,
Bright with orchard gleams.

Mahendra now understood the song and asked Bhavananda to sing again.

He sang:

Mother, I bow to thee!
Rich with thy hurrying streams,
Bright with thy orchard gleams,
Cool with thy winds of delight,
Dark fields waving, Mother of might,
Mother free.
Glory of moonlight dreams
Over thy branches and lordly streams,
Clad in thy blossoming trees,
Mother, giver of ease,
Laughing low and sweet!
Mother, I kiss thy feet,
Speaker sweet and low!
Mother, to thee I bow.
Who hath said thou art weak in thy lands,
When the swords flash out in twice seventy million **hands**
And seventy million voices roar [1]
Thy dreadful name from shore to shore?
With many strengths who are mighty and stored,
To thee I call, Mother and Lord!
Thou who savest, arise and save!
To her I cry who ever her foemen drave
Back from plain and sea
And shook herself free.
Thou art wisdom, thou art law,
Thou our heart, our soul, our breath,
Thou the love divine, the awe
In our hearts that conquers death.
Thine the strength that nerves the arm,
Thine the beauty, thine the charm.
Every image made divine
In our temples is but thine.
Thou art Durga,[2] Lady and Queen,
With her hands that strike and her swords of sheen,
Thou art Lakshmi [3] lotus-throned,

[1] When used as a national anthem, this figure was changed to 300 million.
[2] The Goddess Mother, much-worshiped in Bengal.   [3] The Goddess of Wealth.

And the Muse a hundred-toned.
Pure and Perfect without peer,
Mother, lend thine ear.
Rich with thy hurrying streams,
Bright with thy orchard gleams,
Dark of hue, O candid-fair
In thy soul, with jewelled hair
And thy glorious smile divine,
Loveliest of all earthly lands,
Showering wealth from well-stored hands!
Mother, mother mine!
Mother sweet, I bow to thee
Mother great and free!

Mahendra saw that the outlaw was weeping as he sang. He then asked in wonder, "Who may you be, please?"

Bhavananda answered, "We are the Children."

"Children! Whose children are you?"

"Our mother's."

"Well, but does a child worship its mother with the proceeds of robbery?"

"We do nothing of the sort."

"Presently you looted a cart."

"Was that robbery? Whom did we rob?"

"Why, of course the king!"

"The king! What right has he to take this money?"

"It is the royal portion which goes to the king."

"How do you call him a king who does not rule his kingdom?"

"I fear you will be blown up before the sepoy's cannons one of these days."

"We have seen plenty of sepoys; even today we have had some."

"You haven't yet known them aright, you will know them one day however."

"What then? One never dies more than once."

"But why should you willingly invite death?"

"Mahendra Sinha, I thought you to be a man amongst men, but I now see there is little to choose between you and the rest of your lot—you are only the sworn consumer of milk and butter. Just think of the snake. It creeps on the ground; I cannot think of any creature lower and meaner

[160]

than it; but put your foot on its neck and it will spread its fangs to bite you. But can nothing disturb *your* equanimity? Look round and see, look at Magadha, Mithila, Kasi, Kanchi,[4] Delhi, Kashmir—where do you find such misery as here? Where else do the people eat grass for want of better food? Where do they eat thorns and white-ants' earth and wild creepers? Where do men think of eating dogs and jackals and even carcasses? Where else can you find men getting so anxious about the money in their coffers, the *salgram* [5] in their temples, the females in the Zenana,[6] and the child in the mother's womb? Yes, here they even rip open the womb! In every country the bond that binds a sovereign to his subjects is the protection that he gives; but our Mussulman king—how does he protect us? Our religion is gone; so is our caste, our honor and the sacredness of our family even! Our lives even are now to be sacrificed. Unless we drive these tipsy longbeards away, a Hindu can no longer hope to save his religion."

"Well, but how can you drive them away?"

"We will beat them."

"Alone, will you? With a slap, I presume."

The outlaw sang:

> Who hath said thou art weak in thy lands,
> When the swords flash out in twice seventy million hands
> And seventy million voices roar
> Thy dreadful name from shore to shore?

M: "But I see you are alone."

Bh: "Why, only now you saw two hundred of us."

M: "Are they all children?"

Bh: "They are, all of them."

"How many more are there?"

"Thousands of them; we will have more by and by."

"Suppose you get ten or twenty thousands. Could you hope to depose the Mussulman king with them?"

"How many soldiers had the English at Plassey?"

"Tut! to compare the English with the Bengali!"

"Why not? Physical strength does not count for much; the bullet won't be running faster, I ween, if I am stronger."

---

[4] Names of ancient Indian cities and kingdoms, used here in lieu of modern place-names.
[5] Family idol.   [6] The rooms of a house in which women are secluded.

"Then why this great difference between the English and the Mussulman?"

"Because an Englishman would die sooner than fly; the Mussulman will fly with the first breath of fire and look about for *sherbet*.[7] Secondly, the English have determination: what they want to do they will see done. The Mussulman soldiers come to die for pay, and even that they don't always get. Lastly there is courage. A cannon ball falls only on one spot and cannot kill two hundred men together. Yet, when such a ball falls before the Mussulmans, they fly away in a body, while no Englishman would even fly before a shower of balls."

"Have you these qualities?"

"No, but you don't pluck them like ripe fruits from trees; they come by practice."

"What is your practice?"

"Don't you see we are all anchorites? Our renunciation is for the sake of this practice alone. When our mission is done or the practice is completed, we shall go back to our homes. We too have wives and children."

"You have left them all? How could you break the ties of family life?"

"A Child must not lie! I will not brag in vain to you. No body can ever cut the bond. He who says that he never cares for the family bonds either did never love or merely brags. We don't get rid of the bonds but simply keep our pledge. Will you enter our order?"

"Till I hear of my wife and child, I can say nothing."

"Come and you will see them."

So saying they began to walk along. Bhavananda sang the song "Hail Mother" again. Mahendra had a good voice and had some proficiency in music which he loved; so he joined Bhavananda in his song. He found that it really brought tears to the eye. "If I have not got to renounce my wife and daughter," said he, "you may initiate me into your order."

"He who takes this vow," said Bhavananda, "has to give up his wife and children. If you take it, you need not see your wife and daughter. They will be well kept, but till the mission is fulfilled, you are not to see their face[s]."

"I don't care to take your vow," blurted out Mahendra.

Mahendra does take the vow, but is later reunited with his wife and daughter.

[7] A chilled sweet drink.

Why the British Came to Rule India

In the final chapter of *The Abbey of Bliss*, after the sannyāsīs have routed both the Muslims and the British, Bankim has a supernatural figure explain to their leader Satyānanda, that the British have been forced to rule in India in order that Hinduism might regain its pristine power.

[From *Ānandamath*, Part IV, Chapter 8. Tr. by T. W. Clark]

S: Come, I'm ready. But, my lord, clear up this doubt in my mind. Why at the very moment in which I have removed all barriers from before our eternal Faith, do you order me to cease?

He: Your task is accomplished. The Muslim power is destroyed. There is nothing else for you to do. No good can come of needless slaughter.

S: The Muslim power has indeed been destroyed, but the dominion of the Hindus has not yet been established. The British still hold Calcutta.

He: Hindu dominion will not be established now. If you remain at your work, men will be killed to no purpose. Therefore come.

S: (greatly pained) My lord, if Hindu dominion is not going to be established, who will rule? Will the Muslim kings return?

He: No. The English will rule.

S: (turning tearfully to the image of her who symbolized the land of his birth) Alas, my Mother! I have failed to set you free. Once again you will fall into the hands of infidels. Forgive your son. Alas, my Mother! Why did I not die on the battlefield?

He: Grieve not. You have won wealth; but it was by violence and robbery, for your mind was deluded. No pure fruit can grow on a sinful tree. You will never set your country free in that way. What is going to happen now is for the best. If the English do not rule, there is no hope of a revival of our eternal Faith. I tell you what the wise know. True religion is not to be found in the worship of 33 crores of gods; that is a vulgar, debased religion, which has obscured that which is true. True Hinduism consists in knowledge not in action. Knowledge is of two kinds, physical and spiritual. Spiritual knowledge is the essential part of Hinduism. If however physical knowledge does not come first, spiritual knowledge will never comprehend the subtle spirit within. Now physical knowledge has long since disappeared from our land, and so true religion has gone too. If you wish to restore true religion, you must first teach this physical knowledge. Such knowledge is unknown in this country because there is no one to teach it. So we must learn it from foreigners. The English are wise in this knowledge, and they are good teachers. Therefore we must make the English rule. Once the people of India have acquired knowledge of the physical world from the English, they will be able to comprehend the nature of the spiritual. There will then be no obstacle to the true Faith. True religion will then shine forth again of itself. Until that happens, and until Hindus are wise and virtuous and strong, the English power will remain unbroken. Under the English our people will be happy; and there will be no impediment to our teaching our faith. So, wise one, stop fighting against the English and follow me.

S: My lord, if it was your intention to set up a British government, and if at this time a British government is good for the country, then why did you make use of me to fight this cruel war?

He: At the present moment the English are traders. Their minds are set on amassing wealth. They have no desire to take up the responsibilities of government. But as a result of the rebellion of the Children, they will have to; because they will get no money if they do not. The rebellion took place to make the English ascend the throne. Come with me now. Know and you will understand.

S: My lord. I do not desire knowledge. It cannot help me. I have vowed a vow and I must keep it. Bless me, and let me not be shaken in my devotion to my Mother.

He: Your vow is fulfilled. You have brought fortune to your Mother. You have set up a British government. Give up your fighting. Let the people take to their plows. Let the earth be rich with harvest and the people rich with wealth.

S: (weeping hot tears) I will make my Mother rich with harvest in the blood of her foes.

He: Who is the foe? There are no foes now. The English are friends as well as rulers. And no one can defeat them in battle.

S: If that is so, I will kill myself before the image of my Mother.

He: In ignorance? Come and know. There is a temple of the Mother in the Himalayas. I will show you her image there.

So saying, He took Satyānanda by the hand. What incomparable beauty! In the dim light, in the deep recesses of Vishnu's temple, two human forms radiant with light stood before a mighty four-armed figure.

One held the other by the hand. Who held the hand; and whose was the hand he held? Knowledge was holding Devotion by the hand; Faith that of Action; Self-sacrifice that of Glory; Heavenly Joy that of Earthly Peace. Satyānanda was the Earthly Peace; He was Heavenly Joy. Satyānanda was Glory; He was Self-sacrifice.

And Self-sacrifice led away Glory.

BĀL GANGĀDHAR TILAK: "FATHER OF INDIAN UNREST"

Impressed by his grandfather's recollections of the days before British rule reached Mahārāshtra, and of the Mutiny and Rebellion of 1857–58, it is not surprising that Bāl Gangādhar Tilak (1856–1920) should have grown up questioning the right of the British to govern his land. Like Rānade and Gokhale (with whom he fought a running political duel for many years) Tilak was descended from the Chitpavan brāhman caste, but unlike them he maintained an uncompromising hostility to foreign domination.

In addition to the Marāthā history he imbibed at his grandfather's knee, Tilak learned Sanskrit and English from his father, a schoolteacher and deputy inspector of education in a small town on India's western seacoast. When he was ten, the family moved to Poona, but at sixteen Tilak was an orphan. A self-reliant but weak-bodied youth, he devoted a year to building up his physique with exercises. After receiving his B.A., he took a Bachelor of Laws degree, but refused to enter government service, the usual haven of educated Indians in those days. Instead, with a few like-minded friends he started a school and two newspapers in order to spread Western knowledge among the people of their native region of Mahārāshtra. After helping to found the Deccan Education Society and Fergusson College, Tilak opposed the reform program of Agarkar and Gokhale and resigned from the group in 1890.

Tilak now purchased from the group the Marāthī weekly *Kesari* (The Lion), which he had named and helped to edit, and its English counterpart, the *Mahratta*.[1] Henceforth he poured his energies into educating the people of his province through the columns of these newspapers.

[1] The old spelling for Marāthā.

His Marāthī style was particularly effective and made a direct appeal to the villagers who would gather to have it read to them. Tilak also promoted in his papers the celebration of two new annual festivals—one dedicated to the Hindu god Ganesh, the other honoring the Marāthā hero Shivaji. His purpose in organizing these festivals was to develop in the Mahārāshtrian people a sense of pride in their common history and religion; however, the Muslim community could not ignore the fact that one of them was made to coincide with their own festival of Muharram, and the other extolled the Mughal empire's fiercest enemy. As eaters of beef, Muslims were further alarmed at the anti-cowkilling agitation which had been started by Dayānanda, and which Tilak continued to sponsor.

Tilak's success in arousing popular enthusiasm through these activities began to worry the government after the assassination of two British officials in Poona in 1897. Tilak was accused of fanning hatred for the officials with his *Kesari* articles, and was sentenced to jail for eighteen months. Imprisonment only whetted his fighting spirit, and the Bengal agitation of 1905 found him in the front lines of the fray. "Militancy—not mendicancy" was the slogan the Extremist faction used to disparage the Moderates, and his cry "Freedom is my birthright and I will have it" swept the country. When the Extremists failed to wrest control of the Congress from the Moderates at the 1907 session, Tilak defied the chairman (who had refused to recognize him); whereupon the meeting degenerated into a riot in which shoes and chairs flew through the air.

Shortly afterward Tilak was again arrested and tried for countenancing political assassination in his speeches and writings. He was sentenced to six years' rigorous confinement in Mandalay, Upper Burma. Books helped him to pass the time, and he returned to his Sanskrit studies. Earlier he had written two books arguing that the Vedas were over six thousand years old. His *magnum opus,* written in prison, was his lengthy commentary on the *Bhagavad Gītā.*

Tilak's interpretation of the *Gītā,* emphasizing as it does the importance of action in this world, gives us the key to his own character and to the influence he has had on political thought in twentieth-century India. He stressed that Hinduism's most popular sacred poem preached political as well as religious activity, and hinted that violence in a righteous cause was morally justifiable. His followers, however, cut themselves loose from the known but foreign standards to which the

[166]

Moderates remained attached and drifted into the uncharted depths of revolutionary violence and terrorism. Tilak himself never used such methods, but when others used them he maintained a silence which implied assent. The "father of Indian unrest," as the British journalist Valentine Chirol called him, was not the man to reprimand his own offspring.

By the time of his death in 1920 Tilak had tempered his opposition to British rule sufficiently to favor contesting the elections provided for under the Montagu-Chelmsford Reforms of 1919, in contrast to the younger Gandhi, who wished to boycott them. But Tilak's example of fearless defiance was remembered by those who came after him, and the title of Lokamānya—"Honored by the People"—is still used as a reminder of his efforts to transform the nationalist cause from an upper-class into a truly popular movement.

BĀL GANGĀDHAR TILAK
The Tenets of the New Party

At the end of the Congress session of 1906, it was clear that the gap between the Moderates and the Extremists had been bridged only temporarily by the mediation of Dadabhai Naoroji. At this juncture Tilak delivered an address summarizing the aims and methods of the new party of which he was the leader.
[From *Bal Gangadhar Tilak: His Writings and Speeches*, pp. 55–57, 61, 63–67]

Calcutta, 2d January, 1907

Two new words have recently come into existence with regard to our politics, and they are *Moderates* and *Extremists*. These words have a specific relation to time, and they, therefore, will change with time. The Extremists of today will be Moderates tomorrow, just as the Moderates of today were Extremists yesterday. When the National Congress was first started and Mr. Dadabhai's views, which now go for Moderates, were given to the public, he was styled an Extremist, so that you will see that the term Extremist is an expression of progress. We are Extremists today and our sons will call themselves Extremists and us Moderates. Every new party begins as Extremists and ends as Moderates. The sphere of practical politics is not unlimited. We cannot say what will or will

[167]

not happen 1,000 years hence—perhaps during that long period, the whole of the white race will be swept away in another glacial period. We must, therefore, study the present and work out a program to meet the present condition.

It is impossible to go into details within the time at my disposal. One thing is granted, namely, that this government does not suit us. As has been said by an eminent statesman—the government of one country by another can never be a successful, and therefore, a permanent government. There is no difference of opinion about this fundamental proposition between the old and new schools. One fact is that this alien government has ruined the country. In the beginning, all of us were taken by surprise. We were almost dazed. We thought that everything that the rulers did was for our good and that this English government has descended from the clouds to save us from the invasions of Tamerlane and Chingis Khan, and, as they say, not only from foreign invasions but from internecine warfare, or the internal or external invasions, as they call it. We felt happy for a time, but it soon came to light that the peace which was established in this country did this, as Mr. Dadabhai has said in one place—that we were prevented from going at each other's throats, so that a foreigner might go at the throat of us all. *Pax Britannica* has been established in this country in order that a foreign government may exploit the country. That this is the effect of this *Pax Britannica* is being gradually realized in these days. It was an unhappy circumstance that it was not realised sooner. We believed in the benevolent intentions of the government, but in politics there is no benevolence. Benevolence is used to sugar-coat the declarations of self-interest and we were in those days deceived by the apparent benevolent intentions under which rampant self-interest was concealed. That was our state then. But soon a change came over us. English education, growing poverty, and better familiarity with our rulers, opened our eyes and our leaders; especially, the venerable leader who presided over the recent Congress was the first to tell us that the drain from the country was ruining it, and if the drain was to continue, there was some great disaster awaiting us. So terribly convinced was he of this that he went over from here to England and spent twenty-five years of his life in trying to convince the English people of the injustice that is being done to us. He worked very hard. He had conversations and interviews with secretaries of state, with members of Parliament—and with what result?

He has come here at the age of eighty-two to tell us that he is bitterly disappointed. Mr. Gokhale, I know, is not disappointed. He is a friend of mine and I believe that this is his honest conviction. Mr. Gokhale is not disappointed but is ready to wait another eighty years till he is disappointed like Mr. Dadabhai. . . .

You can now understand the difference between the old and the new parties. Appeals to the bureaucracy are hopeless. On this point both the new and old parties are agreed. The old party believes in appealing to the British nation and we do not. That being our position, it logically follows we must have some other method. There is another alternative. We are not going to sit down quiet. We shall have some other method by which to achieve what we want. We are not disappointed, we are not pessimists. It is the hope of achieving the goal by our own efforts that has brought into existence this new party.

There is no empire lost by a free grant of concession by the rulers to the ruled. History does not record any such event. Empires are lost by luxury, by being too much bureaucratic or overconfident or from other reasons. But an empire has never come to an end by the rulers conceding power to the ruled. . . .

We have come forward with a scheme which if you accept [it], shall better enable you to remedy this state of things than the scheme of the old school. Your industries are ruined utterly, ruined by foreign rule; your wealth is going out of the country and you are reduced to the lowest level which no human being can occupy. In this state of things, is there any other remedy by which you can help yourself? The remedy is not petitioning but boycott. We say prepare your forces, organize your power, and then go to work so that they cannot refuse you what you demand. A story in *Mahabharata* tells that Sri Krishna was sent to effect a compromise, but the Pandavas and Kauravas were both organizing their forces to meet the contingency of failure of the compromise. This is politics. Are you prepared in this way to fight if your demand is refused? If you are, be sure you will not be refused; but if you are not, nothing can be more certain than that your demand will be refused, and perhaps, forever. We are not armed, and there is no necessity for arms either. We have a stronger weapon, a political weapon, in boycott. We have perceived one fact, that the whole of this administration, which is carried on by a handful of Englishmen, is carried on with our assistance. We are all in subordinate service. This whole government is carried on with our assistance and they try to keep us in ignorance of our power of cooperation between ourselves by which that which is in our own hands at present can be claimed by us and administered by us. The point is to have the entire control in our hands. I want to have the key of my house, and not merely one stranger turned out of it. Self-government is our goal; we want a control over our administrative machinery. We don't want to become clerks and remain [clerks]. At present, we are clerks and willing instruments of our own oppression in the hands of an alien government, and that government is ruling over us not by its innate strength but by keeping us in ignorance and blindness to the perception of this fact. Professor Seely [1] shares this view. Every Englishman knows that they are a mere handful in this country and it is the business of every one of them to befool you in believing that you are weak and they are strong. This is politics. We have been deceived by such policy so long. What the new party wants you to do is to realize the fact that your future rests entirely in your own hands. If you mean to be free, you can be free; if you do not mean to be free, you will fall and be for ever fallen. So many of you need not like arms; but if you have not the power of active resistance, have you not the power of self-denial and self-abstinence in such a way as not to assist this foreign government to rule over you? This is boycott and this is what is meant when we say, boycott is a political weapon. We shall not give them assistance to collect revenue and keep peace. We shall not assist them in fighting beyond the frontiers or outside India with Indian blood and money. We shall not assist them in carrying on the administration of justice. We shall have our own courts, and when time comes we shall not pay taxes. Can you do that by your united efforts? If you can, you are free from tomorrow. Some gentlemen who spoke this evening referred to half bread as against the whole bread. I say I want the whole bread and that immediately. But if I can not get the whole, don't think that I have no patience.

I will take the half they give me and then try for the remainder. This is the line of thought and action in which you must train yourself. We have not raised this cry from a mere impulse. It is a reasoned impulse. Try to understand that reason and try to strengthen that impulse by your logical convictions. I do not ask you to blindly follow us. Think

[1] Refers to Sir John Robert Seely, author of *The Expansion of England* (London, 1895).

[170]

over the whole problem for yourselves. If you accept our advice, we feel sure we can achieve our salvation thereby. This is the advice of the new party. Perhaps we have not obtained a full recognition of our principles. Old prejudices die very hard. Neither of us wanted to wreck the Congress, so we compromised, and were satisfied that our principles were recognized, and only to a certain extent. That does not mean that we have accepted the whole situation. We may have a step in advance next year, so that within a few years our principles will be recognized, and recognized to such an extent that the generations who come after us may consider us Moderates. This is the way in which a nation progresses, and this is the lesson you have to learn from the struggle now going on. This is a lesson of progress, a lesson of helping yourself as much as possible, and if you really perceive the force of it, if you are convinced by these arguments, then and then only is it possible for you to effect your salvation from the alien rule under which you labor at this moment.

There are many other points but it is impossible to exhaust them all in an hour's speech. If you carry any wrong impression come and get your doubts solved. We are prepared to answer every objection, solve every doubt, and prove every statement. We want your cooperation; without your help we cannot do anything singlehanded. We beg of you, we appeal to you, to think over the question, to see the situation, and realize it, and after realizing it to come to our assistance, and by our joint assistance to help in the salvation of the country.

The Message of the Bhagavad Gītā

Differing from the nondualistic interpretation of the *Gītā* as pointing the path to renunciation of the world, Tilak held that it preached a life of desireless action *in* the world. In the conclusion to his *Mystic Import of the Bhagavad Gītā* he linked this message with the revival of India's political fortunes.

[From Tilak, *Śrīmad Bhagavadgītā Rahasya*, II, 712–13]

The religion of the *Gītā*, which is a combination of spiritual knowledge, devotion, and action, which is in all respects undauntable and comprehensive, and is further perfectly equable, that is, which does not maintain any distinction, but gives release to everyone in the same measure, and at the same time shows proper forbearance towards other religions, is thus seen to be the sweetest and immortal fruit of the tree of the Vedic religion. In the Vedic religion, higher importance was given in the beginning principally to the sacrifice of wealth or of animals, that is to say, principally to action in the shape of ritual; but, when the knowledge expounded in the Upanishads taught later on that this ritualistic religion of the Shrutis was inferior, Sānkhya philosophy came into existence out of it. But as this knowledge was unintelligible towards abandonment of action, it was not possible for ordinary people to be satisfied merely by the religion of the Upanishads, or by the unification of the Upanishads and the Sānkhya philosophy in the Smritis. Therefore, the *Gītā* religion fuses the knowledge of the Brahman contained in the Upanishads, which is cognoscible only to the intelligence, with the "king of mysticisms" (*rāja-guhya*) of the worship of the perceptible which is accessible to love, and consistently with the ancient tradition of ritualistic religion, it proclaims to everybody, though nominally to Arjuna, that, "[to] perform lifelong your several worldly duties according to your respective positions in life, desirelessly, for the universal good, with a self-identifying vision, and enthusiastically, and thereby perpetually worship the deity in the shape of the Paramātman (the Highest Ātman), which is eternal, and which uniformly pervades the body of all created things as also the cosmos; because, therein lies your happiness in this world and in the next"; and on that account, the mutual conflict between action, spiritual knowledge (jnāna), and love (devotion) is done away with, and the single *Gītā* religion, which preaches that the whole of one's life should be turned into a sacrifice (yajna), contains the essence of the entire Vedic religion. When hundreds of energetic noble souls and active persons were busy with the benefit of all created things, because they looked upon that as their duty, as a result of their having realized this eternal religion, this country was blessed with the favor of the Parameshvara,[1] and reached the height not only of knowledge but also of prosperity; and it need not be said in so many words, that when this ancient religion, which is beneficial in this life and in the next, lost following in our country, it (our country) reached its present fallen state. I, therefore, now pray to the Parameshvara, at the end of this book, that there should come to birth again in this our country such noble and pure men as will worship the Parameshvara according to this equable and brilliant religion of the *Gītā,* which harmonizes devotion, spiritual knowledge, and energism. . . .

[1] The Highest God.

[172]

AUROBINDO GHOSE: MYSTIC PATRIOT

The agitation against the Partition of Bengal drew into public life one of the most fascinating figures modern India has produced—a completely Westernized intellectual who became a fanatic nationalist and ended his days an accomplished yogi. Aurobindo Ghose (1872–1950)— or Sri Aurobindo, as he is known to his followers—spent only four years in active politics, but in that brief span his passionate devotion to the national cause won him reknown as an Extremist leader second only to Tilak in nation-wide popularity.

Aurobindo's father, an English-educated Bengali doctor, was so determined to give his son a completely European education that he sent him to a convent school at five and to England at seven. Isolated from all Indian influences, Aurobindo studied in England until he was twenty. Leaving Cambridge University, he returned to India in 1893 to enter the civil service of the progressive princely state of Baroda. Sensing himself "denationalized" by his foreign education, he turned his attention to Indian culture and politics. He was inspired by the writings of Rāmakrishna, Vivekānanda, and the novels of Bankim Chandra Chatterjee, and after studying Sanskrit was able to appreciate in the original the Upanishads and the *Gītā*.

His fascination with Hindu culture, when combined with the sense of patriotism he had imbibed along with the rest of his English education, naturally led Aurobindo to sympathize with the Extremist politicians. Despite the fact that he was unusually shy, during the agitation against the Partition of Bengal he gave up his post as vice-principal of Baroda College and threw himself into the maelstrom of Bengal politics. His articles in the English-language weekly *Bande Mataram* made him famous, especially after the government tried and failed to prove seditious their deftly phrased innuendos. In 1907 Aurobindo led a large Bengali delegation to the crucial Congress session at Tilak's request, and served as Lokamanya's right-hand man during the stormy days of the split between the Moderates and the Extremists.

Shortly afterward Aurobindo consulted a Hindu holy man who advised him to void his mind of all thought so as to be able to receive supermental inspiration. He followed this advice faithfully, and when he found himself jailed as a suspected member of a bombing plot, he heard the voice of Vivekānanda guiding him in his practice of yoga, and saw all men as incarnations of God. After his release Aurobindo gradually withdrew from political life, and in 1910 abandoned Bengal—and his wife—for the French settlement of Pondichéry, where he spent his remaining forty years doing spiritual exercises and writing. All efforts to bring him back into the political arena proved ineffectual.

Brief as his political career was, Aurobindo defined the essence of religious nationalism in a manner which for sheer passion has never been surpassed. Because of his prolonged absence from India, Aurobindo came to idealize both his native land and its ancestral faith and to identify one with the other in a way no previous thinker had dared to do. The very fervor of his faith in "India" helped his Hindu countrymen to transcend the many differences of caste, language, and custom which had hindered the development among them of allegiance to one nation.

Aurobindo was free of the region-centered nationalism which limited the effectiveness of a Bengali like Bankim or a Mahārāshtrian like Tilak. Along with Bankim and Tilak, however, he failed to perceive that the greater the zeal of the Hindu nationalists became, the more difficult grew the task of uniting both Hindus and Muslims in loyalty to a single non-British government.

AUROBINDO GHOSE
The Doctrine of Passive Resistance

In a series of articles under this heading penned in April, 1907, Aurobindo outlined the Extremists' program of national self-reliance. Both the negative and the positive aspects of this program were later utilized by Gāndhi.

[From Ghose, *The Doctrine of Passive Resistance*, pp. 73–74, 77–79]

We desire to put an end to petitioning until such a strength is created in the country that a petition will only be a courteous form of demand. We wish to kill utterly the pernicious delusion that a foreign and adverse interest can be trusted to develop us to its own detriment, and entirely to do away with the foolish and ignoble hankering after help from our natural adversaries. Our attitude to bureaucratic concession is that of Laocoon: "We fear the Greeks even when they bring us gifts." Our policy is self-development and defensive resistance. But we would extend the policy of self-development to every department of national life; not only

Swadeshi and National Education, but national defense, national arbitration courts, sanitation, insurance against famine or relief of famine—whatever our hands find to do or urgently needs doing, we must attempt ourselves and no longer look to the alien to do it for us. And we would universalize and extend the policy of defensive resistance until it ran parallel on every line with our self-development. We would not only buy our own goods, but boycott British goods; not only have our own schools, but boycott government institutions; not only organize our league of defense, but have nothing to do with the bureaucratic executive except when we cannot avoid it. At present even in Bengal where boycott is universally accepted, it is confined to the boycott of British goods and is aimed at the British merchant and only indirectly at the British bureaucrat. We would aim it directly both at the British merchant and at the British bureaucrat who stands behind and makes possible exploitation by the merchant. . . .

The double policy of self-development and defensive resistance is the common standing-ground of the new spirit all over India. Some may not wish to go beyond its limits, others may look outside it; but so far all are agreed. For ourselves we avow that we advocate passive resistance without wishing to make a dogma of it. In a subject nationality, to win liberty for one's country is the first duty of all, by whatever means, at whatever sacrifice; and this duty must override all other considerations. The work of national emancipation is a great and holy yajna [1] of which boycott, Swadeshi, national education, and every other activity, great and small, are only major or minor parts. Liberty is the fruit we seek from the sacrifice and the Motherland the goddess to whom we offer it; into the seven leaping tongues of the fire of the yajna we must offer all that we are and all that we have, feeding the fire even with our blood and lives and happiness of our nearest and dearest; for the Motherland is a goddess who loves not a maimed and imperfect sacrifice, and freedom was never won from the gods by a grudging giver. But every great yajna has its Rakshasas [2] who strive to baffle the sacrifice, to bespatter it with their own dirt, or by guile or violence put out the flame. Passive resistance is an attempt to meet such disturbers by peaceful and self-contained *Brahmatej;* [3] but even the greatest Rishis of old could not, when the Rakshasas were fierce and determined, keep up the sacrifice

[1] Ritual sacrifice.   [2] Demons.   [3] Divine power.

without calling in the bow of the Kshatriya. We should have the bow of the Kshatriya ready for use, though in the background. Politics is especially the business of the Kshatriya, and without Kshatriya strength at its back, all political struggle is unavailing.

Vedantism accepts no distinction of true or false religions, but considers only what will lead more or less surely, more or less quickly to moksha, spiritual emancipation and the realization of the Divinity within. Our attitude is a political Vedantism. India, free, one and indivisible, is the divine realization to which we move, emancipation our aim; to that end each nation must practice the political creed which is the most suited to its temperament and circumstances; for that is the best for it which leads most surely and completely to national liberty and national self-realization. But whatever leads only to continued subjection must be spewed out as mere vileness and impurity. Passive resistance may be the final method of salvation in our case or it may be only the preparation for the final sadhana.[4] In either case, the sooner we put it into full and perfect practice, the nearer we shall be to national liberty.

Nationalism Is the Work of God

Addressing a Bombay audience soon after the Moderate-Extremist split, Aurobindo made his mind a blank and spoke as the spirit moved him. The result was a startling declaration of the religious significance of Indian nationalism.

[From Ghose, *Speeches*, pp. 7-9]

There is a creed in India today which calls itself Nationalism, a creed which has come to you from Bengal. This is a creed which many of you have accepted when you called yourselves Nationalists. Have you realized, have you yet realized what that means? Have you realized what it is that you have taken in hand? Or is it that you have merely accepted it in the pride of a superior intellectual conviction? You call yourselves Nationalists. What is Nationalism? Nationalism is not a mere political program; Nationalism is a religion that has come from God; Nationalism is a creed which you shall have to live. Let no man dare to call himself a Nationalist if he does so merely with a sort of intellectual pride, thinking that he is more patriotic, thinking that he is something higher

[4] Spiritual discipline leading to attainment of the highest good.

[176]

than those who do not call themselves by that name. If you are going to be a nationalist, if you are going to assent to this religion of Nationalism, you must do it in the religious spirit. You must remember that you are the instruments of God. What is this that has happened in Bengal? You call yourselves Nationalists, but when this happens to you, what will you do? This thing is happening daily in Bengal, because, in Bengal, Nationalism has come to the people as a religion, and it has been accepted as a religion. But certain forces which are against that religion are trying to crush its rising strength. It always happens when a new religion is preached, when God is going to be born in the people, that such forces rise with all their weapons in their hands to crush the religion. In Bengal too a new religion, a religion divine and sattwic [1] has been preached, and this religion they are trying with all the weapons at their command to crush. By what strength are we in Bengal able to survive? Nationalism is not going to be crushed. Nationalism survives in the strength of God and it is not possible to crush it, whatever weapons are brought against it. Nationalism is immortal; Nationalism cannot die; because it is no human thing, it is God who is working in Bengal. God cannot be killed, God cannot be sent to jail. When these things happen among you, I say to you solemnly, what will you do? Will you do as they do in Bengal? [Cries of "Yes."] Don't lightly say "yes." It is a solemn thing; and suppose that God puts you this question, how will you answer it? Have you got a real faith? Or is it merely a political aspiration? Is it merely a larger kind of selfishness? Or is it merely that you wish to be free to oppress others, as you are being oppressed? Do you hold your political creed from a higher source? Is it God that is born in you? Have you realized that you are merely the instruments of God, that your bodies are not your own? You are merely instruments of God for the work of the Almighty. Have you realized that? If you have realized that, then you are truly Nationalists; then alone will you be able to restore this great nation. In Bengal it has been realized clearly by some, more clearly by others, but it has been realized and you on this side of the country must also realize it. Then there will be a blessing on our work, and this great nation will rise again and become once more what it was in the days of its spiritual greatness.

[1] Pure, holy.

India's Mission: The Resurrection of Hinduism

In a memorable speech to the Society for the Protection of Religion after his release from prison in 1908, Aurobindo relayed to his countrymen the messages which had mystically come to him during his confinement. He was first of all to dedicate himself to God's work. Secondly, through her national revival, India was to spread the universal truth of Hinduism throughout the world.

[From Ghose, *Speeches*, pp. 76–80]

The second message came and it said: "Something has been shown to you in this year of seclusion, something about which you had your doubts and it is the truth of the Hindu religion. It is this religion that I am raising up before the world, it is this that I have perfected and developed through the rishis, saints, and avatars, and now it is going forth to do my work among the nations. I am raising up this nation to send forth my word. This is the Sanatan Dharma, this is the eternal religion which you did not really know before, but which I have now revealed to you. The agnostic and the sceptic in you have been answered, for I have given you proofs within and without you, physical and subjective, which have satisfied you. When you go forth, speak to your nation always this word, that it is for the Sanatan Dharma that they arise, it is for the world and not for themselves that they arise. I am giving them freedom for the service of the world. When therefore it is said that India shall rise, it is the Sanatan Dharma that shall rise. When it is said that India shall be great, it is the Sanatan Dharma that shall be great. When it is said that India shall expand and extend itself, it is the Sanatan Dharma that shall expand and extend itself over the world. It is for the dharma and by the dharma that India exists. To magnify the religious means to magnify the country. I have shown you that I am everywhere and in all men and in all things, that I am in this movement and I am not only working in those who are striving for the country but I am working also in those who oppose them and stand in their paths. I am working in everybody and whatever men may think or do they can do nothing but help on my purpose. They also are doing my work, they are not my enemies but my instruments. In all your actions you are moving forward without knowing which way you move. You mean to do one thing and you do another. You aim at a result and your efforts subserve one that is different or contrary. It is Shakti [2] that has gone forth and entered into the people. Since long ago I have been preparing this uprising and now the time has come and it is I who will lead it to its fulfillment."

This then is what I have to say to you. The name of your society is "Society for the Protection of Religion." Well, the protection of the religion, the protection and upraising before the world of the Hindu religion, that is the work before us. But what is the Hindu religion? What is this religion which we call Sanatan, eternal? It is the Hindu religion only because the Hindu nation has kept it, because in this Peninsula it grew up in the seclusion of the sea and the Himalayas, because in this sacred and ancient land it was given as a charge to the Aryan race to preserve through the ages. But it is not circumscribed by the confines of a single country, it does not belong peculiarly and forever to a bounded part of the world. That which we call the Hindu religion is really the eternal religion, because it is the universal religion which embraces all others. If a religion is not universal, it cannot be eternal. A narrow religion, a sectarian religion, an exclusive religion can live only for a limited time and a limited purpose. This is the one religion that can triumph over materialism by including and anticipating the discoveries of science and the speculations of philosophy. It is the one religion which impresses on mankind the closeness of God to us and embraces in its compass all the possible means by which man can approach God. It is the one religion which insists every moment on the truth which all religions acknowledge that He is in all men and all things and that in Him we move and have our being. It is the one religion which enables us not only to understand and believe this truth but to realize it with every part of our being. It is the one religion which shows the world what the world is, that it is the Lila of Vasudeva.[3] It is the one religion which shows us how we can best play our part in that Lila, its subtlest laws and its noblest rules. It is the one religion which does not separate life in any smallest detail from religion, which knows what immortality is and has utterly removed from us the reality of death.

This is the word that has been put into my mouth to speak to you today. What I intended to speak has been put away from me, and

[2] Divine creative power.   [3] The play or sport of God.

beyond what is given to me I have nothing to say. It is only the word that is put into me that I can speak to you. That word is now finished. I spoke once before with this force in me and I said then that this movement is not a political movement and that nationalism is not politics but a religion, a creed, a faith. I say it again today, but I put it in another way. I say no longer that nationalism is a creed, a religion, a faith; I say that it is the Sanatan Dharma which for us is nationalism. This Hindu nation was born with the Sanatan Dharma, with it it moves and with it it grows. When the Sanatan Dharma declines, then the nation declines, and if the Sanatan Dharma were capable of perishing, with the Sanatan Dharma it would perish. The Sanatan Dharma, that is nationalism. This is the message that I have to speak to you.

BRAHMABĀNDHAB UPĀDHYĀY: HINDU CATHOLIC NATIONALIST

A Hindu sannyāsī, a Roman Catholic, a fiery nationalist—all three descriptions apply equally well to the Bengali brāhman Brahmabāndhab Upādhyāy (1861–1907).

Brahmabāndhab grew up in a village near Calcutta, the third and youngest son of an inspector of police. His mother had died before he was a year old; one of his uncles, Kāli Charan Banerjee, later a prominent Protestant minister, used to visit the family frequently and teach the boy reading and writing.

Brahmabāndhab was an avid student of Sanskrit literature, and had read the *Mahābhārata* and *Rāmāyaṇa* many times before entering his 'teens. The novels of Bankim Chandra Chatterjee excited his fertile imagination, and Surendranāth Banerjea's speeches inspired him to dedicate himself to patriotic service. At seventeen he ran away from college to "learn the art of fighting and drive out the English."[1] Unable to enlist in the Mahārāja of Gwalior's army, after a period of wandering he returned disillusioned to Calcutta and became a teacher in a boys' school.

Calcutta in the early 1880s was the scene of an unusual religious fer-

[1] Quoted in B. Animananda, *The Blade*, p. 14.

ment. Brahmabāndhab fell under the influence of Keshub Chunder Sen, and through him met Rāmakrishna, with whom he was less deeply impressed. He also became a good friend of Narendranāth Datta, the future Vivekānanda. In 1887 he joined the Brāhmo Samāj and soon emigrated with a few friends to found a school for the teaching of Sanskrit and moral character in the province of Sind, in western India.

Four years later, after much reading and prayer, his restless spirit embraced Christianity, first as a Protestant, and then as a Roman Catholic. He nevertheless continued to consider himself as every inch a Hindu, and from 1894 until his death followed strictly the celibate and dietary regimen of a Hindu sannyāsī. Throughout this period he tried to reconcile Hindu philosophy with Christian theology, but his efforts to this end were regarded with some anxiety by the Catholic hierarchy, which twice forbade him to write on the subject.

In 1901 Brahmabāndhab joined Rabindranāth Tagore in setting up a rural school on classical lines at Shāntiniketan. In 1902 he made a trip to Rome and England, feeling that by lecturing on Indian thought at Oxford and Cambridge he was carrying on the work begun by Vivekānanda.

A new phase in his life began in 1905, when his weekly Calcutta newspaper *Sandhyā* (*Twilight*) became a sort of headquarters for the great anti-Partition agitation. Although less important as a political figure than they, he worked with Aurobindo, Tilak, Bepin Chandra Pāl and other Extremist leaders. In 1907 the government arrested and tried him for seditious journalism, for he had written some passionately anti-British editorials in his paper. During the trial he underwent a minor operation and died of lockjaw from a resulting infection.

The life of Brahmabāndhab Upādhyāy illustrates once more the fact that for Hindu nationalists the religious and political spheres of action were virtually inseparable. Moreover, his success in adopting the Christian faith while retaining his status as a brāhman testifies to the great freedom of thought which Hindu society permits to its members. It is also possible to conclude from his experience that if Christianity is to win future converts in Asia it will depend increasingly on the sort of religious synthesis Brahmabāndhab tried to create.

BRAHMABĀNDHAB UPĀDHYĀY
Hinduism's Contribution to Christianity

In an article of 1897 Brahmabāndhab stated his aim of explaining Christian doctrine in terms of Hindu concepts. The influence of Keshab Chunder Sen is perceptible in this passage.

[From Animananda, *The Blade*, pp. 67–68]

Christianity has again after a long period come in contact with a philosophy which, though it may contain more errors—because the Hindu mind is synthetic and speculative—still unquestionably soars higher than her Western sister. Shall we, Catholics of India, now . . . [let Hindus make] it their weapon against Christianity or shall we look upon it in the same way as St. Thomas looked upon the Aristotelian system? We are of [the] opinion that attempts should be made to win over Hindu philosophy to the service of Christianity as Greek philosophy was won over in the Middle Ages.

We have no definite idea as regards the *modus operandi* of making Hindu philosophy the handmaid of Christianity. The task is difficult and beset with many dangers. But we have a conviction and it is growing day by day that the Catholic Church will find it hard to conquer India unless she makes Hindu philosophy hew wood and draw water for her. The more we meditate on the cogitations of Hindu philosophy concerning the Supreme Being, on its marvelous but fruitless effort to penetrate into His inner nature . . . the more light is thrown upon the ever-mysterious Christian doctrine of the One God, one yet multiple, absolute yet related within Himself, discovering in it a new fitness to appease the noblest cravings of man and satisfy the demands of the loftiest intellect. . . .

The development of the Christian religion has not come to an end. It will grow, blossom, and fructify till the end of time. Indian soil is humid and its humidity will make the ever-new Christian revelation put forth newer harmonies and newer beauties revealing more clearly the invincible integrity of the Universal Faith deposited in the Church by the Apostles of Jesus Christ. The Hindu mind and heart, coming under the dominion of the One, Holy, Apostolic and Catholic Church,

[182]

will sing a *new* canticle which will fill the earth with sweetness from
end to end.

Hindu Catholicism

Pride in Hindu upbringing, Brahmabāndhab asserted, is totally compatible
with Catholic faith, which is universal.
[From Animananda, *The Blade*, pp. 71–73]

By birth we are Hindus and shall remain *Hindu* till death. But as
dvija (twice-born) by virtue of our sacramental rebirth, we are *Catholic,*
we are members of an indefectible communion embracing all ages and
climes.

In customs and manners, in observing caste and social distinctions, in
eating and drinking, in our life and living, we are genuine Hindus; but
in our faith we are neither Hindus nor European, nor American, nor
Chinese, but all inclusive. Our faith fills the whole world and is not
confined to any country or race; our faith is universal and consequently
includes all truths.

Our thought and thinking is emphatically Hindu. We are more speculative than practical, more given to synthesis than analysis, more con-
templative than active. It is extremely difficult for us to learn how to
think like the Greeks of old or the scholastics of the Middle Ages. Our
brains are molded in the philosophic cast of our ancient country.

We are proud of the stability of the Hindu race. Many a mighty race
did rise and fall, but we continue to exist, though we had to buffet many
a religious deluge and weather many a political storm. We believe in
the future greatness of our race and in this belief we shall live and die.

The more strictly we practice our universal faith, the better do we
grow as Hindus. All that is noblest and best in the Hindu character, is
developed in us by the genial inspiration of the perfect Narahari (God-
man) [Jesus Christ], our pattern and guide. The more we love Him,
the more we love our country, the prouder we become of our past
glory.

Do we really believe in Hinduism? The question must be understood before it can be answered. Hinduism has no definite creed. Kapila
and Vyasa [1] were opposed to each other and yet both of them are con-

[1] The founders of the Sānkhya and Vedanta systems respectively.

sidered to be rishis. The Hindu Vedantists of the school of *Ramanuja* look down upon the Hindu Vedantists of the school of *Sankara* as blasphemers; the *Vaishnava* doctrines differ as widely as the poles from the Shaiva doctrine; even the gods have been made to fight one another in the Puranas. The test of being a Hindu cannot therefore lie in religious opinions.

However we are fully imbued with the *spirit* of Hinduism. We hold with the Vedantists that there is one eternal Essence from which proceed all things. We believe with the *Vaishnavas* in the necessity of incarnation and in the doctrine that man cannot be saved without grace. We agree in spirit with Hindu lawgivers in regard to their teaching that sacramental rites (Sankaras) are vehicles of sanctification. With wondering reverence do we look upon their idea of establishing a sacerdotal hierarchy vested with the highest authority in religious and social matters.

In short, we are Hindus so far as our physical and mental constitution is concerned, but in regard to our immortal souls we are Catholic. We are Hindu Catholics.

Independence for India

Love of India and scorn of the foreigner are expressed in these excerpts from the *Sandhyā* of the anti-Partition days.
[From Animananda, *The Blade*, pp. 136, 137]

I swear by the moon and the sun that I have heard in my heart of hearts this message of freedom. As the tree in winter gets a new life with the touch of the breeze of spring, as you feel joy at the return of love, as the heart of a hero dances to the call of the trumpet of war, so a feeling has throbbed in my heart.

But independence will mean both freedom from our slave complex and freedom from gerrymandering politics.

With the spread of English rule and culture, India lost her own ideal of civilization. Our educated classes think as they have been taught by their Firinghi [2] masters. Our minds have been conquered. We have become slaves. The faith in our own culture and the love for things Indian are gone. India will reach Swaraj the day she will again have a faith in herself. Rāmakrishna had gone in that line. So did Bamkim. So did

[2] Foreigner.

Vivekānanda. The whole mass of our people must now be made to appreciate things Indian and to return to our ancient way. That is Swadesh as opposed to Bidesh.[3] [p. 136]

I see the fort of *Swaraj* built in various places. There shall be no connection with the foreigner. These forts will be purified by the incense of sacrifice, resounding with the cry of victory, filled to overflowing with corn and grain.

Foreigners will not enter there. There we shall be our own masters, from the Thakurghar [4] to the cowshed. All our laws will be observed there, our own Varna-Asram. Let the Englishman be like the *Chaukidar* or *Jamadar*,[5] like the watching dog at the door: "If the dog enters your kitchen you break the cooking pot and chase him out." Outside this, our own jurisdiction, we shall observe the laws of the Firinghi for fear of assault and we shall pay the taxes. But if he were to trespass on our God-given rights, woe betide him? We shall give thrashing for thrashing. [p. 137]

"First Let the Mother Be Free . . ."

The sedition charge for which Brahmabāndhab was tried in 1907 rested primarily on this editorial, which extols India as the Mother in the same way as did the sannyāsīs of Bankim's *Abbey of Bliss*.

[From Animananda, *The Blade*, pp. 170–71]

We have said over and over again that we are not Swadeshi only so far as salt and sugar are concerned. Our aspirations are higher than the Himalayas. Our pain is as intense as if we had a volcano in us. What we want is the emancipation of India. Our aim is that India may be free, that the stranger may be driven from our homes, that the continuity of the learning, the civilization and the system of the rishis may be preserved. We have often heard the voice from heaven: Selfish men! We have not entered the lists to play the mudi [grocer].

First free the Mother from her bondage, then seek your own deliverance. The fire of desire has been kindled within our bosom. We do not know whence. Heaven we do not want. Deliverance we seek not. O Mother! let us be born again and again in India till your chains fall

[3] "One's own country" as opposed to "a foreign country."   [4] Lord's house.
[5] Doorkeeper or guard.

[185]

off. First let the Mother be free, and then shall come our own release from the worldly bonds. This is no mere child's play. O Feringhi [*sic*], here I am with my neck outstretched—offer it up as a sacrifice. You will see, I shall again be born in the land of Bengal and shall cause much more serious confusion. Can you intimidate us? Our power is more than human. It is divine. We have heard the voice telling us that the period of India's suffering is about to close, that the day of her deliverance is near at hand. It is because we have heard the voice that we have left our forest-home and came to town. Your overweening pride is due to your possessing a few cannon and guns. Just see to what plight you are reduced. You imagine that by causing a *Kabulyat*[6] of loyalty to be written, you will drive us to a corner. But the signatories of that document are nonentities. We have all the advantages of the ancient greatness of India on our side. We are immortal. If you are wise, you should help towards the attainment of deliverance by India. Otherwise, come, let us descend into the arena of war. We hereby summon you to battle. See what a mighty contest presently begins all over the country. The sons of the Mother are preparing themselves. All the arms—fiery (Agneya), watery (Varuna), airy (Vayabya)—in her vaults, are being polished. Hark, the flapping of the fourfold arms of the Mother? Are we afraid of your cannon and guns? Arm brothers, arm! The day of deliverance is near. We have heard the voice and we cannot fail to see the chains of India removed before we die. It is now too late to recede.

[6] Certificate.

CHAPTER XXIV

THE MUSLIM REVIVAL

The coming of the British and of Western civilization had, initially at least, a very different impact on the Hindus and Muslims of India. The former, as we have seen, responded to the new situation with both an eagerness to learn from the British whatever would contribute to their own advancement, and a desire to preserve their own sense of national identity by returning to Hindu traditions long neglected. Thus, during the period of British ascendancy, Hindus who had, under Mughal dom-inance, tended to accept as their own much that was most glorious in Indo-Muslim civilization, found their loyalty to it seriously undermined by these new interests or allegiances. Indian Muslims, on the other hand, clung tenaciously to cultural traditions bound up with the practice of their religion and to the memory of a brilliant civilization which, in their eyes, was irreplaceable by anything the West had to offer.

As time passed the divergent loyalties of Hindus and Muslims were manifested particularly in their differing views of history. The Hindu re-vival and a new sense of nationalism led to reexamination and, to some extent, recreation of the past. It was, however, a past which Muslims felt they could not share, a "heathen past" in which they could take no pride. For them it was the days of Muslim domination and the exploits of Mus-lim conquerors to which they turned for inspiration. For Hindus, on the other hand, the period before the Muslim conquest was the age of free-dom and national glory, while the long centuries of Muslim domination came to be looked upon as a humiliation, openly referred to as "the days of subjugation and slavery." Hindu rebels against Muslim authority were hailed as patriots who bravely resisted the alien invader and ruler. To Muslims these same men were the villains of history, who had weakened

The present chapter, as well as Chapter XXVI, "Pakistan: Its Founding and Future," has been prepared by Dr. I. H. Qureshī, Vice-Chancellor of the University of Karachi, par-ticularly with a view to highlighting those developments in the recent past which have contributed to the consciousness among Indian Muslims of separate nationhood.

India from within and prepared the way for the Western aggressor. Thus, the sense of a common attitude toward a common history, which contributes so much to the feeling of unity among a people, was, if it had ever existed in India, almost wholly dissipated.

In the eighteenth century we have already seen, in the views of Abū Tāleb, the near-contempt in which even this remarkably curious and sophisticated Muslim held the Western civilization he observed in Britain. We have noted, too, his prediction that Indian Muslims would continue to ignore Western learning out of "zeal for their own religion." This attitude, indeed, largely prevailed in the Muslim community until, in the mid-nineteenth century, Syed Ahmad Khān appeared to rouse it to a more forward-looking and realistic view of its mission in the modern world.

SYED AHMAD KHĀN AND THE ALĪGARH MOVEMENT

Muslim nationalism had tried to assert itself in many ways before the Sepoy Mutiny, and yet had failed to retrieve its lost position. Almost everywhere it had met with reverses; and the successes it did achieve, such as the victory over the Mārāthas at Panipat (1761), were short-lived. Muslim participation in the Mutiny itself was a last desperate effort, which succeeded only in convincing the British of the Muslims' responsibility for the outbreak. As a result the Muslims were heavily punished, and would have been completely and irretrievably ruined but for the efforts of Sir Syed Ahmad Khān (1817–1898).

Syed Ahmad was born at Delhi to a noble family respected for its learning and piety. He was given an excellent education in the traditional Muslim style. At the time of the Mutiny he was serving the Company's government in a subordinate judicial post, the higher grades being, at that time, not open to Indians. Farsighted enough to see that the Mutiny was unlikely to succeed, he remained faithful to the British and helped them by saving the lives of those in danger.

Syed Ahmad could see that the Muslims would make no progress if they did not accept the fact that British rule had come to stay indefinitely.

[188]

The Muslims were weak and disorganized as a result of the failure of the Mutiny. They were backward because of their hostility to the new educational system established by the British. Only a constructive program could save them, and such a program, for its success, needed the enthusiasm of the community as well as the cooperation of the British. There was still, however, considerable reluctance on the part of the British to believe that Muslims could be loyal to British rule. The Muslims, for their part, found it hard to swallow their pride and loyally serve a regime which they had come to hate as the source of all their troubles. There were, however, hopeful factors in the situation as well. The British had come to realize that it was not in the interests of the empire for a large and brave community to remain sullen and unreconciled; an effort to win its confidence was worthwhile. Among the Muslims, too, there was an increasing number who saw the need for allaying the suspicions of the British, without whose help the Muslim community could not be rescued from its low condition.

Syed Ahmad started work on all fronts. He wrote voluminously to allay British misgivings about the Muslims and Islam itself. He carried on incessant propaganda among his own people to convince them of the futility of any attempt to overthrow British rule, and the desirability of taking full advantage of the possibilities for self-improvement which the stability of the British empire offered. Syed Ahmad laid the greatest emphasis upon education and scientific knowledge and established a society for popularizing science among the Muslims. His greatest achievement was the founding of the Muhammadan Anglo-Oriental College, which was to educate Muslim youth in Western knowledge without neglecting their religious training. Sir Syed's aim was to produce a progressive, educated, well-informed Muslim, capable of success in the modern world without in any way forswearing his loyalty to the tenets of Islam. This college, founded in 1875, was raised to the status of a university in 1921, as the Muslim University of Aligarh.

Sir Syed published a magazine in Urdu called the *Improvement of Manners and Morals* (*Tahdhīb-ul-Akhlāq*), devoted mainly to social and religious problems. His immediate aim was to assimilate the best in Western life and thought into Indo-Muslim culture without in any way compromising the fundamentals of his faith. Through this, however, he was led further to give a new interpretation to Islam. First of all he criticized those beliefs and opinions which had no basis in scripture and yet had become part and parcel of Muslim belief or practice. Then he took up the Qur'ān and the traditions of the Prophet, attempting to explain them in the light of contemporary scientific knowledge. On account of his strong distaste for the supernatural and the irrational he and his followers were called *necharis*—believers in Nature. Though he was vehemently criticized in his lifetime by the conservative sections of his community, he had a profound influence upon the religious opinions of the Muslims of the subcontinent and today his basic ideas are accepted by all but a handful of ultraconservative theologians.

In politics, Sir Syed was a fearless critic of the government. His treatise on the causes of the Mutiny was not pleasing to the reactionary sections of British officialdom in India, and it was only his record of service as a moderating influence against more violent forms of anti-British feelings that helped him to escape the consequences of such boldness. He was, however, a firm believer in the need for cooperation between his community and the British government. He therefore advised the Muslims to stand aloof from the Indian National Congress when it was organized, and remained throughout a critic of its policies. His opposition to the Congress was based upon the belief that a system of representative government, if introduced in the subcontinent, would ultimately lead to rule by the Hindu majority. He believed that the people of India were not sufficiently integrated to be able to run a democratic government without its becoming a disguised rule of the Hindus over the Muslims. So fearful was he of such an eventuality that despite his bitter memories of the Muslim's treatment at the hands of he British, he accepted British rule in preference to Hindu hegemony. Though the Muslim attitude towards British rule changed again after Sir Syed's death, their misgivings about a government run by Hindus remained. In this respect Sir Syed may be considered one of the founders of the Pakistan Movement, though of course, there is no reference to Pakistan or to a separate Muslim state in his writings, since he foresaw no early end to the British empire in India. As one of the first modernists in the world of Islam, moreover, he laid the groundwork for the synthesis of Indian Islam and Western knowledge which has helped make the Pakistanis one of the most advanced Muslim nations in the world. Above all he manifested in his own person those qualities which he put forward as ideals for his people: devotion to Islam, intolerance of superstition and obscurantism, a willingness to accept all that the progress of human knowledge had to offer, and a readiness to make whatever sacrifice was required in the service of his people.

SYED AHMAD KHĀN

Religion and the Supernatural
[From Syed Ahmad Khān, *Akhari Madamin*, pp. 74–77]

There are so many natural mysteries in the universe which are beyond the understanding of men that they can not be counted. . . . These mysteries which we watch every day no longer strike us as miraculous and we become indifferent to them, but when man begins to believe in some religion or considers a person holy, he always attributes miracles to them. He accepts any miracles which are attributed to them; indeed he does not accept the truth of a religion or the holiness of a person without those miracles. . . .

The Prophet of God (Muhammad), on whom be peace and blessings, reiterated again and again: "I am a man like you; it has been revealed to me that your Lord is the one God;" but people were not content with this, and ascribed miracles to him. They base their faith in the Prophet upon these miracles.

The same attitude is adopted toward the saints; until it is accepted that they performed miracles . . . people do not find it possible to believe that they were saints.

In short it has become a habit with men that they ascribe miracles and supernatural attributes to an object or a person whom they consider to be holy or sacred. This is why men have interpolated supernatural factors into Islam, which are not worthy of belief, but such credulous persons believe in them.

However, this is a grievous mistake. Any religion which is true or claims to be true can not contain such elements in it as are contrary to nature and offend human reason, so that a sensible person would find it impossible to believe in them. A true faith in its pristine purity is absolutely free from such supernatural and irrational elements. It is always at a later time that those who hanker for the supernatural interpolate into it supernatural and miraculous elements. I am sincerely convinced about Islam that it is absolutely free from such strange stories and unnatural and irrational mysteries. May God save us from such mystery worshipers!

The Qur'ān and Science
[From Syed Ahmad Khān, *Akhari Madamin,* p. 84]

The Qur'ān does not prove that the earth is stationary, nor does it prove that the earth is in motion. Similarly it can not be proved from the Qur'ān that the sun is in motion, nor can it be proved from it that the sun is stationary. The Holy Qur'ān was not concerned with these problems of astronomy; because the progress in human knowledge was to decide such matters itself. The Qur'ān had a much higher and a far nobler purpose in view. It would have been tantamount to confusing the simple Bedouins by speaking to them about such matters and to throwing into perplexity even the learned, whose knowledge and experience had not yet made the necessary progress, by discussing such problems. The real purpose of a religion is to improve morality; by raising such questions that purpose would have been jeopardized. In spite of all this I am fully convinced that the Work of God and the Word of God can never be antagonistic to each other; we may, through the fault of our knowledge, sometimes make mistakes in understanding the meaning of the Word.

Western Education
[From a letter to Mawlawi Tasadduq, in *Sir Syed ke chand nadir khutut*]

I have been accused by people, who do not understand, of being disloyal to the culture of Islam, even to Islam itself. There are men who say that I have become a Christian. All this I have drawn upon myself because I advocate the introduction of a new system of education which will not neglect the Islamic basis of our culture, nor, for that matter, the teaching of Islamic theology itself, but which will surely take account of the changed conditions in this land. Today there are no Muslim rulers to patronize those who are well versed in the old Arabic and Persian learning. The new rulers insist upon a knowledge of their language for all advancement in their services and in some of the independent professions like practising law as well. If the Muslims do not take to the system of education introduced by the British, they will not only remain a backward community but will sink lower and lower until there will be no hope of recovery left to them. Is this at all a pleasing prospect? Can we serve the cause of Islam in this way? Shall we then be able to ward off the obliteration of all that we hold dear for any length of time?

If the choice were to lie between giving up Islam itself and saving ourselves from apostasy, I should have unhesitatingly chosen the latter even if it had meant utter destruction for myself and my people. That, however, is not the choice. The adoption of the new system of education does not mean the renunciation of Islam. It means its protection. We are justly proud of the achievements of our forefathers in the fields of learning and culture. We should, however, remember that these achievements were possible only because they were willing to act upon the teachings of the Prophet upon whom be peace and blessings of God. He said that knowledge is the heritage of the believer, and that he should acquire it wherever he can find it. He also said that the Muslims should seek knowledge even if they have to go to China to find it. It is obvious that the Prophet was not referring to theological knowledge in these sayings; China at that time was one of the most civilized countries of the world, but it was a non-Muslim country and could not teach the Muslims anything about their own religion. Islam, Islamic culture, and the Muslims themselves prospered as long as the Prophet was followed in respect of these teachings; when we ceased to take interest in the knowledge of others, we began to decline in every respect. Did the early Muslims not take to Greek learning avidly? Did this in any respect undermine their loyalty to Islam?

It is not only because the British are today our rulers, and we have to recognize this fact if we are to survive, that I am advocating the adoption of their system of education, but also because Europe has made such remarkable progress in science that it would be suicidal not to make an effort to acquire it. Already the leeway between our knowledge and that of Europe is too great. If we go on with our present obstinacy in neglecting it, we shall be left far behind. How can we remain true Muslims or serve Islam, if we sink into ignorance? The knowledge of yesterday is often the ignorance of tomorrow, because knowledge and ignorance are, in this context, comparative terms. The truth of Islam will shine the more brightly if its followers are well educated, familiar with the highest in the knowledge of the world; it will come under an eclipse if its followers are ignorant and backward.

The Muslims have nothing to fear from the adoption of the new education if they simultaneously hold steadfast to their faith, because Islam is not irrational superstition; it is a rational religion which can march hand in hand with the growth of human knowledge. Any fear to the contrary betrays lack of faith in the truth of Islam.

The Indian National Congress
[From Syed Ahmad Khān, *Akhari Madamin,* pp. 46–50]

Long before the idea of founding the Indian National Congress was mooted, I had given thought to the matter whether representative government is suited to the conditions of India. I studied John Stuart Mill's views in support of representative government. He has dealt with this matter exceedingly well in great detail. I reached the conclusion that the first requisite of a representative government is that the voters should possess the highest degree of homogeneity. In a form of government which depends for its functioning upon majorities, it is necessary that the people should have no differences in the matter of nationality, religion, ways of living, customs, mores, culture, and historical traditions. These things should be common among a people to enable them to run a representative government properly. Only when such homogeneity is present can representative government work or prove beneficial. It should not even be thought of when these conditions do not exist.

In a country like India where homogeneity does not exist in any one of these fields, the introduction of representative government can not produce any beneficial results; it can only result in interfering with the peace and prosperity of the land. I sincerely hope that whichever party comes into power in Great Britain—be they the Conservatives, the Liberals, the Unionists, or the Radicals—they will remember that India is a continent; it is not a small and homogeneous country like England, Scotland, Wales, or Ireland. India is inhabited by different peoples, each one of whom is numerically large and different from the others in its culture, its moral code, its social organization, its political outlook, its religion, its physique, and its historical associations. These peoples have never been united since the downfall of the Muslim empire. Instead of being able to organize some other form of government they have just indulged in mutual fighting and internecine wars. . . . All the difficulties with which Ireland has been faced are due to the fact that the British are the rulers and the Irish are the ruled, and the two peoples are different from each other . . . and yet there is great resemblance between the two; they have the same complexion, their religions are not so different; they can intermarry; their cultures are similar; so are their mores. . . .

The aims and objects of the Indian National Congress are based upon an ignorance of history and present-day realities; they do not take into consideration that India is inhabited by different nationalities; they presuppose that the Muslims, the Marathas, the Brahmins, the Kshatriyas, the Banias, the Sudras, the Sikhs, the Bengalis, the Madrasis, and the Peshawaris can all be treated alike and all of them belong to the same nation. The Congress thinks that they profess the same religion, that they speak the same language, that their way of life and customs are the same, that their attitude to History is similar and is based upon the same historical traditions. . . . For the successful running of a democratic government it is essential that the majority should have the ability to govern not only themselves but also unwilling minorities. . . . I consider the experiment which the Indian National Congress wants to make fraught with dangers and suffering for all the nationalities of India, specially for the Muslims. The Muslims are in a minority, but they are a highly united minority. At least traditionally they are prone to take the sword in hand when the majority oppresses them. If this happens, it will bring about disasters greater than the ones which came in the wake of the happenings of 1857. . . . The Congress cannot rationally prove its claim to represent the opinions, ideals, and aspirations of the Muslims.

THE MUSLIM SEARCH FOR FREEDOM

After the death of Sir Syed Ahmad Khān, Muslim leaders from the Alīgarh school maintained the policy of cooperation with the British; but by its very nature such a policy could not endure for long. Though years of constructive effort had improved the position of the Muslims, there was still a good deal of ground to cover before they could reach the level of educational and economic progress already achieved by the Hindus. The Muslims became increasingly conscious of the fact that mere loyalty to the British could not meet their needs. They had to organize if they were to make their voice heard by the government and the other communities of India.

Muslim suspicions of the Indian National Congress were not allayed by the fact that its control had passed from the hands of the liberals and moderate elements into those of the Maratha leader Tilak, whose anti-Muslim opinions and activities were well-known. The partition of Bengal (1905) gave the Muslims of East Bengal a majority in the newly constituted province of East Bengal and Assam, where they could develop the resources of a Muslim majority area to their advantage. Vehement Hindu opposition to the partition seemed to Muslims additional evidence that the Hindus were reluctant to part with their own power and influence. The Muslims had also been alarmed by the growing hostility shown by Hindu revivalist movements like the Ārya Samāj and the Mārātha glorification of Shivaji's rebellion against the Mughal empire. All these factors led them to establish the All-India Muslim League in 1906. Despite Muslim opposition to the introduction of representative institutions, it was already clear that the British could not resist Hindu pressure in this direction indefinitely. Besides, British elections had brought into office a liberal government in 1905, and some change in the Indian system of government was expected. The Muslims, therefore, sent a deputation to the Governor-General, Lord Minto, stressing their fears lest representative institutions be extended without any safeguards to protect Muslim interests. The deputation succeeded in getting from the Governor-General a promise of separate electorates for the Muslims. This was to remain the cornerstone of Muslim policy as long as British rule lasted on the subcontinent. Acceptance of the principle of separate electorates was the first official recognition on the part of the British that the Muslims and the Hindus were not a single people.

At this point Muslim policy entered a new phase. The Muslims began to be stirred again by dreams of freedom but were still apprehensive lest one form of domination be exchanged for another. They therefore continued to look for legal and constitutional safeguards, until the goal of a separate state for Muslims became clearer and better defined. In the meantime Muslims felt their way along amidst much confusion of thought and difference of opinion. The most important figures of this period are Iqbāl and Muhammad Alī. In the religious field the tendency to bring the interpretation of Islam into line with contemporary knowledge gained momentum and produced, among a host of less-known authors, Amīr Alī, who became famous for his *The Spirit of Islam.*

MUHAMMAD IQBĀL: POET AND PHILOSOPHER OF THE ISLAMIC REVIVAL

Sir Syed had brought rationalism and the desire for knowledge and progress to the Indian Muslims; Iqbāl brought them inspiration and a philosophy. Next to the Qur'ān, there is no single influence upon the consciousness of the Pakistani intelligentsia so powerful as Iqbāl's poetry. In his own time it kindled the enthusiasm of Muslim intellectuals for the values of Islam, and rallied the whole Muslim community once again to the banner of their faith. For this reason Iqbāl is looked upon today as the spiritual founder of Pakistan.

Muhammad Iqbāl (1873–1938) was born at Sialkot in the Punjab in the year 1873. His parents, devout and pious Muslims, inculcated in him the teachings of Islam. Eventually Iqbāl was sent to the Government College at Lahore where he graduated in 1899 and was appointed a lecturer in philosophy. After studying philosophy at Cambridge and in Germany, and having also qualified as a barrister-at-law, he came back to his teaching at Lahore in 1908. Two years later, in order to free himself from this type of service to a foreign government, he gave up teaching and started the private practice of law. Still, his heart was not in the legal profession, and he undertook only enough work to keep himself in modest comfort. For the most part, his time was spent in study and writing. It was not long before he came to be recognized as a thinker of importance and the greatest Urdu poet of his time.

While in Europe, Iqbāl had come into contact with the leading schools of Western philosophy, and was particularly influenced by Nietzsche and Bergson. These influences are evident in his own thought, and yet the main source of Iqbāl's ideas is the Islamic tradition itself. His knowledge of Islamic thought and literature, especially of the Persian classics, was profound. Above all he was indebted to the great mystic thinker of Turkey, Jalāl-u'd-dīn Rūmī, whom he quotes again and again with deep appreciation. Iqbāl had an aversion, however, for those Sufis who tended toward a mystical quietism. Their philosophy of inaction he held responsible for the decadence of Islam. Action is life and inaction is death, he taught. In strife with evil, not in the peace of the grave, lies the true meaning of human life. Iqbāl had a burning conviction that Islam provided the remedy for many of the world's ills. The division of humanity into national and racial groups, according to him, was the greatest curse of the day. Injustice in any form was abhorrent and had to be fought. The evils of colonialism, the tyranny of the landlord over the unprotected tenant, the cupidity of capitalism, and the exploitation of the resources of a weaker people by a stronger nation, were all hateful in his eyes. The real remedy lay, according to him, in the cultivation of the innate greatness of the human self, so that realizing its real qualities, it would become incapable of meaner tendencies like greed, injustice, and fear. Such development of the Self, he insisted, is possible only through a true understanding of the relationship between God and man. Even God does not demand the destruction of the Self; He is desirous that the Self should be developed to its fullest capacity. The Self, however, finds its fullest meaning only through identification with the life of the community, and for that purpose the community should be organized on a righteous basis. Such a community is the community of Islam, because its sole foundation is the acceptance of God and the Law, which is the criterion of righteousness. As Islam recognizes no superiority of birth or rank or wealth within its bosom and judges excellence by righteousness alone, the fullest cultivation of the Self is possible within its fold. This community, moreover, is not limited by time or space, according to the Islamic doctrine that all truth from God revealed anywhere at any time is Islam, Muhammad being the final recipient of this truth in its most perfect form. Such a community was not meant to be fragmented into nations. The means by which the Self can develop to its full height is Love, which is the Sufic word for the ecstatic devotion to God. Whereas human reason is limited by time and space, Love is not; it is therefore capable of creating immutable qualities in the Self. Iqbāl thinks that real Time is not the linear time of which we have a feeling, nor the limited time of the scientist, because he must think in terms of transient and limited space, but that it is higher and everlasting. It is infinite and eternal, indeed an attribute of God himself. It is in this Time that the Self finds its ultimate fulfillment.

Realizing the importance of his message to the whole Islamic world Iqbāl began to write in Persian, which is more widely understood and read in the Muslim world than Urdu. Urdu itself was not his mother tongue but had been the literary language of the Punjab for more than a century. In Urdu, he ranks high as a philosophic poet and is considered next only to Ghalib (1796–1869) in charm, depth, and richness of ideas.

Unfortunately Iqbāl's poetry is difficult to translate; even in the excellent translations reproduced below, they lose a good deal of the charm and force of the original.

In 1922, Iqbāl accepted a knighthood conferred upon him in recognition of his greatness as a poet, but only on the understanding that it was not a reward for any service he had rendered the government. He also somewhat halfheartedly participated in the political activities of his province and local community. Elected to the provincial legislature, he participated in its debates, but made no great mark as a legislator. In addition he served as a delegate to the Round Table Conference in London in 1931. Temperamentally, he was not suited to politics, and his only real contribution in this field was made as president of the All-India Muslim League session of 1930, when he declared that he would like to see the Northwestern areas, where Muslims were in a majority, constituted a separate state. Though his ideas on the subject were still vague and aroused no immediate response, this was the first time that the idea of a separate state for the Muslims had been put forward from the platform of a political party.

Toward the end of his life Iqbāl became convinced that the Muslims in India were threatened with extermination. He called the endless succession of Hindu-Muslim riots a virtual civil war, which he foresaw would develop in magnitude as time passed. Feeling that the Muslims were unprepared for a final showdown, ill-organized and without a leader, he singled out Jinnāh as the one person capable of serving the Muslims and in whose capacity and leadership he had the fullest confidence and faith.

Iqbāl died in 1938, deeply mourned by the Muslims in India and by Muslims in other lands as well. Today admirers come from afar to visit his tomb, and Pakistan recognizes him as its national poet. One of the earliest actions of the government of Pakistan was to found an academy for the study of his teachings.

MUHAMMAD IQBĀL

Fate

[From Kiernan, *Poems from Iqbal*, p. 64]

Satan
Oh God, Creator! I did not hate your Adam,
That captive of Far-and-Near and Swift-and-Slow;

[199]

And what presumption could refuse to *You*
Obedience? If I would not kneel to him,
The cause was Your own foreordaining will.

God
When did that mystery dawn on you? before,
Or after your sedition?

Satan
After, oh brightness
Whence all the glory of all being flows.

God (to His angels)
See what a groveling nature taught him this
Fine theorem! His not kneeling, he pretends,
Belonged to My foreordinance; gives his freedom
Necessity's base title;—wretch! his own
Consuming fire he calls a wreath of smoke.

Freedom
[From Kiernan, *Poems from Iqbal,* p. 90]

The freeman's veins are firm as veins of granite;
The bondman's weak as tendrils of the vine,
And his heart too despairing and repining—
The free heart has life's tingling breath to fan it.
Quick pulse, clear vision, are the freeman's treasure;
The unfree, to kindness and affection dead,
Has no more wealth than tears of his own shedding
And those glib words he has in such good measure.

Bondman and free can never come to accord:
One is the heavens' lackey, one their lord.

The Self

In order to stir the Muslims from their lethargy and despair, in the following poems from *The Secrets of the Self* Iqbāl extols a positive, active attitude to the world, rather than the world-negating quietism preached by certain Sufis. He also emphasizes the importance of the individual in the world ("The Self").

[200]

By "desire" Iqbāl meant primarily the striving after ideals as the source of man's activity and progress.

[From Iqbāl, *The Secrets of the Self*, pp. 16, 18–19]

The form of existence is an effect of the Self,
Whatsoever thou seest is a secret of the Self,
When the Self awoke to consciousness,
It revealed the universe of Thought.
A hundred worlds are hidden in its essence:
Self-affirmation brings Not-self to light.

. . . .

Subject, object, means, and causes—
All these are forms which it assumes for the purpose of action.
The Self rises, kindles, falls, glows, breathes,
Burns, shines, walks, and flies.
The spaciousness of time is its arena,
Heaven is a billow of the dust on its road.
From its rose-planting the world abounds in roses;
Night is born of its sleep, day springs from its waking.

Desire

[From Iqbāl, *The Secrets of the Self*, pp. 23, 25–27]

Life is preserved by purpose:
Because of the goal its caravan-bell tinkles.
Life is latent in seeking,
Its origin is hidden in desire.
Keep desire alive in thy heart,
Lest thy little dust become a tomb.

. . . .

'Tis desire that enriches life,
And the mind is a child of its womb.
What are social organization, customs, and laws?
What is the secret of the novelties of science?
A desire which realized itself by its own strength
And burst forth from the heart and took shape.

. . . .

Rise intoxicated with the wine of an ideal,
An ideal shining as the dawn
A blazing fire to all that is other than God,
An ideal higher than Heaven—
Winning, captivating, enchanting men's hearts;
A destroyer of ancient falsehood,
Fraught with turmoil, an embodiment of the Last Day.
We live by forming ideals,
We glow with the sunbeams of desire!

Love

Iqbāl uses Love for the ecstatic love of God, not in any quietist, passive sense, but as the source of the highest inspiration for true knowledge and effective, righteous action.
[From Iqbāl, *The Secrets of the Self,* pp. 28–29]

The luminous point whose name is the Self
Is the life-spark beneath our dust.
By love it is made more lasting,
More living, more burning, more glowing.
From love proceeds the radiance of its being
And the development of its unknown possibilities.
Its nature gathers fire from love,
Love instructs it to illumine the world.
Love fears neither sword nor dagger,
Love is not born of water and air and earth.
Love makes peace and war in the world,
Love is the fountain of life, love is the flashing sword of death.
The hardest rocks are shivered by love's glance:
Love of God at last becomes wholly God.

Time

Iqbāl believed that the conception of time as finite and limited induced a passive attitude toward life; if time itself is limited, nothing that exists in time can be of everlasting value and all that is achieved by human action must perish. To combat this tendency Iqbāl held that time is eternal and, therefore, human action has a lasting importance. This idea militated against both inaction and mere expediency.

[From Iqbāl, *The Secrets of the Self*, pp. 137–38]

The cause of time is not the revolution of the sun:
Time is everlasting, but the sun does not last forever.
Time is joy and sorrow, festival and fast;
Time is the secret of moonlight and sunlight.
Thou hast extended time, like space,
And distinguished yesterday from tomorrow.
Thou hast fled, like a scent, from thine own garden;
Thou hast made thy prison with thine own hand.
Our time which has neither beginning nor end,
Blossoms from the flower bed of our mind.
To know its root quickens the living with new life:
Its being is more splendid than the dawn.
Life is of time, and time is of life.

Muslims Are One in Soul

In the following passages from his *Mysteries of Selflessness* Iqbāl attempts to correct the overindividualistic effect of his previous work, *The Secrets of the Self*, by emphasizing the Muslim community. Reflecting the concern of Muslims at that time over the fate of the Ottoman empire and other Muslim lands conquered or threatened by European powers, Iqbāl propagates pan-Islamism based on the doctrine of an indivisible Muslim community. The Muslims are united throughout space and time by a common faith and a common history.

[From Iqbāl, *The Mysteries of Selflessness*, p. 20]

A common aim shared by the multitude
Is unity which, when it is mature,
Forms the Community; the many live
Only by virtue of the single bond.
The Muslim's unity from natural faith
Derives, and this the Prophet taught us,
So that we lit a lantern on truth's way.
This pearl was fished from his unfathomed sea,
And of his bounty we are one in soul.

[203]

Let not this unity go from our hands,
And we endure to all eternity.

Muslims Profess No Fatherland
[From Iqbāl, *The Mysteries of Selflessness,* p. 29]

Our Essence is not bound to any place;
The vigor of our wine is not contained
In any bowl; Chinese and Indian
Alike the shard that constitutes our jar,
Turkish and Syrian alike the clay
Forming our body; neither is our heart
Of India, or Syria, or Rum,
Nor any fatherland do we profess
Except Islam.

The Concept of Country Divides Humanity
[From Iqbāl, *The Mysteries of Selflessness,* p. 32]

Now brotherhood has been so cut to shreds
That in the stead of community
The country has been given pride of place
In men's allegiance and constructive work;
The country is the darling of their hearts,
And wide humanity is whittled down
Into dismembered tribes. . . .
Vanished is humankind; there but abide
The disunited nations. Politics
Dethroned religion. . . .

The Muslim Community Is Unbounded in Time
[From Iqbāl, *The Mysteries of Selflessness,* pp. 36–37]

. . . When the burning brands
Of time's great revolution ring our mead,
Then Spring returns. The mighty power of Rome,
Conqueror and ruler of the world entire,
Sank into small account; the golden glass
Of the Sassanians was drowned in blood;

Broken the brilliant genius of Greece;
Egypt too failed in the great test of time,
Her bones lie buried neath the pyramids.
Yet still the voice of the muezzin rings
Throughout the earth, still the Community
Of World-Islam maintains its ancient forms.
Love is the universal law of life,
Mingling the fragmentary elements
Of a disordered world. Through our hearts' glow
Love lives, irradiated by the spark
There is no god but God.

The Importance of History
[From Iqbāl, *The Mysteries of Selflessness*, pp. 60–62]

Like to a child is a community
Newborn, an infant in its mother's arms;
All unaware of Self. . . .
But when with energy it falls upon
The world's great labors, stable then becomes
This new-won consciousness; it raises up
A thousand images, and casts them down;
So it createth its own history. . . .
The record of the past illuminates
The conscience of a people; memory
Of past achievements makes it Self-aware;
But if that memory fades, and is forgot,
The folk again is lost in nothingness. . . .
What thing is history, O Self-unaware?
A fable? Or a legendary tale?
Nay, 'tis the thing that maketh thee aware
Of thy true Self, alert unto the task,
A seasoned traveler; this is the source
Of the soul's ardor, this the nerves that knit
The body of the whole community.
This whets thee like a dagger on its sheath,
To dash thee in the face of all the world. . . .
If thou desirest everlasting life,

Break not the thread between the past and now
And the far future. What is Life? A wave
Of consciousness of continuity,
A gurgling wine that flames the revelers.

Muslims Are Bound Together by Faith Alone
[From Iqbāl, *The Mysteries of Selflessness*, pp. 75–76]

The bond of Turk and Arab is not ours,
The link that binds us is no fetter's chain
Of ancient lineage; our hearts are bound
To the beloved Prophet of Hejaz,
And to each other are we joined through him.
Our common thread is simple loyalty
To him alone; the rapture of his wine
Alone our eyes entrances; from what time
This glad intoxication with his love
Raced in our blood, the old is set ablaze
In new creation. As the blood that flows
Within a people's veins, so is his love
Sole substance of our solidarity.
Love dwells within the spirit, lineage
The flesh inhabits; stronger far than race
And common ancestry is love's firm cord.
True loverhood must overleap the bounds
Of lineage, transcend Arabia
And Persia. Love's community is like
The light of God; whatever being we
Possess, from its existence is derived.
"None seeketh when or where God's light was born;
What need of warp and woof, God's robe to spin?" [1]
Who suffereth his foot to wear the chains
Of clime and ancestry is unaware
How *He begat not, neither was begot.*[2]

[1] A quotation from Jalāl-u'd-dīn Rūmī.
[2] One of the most repeated verses of the Qur'ān.

[206]

The Need for Understanding Islam in the Light of Modern Knowledge

[From Iqbāl, *Reconstruction of Religious Thought in Islam*, pp. 7–8]

During the last five hundred years religious thought in Islam has been practically stationary. There was a time when European thought received inspiration from the world of Islam. The most remarkable phenomenon of modern history, however, is the enormous rapidity with which the world of Islam is spiritually moving towards the West. There is nothing wrong in this movement, for European culture, on its intellectual side, is only a further development of some of the most important phases of the culture of Islam. Our only fear is that the dazzling exterior of European culture may arrest our movement and we may fail to reach the true inwardness of that culture. During all the centuries of our intellectual stupor Europe has been seriously thinking on the great problems in which the philosophers and scientists of Islam were so keenly interested. Since the Middle Ages, when the schools of Muslim theology were completed, infinite advance has taken place in the domain of human thought and experience. The extension of man's power over nature has given him a new faith and a fresh sense of superiority over the forces that constitute his environment. New points of view have been suggested, old problems have been restated in the light of fresh experience, and new problems have arisen. It seems as if the intellect of man is outgrowing its own most fundamental categories—time, space, and causality. With the advance of scientific thought even our concept of intelligibility is undergoing a change. The theory of Einstein has brought a new vision of the universe and suggests new ways of looking at the problems common to both religion and philosophy. No wonder then that the younger generation of Islam in Asia and Africa demand a fresh orientation of their faith. With the reawakening of Islam, therefore, it is necessary to examine, in an independent spirit, what Europe has thought and how far the conclusions reached by her can help us in the revision and, if necessary, reconstruction, of theological thought in Islam. Besides this it is not possible to ignore the generally antireligious and especially anti-Islamic propaganda in Central Asia which has already crossed the Indian frontier.

The Role of Religion in the World of Today
[From Iqbāl, *Reconstruction of Religious Thought in Islam,* pp. 186–88]

Thus, wholly overshadowed by the results of his intellectual activity, the modern man has ceased to live soulfully, i.e., from within. In the domain of thought he is living in open conflict with himself; and in the domain of economic and political life he is living in open conflict with others. He finds himself unable to control his ruthless egoism and his infinite gold-hunger which is gradually killing all higher striving in him and bringing him nothing but life-weariness. Absorbed in the "fact," that is to say, the optically present source of sensation, he is entirely cut off from the unplumbed depths of his own being. In the wake of his systematic materialism has at last come that paralysis of energy which Huxley apprehended and deplored. The condition of things in the East is no better. The technique of medieval mysticism by which religious life, in its higher manifestations, developed itself both in the East and in the West has now practically failed. And in the Muslim East it has, perhaps, done far greater havoc than anywhere else. Far from reintegrating the forces of the average man's inner life, and thus preparing him for participation in the march of history, it has taught him a false renunciation and made him perfectly contented with his ignorance and spiritual thralldom. No wonder then that the modern Muslim in Turkey, Egypt, and Persia is led to seek fresh sources of energy in the creation of new loyalties, such as patriotism and nationalism which Nietzsche described as "sickness and unreason," and "the strongest force against culture." Disappointed of a purely religious method of spiritual renewal which alone brings us into touch with the everlasting fountain of life and power by expanding our thought and emotion, the modern Muslim fondly hopes to unlock fresh sources of energy by narrowing down his thought and emotion. Modern atheistic socialism, which possesses all the fervor of a new religion, has a broader outlook; but having received its philosophical basis from the Hegelians of the left wing, it rises in revolt against the very source which could have given it strength and purpose. Both nationalism and atheistic socialism, at least in the present state of human adjustments, must draw upon the psychological forces of hate, suspicion, and resentment which tend to impoverish the soul of man and close up his hidden sources of spiritual energy. Neither the technique of medieval mysticism nor nationalism nor atheistic socialism can cure the ills of a despairing humanity. Surely the present moment is one of great crisis in the history of modern culture. The modern world stands in need of biological renewal. And religion, which in its higher manifestations is neither dogma, nor priesthood, nor ritual, can alone ethically prepare the modern man for the burden of the great responsibility which the advancement of modern science necessarily involves, and restore to him that attitude of faith which makes him capable of winning a personality here and retaining it hereafter. It is only by rising to a fresh vision of his origin and future, his whence and whither, that man will eventually triumph over a society motivated by an inhuman competition, and a civilization which has lost its spiritual unity by its inner conflict of religious and political values.

Islam and Human Dignity

Iqbāl opposed the way of life of the West which according to him looked upon man as "a *thing* to be exploited and not as a *personality* to be developed." He thought that Islam, freed from the shackles of theological thought of the previous ages, was capable of giving a better deal to man by emphasizing its doctrines of equality and regard for human dignity.

[From Iqbāl, *Speeches and Statements. . . .* , pp. 52–56]

The present struggle in India is sometimes described as India's revolt against the West. I do not think it is a revolt against the West; for the people of India are demanding the very institutions which the West stands for. . . . Educated urban India demands democracy. The minorities, feeling themselves as distinct cultural units and fearing that their very existence is at stake, demand safeguards, which the majority community, for obvious reasons, refuses to concede. The majority community pretends to believe in a nationalism theoretically correct, if we start from Western premises, belied by facts, if we look to India. Thus the real parties to the present struggle in India are not England and India, but the majority community and the minorities of India which can ill afford to accept the principle of Western democracy until it is properly modified to suit the actual conditions of life in India.

Nor do Mahātmā Gāndhi's political methods signify a revolt in the psychological sense. These methods arise out of a contact of two opposing types of world-consciousness, Western and Eastern. The Western man's mental texture is chronological in character. He lives and moves and has his being in time. The Eastern man's world-consciousness is nonhistorical. To the Western man things gradually become; they have a past, present, and future. To the Eastern man they are immediately rounded off, timeless, purely present. That is why Islam which sees in the time-movement a symbol of reality appeared as an intruder in the static world-pictures of Asia. The British as a Western people cannot but conceive political reform in India as a systematic process of gradual evolution. Mahātmā Gāndhi as an Eastern man sees in this attitude nothing more than an ill-conceived unwillingness to part with power and tries all sorts of destructive negations to achieve immediate attainment. Both are elementally incapable of understanding each other. The result is the appearance of a revolt.

These phenomena, however, are merely premonitions of a coming storm, which is likely to sweep over the whole of India and the rest of Asia. This is the inevitable outcome of a wholly political civilization which has looked upon man as a *thing* to be exploited and not as a *personality* to be developed and enlarged by purely cultural forces. The peoples of Asia are bound to rise against the acquisitive economy which the West has developed and imposed on the nations of the East. Asia cannot comprehend modern Western capitalism with its undisciplined individualism. The faith which you represent recognizes the worth of the individual, and disciplines him to give away his all to the service of God and man. Its possibilities are not yet exhausted. It can still create a new world where the social rank of man is not determined by his caste or color, or the amount of dividend he earns, but by the kind of life he lives; where the poor tax the rich, where human society is founded not on the equality of stomachs but on the equality of spirits, where an untouchable can marry the daughter of a king, where private ownership is a trust, and where capital cannot be allowed to accumulate so as to dominate the real producer of wealth. This superb idealism of your faith, however, needs emancipation from the medieval fancies of theologians and legists. Spiritually we are living in a prison-house of thoughts and emotions which during the course of centuries we have woven round ourselves. And be it further said to the shame of us—men of [the] older generation —that we have failed to equip the younger generation for the economic, political, and even religious crises that the present age is likely to bring. The whole community needs a complete overhauling of its present mentality in order that it may again become capable of feeling the urge of fresh desires and ideals. The Indian Muslim has long ceased to explore the depths of his own inner life. The result is that he has ceased to live in the full glow and color of life, and is consequently in danger of an unmanly compromise with forces which, he is made to think, he cannot vanquish in open conflict. He who desires to change an unfavorable environment must undergo a complete transformation of his inner being. God changeth not the condition of a people until they themselves take the initiative to change their condition by constantly illuminating the zone of their daily activity in the light of a definite ideal. Nothing can be achieved without a firm faith in the independence of one's own inner life. This faith alone keeps a people's eye fixed on their goal and saves them from perpetual vacillation. . . . The flame of life cannot be borrowed from others; it must be kindled in the temple of one's own soul.

A Separate State for the Muslims

Iqbāl's presidential address before the All-India Muslim League, Allahabad, December 29, 1930, from which this reading is taken, is his most important political statement in relation to the later establishment of a separate state for the Muslims in India. His argument is that a polity making religion a purely private matter, as in European states, dooms religion. Islam, on the other hand, is organically connected with the social order and in India needs an autonomous area for its full expression and development.

[From Iqbāl, *Speeches and Statements* . . . , pp. 3–12, 34–36]

It cannot be denied that Islam, regarded as an ethical ideal plus a certain kind of polity—by which expression I mean a social structure regulated by a legal system and animated by a specific ethical ideal—has been the chief formative factor in the life-history of the Muslims of India. It has furnished those basic emotions and loyalties which gradually unify scattered individuals and groups and finally transform them into a well-defined people. Indeed it is no exaggeration to say that India is perhaps the only country in the world where Islam, as a people-building force, has worked at its best. . . . The ideas set free by European political thinking, however, are now rapidly changing the outlook of the present generation of Muslims both in India and outside India. Our younger men, inspired by these ideas, are anxious to see them as living forces in their own countries, without any critical appreciation of the facts which have determined their evolution in Europe. . . . Islam does not bifurcate the unity of man into an irreconcilable duality of spirit and matter. In Islam God and the universe, spirit and matter, Church and State, are organic to each other. Man is not the citizen of a profane world to be renounced in the interest of a world of spirit situated elsewhere. To Islam matter is spirit realizing itself in space and time. Europe uncritically accepted the duality of spirit and matter probably from Manichaean thought. Her best thinkers are realizing this initial mistake today, but her statesmen are indirectly forcing the world to accept it as an unquestionable dogma. It is, then, this mistaken separation of spiritual and temporal which has largely influenced European religious and political thought and has resulted practically in the total exclusion of Christianity from the life of European states. The result is a set of mutually ill-adjusted states dominated by interests not human but national. . . . In the world of Islam we have a universal polity whose fundamentals are believed to have been revealed, but whose structure, owing to our legists' want of contact with [the] modern world, stands today in need of renewed power by fresh adjustments. I do not know what will be the final fate of the national idea in the world of Islam. Whether Islam will assimilate and transform it, as it has assimilated and transformed before many ideas expressive of a different spirit, or allow a radical transformation of its own structure by the force of this idea, is hard to predict. Professor Wensinck of Leiden (Holland) wrote to me the other day: "It seems to me that Islam is entering upon a crisis through which Christianity has been passing for more than a century. The great difficulty is how to save the foundations of religion when many antiquated notions have to be given up. It seems to me scarcely possible to state what the outcome will be for Christianity, still less what it will be for Islam." At the present moment the national idea is racializing the outlook of Muslims, and thus materially counteracting the humanizing work of Islam. And the growth of racial consciousness may mean the growth of standards different and even opposed to the standards of Islam. . . .

What, then, is the problem and its implications? Is religion a private affair? Would you like to see Islam, as a moral and political ideal, meeting the same fate in the world of Islam as Christianity has already met in Europe? Is it possible to retain Islam as an ethical ideal and to reject it as a polity in favor of national polities, in which a religious attitude is not permitted to play any part? This question becomes of special importance in India where the Muslims happen to be in a minority. The proposition that religion is a private individual experience is not surprising on the lips of a European. In Europe the conception of Christianity as a monastic order, renouncing the world of matter and fixing its gaze entirely on the world of spirit led, by a logical process of thought, to the view embodied in this proposition. The nature of the Prophet's religious experience, as disclosed in the Qur'ān, however, is wholly different. It is not mere experience in the sense of a purely biological event, happening inside the experient and necessitating no reactions on his social environment. It is individual experience creative of a social order. Its immediate outcome is the fundamentals of a polity with implicit legal concepts whose civic significance cannot be belittled merely because their origin is revelational. The religious ideal of Islam, therefore, is organically related to the social order which it has created. The rejection of the one will eventually involve the rejection of the other. Therefore the construction of a polity on national lines, if it means a displacement of the Islamic principle of solidarity, is simply unthinkable to a Muslim. This is a matter which at the present moment directly concerns the Muslims of India. "Man," says Renan, "is enslaved neither by his race, nor by his religion, nor by the course of rivers, nor by the direction of mountain ranges. A great aggregation of men, sane of mind and warm of heart, creates a moral consciousness which is called a nation." Such a formation is quite possible, though it involves the long and arduous process of practically remaking men and furnishing them with a fresh emotional equipment. It might have been a fact in India if the teaching of Kabīr and the Divine Faith of Akbar had seized the imagination of the masses of this country. Experience, however, shows that the various caste-units and religious units in India have shown no inclination to sink their respective individualties in a larger whole. Each group is intensely jealous of its collective existence. The formation of the kind of moral consciousness which constitutes the essence of a nation in Renan's sense demands a price which the peoples of India are not prepared to pay. The unity of an Indian nation, therefore, must be sought, not in the negation but in the mutual harmony and cooperation of the many. True statesmanship cannot ignore facts, however unpleasant they may be. The only practical course is not to assume the existence of a state of things which does not exist, but to recognize facts

[213]

as they are, and to exploit them to our greatest advantage. . . . And it is on the discovery of Indian unity in this direction that the fate of India as well as Asia really depends. India is Asia in miniature. Part of her people have cultural affinities with nations in the east and part with nations in the middle and west of Asia. If an effective principle of cooperation is discovered in India, it will bring peace and mutual goodwill to this ancient land which has suffered so long, more because of her situation in historic space than because of any inherent incapacity of her people. And it will at the same time solve the entire political problem of Asia.

It is, however, painful to observe that our attempts to discover such a principle of internal harmony have so far failed. Why have they failed? Perhaps we suspect each other's intentions and inwardly aim at dominating each other. Perhaps in the higher interests of mutual cooperation, we cannot afford to part with the monopolies which circumstances have placed in our hands and conceal our egoism under the cloak of a nationalism, outwardly stimulating a large-hearted patriotism, but inwardly as narrow-minded as a caste or a tribe. Perhaps, we are unwilling to recognize that each group has a right to free development according to its own cultural traditions. But whatever may be the causes of our failure, I still feel hopeful. Events seem to be tending in the direction of some sort of internal harmony. And as far as I have been able to read the Muslim mind, I have no hesitation in declaring that if the principle that the Indian Muslim is entitled to full and free development on the lines of his own culture and tradition in his own Indian home-lands is recognized as the basis of a permanent communal settlement, he will be ready to stake his all for the freedom of India. The principle that each group is entitled to free development on its own lines is not inspired by any feeling of narrow communalism. There are communalisms and communalisms. A community which is inspired by feelings of ill-will toward other communities is low and ignoble. I entertain the highest respect for the customs, laws, religious, and social institutions of other communities. Nay, it is my duty according to the teaching of the Qur'ān, even to defend their places of worship, if need be. Yet I love the communal group which is the source of my life and behavior and which has formed me what I am by giving me its religion, its literature, its thought, its culture and thereby recreating its whole past as a living factor in my present consciousness. . . .

Communalism in its higher aspect, then, is indispensable to the formation of a harmonious whole in a country like India. The units of Indian society are not territorial as in European countries. India is a continent of human groups belonging to different races, speaking different languages and professing different religions. Their behavior is not at all determined by a common race-consciousness. Even the Hindus do not form a homogeneous group. The principle of European democracy cannot be applied to India without recognizing the fact of communal groups. The Muslim demand for the creation of a Muslim India within India is, therefore, perfectly justified. The resolution of the All-Parties Muslim Conference at Delhi, is, to my mind, wholly inspired by this noble ideal of a harmonious whole which, instead of stifling the respective individualities of its component wholes, affords them chances of fully working out the possibilities that may be latent in them. And I have no doubt that this House will emphatically endorse the Muslim demands embodied in this resolution. Personally, I would go further than the demands embodied in it. *I would like to see the Punjab, North-West Frontier Province, Sind and Baluchistan amalgamated into a single State. Self-government within the British empire or without the British empire, the formation of a consolidated North-West Indian Muslim State appears to me to be the final destiny of the Muslims, at least of North-West India.*[1]

MUSLIM UNITY OF WILL TO BE PROVIDED BY ISLAM

In conclusion I cannot but impress upon you that the present crisis in the history of India demands complete organization and unity of will and purpose in the Muslim community, both in your own interest as a community, and in the interest of India as a whole. The political bondage of India has been and is a source of infinite misery to the whole of Asia. It has suppressed the spirit of the East and wholly deprived her of that joy of self-expression which once made her the creator of a great and glorious culture. We have a duty towards India where we are destined to live and die. We have a duty towards Asia, especially Muslim Asia. And since 70 millions of Muslims in a single country constitute a far more valuable

[1] The italics are Dr. Qureshī's.

asset to Islam than all the countries of Muslim Asia put together, we must look at the Indian problem not only from the Muslim point of view but also from the standpoint of the Indian Muslim as such. Our duty towards Asia and India cannot be loyally performed without an organized will fixed on a definite purpose. In your own interest, as a political entity among other political entities of India, such an equipment is an absolute necessity. Our disorganized condition has already confused political issues vital to the life of the community. I am not hopeless of an intercommunal understanding, but I cannot conceal from you the feeling that in the near future our community may be called upon to adopt an independent line of action to cope with the present crisis. And an independent line of political action, in such a crisis, is possible only to a determined people, possessing a will focalized by a single purpose. Is it possible for you to achieve the organic wholeness of a unified will? Yes, it is. Rise above sectional interests and private ambitions, and learn to determine the value of your individual and collective action, however directed on material ends, in the light of the ideal which you are supposed to represent. Pass from matter to spirit. Matter is diversity; spirit is light, life and unity. One lesson I have learnt from the history of Muslims. At critical moments in their history it is Islam that has saved Muslims and not vice versa. If today you focus your vision on Islam and see inspiration from the ever-vitalizing idea embodied in it, you will be only reassembling your scattered forces, regaining your lost integrity, and thereby saving yourself from total destruction. One of the profoundest verses in the Holy Qur'ān teaches us that the birth and rebirth of the whole of humanity is like the birth of a single individual. Why cannot you who, as a people, can well claim to be the first practical exponents of this superb conception of humanity, live and move and have your being as a single individual? . . . In the words of the Qur'ān: "Hold fast to yourself; no one who erreth can hurt you, provided you are well guided."

MUHAMMAD ALĪ AND THE KHILĀFAT MOVEMENT

If Iqbāl was the philosopher of the new awakening of the Indian Muslims, Muhammad Alī (1879–1930) was its man of action. To Muslim political life he contributed a most vital asset—mass support. Hitherto politics had been the preserve of a few intellectuals; now popular opinion began to play a part in the determination of policy. Thus when Jinnāh later launched his campaign for Pakistan, it was the support given him by the Muslim masses which brought success, as well as the help of trained workers who had received their political baptism under Muhammad Alī in the Khilāfat Movement.

Muhammad Alī was born at Rampur, a small Muslim princely state in northern India. Following his education at Aligarh and Oxford, he entered the civil service of Baroda, which, at that time, was one of the most progressive Indian states. Gradually, however, his interest in public affairs and particularly in the welfare of his community drew him away from civil service. After starting an independent weekly review, the *Comrade,* which attracted the attention of educated Muslims, Muhammad Alī found himself engaged in politics. He was one of the original members of the Muslim League, and it was through his efforts that the founder of Pakistan, Muhammad Alī Jinnāh, was persuaded to join the League in 1913.

An ardent Muslim, Muhammad Alī's loyalty was not limited to Islam in India; the difficulties of Muslims anywhere in the world elicited his sympathy and active concern. In this he was a true representative of the ideals of Islam and the feelings of Indian Muslims. The European onslaught upon the Ottoman empire, beginning with the Italian occupation of Tripoli, the Balkan Wars, and the events leading up to the First World War created grave misgivings in the minds of the Indian Muslims regarding the future of the secular power of Islam in the world and the freedom of the Muslim peoples. They had themselves tasted the humiliation of subjugation and there was a great upsurge of sympathy among them for suffering Muslims elsewhere, as well as of antagonism toward the West and in particular Great Britain. These feelings were powerfully expressed and represented by Muhammad Alī.

When the First World War came, he saw that the Turks might be tempted to join the Germans in the hope of recovering the territories they had lost to Great Britain, especially Egypt. A long article of his in the *Comrade* entitled "The Choice of the Turks," begged the Allies to win over the Turks by making good the losses which had been inflicted upon the Ottoman empire despite its traditional friendship with Great Britain.

[217]

This article, though well intentioned, was so outspoken about the record of British relations with Turkey that it was proscribed by the government, and in spite of Muhammad Alī's earlier support of the Allied cause, his press, review, and Urdu daily, the *Hamdard,* were suppressed. Muhammad Alī himself was jailed.

The British, nevertheless, realized that the war between Britain and Turkey placed a great strain upon the loyalty of Indian Muslims to the British Empire. To allay Muslim fears Lloyd George stated in Parliament that it was not the intention of the British government to deprive the Turks of their homelands. When, despite these assurances, territories inhabited by the Turks, such as parts of Anatolia, were wrested from Turkey after the war (1920), Muslim opinion on the subcontinent was shocked. Even the release of Muhammad Alī did not allay mounting feeling over this betrayal, and he soon found himself in the forefront of popular agitation.

It was on the issue of the Caliphate (*Khilāfat*) that Muslim leaders felt they could most effectively appeal to the non-Muslim world including Great Britain. The Ottoman sultans had long claimed to be the caliphs, or supreme religious authority of the Muslim world, a claim never seriously challenged because, within the Ottoman empire, it was identified with the political sovereignty of the sultanate, and, outside the Ottoman empire, had no practical significance. But now that the Indian Muslims had lost their own liberty, they had reason to feel a strong emotional attachment to a caliph whom they could claim as their own sovereign, even though only in a nominal and religious sense. Indeed, before the First World War, prayers for the Turkish sultan had already come to be included in the Friday *Khutbah* (sermon) in the mosques of India.

The Indian Muslims, therefore, based their case for Turkey upon loyalty to the caliphate, arguing that in so far as it was necessary that the caliph should possess sufficient power to defend the vital interests of Islam, any further diminution in his territories would reduce the institution to a farce. Moreover it was necessary that the sacred places of Islam, Mecca and Medina, should be free from non-Muslim influence, and since the Sharif of Mecca, Husain, was merely a British puppet, he could not serve as true guardian of the sanctuaries. To Indian Muslims these arguments had a strong religious appeal, and the Khilāfat Movement quickly gathered momentum.

The time was ripe for a genuine mass movement in India. Gāndhi was now home from South Africa, having perfected his methods of passive resistance and nonviolent noncooperation. Believing that if the Hindus and Muslims joined forces they could seriously embarrass the government, he supported the Khilāfat Movement; and the Muslims, in turn, guided by Muhammad Alī, accepted Gāndhi's leadership. As the movement gathered strength, Hindus and Muslims fraternized and it seemed that communal unity had been achieved. However, scattered outbreaks of violence convinced Gāndhi that the movement was getting out of hand and might give the British an opportunity to retaliate with superior force. He therefore called off the militant part of the movement. In the meantime, Muhammad Alī and others had been put on trial and sentenced to two years' imprisonment for a resolution they had passed at a meeting asking Indian troops not to serve the British. On the other hand, Gāndhi's calling off of the campaign was interpreted by the British as a confession of weakness on his part. As a result Gāndhi and many other leaders were imprisoned, and the noncooperation movement came to an end. The Khilāfat Movement itself hung on a while longer until the Turks unexpectedly delivered the coup de grace by abolishing the caliphate in 1924.

Muslims felt that they could have gone no further than they did in the Khilāfat Movement to cultivate good relations with the Hindus, without yielding on matters of fundamental principle. Nevertheless, violent agitation was stirred up by the Hindu Ārya Samāj in protest against injuries done Hindus by Muslims during one of the outbreaks. After the imprisonment of the Congress and Khilāfat leaders, the Ārya Samājists launched two movements aimed at Muslims. One of these, called *Sangathan* (lit. holding-together), sought to organize the Hindus into a militant group "capable of defending themselves" against the Muslims, who were called bullies in this connection even by Gandhi. A secret militant branch of this movement was the Rāshtrīya Svayam Sevak Sangh (National Self-Help Society), established in 1926, which finally came out into the open in the pre-Partition days. The other movement was called *Suddhi* (purification), which aimed at the mass conversion of the Muslims to Hinduism. Muhammad Alī took the attitude that if the Hindus wanted to organize themselves, no one could object; likewise he held that the Muslims, who themselves belonged to a missionary religion, could not well object to the Hindus organizing missionary activities even on a mass scale. However, his view was not shared by Muslims, and good will yielded to animosity on both sides until a wave of communal riots had begun. The causes of these riots were often trivial, but they were symptoms of a deeper malady.

Soon differences of opinion sprang up between the Hindu and Muslim Congress leaders. Muslim leaders, including Muhammad Alī, complained that the Hindu leaders did not try to curb the growing anti-Muslim feeling among the Hindus; nor did they exercise their influence with their own community to remove the causes of discord. About Gāndhi, Muhammad Alī said: "The Mussalmans have been oppressed and persecuted by the excesses of the Hindu majority in the last ten years, but Mr. Gāndhi never tried to improve matters or condemn Hindu terrorism against the Muslims. He never denounced the movements of Shuddhi and Sangathan . . . which openly and clearly aimed at the annihilation of the Muslims in India."

Muhammad Alī now moved further and further away from the Congress of which he had once been president. He was dissatisfied with the provisions of the Nehru Report,[1] which, he argued, would result in Hindu domination. The final break came in 1930, when Gāndhi started the second civil disobedience movement; Muhammad Alī advised the Muslims to stand aloof from it, and they did. That same year Muhammad Alī died in London, where he had gone against the advice of his doctors to participate in the first Round Table Conference. He had sworn that he would not return again to a "slave country" and at the request of Muslims in Palestine, who respected him as a great Muslim leader, he was buried in Jerusalem.

MUHAMMAD ALĪ

The Communal Patriot

In this famous article written for the *Comrade* in 1912 Muhammad Alī pleaded for mutual understanding of the very real factors creating communal feeling, and argued that genuine Indian nationalism, which he then still supported,

[1] As a challenge to the British Simon Commission, an Indian All-Parties Convention met in 1928. The Convention, with a large Hindu majority, appointed a commission under Motīlāl Nehru (Jawāharlāl Nehru's father) to draw a draft constitution. The Convention accepted the principle of reservation of seats for the minorities, but not separate electorates, which the Muslims demanded. Jinnāh split with the Congress on this occasion and held an All-India Muslim Conference on January 1, 1929. The Nehru Report came out later in 1929.

could only be achieved by allowing for basic differences of interest rather than suppressing them.

[From Muhammad Alī, *Select Writings* . . . , pp. 65–70]

How does India justify her "communal patriots"? The "Nationalist" of the Congress school would swear by "nationality" and patriotism and vehemently deny that any such monster could exist in his ranks, and point, with a mild, deprecating gesture, to "Muslim Leaguers" and their cries for "separate electorates." The Muslims would hold forth on the woes of "minorities," the imperative duty of self-preservation, and the aggressive spirit and character of Hindu "nationalism." These self-righteous attitudes prove not only that the problem is not even half-understood, but also that the "patriotism" in vogue in this country is exclusively Hindu or Muslim. Discussions on this subject have seldom been inspired by intellectual honesty and courage. Much of the "patriotic" literature is fumbling, shallow, and jejune. Not only it lacks sincerity and breadth of outlook, but it also betrays inordinate fondness for crude subterfuges and cheap claptrap with a view to secure some paltry advantage in the struggle for race ascendancy. The "communal patriot" only reflects in his inadequacy, narrowness, and fanaticism, the temper of his people. Without attempting a detailed analysis of the factors that hamper the growth of a truly Indian patriotism, it may be worth while studying how the communal fanatic has been evolved. Many centuries of Muslim rule in India had given the Hindus an immense power of adaptability to varying political conditions. They readily availed themselves of the facilities for education and material progress which British rule brought within their reach, because they were not burdened like the Muslims with a pride of race and powerful traditions of empire. Western literature gave them a free access to ideas of political freedom and democracy and they naturally and justly began to dream of self-government and organized national existence. They looked back and searched for fresh inspiration, but the oracles of the past were dumb. Before them lay a boundless sea of hope, aspiration, and experiment. If the past could not offer a chart and compass for the new voyage, clearly the fault lay with the Muslims who had viciously strayed into Bharat and demolished its political features and landmarks. Instead of accepting philosophically what could not be undone, they began to quarrel with history. This attitude speedily produced amongst the majority of the educated Hindus the unfortunate habit of ignoring the one great reality of the Indian situation—the existence of about 70 million Muslims who had made a permanent home in this country. Whatever may be the inspiration of Hinduism as a religious creed, the educated Hindus made it a rallying symbol for political unity. The aspiration for self-government arrested all movements for social reform which the early impulse towards liberalism had called forth amongst the educated Hindus. Past history was ransacked for new political formulas; and by a natural and inevitable process "nationality" and "Patriotism" began to be associated with Hinduism. The Hindu "communal patriot" sprang into existence with "Swaraj" as his war-cry. He refuses to give quarter to the Muslims unless the latter quietly shuffles off his individuality and becomes completely Hinduized. He knows, of course, the use of the words like "India" and "territorial nationality," and they form an important part of his vocabulary. But the Muslims weigh on his consciousness all the same, as a troublesome irrelevance; and he would thank his stars if some great exodus or even a geological cataclysm could give him riddance.

The Muslim "communal patriot" owes his origin to a very different set of circumstances. His community lagged behind in the race by moodily sulking in its tents and declining, for a considerable time, to avail itself of the facilities for intellectual and material progress. When it made up its mind to accept the inevitable and move with the times, it suddenly found itself face to face with a community vastly superior to it in number, in wealth, in education, in political organization and power, in a word a united community uttering new accents and pulsating with a new hope. The spectacle of a go-ahead Hinduism, dreaming of self-government and playing with its ancient gods, clad in the vesture of democracy, dazed the conservative Muslim, who was just shaking himself free from the paralyzing grip of the past. He realized that the spirit of the fight had changed. The weapons were new and so were the ways to use those weapons. He felt as if he was being treated as an alien, as a meddlesome freak, who had wantonly interfered with the course of Indian history. Strange incidents were raked up from his long and eventful career, which he was called upon to justify. He had come as a conqueror and had freely given to India the best that was in him. With the loss of empire he felt as if he were to lose his self-respect as well. The "communal patriots" amongst the Hindus treated him as a prisoner in the dock, and loudly complained of him as an impossible factor in the scheme of India's future. Then, again, the new conditions of political success alarmed him. It was to him a painful education to learn that wisdom consisted in lung-power multiplied by the millions and political strength lay in the counting of heads. His community was small in numbers, ignorant, and poor. He was a negligible quantity in the visions of the Hindu "patriot." His religion and history had given him an individuality which he was very loth to lose. As a consequence he drew within his shell and nursed ideals of communal patriotism. He has been scared into this attitude in self-defense. The Hindu "communal patriot" has an advantage over him in the choice of his formulas. While the former boldly walks a road in the garb of India's champion, the latter, less mobile and more unfortunate, formulates even his unimpeachable right to live in terms of apology.

This is, in broad outline, the atmosphere in which the Hindu-Muslim problem has taken its rise. The race antagonism owes its virulence mainly to a false reading of history. The past has flung out its dead hand to paralyze the present. Practical issues of politics are swayed by the foolish but eminently real resentment of the Hindu "patriot" at the political domination of the Muslim in a bygone period of Indian history and by the equally foolish yet powerful sentiment of the Muslim about his vanished power and prestige and empire. The temper of the "communal patriots" has grown aggressive and bellicose on the one hand, and suspicious, sensitive, and irritable on the other. The Hindu tries to ignore the Muslim, the latter retaliates by assuming that all "nationalist" desires are a snare, if not a delusion. Yet the fiction is industriously kept up about the identity of interests, and the organs of Hindu "nationalism" use facile phrases about Indian unity, as if there existed no vital differences of feeling, temper, ideals, and standpoints. The first step towards the solution of the problem is to recognize honestly and courageously that the problem in all its magnitude and many-sided aspects exists. We must clearly recognize that the Hindus and the Muslims dwell apart in thought and sentiment, that the Hindu "patriot" is at times intolerant and grasping, that he dreams of the India that is to be as a modern shrine he is going to build for his gods, that the Muslim is getting a little too clannish, that he is only dimly aware of what it means to feel a generous enthusiasm for such great secular causes as self-government and nationality, and that he broods over his loss and moves about in a world of unsubstantial shadows. It is when we have recognized all this that any progress in the direction of Hindu-Muslim *rapprochement* will become possible. The Muslim who imagines his community to be entirely free of blame is either a man of simple texture or a politician of a very complex type. The Hindu who talks of his community as wholly innocent must be talking with his tongue in his cheek.

Let us look at the facts. To take an important instance, separate representation of the Muslims in the legislative chambers of the country has been denounced with a vehemence that must have struck even the Hindu "communal patriots" themselves as a little tactless and crude. With the existing state of racial feeling, the cry for mixed electorates cannot but alarm the Muslims and create in their minds a strong suspicion of Hindu motives. . . . It is because the immediate, the practical issues of the day divide the Hindus and the Muslims that communal representation has become a cardinal feature in the political evolution of the country. If the Hindu "patriot" is not thinking of an exclusively Hindu India, if he wants the Muslims to exercise their due influence on Indian affairs his demand for the mixed electorates is an insoluble riddle. . . . Let us take another question which is said to have been a powerful factor in the growth of racial bitterness. Cows have been responsible for many riots in the country and many riotous campaigns in the Press. If only the Muslims gave up eating beef, we are told by many well-meaning persons, the Hindu-Muslim relations would grow in good will and cordiality at a bound. . . . It is sometimes forgotten that to a non-Hindu a cow is an ordinary quadruped and no more. A Muslim who eats beef does so on the score of its comparative cheapness. It is not possible that the Hindu, while retaining all his reverence for the animal, should leave others to their own notions of its utility, as long as they are not wantonly offensive? The educated Hindu who assures us that cow-killing lies at the root of racial bitterness makes rather a large demand on our credulity. India may be in varying stages of development from the twelfth century onward, but the sense of proportion of her educated sons is surely quite abreast of the twentieth's.

We need not multiply instances to show how the attitude of the Hindu "communal patriots" has alarmed the Muslims and driven them into a comparative isolation. The walls of separation can be broken down only if a radical change takes place in the conceptions of communal duty and patriotism. The responsibility of the Hindus is much greater in the matter, because they are more powerful and have sometimes used their strength with strange disregard to consequences. The Muslims stand aloof because they are afraid of being completely swallowed up. Any true patriot of India working for the evolution of Indian nationality will have to accept the communal individuality of the Muslims as the basis of his constructive effort. This is the irreducible factor of the situation, and the politician who ignores it has no conception of the task that awaits India's states-men. People talk sometimes of the need of the Muslims joining hands with the Hindus, because some incidents in contemporary history have not been exactly to their liking. They conceive of Muslim "policy" as something wholly apart from Muslim interests, entirely unrelated to con-temporary facts and past history, something necessary for a bargain, a toy that one might have for the mere fun of politics. Soft-headed and some self-advertising folk have gone about proclaiming that the Muslims should join the Congress because the government had revoked the Partition of Bengal or because Persia and Turkey are in trouble. We were simply amused at this irresponsible fatuity. But when a responsible body like the London Branch of the All-India Muslim League talks of closer cooperation between the Hindus and Muslims because the Muslims of Tripoli and Persia have been the victims of European aggressions, we realize for the first time that even sane and level-headed men can run off at a tangent and confuse the issues. What has the Muslim situation abroad to do with the conditions of the Indian Muslims? Either their interests come actually into conflict with those of the Hindus, or they have been all along guilty of a great political meanness and hypocrisy. Has the Indian situation undergone a change? Are the Hindu "communal pa-triots" less militant today and have they grown more considerate and careful about Muslim sentiments? Have the questions that really divide the two communities lost their force and meaning? If not, then the prob-lem remains exactly where it was at any time in recent Indian history. Boards of arbitration, peace syndicates and solemn pacts about cows cannot solve it any more than we can by a spell of occult words control the winds and the tides. The communal sentiment and temper must change, and interests must grow identical before the Hindus and the Muslims can be welded into a united nationality. The problem is great, in fact, one of the greatest known to history. None, however, need despair, as the influences of education, and the leveling, liberalizing tendencies of the times are bound to succeed in creating political individuality out of the diversity of creed and race. Any attempt to impose artificial unity is sure to end in failure, if not in disaster.

The Muslim and Urdu

One of the most sensitive issues which developed with the rise of Indian nationalism arose over the drive for unification of language and script, which some considered a prerequisite to greater unity of thought and action. As a Muslim, Muhammad Alī was deeply concerned over the fate of Islamic culture and religion if the common language of the Muslim minority should be set aside. In this article he deals with the question of linguistic nationalism which even today is one of the most serious unresolved problems of independent India and Pakistan.

[From Muhammad Alī, *Select Writings* . . . , p. 40–43]

The question then arises, what shall be the fate of Urdu? It is our hope that there will always be a body of Hindu lovers of literature who will not willingly let it die. But our fear is that the tidal wave of a narrow and aggressive politics may sweep them away also, and party passions may prove too much for poetic sensibility. Prudence does not sanction an indolent optimism. But another question arises. Why not let Urdu be swept away altogether? Why not let that share the hecatomb of many good things which the "nationalism" of today has ordered? Let it also be the peace offering of Muslim India to the insatiable goddess of numbers!

The answer to this question, suggested as it is by the policy of working on the lines of least resistance, cannot be given till we have examined fully what Urdu now means to [the] Muslims of India. It will not perhaps be contradicted that Urdu is the vernacular of the Muslims of Northern India, if we exclude the portions of the North-West Frontier Province where Pushtu is mostly spoken. In the United Provinces, whatever language may be the vernacular of the Hindus, Urdu is undoubtedly the vernacular of the Muslims. In the Punjab, too, although Punjabi is often spoken at home, Urdu is the written language and the language of refined intercourse, while in Eastern Punjab, in which Delhi and its neighboring districts are included, Urdu is, of course, the only vernacular. In Behar, Rajputana, Central India, and the Central Provinces, Urdu is the mother tongue of the Muslims. Even in the South, in the Dominions of His Highness the Nizam, Urdu is the vernacular of the Muslims. There now remain for consideration the extreme South and Eastern and Western India. In these parts Muslims are somewhat sharply divided into two classes, the descendants of Muslim officials who were sent from Delhi to the outlying provinces, and were originally, at least, of non-Indian extraction; and the Neo-Muslims, the converts whose Indian origin is beyond doubt and the period of whose ancestors is often not very remote.

Those who belong to the former class still retain Urdu, which they brought from Delhi as their mother tongue, although they have learnt the commoner languages of their respective provinces. In Gujarat, for instance, they speak and write in Gujarati like the best of Hindus, but one would never hear them converse amongst themselves and at home in anything but what is known there as Mussalmani and is, of course, no other than Urdu as spoken in Gujarat. Urdu, then is the language in which they think although they may carry on business in the languages used generally by the Hindus of their province, such as Gujarati, Marathi, Sindhi, Kachhi, or Bengali.

Those who come under the latter category have retained the use of the vernacular which their Hindi ancestors used before and which their neighbors use now, for instance, the Khojas of Bombay speak Kachhi and write in Gujarati. Exceptions, of course, exist, such as the well-known and highly cultured Tayebji family of Bombay in which Urdu has been deliberately adopted as the language of daily intercourse, although Gujarati has not been given up for business purposes. But it may safely be asserted that, as a general rule, the literates among these Neo-Muslims have learnt some Urdu partly for purposes of intercourse with other Muslims and partly for religious purposes. For, incredible as it may seem, in spite of the fact that until recently and for long centuries Persian was the court language and the language of literary composition and Arabic was the classical language which the Muslims studied both for general culture and religious purposes, Urdu has been enriched during the last two generations by translations of almost every important work on Muslim theology. The Qur'ān and the Traditions and Commentaries have all been translated by more than one writer into Urdu.

If Urdu is to be sacrificed, we deprive millions of Muslims—and these the best of Muslims, if heredity counts for anything—of their tongue in which they lisped as children and in which they think today. In addition to this we deprive them and the remaining millions of Muslims of the consolation which their religion has to offer to them. For our part we think it is the loss to the latter whose mother tongue is not Urdu that is irreparable. It is possible for Muslims, as it is being made possible for Hindus in Northern India, to give up the use of a familiar Persian word or Arabic expression and substitute for it a strange word or expression from Sanskrit for ordinary purposes of life. Time and use would make strange phrases familiar and time and disuse would make familiar phrases strange. But what of the familiar word and phrase of religious literature? Language is the expression of thought, and where thought differs so radically as in Islam and Hinduism can the same language express it adequately in each case? Consider it whichever way we like, it has to be confessed in the end that Urdu is [the] irreducible minimum to which the most compromising Muslims would consent. Not that there is no room in Urdu for a longer admixture of Sanskrit words, but they can glide in naturally and smoothly; they cannot be pushed by force. If Muslims study Sanskrit in larger numbers than they do today, they are bound to use a larger number of such words. . . . Nor would there be a keen desire on the part of the Muslims to enrich Urdu with such words if the Hindus follow the opposite policy of excluding words of Arabic and Persian origin. . . .

This brings us to the question of a script, though we are concerned here mainly with that of language. Islam was neither insular nor peninsular, and if Muslims lacked something in their love for the land they lived in, they have been charged with a little too much of it for the lands of others. Their conquest brought them worldly gain and afforded them facilities for conversion. Just as in the case of European nations today, commerce follows conquest, in the history of Islam the faith followed the flag. For a world-wide empire, a common language was an impossibility, and, as we have shown, Arabic was not imposed on the conquered lands. But a common script facilitated a common understanding, and today, while Arabic, Persian, Turki, Pushtu, Urdu, and many other languages are used by Muslims, the Arabic script is common to all. Herein, again, the irreducible minimum was found by people ready to compromise. Efforts are now being made in India to have a common script. So long as Islam remains a world-wide religion and Muslims retain their present sympathies with other Muslims no matter where they be, Indian Muslims cannot give up their present script for Devanāgrī. We have heard a great deal of the scientific character of the latter, but few of its advocates have examined its suitability for transcription of Arabic words, and all seem to ignore the fact that the Arabic script is perhaps the only form of shorthand which is a common blessing for many millions. Granting, for argument's sake, that Devanāgrī is more scientific, does it entitle it to any greater consideration than that which such a shrewd and businesslike nation as the Americans paid to Mr. Roosevelt's short list of phonetically spelt words? And, finally, in the matter of script, even more than in the case of language, the general adoption of Devanāgrī to the exclusion of Arabic character would be to curtail the facilities of intercourse between India and other Asiatic countries.

The only conclusion at which we can arrive is that neither in the matter of language nor in that of script can the Muslims afford to concede more than what they have already done in adopting Urdu as their only vernacular or their second vernacular, and retaining the script that is practically common to the Islamic world. But unless we take practical steps to safeguard the language and the script, both are endangered by the narrow and exclusive "nationalism" which is growing more and more militant every day.

CHAPTER XXV

TAGORE AND GĀNDHI

Two towering figures dominated the Indian scene in the first half of the twentieth century, overshadowing all rivals in their respective fields of endeavor. Each achieved such international renown that he thereby automatically increased India's prestige abroad. Each in his own way spent many years in the service of his countrymen. And yet there could scarcely be two men more different from one another in temperament and interests. Tagore's nature was that of a poet; Gāndhi's that of a statesman. Tagore's realm was artistic expression; Gāndhi's ethical action. Even the clothes they chose reflected the contrast between them, for Tagore was fond of dressing in flowing silken robes, while Gāndhi wore nothing but the simplest hand-spun garments.

In a sense these two remarkable men brought to their finest fruition the potentialities created in modern India by the engrafting of new patterns of thought and action onto various "stems" of traditional culture. Both Tagore and Gāndhi made themselves masters of the English language and were considerably affected by their contact with Western culture. How then can one explain the contrary directions in which their minds developed? Perhaps the distinctive regional cultures in which they grew to manhood affected them most decisively. Cosmopolitan Bengal, where English thought left its deepest imprint, produced the Brāhmo Samāj in whose bosom Tagore was born. Isolated Gujarāt, on the opposite side of the subcontinent, and the home of the Vedist Dayānanda, clung longer to the older Vaishnava and Jaina traditions which influenced Gāndhi so deeply.

For whatever reasons, Tagore and Gāndhi certainly disagreed fundamentally in their diagnoses of India's ills and their prescriptions for her cure. For a time this disagreement clouded their personal friendship, which had dated from 1915 when Tagore had invited Gāndhi, fresh from South Africa, to bring his followers to Shāntiniketan for want of a more congenial temporary haven. Addressing Gāndhi on this occasion as Mahātmā (great soul), Tagore seems to have been the first to use the famous title. Their public controversy over the methods of Gāndhi's noncooperation movement flared up in 1921, and passages from their eloquent debate are reproduced in this chapter. Gāndhi's 1933 fast against untouchability brought about a dramatic reconciliation between the two men, and Gāndhi ended his fast with a sip of fruit juice while Tagore sat nearby. Visiting Shāntiniketan after the poet's death, Gāndhi is said to have remarked that he had begun by thinking that he and Tagore were poles apart, but now believed that in fundamentals they were one.

Jawaharlāl Nehru, who admired both men greatly (perhaps because they served as models for the two sides of his own personality) has written: "Tagore was primarily the man of thought, Gandhi of concentrated and ceaseless activity. Both, in their different ways, had a world outlook, and both were at the same time wholly India. They seemed to represent different but harmonious aspects of India and to complement one another." [1]

RABĪNDRANĀTH TAGORE: POET, EDUCATOR, AND AMBASSADOR TO THE WORLD

The fourteenth of Maharshi Debendranāth Tagore's fifteen children, Rabīndranāth Tagore (1861–1941) grew to manhood in a highly cultured family environment. A number of his brothers and sisters were artistically inclined—one composed music, another staged amateur theatricals, and several contributed to the literary magazine edited by their eldest brother, who was also a philosopher. The venerable Debendranāth gave special attention to his youngest son's education, and after investing him with the brāhmanical sacred thread, took him on an extended pilgrimage to Amritsar and the Himalayas. Rabīndranāth's religious views were decisively shaped by his father's influence.

A steady income from the family's landed estates deprived Rabīndranāth of the necessity of earning his own livelihood, and he was allowed to give up formal studies at the age of thirteen. Living at home, he began to experiment with writing verse. Encouraged by his older

[1] Jawaharlāl Nehru, *The Discovery of India*, 342–43.

[231]

siblings, he went on to win renown at twenty with his first volume of Bengali poems, Bankim Chandra Chatterjee himself hailing their appearance. Year after year his writing matured in style and grew richer in content. Translating into English from the devotional poems written after the death of his wife and three of his five children, he published in 1912 the collection entitled *Gītāñjali* (*Song Offerings*). A year later the world was startled to hear that he had been awarded the Nobel Prize for Literature. Educated India went wild with excitement, sensing that Rabīndranāth had vindicated Indian culture in the eyes of the West. As for the poet, he is said to have cried, "I shall never have any peace again." [1]

Although his prediction proved correct, the ceaseless activity in which he spent the rest of his life was mostly of his own making. He had already founded a school at Shāntiniketan, the rural retreat where his father used to pass days in meditation. He now began to develop there a center of Indian culture, where all the creative and performing arts could thrive in a new birth. In 1921, as a crowning step in his educational work, Tagore opened his Vishva-Bhāratī [2] University at Shāntiniketan, dedicating it to his ideal of world brotherhood and cultural interchange.

Like his father, Rabīndranāth loved to travel, and he seldom refused the many invitations which came to him from all parts of the world. In addition to many tours within India, he lectured on five occasions in the United States, five times in Europe, three times in Japan, and once each in China, South America, Soviet Russia, and Southeast Asia. He made good use of his opportunities to address important audiences by denouncing—especially after the First World War—the evils of nationalism and materialism. Mankind could only save itself from destruction, he declared, by a return to the spiritual values which permeate all religions. Asia, the home of the world's great faiths, lay under a special obligation to lead this religious revival, and to India, the home of both Hinduism and Buddhism, belonged the mission of reawakening herself, Asia, and the world. Although this message, like that of Vivekānanda, stressed India's role as spiritual teacher to mankind, Tagore

[1] E. J. Thompson, *Rabindranath Tagore, His Life and Work*, p. 44.
[2] Translatable as either "universal learning" or "all-India."

never tired of reminding his countrymen that they also needed to learn from the West's vitality and dedicated search for truth.

Through an irony of fate, this preacher of the complementary relationship between Asian and Western cultures returned from a triumphant European tour in 1921 to find Gāndhi leading a mass movement of noncooperation with every aspect of British influence in India, including the prevailing form of English education. Rabīndranāth publicly opposed the Mahātmā and was accordingly accused of taking an "unpatriotic" position. He had already been virtually ostracized for his withdrawal in 1908 from Bengal politics in disgust at the extremist excesses of the anti-Partition agitation. On both occasions he bore his isolation stoically and without yielding his ground, much like the great Bengali whom he considered his spiritual kinsman—Rāmmohun Roy.

Shy and aloof, Tagore was able to look more dispassionately on the events of his time than those who hurled themselves into the struggle against British rule. Reversing Tilak's dictum that social reform diverted and divided the movement for independence, Tagore held that the clamor for political rights distracted men from more fundamental tasks such as erasing caste barriers, reconciling Hindus and Muslims, uplifting the poor and helpless villagers, and liberating men's minds and bodies from a host of self-made but unnecessary burdens.

Right down to his eightieth year, Tagore never lost his childlike wonderment at the variety and beauty of the creation and he expressed his delight with life in a ceaseless outpouring of poetry, prose, drama, and song. By making the speech of the common people the medium for his masterly style he revolutionized and revitalized Bengali literature. His interests, although basically esthetic, were truly universal; in his seventies he wrote a textbook on elementary science which explained the theory of relativity and the working of the solar system. In an age of growing xenophobia he sought to keep India's windows open on the world. For his creativity, his breadth of vision, and his zeal in championing man's freedom from arbitrary restraints—whether social, political or religious—Tagore deserves comparison with the great artist-philosophers of Renaissance humanism in the West.

RABĪNDRANĀTH TAGORE
The Sunset of the Century

Written originally in Bengali on the last day of the nineteenth century, this poem embodied Tagore's protest against the aggressive nationalism which brought on the Boer War then raging in South Africa. He implied that by patient cultivation of spiritual virtues India and "the East" would take their proper place in world civilization after the militant power of Western nationalism had ceased to control mankind.

[From Tagore, *Nationalism*, 133–35]

I

The last sun of the century sets amidst the blood-red clouds of the West and the whirlwind of hatred.

The naked passion of self-love of Nations, in its drunken delirium of greed, is dancing to the clash of steel and the howling verses of vengeance.

2

The hungry self of the Nation shall burst in a violence of fury from its own shameless feeding.

For it has made the world its food.

And licking it, crunching it, and swallowing it in big morsels,

It swells and swells,

Till in the midst of its unholy feast descends the sudden shaft of heaven piercing its heart of grossness.

3

The crimson glow of light on the horizon is not the light of thy dawn of peace, my Motherland.

It is the glimmer of the funeral pyre burning to ashes the vast flesh—the self-love of the Nation—dead under its own excess.

Thy morning waits behind the patient dark of the East,

Meek and silent.

4

Keep watch, India.

Bring your offerings of worship for that sacred sunrise.

Let the first hymn of its welcome sound in your voice and sing

"Come, Peace, thou daughter of God's own great suffering.

[234]

Come with thy treasure of contentment, the sword of fortitude,
And meekness crowning thy forehead."

5

Be not ashamed, my brothers, to stand before the proud and the powerful
With your white robe of simpleness.
Let your crown be of humility, your freedom the freedom of the soul.
Build God's throne daily upon the ample bareness of your poverty
And know that what is huge is not great and pride is not everlasting.

"Where the Mind Is Without Fear"

One of the hundred-odd poems which comprise the prize-winning volume
Gītāñjali listed in a rising crescendo Tagore's ambitions for his native India.
[From *Collected Poems and Plays of Rabindranath Tagore*, p. 16]

Where the mind is without fear and the head is held high;
Where knowledge is free;
Where the world has not been broken up into fragments by narrow
  domestic walls;
Where words come out from the depth of truth;
Where tireless striving stretches its arms towards perfection;
Where the clear stream of reason has not lost its way into the dreary
  desert sand of dead habit;
Where the mind is led forward by thee into everwidening thought and
  action—
Into that heaven of freedom, my Father, let my country awake.

Jana Gana Mana

In addition to composing the melody for the famous *Bande Mātaram* song
in 1912, Tagore wrote both words and music for the hymn *Jana Gana Mana*
(The Mind of the Multitude of the People), which after independence became the national anthem of India.
[From Sykes, *Rabindranath Tagore*, p. 69]

Thou art the ruler of the minds of all people,
  Thou Dispenser of India's destiny.
Thy name rouses the hearts
  Of the Punjab, Sind, Gujrat, and Maratha,

[235]

Of Dravid, Orissa, and Bengal.
It echoes in the hills of the Vindhyas and Himālayas,
  Mingles in the music of Jumna and Ganges,
  And is chanted by the waves of the Indian sea.
They pray for Thy blessing and sing Thy praise,
  Thou Dispenser of India's destiny,
Victory, Victory, Victory to Thee.

The Evils of Nationalism

Lecturing to American audiences in 1917, Tagore denounced the nationalistic trend of the times. Crucial to his argument was the distinction he drew between the Western nation and the spirit of the West.

[From Tagore, *Nationalism*, pp. 18–22]

Before the Nation came to rule over us we had other governments which were foreign, and these, like all governments, had some element of the machine in them. But the difference between them and the government by the Nation is like the difference between the hand-loom and the power-loom. In the products of the hand-loom the magic of man's living fingers finds its expression, and its hum harmonizes with the music of life. But the power-loom is relentlessly lifeless and accurate and monotonous in its production.

We must admit that during the personal government of the former days there have been instances of tyranny, injustice, and extortion. They caused sufferings and unrest from which we are glad to be rescued. The protection of law is not only a boon, but it is a valuable lesson to us. It is teaching us the discipline which is necessary for the stability of civilization and for continuity of progress. We are realizing through it that there is a universal standard of justice to which all men, irrespective of their caste and color, have their equal claim.

This reign of law in our present government in India has established order in this vast land inhabited by peoples different in their races and customs. It has made it possible for these peoples to come in closer touch with one another and cultivate a communion of aspiration.

But this desire for a common bond of comradeship among the different races of India has been the work of the spirit of the West, not that of the Nation of the West. Wherever in Asia the people have received the true lesson of the West it is in spite of the Western Nation. Only because Japan had been able to resist the dominance of this Western Nation could she acquire the benefit of the Western civilization in fullest measure. Though China has been poisoned at the very spring of her moral and physical life by this Nation, her struggle to receive the best lessons of the West may yet be successful if not hindered by the Nation. It was only the other day that Persia woke up from her age-long sleep at the call of the West to be instantly trampled into stillness by the Nation. The same phenomenon prevails in this country also, where the people are hospitable, but the Nation has proved itself to be otherwise, making an Eastern guest feel humiliated to stand before you as a member of the humanity of his own motherland.

In India we are suffering from this conflict between the spirit of the West and the Nation of the West. The benefit of the Western civilization is doled out to us in a miserly measure by the Nation, which tries to regulate the degree of nutrition as near the zero-point of vitality as possible. The portion of education allotted to us is so raggedly insufficient that it ought to outrage the sense of decency of a Western humanity. We have seen in these countries how the people are encouraged and trained and given every facility to fit themselves for the great movements of commerce and industry spreading over the world, while in India the only assistance we get is merely to be jeered at by the Nation for lagging behind. While depriving us of our opportunities and reducing our education to the minimum required for conducting a foreign government, this Nation pacifies its conscience by calling us names, by sedulously giving currency to the arrogant cynicism that the East is East and the West is West and never the twain shall meet. If we must believe our schoolmaster in his taunt that, after nearly two centuries of his tutelage, India not only remains unfit for self-government but unable to display originality in her intellectual attainments, must we ascribe it to something in the nature of Western culture and our inherent incapacity to receive it or to the judicious niggardliness of the Nation that has taken upon itself the white man's burden of civilizing the East? That Japanese people have some qualities which we lack we may admit, but that our intellect is naturally unproductive compared to theirs we cannot accept even from them whom it is dangerous for us to contradict.

The truth is that the spirit of conflict and conquest is at the origin and in the center of Western nationalism; its basis is not social cooperation. It has evolved a perfect organization of power, but not spiritual idealism. It is like the pack of predatory creatures that must have its victims. With all its heart it cannot bear to see its hunting-grounds converted into cultivated fields. In fact, these nations are fighting among themselves for the extension of their victims and their reserve forests. Therefore the Western Nation acts like a dam to check the free flow of Western civilization into the country of the No-Nation. Because this civilization is the civilization of power, therefore it is exclusive, it is naturally unwilling to open its sources of power to those whom it has selected for its purposes of exploitation.

But all the same moral law is the law of humanity, and the exclusive civilization which thrives upon others who are barred from its benefit carries its own death-sentence in its moral limitations. The slavery that it gives rise to unconsciously drains its own love of freedom dry. The helplessness with which it weighs down its world of victims exerts its force of gravitation every moment upon the power that creates it. And the greater part of the world which is being denuded of its self-sustaining life by the Nation will one day become the most terrible of all its burdens, ready to drag it down into the bottom of destruction. Whenever Power removes all checks from its path to make its career easy, it triumphantly rides into its ultimate crash of death. Its moral brake becomes slacker every day without its knowing it, and its slippery path of ease becomes its path of doom.

Gāndhi—The Frail Man of Spirit

Tagore was lecturing in Europe and America when Gāndhi started his first great noncooperation campaign. From this distance the poet began to see the significance of Gāndhi's methods, and his admiration is shown in the following letter to his friend C. F. Andrews.

[From Andrews, *Letters to a Friend,* pp. 127–28]

Chicago, March 2d, 1921

Your last letter gives wonderful news about our students in Calcutta.[1] I hope that this spirit of sacrifice and willingness to suffer will grow in

[1] Referring to the boycott of schools and colleges by thousands of students.

strength; for to achieve this is an end in itself. This is the true freedom! Nothing is of higher value—be it national wealth or independence—than disinterested faith in ideals, in the moral greatness of man.

The West has its unshakable faith in material strength and prosperity; and therefore, however loud grows the cry for peace and disarmament, its ferocity growls louder, gnashing its teeth and lashing its tail in impatience. It is like a fish, hurt by the pressure of the flood, planning to fly in the air. Certainly the idea is brilliant, but it is not possible for a fish to realize. We, in India, have to show the world what is that truth which not only makes disarmament possible but turns it into strength.

The truth that moral force is a higher power than brute force will be proved by the people who are unarmed. Life, in its higher development, has thrown off its tremendous burden of armor and a prodigious quantity of flesh, till man has become the conqueror of the brute world. The day is sure to come when the frail man of spirit, completely unhampered by airfleets and dreadnoughts, will prove that the meek are to inherit the earth.

It is in the fitness of things that Mahātmā Gāndhi, frail in body and devoid of all material resources, should call up the immense power of the meek that has been waiting in the heart of the destitute and insulted humanity of India. The destiny of India has chosen for its ally the power of soul, and not that of muscle. And she is to raise the history of man from the muddy level of physical conflict to the higher moral altitude.

What is *Swarāj!* [2] It is māyā; [3] it is like a mist that will vanish, leaving no stain on the radiance of the Eternal. However we may delude ourselves with the phrases learnt from the West, *Swarāj* is not our objective. Our fight is a spiritual fight—it is for Man. We are to emancipate Man from the meshes that he himself has woven round him—these organizations of national egoism. The butterfly will have to be persuaded that the freedom of the sky is of higher value than the shelter of the cocoon. If we can defy the strong, the armed, the wealthy—revealing to the world the power of the immortal spirit—the whole castle of the Giant Flesh will vanish in the void. And then Man will find his *Swarāj.*

We, the famished ragged ragamuffins of the East, are to win freedom for all humanity. We have no word for "Nation" in our language. When

[2] Self-rule.   [3] Illusion.

[239]

we borrow this word from other people, it never fits us. For we are to make our league with *Nārāyan*,[4] and our triumph will not give us anything but victory itself: victory for God's world. I have seen the West; I covet not the unholy feast in which she revels every moment, growing more and more bloated and red and dangerously delirious. Not for us is this mad orgy of midnight, with lighted torches, but awakenment in the serene light of the morning.

Gāndhi versus Truth

Even before Tagore returned to India in 1921, he saw that Gāndhi's nationalism clashed with his own internationalism. A meeting between the two at Tagore's Calcutta house failed to resolve their differences. Finally, Tagore published an article entitled "The Call of Truth," expressing his criticisms of Gāndhi's narrow conception of *Swarāj* and the way to achieve it.

[From Tagore, "The Call of Truth," in *Modern Review*, XXX, 4, 429-33]

The Mahātmā has won the heart of India with his love; for that we have all acknowledged his sovereignty. He has given us a vision of the shakti [1] of truth; for that our gratitude to him is unbounded. We read about truth in books: we talk about it: but it is indeed a red-letter day, when we see it face to face. Rare is the moment, in many a long year, when such good fortune happens. We can make and break Congresses every other day. It is at any time possible for us to stump the country preaching politics in English. But the golden rod which can awaken our country in Truth and Love is not a thing which can be manufactured by the nearest goldsmith. To the wielder of that rod our profound salutation! But if, having seen truth, our belief in it is not confirmed, what is the good of it all? Our mind must acknowledge the truth of the intellect, just as our heart does the truth of love. No Congress or other outside institution succeeded in touching the heart of India. It was roused only by the touch of love. Having had such a clear vision of this wonderful power of Truth, are we to cease to believe in it, just where the attainment of *Swarāj* is concerned? Has the truth, which was needed in the process of awakenment, to be got rid of in the process of achievement? . . .

From our master, the Mahātmā—may our devotion to him never grow

[4] The godlike element in man.   [1] Divine creative power.

less!—we must learn the truth of love in all its purity, but the science and art of building up *Swarāj* is a vast subject. Its pathways are difficult to traverse and take time. For this task, aspiration and emotion must be there, but no less must study and thought be there likewise. For it, the economist must think, the mechanic must labor, the educationist and statesman must teach and contrive. In a word, the mind of the country must exert itself in all directions. Above all, the spirit of inquiry throughout the whole country must be kept intact and untrammelled, its mind not made timid or inactive by compulsion, open or secret.

We know from past experience that it is not any and every call to which the country responds. It is because no one has yet been able to unite in Yoga [2] all the forces of the country in the work of its creation, that so much time has been lost over and over again. And we have been kept waiting and waiting for him who has the right and the power to make the call upon us. In the old forests of India, our gurus, in the fullness of their vision of the Truth had sent forth such a call saying: "As the rivers flow on their downward course, as the months flow on to the year, so let all seekers after truth come from all sides." The initiation into Truth of that day has borne fruit, undying to this day, and the voice of its message still rings in the ears of the world.

Why should not our Guru of today, who would lead us on the paths of Karma, send forth such a call? Why should he not say: "Come ye from all sides and be welcome. Let all the forces of the land be brought into action, for then alone shall the country awake. Freedom is in complete awakening, in full self-expression." God has given the Mahātmā the voice that can call, for in him there is the Truth. Why should this not be our long-awaited opportunity?

But his call came to one narrow field alone. To one and all he simply says: Spin and weave, spin and weave. Is this the call: "Let all seekers after truth come from all sides"? Is this the call of the New Age to new creation? When nature called to the bee to take refuge in the narrow life of the hive, millions of bees responded to it for the sake of efficiency, and accepted the loss of sex in consequence. But this sacrifice by way of self-atrophy led to the opposite of freedom. Any country, the people of which can agree to become neuters for the sake of some temptation, or command, carries within itself its own prison-house. To spin

[2] Here used in the sense of "a harmonious union."

is easy, therefore for all men it is an imposition hard to bear. The call to the ease of mere efficiency is well enough for the Bee. The wealth of power that is Man's can only become manifest when his utmost is claimed.

Sparta tried to gain strength by narrowing herself down to a particular purpose, but she did not win. Athens sought to attain perfection by opening herself out in all her fullness—and she did win. Her flag of victory still flies at the masthead of man's civilization. It is admitted that European military camps and factories are stunting man, that their greed is cutting man down to the measure of their own narrow purpose, that for these reasons joylessness darkly lowers over the West. But if man be stunted by big machines, the danger of his being stunted by small machines must not be lost sight of. The charkha [3] in its proper place can do no harm, but will rather do much good. But where, by reason of failure to acknowledge the differences in man's temperament, it is in the wrong place, there thread can only be spun at the cost of a great deal of the mind itself. Mind is no less valuable than cotton thread.

Some are objecting: "We do not propose to curb our minds forever, but only for a time." But why should it be even for a time? Is it because within a short time spinning will give us *Swarāj?* But where is the argument for this? *Swarāj* is not concerned with our apparel only —it cannot be established on cheap clothing; its foundation is in the mind, which, with its diverse powers and its confidence in those powers, goes on all the time creating *Swarāj* for itself. In no country in the world is the building up of *Swarāj* completed. In some part or other of every nation, some lurking greed or illusion still perpetuates bondage. And the root of such bondage is always within the mind. Where then, I ask again, is the argument, that in our country *Swarāj* can be brought about by everyone engaging for a time in spinning? A mere statement, in lieu of argument, will surely never do. If once we consent to receive fate's oracle from human lips, that will add once more to the torments of our slavery, and not the least one either. If nothing but oracles will serve to move us, oracles will have to be manufactured, morning, noon and night, for the sake of urgent needs, and all other voices would be defeated. Those for whom authority is needed in place of reason will invariably accept despotism in place of freedom. It is like cutting at the

[3] Spinning wheel.

root of a tree while pouring water on the top. This is not a new thing, I know. We have enough magic in the country—magical revelation, magical healing, and all kinds of divine intervention in mundane affairs. That is exactly why I am so anxious to reinstate reason on its throne. As I have said before, God himself has given the mind sovereignty in the material world. And I say today, that only those will be able to get and keep *Swarāj* in the material world who have realized the dignity of self-reliance and self-mastery in the spiritual world, those whom no temptation, no delusion, can induce to surrender the dignity of intellect into the keeping of others.

Consider the burning of cloth, heaped up before the very eyes of our motherland shivering and ashamed in her nakedness. What is the nature of the call to do this? Is it not another instance of a magical formula? The question of using or refusing cloth of a particular manufacture belongs mainly to economic science. The discussion of the matter by our countrymen should have been in the language of economics. If the country has really come to such a habit of mind that precise thinking has become impossible for it, then our very first fight should be against such a fatal habit, to the temporary exclusion of all else if need be. Such a habit would clearly be the original sin from which all our ills are flowing. But far from this, we take the course of confirming ourselves in it by relying on the magical formula that foreign cloth is "impure." Thus economics is bundled out and a fictitious moral dictum dragged into its place. . . .

The command to burn our foreign clothes has been laid on us. I, for one, am unable to obey it. Firstly, because I conceive it to be my very first duty to put up a valiant fight against this terrible habit of blindly obeying orders, and this fight can never be carried on by our people being driven from one injunction to another. Secondly, I feel that the clothes to be burnt are not mine, but belong to those who most sorely need them. If those who are going naked should have given us the mandate to burn, it would, at least, have been a case of self-immolation and the crime of incendiarism would not lie at our door. But how can we expiate the sin of the forcible destruction of clothes which might have gone to women whose nakedness is actually keeping them prisoners, unable to stir out of the privacy of their homes?

I have said repeatedly and must repeat once more that we cannot afford to lose our mind for the sake of any external gain. Where Mahātmā Gāndhi has declared war against the tyranny of the machine which is oppressing the whole world, we are all enrolled under his banner. But we must refuse to accept as our ally the illusion-haunted, magic-ridden, slave-mentality that is at the root of all the poverty and insult under which our country groans. Here is the enemy itself, on whose defeat alone *Swarāj* within and without can come to us.

The time, moreover, has arrived when we must think of one thing more, and that is this. The awakening of India is a part of the awakening of the world. The door of the New Age has been flung open at the trumpet blast of a great war. We have read in the *Mahābhārata* how the day of self-revelation had to be preceded by a year of retirement. The same has happened in the world today. Nations had attained nearness to each other without being aware of it, that is to say, the outside fact was there, but it had not penetrated into the mind. At the shock of the war, the truth of it stood revealed to mankind. The foundation of modern, that is Western, civilization was shaken; and it has become evident that the convulsion is neither local nor temporary, but has traversed the whole earth and will last until the shocks between man and man, which have extended from continent to continent, can be brought to rest, and a harmony be established.

From now onward, any nation which takes an isolated view of its own country will run counter to the spirit of the New Age, and know no peace. From now onward, the anxiety that each country has for its own safety must embrace the welfare of the world. . . .

I have condemned, in unsparing terms, the present form and scope of the League of Nations and the Indian Reform Councils. I therefore feel certain that there will be no misunderstanding when I state that, even in these, I find signs of the Time Spirit, which is moving the heart of the West. Although the present form is unacceptable, yet there is revealed an aspiration, which is towards the truth, and this aspiration must not be condemned. In this morning of the world's awakening, if in only our own national striving, there is no response to its universal aspiration, that will betoken the poverty of our spirit. I do not say for a moment that we should belittle the work immediately to hand. But when the bird is roused by the dawn, all its awakening is not absorbed in its search for food. Its wings respond unweariedly to the call of the sky, its throat pours forth songs for joy of the new light. Universal humanity has sent us its call today. Let our mind respond in its own language; for response is the only true sign of life. When of old we were immersed in the politics of dependence on others, our chief business was the compilation of others' shortcomings. Now that we have decided to dissociate our politics from dependence, are we still to establish and maintain it on the same recital of others' sins? The state of mind so engendered will only raise the dust of angry passion, obscuring the greater world from our vision, and urge us more and more to take futile short cuts for the satisfaction of our passions. It is a sorry picture of India, which we shall display if we fail to realize for ourselves the greater India. This picture will have no light. It will have in the foreground only the business side of our aspiration. Mere business talent, however, has never created anything.

In the West, a real anxiety and effort of their higher mind to rise superior to business considerations is beginning to be seen. I have come across many there whom this desire has imbued with the true spirit of the sannyasin,[4] making them renounce their home-world in order to achieve the unity of man, by destroying the bondage of nationalism; men who have within their own soul realized the advaita [5] of humanity. Many such have I seen in England who have accepted persecution and contumely from their fellow-countrymen in their struggles to free other peoples from the oppression of their own country's pride of power. Some of them are amongst us here in India. I have seen sannyāsins too in France—Romain Rolland for one, who is an outcast from his own people. I have also seen them in the minor countries of Europe. I have watched the faces of European students all aglow with the hope of a united mankind, prepared manfully to bear all the blows, cheerfully to submit to all the insults, of the present age for the glory of the age to come. And are we alone to be content with telling the beads of negation, harping on others' faults and proceeding with the erection of *Swarāj* on a foundation of quarrelsomeness? Shall it not be our first duty in the dawn to remember Him, who is One, who is without distinction of class or color, and who with his varied shakti makes true provision for the inherent need of each and every class; and to pray to the Giver of Wisdom to unite us all in right understanding.

---

[4] Religious mendicant.   [5] Non-duality.

The Spirit of Asia

Like Keshub Chunder Sen and Swāmī Vivekānanda, Tagore believed that all Asia was united by a profound spirituality from which the more materialistic nations of the West could benefit. In his lectures of 1924 to audiences in China he stressed Asia's need to find her own soul, in order that her message to mankind might not perish.

[From Tagore, *Talks in China,* pp. 64, 66–67, 156–57]

My friends, I have come to ask you to reopen the channel of communion which I hope is still there; for though overgrown with weeds of oblivion its lines can still be traced. I shall consider myself fortunate if, through this visit, China comes nearer to India and India to China—for no political or commercial purpose, but for disinterested human love and for nothing else. . . .

In Asia we must seek our strength in union, in an unwavering faith in righteousness, and. never in the egotistic spirit of separateness and self-assertion. It is from the heart of the East that the utterance has sprung forth: "The meek shall inherit the earth." For the meek never waste energy in the display of insolence, but are firmly established in true prosperity through harmony with the All.

In Asia we must unite, not through some mechanical method of organization, but through a spirit of true sympathy. The organized power of the machine is ready to smite and devour us, from which we must be rescued by that living power of spirit which grows into strength, not through mere addition, but through organic assimilation. . . .

It will never do for the Orient to trail behind the West like an overgrown appendix, vainly trying to lash the sky in defiance of the divine. For humanity this will not only be a useless excess, but a disappointment and a deception. For if the East ever tries to duplicate Western life, the duplicate is bound to be a forgery.

The West has no doubt overwhelmed us with its flood of commodities, tourists, machine guns, school masters, and a religion which is great, but whose followers are intent upon lengthening the list of its recruits, and not upon following it in details that bring no profit, or in practices that are inconvenient. But one great service the West has done us by bringing the force of its living mind to bear upon our life; it has stirred our

[246]

thoughts into activity. For its mind is great; its intellectual life has in
its center intellectual probity, the standard of truth.

The first effect of our mind being startled from its sleep was to make it
intensely conscious of what was before it; but now that the surprise of
awakening has subsided, the time has come to know what is within. We
are beginning to know ourselves. We are finding our own mind, because
the mind of the West claims our attention.

I have no doubt in my own mind that in the East our principal characteristic is not to set too high a price upon success through gaining
advantage, but upon self-realization through fulfilling our dharma, our
ideals. Let the awakening of the East impel us consciously to discover the
essential and the universal meaning of our own civilization, to remove
the debris from its path, to rescue it from the bondage of stagnation that
produces impurities, to make it a great channel of communication between all human races.

M. K. GĀNDHI: INDIA'S "GREAT SOUL"

Known to the world as the greatest Indian of modern times, Mohandās
Karamchand Gāndhi (1869–1948) was more a man of action, a karmayo-
gin, than a thinker. He himself declared, when asked for his message to
mankind, "My life is my message." Nevertheless, in working out the philosophy which sustained him through a lifetime of striving, Gāndhi
wove together and gave new strength to many strands of both Indian and
Western thought.

From his pious mother, young Mohandās imbibed the devotional spirit
of Vaishnavite Hinduism. Western secular influences were weak and
Jain influences strong in his native Gujarat, and the importance of
ahimsā (noninjury or nonviolence to all creatures) and ascetic self-
discipline was impressed on him by the examples of his mother, who
fasted frequently, and of Jain friends of the family. Although the Gāndhis
belonged to the vaishya caste and were originally merchants, Mohandās'
father, uncle, and grandfather had served as prime ministers to several
small princely states.

A youngest son, and an unusually bright and ambitious youth, Mohandās resolved to study law in order to follow in his father's footsteps.

By the time he sailed for England at eighteen, leaving behind his wife and infant son, his mind had been deeply and permanently molded by traditional Indian influences.

His three years as a student in London turned Gāndhi into a Westernized and nattily dressed young barrister. His associations with Englishmen were pleasant: he became an active member of the London Vegetarian Society and was introduced by English theosophists to the *Bhagavad Gītā* in Sir Edwin Arnold's translation. He studied the New Testament and often attended church in order to hear sermons by the best preachers of the day. He returned to Gujarāt at twenty-one, convinced that "next to India, I would rather live in London than in any other place in the world." [1]

After two years of unsuccessful law practice, Gāndhi was called to South Africa to help a Gujarātī Muslim merchant with a court case. Insisting on traveling first class, he was shoved out of carriages and beaten by a white South African. These brutal encounters with racial intolerance came as a great shock to him after his close relations with English friends in London. He decided to stay on in South Africa to help the Indians there fight for their rights. To unite the disorganized Indian community he founded the Natal Indian Congress. At twenty-seven he toured India to enlist support for the cause he had made his own. On this mission he met Banerjea, Rānade, Gokhale, and Tilak, and felt so drawn to Gokhale that he came to consider himself as the latter's disciple.

Twenty years in the invigorating climate of the South African frontier, far from the restrictions of caste- and custom-conscious India, gave Gāndhi a unique opportunity to evolve religious and ethical beliefs of his own. The seed of pacifist anarchism had already been sown in his mind by his reading of Kropotkin's essays, which were being published in London during his student days there. Tolstoy's *The Kingdom of God Is Within You* now "overwhelmed" him with its message of Christian pacifism. Ruskin's *Unto This Last* made real to him the significance of manual labor as an expression of solidarity between the educated and the uneducated, and he acted immediately on this insight by starting a rural settlement for his growing band of followers. His studies of the Sermon on the Mount and the *Gītā* led him to the conclusion that the ideal life was one of selfless action in the service of one's fellow men, and the best

---

[1] D. G. Tendulkar, *Mahātmā. Life of Mohandas Karamchand Gandhi,* I, 39.

method of righting wrongs was to protest nonviolently and to suffer lovingly rather than submit to injustice. Last but not least, as he testified in his autobiography, *The Story of My Experiments with Truth,* the example of his wife, Kasturbā, proved to him how passive resistance to a wrong-doer could shame him into repentance.

Applying these principles to the struggle for fair treatment to the Indian community in South Africa, Gāndhi coined the term *satyāgraha* (literally, truth-insistence), defining it as "soul-force" or "the force which is born of truth and love or nonviolence." Time and again he and his followers deliberately and gladly went to jail rather than obey anti-Indian legislation. Thoreau's essay on "Civil Disobedience," read during one of his imprisonments, confirmed his view that an honest man is duty-bound to violate unjust laws. To fit himself for a life of voluntary hardship, Gāndhi continued to simplify his diet and dress, took a vow of celibacy, and disciplined his mind and body with prayer and fasting. His great *satyāgraha* campaign of 1913–14 ending successfully, he returned to India in 1915.

Gāndhi's use of peasant dress, his tireless advocacy of hand spinning and weaving, and his devotion to the cause of India's untouchables startled the older school of nationalist leaders and won the admiration of younger middle-class patriots. Because he had given up all worldly attachments, illiterate villagers trusted him unquestioningly. With the death of Tilak in 1920, he became the unchallenged master of the Congress. He brought to the task a Moderate's abhorrence of violence and willingness to arrive at compromises, together with an Extremist's passion for action and quasireligious appeal to the masses. Under his leadership the Congress was transformed into a fighting political army with hundreds of thousands of active members and sympathizers. In three major campaigns, spaced roughly ten years apart, he and his nonviolent army demonstrated their dissatisfaction with British reforms by inviting imprisonment and filling the jails to overcrowding.

Gāndhi's method of nonviolent noncooperation with British rule proved uniquely effective in the Indian situation where a resort to violence would have provoked severe repression and also embarrassed those English liberals and Laborites who were instrumental in finally freeing India. Whether *satyāgraha* would, as Gāndhi claimed, have worked equally well against a government of men fettered neither by Christian consciences nor by the sovereign rule of law has yet to be proved. The eventual achievement of Indian independence in 1947 was the outcome of a combination of circumstances—probably the most important being the weakening effect of two world wars on Britain's power and prestige in Asia—but the presence of a disciplined political organization under a revered leader greatly facilitated the transfer of power. Gāndhi, however, was deeply grieved at the partition of British India into the two states of India and Pakistan, and heartbroken at the ensuing communal warfare between Hindus and Sikhs on the one hand and Muslims on the other. His last of many political fasts were undertaken to persuade the rioters to come to their senses and to promote amity between the rival governments. On January 30, 1948, a Mahārāshtrian Hindu nationalist, feeling that Gāndhi had been too conciliatory to the Muslims, fatally shot him at his daily prayer meeting.

Gāndhi's remarkably protean thought mirrored the many influences, both Indian and Western, to which he subjected himself. The most ardent of Indian nationalists, he can also be considered the greatest representative of the renascence of Hinduism. At the same time, his long residence in Christian communities sharpened his unusual sense of sinfulness and his desire to serve the humblest of his fellow men. Gāndhi took seriously the New Testament injunction to return good for evil, and often referred to Jesus as "the Prince of Civil Resisters." A child of the Victorian era, he developed a puritanical zeal which spurred him on to act in strict accordance with his conscience, whatever the consequences. Significantly, Newman's "Lead, kindly light . . . one step enough for me," was his favorite hymn.

Harmony between thought and deed thus meant far more to Gāndhi than consistency between one thought and another. Because his mind operated in two different dimensions—the religious, with its insistence on absolute perfection and purity, and the political, with its emphasis on practicality and expediency—he often seemed to contradict himself. Summing up the conflict between these two sides of his nature, he once remarked, "Men say I am a saint losing myself in politics. The fact is I am a politician trying my hardest to be a saint." [2] Gāndhi's great strength as a political leader, however, and the key to his compelling personality,

[2] L. Fischer, *Gandhi, His Life and Message for the World*, p. 35, citing Henry Polak as his source.

lay precisely in his saintliness, his transparent honesty, and his constant willingness to see new points of view, to admit mistakes, but above all to be faithful to the truth as he saw it at the moment.

MOHANDĀS K. GĀNDHI
Hind Swarāj

Hind Swarāj (Indian Home Rule) was Gāndhi's first full-dress statement of his social and political ideals. Written in 1909 during a sea-voyage from London to South Africa, it took the form of a dialogue between the author and a skeptical friend. In a preface to a later edition Gāndhi explained that he wrote it to stop the "rot" of extremism and anarchism that was setting in among Indians in South Africa and elsewhere. To accomplish this end, Gāndhi seems to go the anarchists one better by advocating the complete rejection of modern Western civilization. In his conclusion he set forth clearly the doctrine of passive resistance, which follows as a logical corollary of his antagonism to "modern" civilization and all its ways.

Although Gāndhi was later forced to modify some of the extreme positions taken in *Hind Swarāj*, he never recanted the basic principles outlined in this manifesto. In his preface to the edition of 1938, he wrote that ". . . after the stormy thirty years through which I have . . . passed [since writing it], I have seen nothing to make me alter the views expounded in it."

Starting with a discussion of the political situation in India, Gāndhi criticized the British system of parliamentary government, and concluded:

[From Gāndhi, *Hind Swarāj*, pp. 24–76]

If India copies England, it is my firm conviction that she will be ruined.

Reader: To what do you ascribe this state of England?

Editor: It is not due to any peculiar fault of the English people, but the condition is due to modern civilization. It is a civilization only in name. Under it the nations of Europe are becoming degraded and ruined day by day.

Reader: Now you will have to explain what you mean by civilization.

Editor: It is not a question of what I mean. Several English writers refuse to call that civilization which passes under that name. Many books have been written upon that subject. Societies have been formed to cure the nation of the evils of civilization. A great English writer has written a work called "Civilization: Its Cause and Cure." Therein he has called it a disease.

Reader: Why do we not know this generally?

Editor: The answer is very simple. We rarely find people arguing against themselves. Those who are intoxicated by modern civilization are not likely to write against it. Their care will be to find out facts and arguments in support of it, and this they do unconsciously, believing it to be true. A man whilst he is dreaming, believes in his dream; he is undeceived only when he is awakened from his sleep. A man laboring under the bane of civilization is like a dreaming man. What we usually read are the works of defenders of modern civilization, which undoubtedly claims among its votaries very brilliant and even some very good men. Their writings hypnotize us. And so, one by one, we are drawn into the vortex.

Reader: This seems to be very plausible. Now will you tell me something of what you have read and thought of this civilization?

Editor: Let us first consider what state of things is described by the word "civilization." Its true test lies in the fact that people living in it make bodily welfare the object of life. We will take some examples. The people of Europe today live in better-built houses than they did a hundred years ago. This is considered an emblem of civilization, and this is also a matter to promote bodily happiness. Formerly, they wore skins, and used spears as their weapons. Now, they wear long trousers, and, for embellishing their bodies, they wear a variety of clothing, and, instead of spears, they carry with them revolvers containing five or more chambers. If people of a certain country, who have hitherto not been in the habit of wearing much clothing, boots, etc., adopt European clothing, they are supposed to have become civilized out of savagery. Formerly, in Europe, people plowed their lands mainly by manual labor. Now, one man can plow a vast tract by means of steam engines and can thus amass great wealth. This is called a sign of civilization. Formerly, only a few men wrote valuable books. Now, anybody writes and prints anything he likes and poisons people's minds. Formerly, men traveled in wagons. Now, they fly through the air in trains at the rate of four hundred and more miles per day. This is considered the height of civilization. It has been stated that, as men progress, they shall be able to travel in airships and reach any part of the world in a few hours. Men will not need the use of their hands and feet. They will press a button, and they will have their clothing by their side. They will press another button, and they will have their newspaper. A third, and a motor-car will be in waiting for them. They will have a variety of delicately dished up food. Everything will be done by machinery. Formerly, when people wanted to fight with one another, they measured between them their bodily strength; now it is possible to take away thousands of lives by one man working behind a gun from a hill. This is civilization. Formerly, men worked in the open air only as much as they liked. Now thousands of workmen meet together and for the sake of maintenance work in factories or mines. Their condition is worse than that of beasts. They are obliged to work, at the risk of their lives, at most dangerous occupations, for the sake of millionaires. Formerly, men were made slaves under physical compulsion. Now they are enslaved by temptation of money and of the luxuries that money can buy. There are now diseases of which people never dreamt before, and an army of doctors is engaged in finding out their cures, and so hospitals have increased. This is a test of civilization. Formerly, special messengers were required and much expense was incurred in order to send letters; today, anyone can abuse his fellow by means of a letter for one penny. True, at the same cost, one can send one's thanks also. Formerly, people had two or three meals consisting of home-made bread and vegetables; now, they require something to eat every two hours so that they have hardly leisure for anything else. What more need I say? All this you can ascertain from several authoritative books. These are all true tests of civilization. And if anyone speaks to the contrary, know that he is ignorant. This civilization takes note neither of morality nor of religion. Its votaries calmly state that their business is not to teach religion. Some even consider it to be a superstitious growth. Others put on the cloak of religion, and prate about morality. But, after twenty years' experience, I have come to the conclusion that immorality is often taught in the name of morality. Even a child can understand that in all I have described above there can be no inducement to morality. Civilization seeks to increase bodily comforts, and it fails miserably even in doing so.

This civilization is irreligion, and it has taken such a hold on the people in Europe that those who are in it appear to be half-mad. They lack real physical strength or courage. They keep up their energy by intoxication. They can hardly be happy in solitude. Women, who should be the queens of households, wander in the streets or they slave away in factories. For the sake of a pittance, half a million women in England alone are laboring under trying circumstances in factories or similar institutions. This awful fact is one of the causes of the daily growing suffragette movement.

This civilization is such that one has only to be patient and it will be self-destroyed. According to the teaching of Mahomed this would be considered a Satanic Civilization. Hinduism calls it the Black Age. I cannot give you an adequate conception of it. It is eating into the vitals of the English nation. It must be shunned. Parliaments are really emblems of slavery. If you will sufficiently think over this, you will entertain the same opinion and cease to blame the English. They rather deserve our sympathy. They are a shrewd nation and I therefore believe that they will cast off the evil. They are enterprising and industrious, and their mode of thought is not inherently immoral. Neither are they bad at heart. I therefore respect them. Civilization is not an incurable disease, but it should never be forgotten that the English people are at present afflicted by it. [pp. 24–27]

Gāndhi next explained that the English gained India because Indians yielded to the blandishments of their silver bullion; he condemned the railway as a "distributing agency for the evil one," and "a most dangerous institution"; charged lawyers with enslaving India by their cooperation with the British legal system; and ridiculed doctors for encouraging vice by curing the diseases acquired through overindulgence. He went on to draw an idyllic picture of pre-British India, whose civilization he characterized as "unquestionably" the world's best.

Reader: You have denounced railways, lawyers and doctors. I can see that you will discard all machinery. What then, is civilization?

Editor: The answer to that question is not difficult. I believe that the civilization India has evolved is not to be beaten in the world. Nothing can equal the seeds sown by our ancestors. Rome went, Greece shared the same fate; the might of the Pharaohs was broken; Japan has become Westernized; of China nothing can be said; but India is still, somehow or other, sound at the foundation. The people of Europe learn their lessons from the writings of the men of Greece or Rome, which exist no longer in their former glory. In trying to learn from them, the Europeans imagine that they will avoid the mistakes of Greece and Rome. Such is their pitiable condition. In the midst of all this India remains immovable and that is her glory. It is a charge against India that her people are so uncivilized, ignorant, and stolid, that it is not possible to induce them to adopt any changes. It is a charge really against our merit. What we have tested and found true on the anvil of experience, we dare not change. Many thrust their advice upon India, and she remains steady. This is her beauty: it is the sheet-anchor of our hope.

Civilization is that mode of conduct which points out to man the path of duty. Performance of duty and observance of morality are convertible terms. To observe morality is to attain mastery over our mind and our passions. So doing, we know ourselves. The Gujarati equivalent for civilization means "good conduct."

If this definition be correct, then India, as so many writers have shown, has nothing to learn from anybody else, and this is as it should be. We notice that the mind is a restless bird; the more it gets the more it wants, and still remains unsatisfied. The more we indulge our passions the more unbridled they become. Our ancestors, therefore, set a limit to our indulgences. They saw that happiness was largely a mental condition. A man is not necessarily happy because he is rich, or unhappy because he is poor. The rich are often seen to be unhappy, the poor to be happy. Millions will always remain poor. Observing all this, our ancestors dissuaded us from luxuries and pleasures. We have managed with the same kind of plow as existed thousands of years ago. We have retained the same kind of cottages that we had in former times and our indigenous education remains the same as before. We have had no system of life-corroding competition. Each followed his own occupation or trade and charged a regulation wage. It was not that we did not know how to invent machinery, but our forefathers knew that, if we set our hearts after such things, we would become slaves and lose our moral fibre. They, therefore, after due deliberation decided that we should only do what we could with our hands and feet. They saw that our real happiness and health consisted in a proper use of our hands and feet. They further reasoned that large cities were a snare and a useless encumbrance and that people would not be happy in them, that there would be gangs of thieves and robbers, prostitution, and vice flourishing in them and that poor men would be robbed by rich men. They were, therefore, satisfied with small villages. They saw that kings and their swords were inferior to the sword of ethics, and they, therefore, held the sovereigns of the earth to be inferior to the Rishis and the Fakirs. A nation with a constitution like this is fitter to teach others than to learn from others. This nation had courts, lawyers, and doctors, but they were all within bounds. Everybody knew that these professions were not particularly superior; moreover, these *vakils* and *vaids*[1] did not rob people; they were considered people's dependants, not their masters. Justice was tolerably fair. The ordinary rule was to avoid courts. There were no touts to lure people into them. This evil, too, was noticeable only in and around capitals. The common people lived independently and followed their agricultural occupation. They enjoyed true Home Rule.

And where this cursed modern civilization has not reached, India remains as it was before. The inhabitants of that part of India will very properly laugh at your new-fangled notions. The English do not rule over them, nor will you ever rule over them. Those in whose name we speak we do not know, nor do they know us. I would certainly advise you and those like you who love the motherland to go into the interior that has not yet been polluted by the railways and to live there for six months; you might then be patriotic and speak of Home Rule.

Now you see what I consider to be real civilization. Those who want to change conditions such as I have described are enemies of the country and are sinners.

Reader: It would be all right if India were exactly as you have described it, but it is also India where there are hundreds of child widows, where two-year-old babies are married, where twelve-year-old girls are mothers and housewives, where women practice polyandry, where the practice of *niyoga*[2] obtains, where, in the name of religion, girls dedicate themselves to prostitution, and in the name of religion sheep and goats are killed. Do you consider these also symbols of the civilization that you have described?

Editor: You make a mistake. The defects that you have shown are defects. Nobody mistakes them for ancient civilization. They remain in spite of it. Attempts have always been made and will be made to remove them. We may utilize the new spirit that is born in us for purging ourselves of these evils. But what I have described to you as emblems of modern civilization are accepted as such by its votaries. The Indian civilization, as described by me, has been so described by its votaries. In no part of the world, and under no civilization, have all men attained

---

[1] Lawyers and doctors.
[2] Temporary cohabitation, enjoined for the sake of giving a childless widow a son.

perfection. The tendency of the Indian civilization is to elevate the moral being, that of the Western civilization is to propagate immorality. The latter is godless, the former is based on a belief in God. So understanding and so believing, it behoves every lover of India to cling to the old Indian civilization even as a child clings to the mother's breast.

Reader: I appreciate your views about civilization. I will have to think over them. I cannot take them in all at once. What, then, holding the views you do, would you suggest for freeing India?

Editor: I do not expect my views to be accepted all of a sudden. My duty is to place them before readers like yourself. Time can be trusted to do the rest. We have already examined the conditions for freeing India, but we have done so indirectly; we will now do so directly. It is a world-known maxim that the removal of the cause of a disease results in the removal of the disease itself. Similarly if the cause of India's slavery be removed, India can become free.

Reader: If Indian civilization is, as you say, the best of all, how do you account for India's slavery?

Editor: This civilization is unquestionably the best, but it is to be observed that all civilizations have been on their trial. That civilization which is permanent outlives it. Because the sons of India were found wanting, its civilization has been placed in jeopardy. But its strength is to be seen in its ability to survive the shock. Moreover, the whole of India is not touched. Those alone who have been affected by Western civilization have become enslaved. We measure the universe by our own miserable foot-rule. When we are slaves, we think that the whole universe is enslaved. Because we are in an abject condition, we think that the whole of India is in that condition. As a matter of fact, it is not so, yet it is as well to impute our slavery to the whole of India. But if we bear in mind the above fact, we can see that if we become free, India is free. And in this thought you have a definition of *Swarāj*. It is *Swarāj* when we learn to rule ourselves. It is, therefore, in the palm of our hands. Do not consider this *Swarāj* to be like a dream. There is no idea of sitting still. The *Swarāj* that I wish to picture is such that, after we have once realized it, we shall endeavor to the end of our lifetime to persuade others to do likewise. But such *Swarāj* has to be experienced, by each one for himself. One drowning man will never save another. Slaves ourselves, it would be a mere pretension to think of freeing others. Now you will have seen that it is not necessary for us to have as our goal the expulsion of the English. If the English become Indianized, we can accommodate them. If they wish to remain in India along with their civilization, there is no room for them. It lies with us to bring about such a state of things.

Reader: It is impossible that Englishmen should ever become Indianized.

Editor: To say that is equivalent to saying that the English have no humanity in them. And it is really beside the point whether they become so or not. If we keep our own house in order, only those who are fit to live in it will remain. Others will leave of their own accord. Such things occur within the experience of all of us.

Reader: But it has not occurred in history.

Editor: To believe that what has not occurred in history will not occur at all is to argue disbelief in the dignity of man. At any rate, it behoves us to try what appeals to our reason. All countries are not similarly conditioned. The condition of India is unique. Its strength is immeasurable. We need not, therefore, refer to the history of other countries. I have drawn attention to the fact that, when other civilizations have succumbed, the Indian has survived many a shock. [pp. 43-47]

. . . .

Reader: I cannot follow this. There seems little doubt that we shall have to expel the English by force of arms. So long as they are in the country we cannot rest. . . .

Editor: . . . I believe that you want the millions of India to be happy, not that you [merely] want the reins of government in your hands. If that be so, we have to consider only one thing: how can the millions obtain self-rule? You will admit that people under several Indian princes are being ground down. The latter mercilessly crush them. Their tyranny is greater than that of the English, and if you want such tyranny in India, then we shall never agree. My patriotism does not teach me that I am to allow people to be crushed under the heel of Indian princes if only the English retire. If I have power, I should resist the tyranny of Indian princes just as much as that of the English. By patriotism I mean the welfare of the whole people, and if I could secure it at the hands of the English, I should bow down my head to them. If any Englishman dedicated his life to securing the freedom of India, resisting tyranny, and serving the land, I should welcome that Englishman as an Indian.

[258]

Again [you say that] India can fight . . . only when she has arms. You have not considered this problem at all. The English are splendidly armed; that does not frighten me, but it is clear that, to pit ourselves against them in arms, thousands of Indians must be armed. If such a thing be possible, how many years will it take? Moreover, to arm India on a large scale is to Europeanize it. Then her condition will be just as pitiable as that of Europe. This means, in short that India must accept European civilization, and if that is what we want, the best thing is that we have among us those who are so well trained in that civilization. We will then fight for a few rights, will get what we can and so pass our days. But the fact is that the Indian nation will not adopt arms, and it is well that it does not. [p. 49]

Introducing the concept of "soul-force" or "passive resistance," Gāndhi argued that it was the only method by which home rule could be regained.

Thousands, indeed tens of thousands, depend for their existence on a very active working of this force. Little quarrels of millions of families in their daily lives disappear before the exercise of this force. Hundreds of nations live in peace. History does not and cannot take note of this fact. History is really a record of every interruption of the even working of the force of love or of the soul. Two brothers quarrel; one of them repents and reawakens the love that was lying dormant in him; the two again begin to live in peace; nobody takes note of this. But if the two brothers, through the intervention of solicitors or some other reason, take up arms or go to law—which is another form of the exhibition of brute force—their doings would be immediately noticed in the press, they would be the talk of their neighbors and would probably go down to history. And what is true of families and communities is true of nations. There is no reason to believe that there is one law for families and another for nations. History, then, is a record of an interruption of the course of nature. Soul-force, being natural, is not noted in history.

Reader: According to what you say, it is plain that instances of this kind of passive resistance are not to be found in history. It is necessary to understand this passive resistance more fully. It will be better, therefore, if you enlarge upon it.

Editor: Passive resistance is a method of securing rights by personal suffering; it is the reverse of resistance by arms. When I refuse to do a thing that is repugnant to my conscience, I use soul-force. For instance, the government of the day has passed a law which is applicable to me. I do not like it. If by using violence I force the government to repeal the law, I am employing what may be termed body-force. If I do not obey the law and accept the penalty for its breach, I use soul-force. It involves sacrifice of self.

Everybody admits that sacrifice of self is infinitely superior to sacrifice of others. Moreover, if this kind of force is used in a cause that is unjust, only the person using it suffers. He does not make others suffer for his mistakes. Men have before now done many things which were subsequently found to have been wrong. No man can claim that he is absolutely in the right or that a particular thing is wrong because he thinks so, but it is wrong for him so long as that is his deliberate judgment. It is therefore meet that he should not do that which he knows to be wrong, and suffer the consequence whatever it may be. This is the key to the use of soul-force.

Reader: You would then disregard laws—this is rank disloyalty. We have always been considered a law-abiding nation. You seem to be going even beyond the extremists. They say that we must obey the laws that have been passed, but that if the laws be bad, we must drive out the law-givers even by force.

Editor: Whether I go beyond them or whether I do not is a matter of no consequence to either of us. We simply want to find out what is right and to act accordingly. The real meaning of the statement that we are a law-abiding nation is that we are passive resisters. When we do not like certain laws, we do not break the heads of law-givers but we suffer and do not submit to the laws. That we should obey laws whether good or bad is a new-fangled notion. There was no such thing in former days. The people disregarded those laws they did not like and suffered the penalties for their breach. It is contrary to our manhood if we obey laws repugnant to our conscience. Such teaching is opposed to religion and means slavery. If the government were to ask us to go about without any clothing, should we do so? If I were a passive resister, I would say to them that I would have nothing to do with their law. But we have so forgotten ourselves and become so compliant that we do not mind any degrading law.

A man who has realized his manhood, who fears only God, will fear no one else. Man-made laws are not necessarily binding on him. Even the government does not expect any such thing from us. They do not say:

"You must do such and such a thing," but they say: "If you do not do it, we will punish you." We are sunk so low that we fancy that it is our duty and our religion to do what the law lays down. If man will only realize that it is unmanly to obey laws that are unjust, no man's tyranny will enslave him. This is the key to self-rule or home-rule.

It is a superstition and ungodly thing to believe that an act of a majority binds a minority. Many examples can be given in which acts of majorities will be found to have been wrong and those of minorities to have been right. All reforms owe their origin to the initiation of minorities in opposition to majorities. If among a band of robbers a knowledge of robbing is obligatory, is a pious man to accept the obligation? So long as the superstition that men should obey unjust laws exists, so long will their slavery exist. And a passive resister alone can remove such a superstition.

To use brute-force, to use gunpowder, is contrary to passive resistance, for it means that we want our opponent to do by force that which we desire but he does not. And if such a use of force is justifiable, surely he is entitled to do likewise by us. And so we should never come to an agreement. We may simply fancy, like the blind horse moving in a circle round a mill, that we are making progress. Those who believe that they are not bound to obey laws which are repugnant to their conscience have only the remedy of passive resistance open to them. Any other must lead to disaster.

Reader: From what you say I deduce that passive resistance is a splendid weapon of the weak, but that when they are strong they may take up arms.

Editor: This is gross ignorance. Passive resistance, that is, soul-force, is matchless. It is superior to the force of arms. How, then, can it be considered only a weapon of the weak? Physical-force men are strangers to the courage that is requisite in a passive resister. Do you believe that a coward can ever disobey a law that he dislikes? Extremists are considered to be advocates of brute force. Why do they, then, talk about obeying laws? I do not blame them. They can say nothing else. When they succeed in driving out the English and they themselves become governors, they will want you and me to obey their laws. And that is a fitting thing for their constitution. But a passive resister will say he will not obey a law that is against his conscience, even though he may be blown to pieces at the mouth of a cannon.

What do you think? Wherein is courage required—in blowing others to pieces from behind a cannon, or with a smiling face to approach a cannon and be blown to pieces? Who is the true warrior—he who keeps death always as a bosom-friend, or he who controls the death of others? Believe me that a man devoid of courage and manhood can never be a passive resister.

This however, I will admit: that even a man weak in body is capable of offering this resistance. One man can offer it just as well as millions. Both men and women can indulge in it. It does not require the training of an army; it needs no jiu-jitsu. Control over the mind is alone necessary, and when that is attained, man is free like the king of the forest and his very glance withers the enemy.

Passive resistance is an all-sided sword, it can be used anyhow; it blesses him who uses it and him against whom it is used. Without drawing a drop of blood it produces far-reaching results. It never rusts and cannot be stolen. Competition between passive resisters does not exhaust. The sword of passive resistance does not require a scabbard. It is strange indeed that you should consider such a weapon to be a weapon merely of the weak.

Reader: You have said that passive resistance is a specialty of India. Have cannons never been used in India?

Editor: Evidently, in your opinion, India means its few princes. To me it means its teeming millions on whom depends the existence of its princes and our own.

Kings will always use their kingly weapons. To use force is bred in them. They want to command, but those who have to obey commands do not want guns: and these are in a majority throughout the world. They have to learn either body-force or soul-force. Where they learn the former, both the rulers and the ruled become like so many madmen; but where they learn soul-force, the commands of the rulers do not go beyond the point of their swords, for true men disregard unjust commands. Peasants have never been subdued by the sword, and never will be. They do not know the use of the sword, and they are not frightened by the use of it by others. That nation is great which rests its head upon death as its pillow. Those who defy death are free from all fear. For those who are laboring under the delusive charms of brute-force, this picture is not overdrawn. The fact is that, in India, the nation at large has generally used passive resistance in all departments of life. We cease to cooperate with our rulers when they displease us. This is passive resistance.

I remember an instance when, in a small principality, the villagers were offended by some command issued by the prince. The former immediately began vacating the village. The prince became nervous, apologized to his subjects, and withdrew his command. Many such instances can be found in India. Real Home Rule is possible only where passive resistance is the guiding force of the people. Any other rule is foreign rule.

Reader: Then you will say that it is not at all necessary for us to train the body?

Editor: I will certainly not say any such thing. It is difficult to become a passive resister unless the body is trained. As a rule, the mind, residing in a body that has become weakened by pampering, is also weak, and where there is no strength of mind there can be no strength of soul. We shall have to improve our physique by getting rid of infant marriages and luxurious living. If I were to ask a man with a shattered body to face a cannon's mouth I should make a laughing-stock of myself.

Reader: From what you say, then, it would appear that it is not a small thing to become a passive resister, and, if that is so, I should like you to explain how a man may become one.

Editor: To become a passive resister is easy enough but it is also equally difficult. I have known a lad of fourteen years become a passive resister; I have known also sick people do likewise; and I have also known physically strong and otherwise happy people unable to take up passive resistance. After a great deal of experience it seems to me that those who want to become passive resisters for the service of the country have to observe perfect chastity, adopt poverty, follow truth, and cultivate fearlessness.

Chastity is one of the greatest disciplines without which the mind cannot attain requisite firmness. A man who is unchaste loses stamina, becomes emasculated and cowardly. He whose mind is given over to animal passions is not capable of any great effort. This can be proved by innumerable instances. What, then, is a married person to do is the question that arises naturally; and yet it need not. When a husband and wife gratify the passions, it is no less an animal indulgence on that account. Such an indulgence, except for perpetuating the race, is strictly prohibited. But a passive resister has to avoid even that very limited indulgence because he can have no desire for progeny. A married man, therefore, can observe perfect chastity. This subject is not capable of being treated at greater length. Several questions arise: How is one to carry one's wife with one? what are her rights? and other similar questions. Yet those who wish to take part in a great work are bound to solve these puzzles.

Just as there is necessity for chastity, so is there for poverty. Pecuniary ambition and passive resistance cannot well go together. Those who have money are not expected to throw it away, but they *are* expected to be indifferent about it. They must be prepared to lose every penny rather than give up passive resistance.

Passive resistance has been described in the course of our discussion as truth-force. Truth, therefore, has necessarily to be followed and that at any cost. In this connection, academic questions such as whether a man may not lie in order to save a life, etc., arise, but these questions occur only to those who wish to justify lying. Those who want to follow truth every time are not placed in such a quandry; and if they are, they are still saved from a false position.

Passive resistance cannot proceed a step without fearlessness. Those alone can follow the path of passive resistance who are free from fear, whether as to their possessions, false honor, their relatives, the government, bodily injuries or death.

These observances are not to be abandoned in the belief that they are difficult. Nature has implanted in the human breast ability to cope with any difficulty or suffering that may come to man unprovoked. These qualities are worth having, even for those who do not wish to serve the country. Let there be no mistake, as those who want to train themselves in the use of arms are also obliged to have these qualities more or less. Everybody does not become a warrior for the wish. A would-be warrior will have to observe chastity and to be satisfied with poverty as his lot. A warrior without fearlessness cannot be conceived of. It may be thought that he would not need to be exactly truthful, but that quality follows real fearlessness. When a man abandons truth, he does so owing to fear in some shape or form. The above four attributes, then, need not frighten anyone. It may be as well here to note that a physical-force man has to have many other useless qualities which a passive resister never needs. And you will find that whatever extra effort a swordsman needs is due to lack of fearlessness. If he is an embodiment of the latter, the sword will drop from his hand that very moment. He does not need its support. One who is free from hatred requires no sword. A man with a stick suddenly came face to face with a lion and instinctively raised his weapon in self-defense. The man saw that he had only prated about fearlessness when there was none in him. That moment he dropped the stick and found himself free from all fear. [pp. 57–63]

In the manner of a lawyer summing up his brief, Gāndhi reduced his argument to its essentials in this final portion of *Hind Swarāj*. After his prophetic last sentence, he appended a list of twenty authoritative books, eighteen of them by Europeans, and eight testimonies to the superiority of Indian civilization, all of them by Englishmen.

Reader: What then, would you say to the English?

Editor: To them I would respectfully say: "I admit you are my rulers. It is not necessary to debate the question whether you hold India by the sword or by my consent. I have no objection to your remaining in my country, but although you are the rulers, you will have to remain as servants of the people. It is not we who have to do as you wish, but it is you who have to do as we wish. You may keep the riches that you have drained away from this land, but you may not drain riches henceforth. Your function will be, if you so wish, to police India; you must abandon the idea of deriving any commercial benefit from us. We hold the civilization that you support to be the reverse of civilization. We consider our civilization to be far superior to yours. If you realize this truth, it will be to your advantage and, if you do not, according to your own proverb, you should only live in our country in the same manner as we do. You must not do anything that is contrary to our religions. It is your duty as rulers that for the sake of the Hindus you should eschew beef, and for the sake of Mahomedans you should avoid bacon and ham. We have hitherto said nothing because we have been cowed down, but you need not consider that you have not hurt our feelings by your conduct. We are not expressing our sentiments either through base selfishness or fear, but because it is our duty now to speak out boldly. We consider your schools and law courts to be useless. We want our own ancient schools and courts to be restored. The common language of India is not

English but Hindi. You should, therefore, learn it. We can hold communication with you only in our national language.

"We cannot tolerate the idea of your spending money on railways and the military. We see no occasion for either. You may fear Russia;[3] we do not. When she comes we shall look after her. If you are with us, we may then receive her jointly. We do not need any European cloth. We shall manage with articles produced and manufactured at home. You may not keep one eye on Manchester and the other on India. We can work together only if our interests are identical.

"This has not been said to you in arrogance. You have great military resources. Your naval power is matchless. If we wanted to fight with you on your own ground, we should be unable to do so, but if the above submissions be not acceptable to you, we cease to play the part of the ruled. You may, if you like cut us to pieces. You may shatter us at the cannon's mouth. If you act contrary to our will, we shall not help you; and without our help, we know that you cannot move one step forward.

"It is likely that you will laugh at all this in the intoxication of your power. We may not be able to disillusion you at once; but if there be any manliness in us, you will see shortly that your intoxication is suicidal and that your laugh at our expense is an aberration of intellect. We believe that at heart you belong to a religious nation. We are living in a land which is the source of religions. How we came together need not be considered, but we can make mutual good use of our relations.

"You, English, who have come to India are not good specimens of the English nation, nor can we, almost half-Anglicized Indians, be considered good specimens of the real Indian nation. If the English nation were to know all you have done, it would oppose many of your actions. The mass of the Indians have had few dealings with you. If you will abandon your so-called civilization and search into your own scriptures, you will find that our demands are just. Only on condition of our demands being fully satisfied may you remain in India; and if you remain under those conditions, we shall learn several things from you and you will learn many from us. So doing we shall benefit each other and the world. But that will happen only when the root of our relationship is sunk in a religious soil."

[3] Russia's conquest of Central Asia in the latter half of the nineteenth century had alarmed the British, who feared a possible invasion of India through Afghānistān.

Reader: What will you say to the nation?

Editor: Who is the nation?

Reader: For our purposes it is the nation that you and I have been thinking of, that is those of us who are affected by European civilization, and who are eager to have Home Rule.

Editor: To these I would say: "It is only those Indians who are imbued with real love who will be able to speak to the English in the above strain without being frightened, and only those can be said to be so imbued who conscientiously believe that Indian civilization is the best and that the European is a nine-days' wonder. Such ephemeral civilizations have often come and gone and will continue to do so. Those only can be considered to be so imbued who, having experienced the force of the soul within themselves, will not cower before brute-force, and will not, on any account, desire to use brute-force. Those only can be considered to have been so imbued who are intensely dissatisfied with the present pitiable condition, having already drunk the cup of poison.

"If there be only one such Indian, he will speak as above to the English and the English will have to listen to him." [pp. 72–74]

Reader: This is a large order. When will all carry it out?

Editor: You make a mistake. You and I have nothing to do with the others. Let each do his duty. If I do my duty, that is, serve myself, I shall be able to serve others. Before I leave you, I will take the liberty of repeating;

1. Real home-rule is self-rule or self-control.

2. The way to it is passive resistance: that is soul-force or love-force.

3. In order to exert this force, Swadeshī in every sense is necessary.

4. What we want to do should be done, not because we object to the English or because we want to retaliate, but because it is our duty to do so. Thus, supposing that the English remove the salt-tax, restore our money, give the highest posts to Indians, withdraw the English troops, we shall certainly not use their machine-made goods, nor use the English language, nor many of their industries. It is worth noting that these things are, in their nature, harmful; hence we do not want them. I bear no enmity towards the English but I do towards their civilization.

In my opinion, we have used the term *Swarāj* without understanding its real significance. I have endeavored to explain it as I understand it, and my conscience testifies that my life henceforth is dedicated to its attainment. [p. 76]

Reply to Tagore

Referring to the poet as "the great sentinel" who was exquisitely jealous of India's honor, Gāndhi answered Tagore's criticisms in his weekly magazine, *Young India*. He justified his program of spinning, burning foreign cloth, and boycotting English education by an eloquent appeal on behalf of the starving millions with whom he had identified himself.

[From Gāndhi, *Young India, 1919–1922,* pp. 670–74]

To a people famishing and idle, the only acceptable form in which God can dare appear is work and promise of food as wages. God created man to work for his food, and said that those who ate without work were thieves. Eighty percent of India are compulsory thieves half the year. Is it any wonder if India has become one vast prison? Hunger is the argument that is driving India to the spinning wheel. The call of the spinning wheel is the noblest of all. Because it is the call of love. And love is *Swarāj*. The spinning wheel will "curb the mind" when the time is spent on necessary physical labor can be said to do so. We must think of millions who are today less than animals, who are almost in a dying state. The spinning wheel is the reviving draught for the millions of our dying countrymen and countrywomen. "Why should I who have no need to work for food, spin?" may be the question asked. Because I am eating what does not belong to me. I am living on the spoliation of my countrymen. Trace the course of every pice[1] that finds its way into your pocket, and you will realize the truth of what I write. *Swarāj* has no meaning for the millions if they do not know how to employ their enforced idleness. The attainment of this *Swarāj* is possible within a short time and it is so possible only by the revival of the spinning wheel.

I do want growth, I do want self-determination, I do want freedom, but I want all these for the soul. I doubt if the steel age is an advance upon the flint age. I am indifferent. It is the evolution of the soul to which the intellect and all our faculties have to be devoted. I have no difficulty in imagining the possibility of a man armored after the modern style making some lasting and new discovery for mankind, but I have less difficulty in imagining the possibility of a man having nothing but a bit of flint and a dail for lighting his path or his matchlock ever singing new hymns of praise and delivering to an aching world a message

[1] One-fourth anna, or one forty-eighth of a rupee.

[268]

of peace and good will upon earth. A plea for the spinning wheel is a plea for recognizing the dignity of labor.

I claim that in losing the spinning wheel we lost our left lung. We are therefore suffering from galloping consumption. The restoration of the wheel arrests the progress of the fell disease. There are certain things which all must do in all climes. There are certain things which all must do in certain climes. The spinning wheel is the thing which all must turn in the Indian clime for the transition stage at any rate and the vast majority must for all time.

It was our love of foreign cloth that ousted the wheel from its position of dignity. Therefore I consider it a sin to wear foreign cloth. I must confess that I do not draw a sharp or any distinction between economics and ethics. Economics that hurt the moral well-being of an individual or a nation are immoral and therefore sinful. Thus the economics that permit one country to prey upon another are immoral. It is sinful to buy and use articles made by sweated labor. It is sinful to eat American wheat and let my neighbor the grain dealer starve for want of custom. Similarly it is sinful for me to wear the latest finery of Regent Street, when I know that if I had but worn the things woven by the neighboring spinners and weavers, that would have clothed me, and fed and clothed them. On the knowledge of my sin bursting upon me, I must consign the foreign garments to the flames and thus purify myself, and henceforth rest content with the rough khādī[2] made by my neighbors. On knowing that my neighbors may not, having given up the occupation, take kindly to the spinning wheel, I must take it up myself and thus make it popular.

I venture to suggest to the Poet that the clothes I ask him to burn must be and are his. If they had to his knowledge belonged to the poor or the ill-clad, he would long ago have restored to the poor what was theirs. In burning *my* foreign clothes I burn my shame. I must refuse to insult the naked by giving them clothes they do not need, instead of giving them work which they sorely need. I will not commit the sin of becoming their patron, but on learning that I had assisted in impoverishing them, I would give them a privileged position and give them neither crumbs nor cast off clothing, but the best of my food and clothes and associate myself with them in work.

[2] Homespun cloth.

Nor is the scheme of noncooperation or Swadeshī an exclusive doctrine. My modesty has prevented me from declaring from the house top that the message of noncooperation, nonviolence, and Swadeshī, is a message to the world. It must fall flat, if it does not bear fruit in the soil where it has been delivered. At the present moment India has nothing to share with the world save her degradation, pauperism and plagues. Is it her ancient Shāstras that we should send to the world? Well they are printed in many editions, and an incredulous and idolatrous world refuses to look at them, because we, the heirs and custodians, do not live them. Before, therefore, I can think of sharing with the world, I must possess. Our noncooperation is neither with the English nor with the West. Our noncooperation is with the system the English have established, with the material civilization and its attendant greed and exploitation of the weak. Our noncooperation is a retirement within ourselves. Our non-cooperation is a refusal to cooperate with the English administrators on their own terms. We say to them, "Come and cooperate with us on our terms, and it will be well for us, for you and the world." We must refuse to be lifted off our feet. A drowning man cannot save others. In order to be fit to save others, we must try to save ourselves. Indian nationalism is not exclusive, nor aggressive, nor destructive. It is health-giving, religious, and therefore humanitarian. India must learn to live before she can aspire to die for humanity. The mice which helplessly find themselves between the cat's teeth acquire no merit from their enforced sacrifice.

True to his poetical instinct the Poet lives for the morrow and would have us do likewise. He presents to our admiring gaze the beautiful picture of the birds early in the morning singing hymns of praise as they soar into the sky. These birds had their day's food and soared with rested wings in whose veins new blood had flown during the previous night. But I have had the pain of watching birds who for want of strength could not be coaxed even into a flutter of their wings. The human bird under the Indian sky gets up weaker than when he pretended to retire. For millions it is an eternal vigil or an eternal trance. It is an indescribably painful state which has to be experienced to be realized. I have found it impossible to soothe suffering patients with a song from Kabīr. The hungry millions ask for one poem—invigorating food. They cannot be given it. They must earn it. And they can earn only by the sweat of their brow.

Through Love to God

In bringing to a close his exceedingly frank autobiography (which is a classic of its kind), Gāndhi gave a succinct statement of his ethico-religious beliefs. For him, Truth is God, and ahimsā (which in Gāndhi's usage of the term corresponds closely to the Christian concept of love) is the way to achieve the traditional Hindu ideal of "God-realization."
[From Gāndhi, *Autobiography*, pp. 615–16]

My uniform experience has convinced me that there is no other God than Truth. And if every page of these chapters does not proclaim to the reader that the only means for the realization of Truth is ahimsā, I shall deem all my labor in writing these chapters to have been in vain. And, even though my efforts in this behalf may prove fruitless, let the readers know that the vehicle, not the great principle, is at fault. After all, however sincere my strivings after ahimsā may have been, they have still been imperfect and inadequate. The little fleeting glimpses, therefore, that I have been able to have of Truth can hardly convey an idea of the indescribable luster of Truth, a million times more intense than that of the sun we daily see with our eyes. In fact what I have caught is only the faintest glimmer of that mighty effulgence. But this much I can say with assurance, as a result of all my experiments, that a perfect vision of Truth can only follow a complete realization of ahimsā.

To see the universal and all-pervading Spirit of Truth face to face one must be able to love the meanest of creation as oneself. And a man who aspires after that cannot afford to keep out of any field of life. That is why my devotion to Truth has drawn me into the field of politics; and I can say without the slightest hesitation, and yet in all humility, that those who say that religion has nothing to do with politics do not know what religion means.

Identification with everything that lives is impossible without self-purification; without self-purification the observance of the law of ahimsā must remain an empty dream; God can never be realized by one who is not pure of heart. Self-purification therefore must mean purification in all the walks of life. And purification being highly infectious, purifica-

tion of oneself necessarily leads to the purification of one's surroundings.
But the path of self-purification is hard and steep. To attain to perfect purity one has to become absolutely passion-free in thought, speech,
and action; to rise above the opposing currents of love and hatred, attachment and repulsion. I know that I have not in me as yet that triple
purity, in spite of constant ceaseless striving for it. That is why the
world's praise fails to move me, indeed it very often stings me. To conquer the subtle passions seems to me to be harder far than the physical
conquest of the world by the force of arms. Ever since my return to
India I have had experiences of the dormant passions lying hidden within
me. The knowledge of them has made me feel humiliated though not
defeated. The experiences and experiments have sustained me and given
me a great joy. But I know that I have still before me a difficult path
to traverse. I must reduce myself to zero. So long as a man does not of
his own free will put himself last among his fellow creatures, there is
no salvation for him. Ahimsā is the farthest limit of humility.

In bidding farewell to the reader, for the time being at any rate, I
ask him to join with me in prayer to the God of Truth that He may
grant me the boon of ahimsā in mind, word, and deed.

Hindu-Muslim Unity

The following passages from a statement issued shortly before a meeting in
1938 with Muslim League leader Jinnāh show Gāndhi's deep longing to
establish concord between Hindus and Muslims. By the very nature of orthodox Islam, however, most Indian Muslims were unable to reciprocate his
readiness to include the best of their religion in his.
[From Gāndhi, *Communal Unity*, pp. 217–18]

My Hinduism is not sectarian. It includes all that I know to be best in
Islam, Christianity, Buddhism, and Zoroastrianism. I approach politics
as everything else in a religious spirit. Truth is my religion and ahimsā
is the only way of its realization. I have rejected once and for all the
doctrine of the sword. The secret stabbings of innocent persons, and the
speeches I read in the papers, are hardly the thing leading to peace or an
honorable settlement.

Again I am not approaching the forthcoming interview in any representative capacity. I have purposely divested myself of any such. If there
are to be any formal negotiations, they will be between the President of

the Congress and the President of the Muslim League. I go as a lifelong worker in the cause of Hindu-Muslim unity. It has been my passion from early youth. I count some of the noblest of Muslims as my friends. . . .

I may not leave a single stone unturned to achieve Hindu-Muslim unity. God fulfills Himself in strange ways. He may, in a manner least known to us, both fulfill Himself through the interview and open a way to an honorable understanding between the two communities. It is in that hope that I am looking forward to the forthcoming talk. We are friends, not strangers. It does not matter to me that we see things from different angles of vision. I ask the public not to attach any exaggerated importance to the interview. But I ask all lovers of communal peace to pray that the God of truth and love may give us both the right spirit and the right word and use us for the good of the dumb millions of India.

The Message of Asia

Addressing the Inter-Asian Relations Conference convened at Delhi in April, 1947, Gāndhi reiterated the belief of many Indian intellectuals that all Asia shared their traditional concern for religious and spiritual values.
[From Gāndhi, *Communal Unity*, pp. 579–80]

What I want you to understand is the message of Asia. It is not to be learnt through Western spectacles or by imitating the atom bomb. If you want to give a message to the West, it must be the message of love and the message of truth. I do not want merely to appeal to your head. I want to capture your heart.

In this age of democracy, in this age of awakening of the poorest of the poor, you can redeliver this message with the greatest emphasis. You will complete the conquest of the West not through vengeance because you have been exploited, but with real understanding. I am sanguine if all of you put your hearts together—not merely heads—to understand the secret of the message these wise men [1] of the East have left to us, and if we really become worthy of that great message, the conquest of the West will be completed. This conquest will be loved by the West itself.

---

[1] He had previously mentioned Zoroaster, Buddha, Moses, Jesus, Muhammad, Krishna, and Rāma.

The West is today pining for wisdom. It is despairing of a multiplication of atom bombs, because atom bombs mean utter destruction not merely of the West but of the whole world, as if the prophecy of the Bible is going to be fulfilled and there is to be a perfect deluge. It is up to you to tell the world of its wickedness and sin—that is the heritage your teachers and my teachers have taught Asia.

CHAPTER XXVI

PAKISTAN: ITS FOUNDING AND FUTURE

When Iqbāl told the All-India Muslim League in December, 1930, that he hoped to see the Muslim areas of the subcontinent become a separate state, it was not the first time this idea had been put forward. Earlier the famous pan-Islamist thinker, Saiyid Jamāl-u'd-dīn al-Afghānī (1838/39–1897) had written that the destiny of the Muslims of Central Asia was to form a state with Afghanistan and the Muslim majority area in northwestern India. Some kind of separation from the other areas of India and autonomous integration into a single entity was also advocated by several other contemporary thinkers. An Indian Muslim student at Cambridge, Chaudhari Rahmat Alī, coined the word Pakistan, by taking the *P* from Punjab, *A* from Afghania (by which name he preferred to call the North-Western Frontier Province), *K* from Kashmir, *S* from Sind, and *Tan* from Baluchistan. The *I* between *K* and *S* does not occur if the name Pakistan is written in Urdu. The synthetic name also has a meaning—the Land of the Pure.

Rahmat Alī had had no political experience. He expressed his ideas with greater fervor and enthusiasm than practical reasoning. In the propagation of the idea of Pakistan, however, the part played by him should not be underestimated. Gradually the majority of Indian Muslim students studying in Great Britain came to subscribe to his ideal. This was no mean achievement, as they represented the future leadership of the Indo-Muslim intelligentsia. Moreover, he had to wean them away from Communism, which was then quite fashionable among the students. His deep influence upon them was soon shown in their personal lives, when they withdrew from the frivolities of undergraduate life and became sincere and practicing Muslims. So great was their enthusiasm that sometimes to get a manifesto printed or a note inserted in a newspaper they would go without lunch for weeks to save the necessary money.

Rahmat Alī issued his first manifesto in 1933. At that time his ideas were dismissed with contempt by practical politicians as the wild musings of an irresponsible student. But by the end of 1937, the idea of a separate Muslim state had begun to spread with such rapidity that the politicians themselves were astonished. In 1940, the All-India Muslim League in its Lahore session demanded that Muslim majority areas lying in contiguity should become sovereign states. This idea won at least partial acceptance in the Cripps proposals of 1942. By 1947 Pakistan itself had been achieved. Rahmat Alī died in 1948, disappointed because the Muslim League had accepted a much smaller Pakistan than he had envisaged. Nevertheless, few other university students have lived to see a dream of such magnitude so substantially realized in so short a time.

RAHMAT ALĪ

Sovereign Nations in Homeland or Sub-Nations in Hindoolands?

[From Rahmat Alī, India . . . , pp. 3–5]

Nations of Dinia:[1]

It is time to realize that we, the non-Indian nations, who comprise the Muslims, Dravidians, Akhoots [the untouchables],[2] Christians, Sikhs, Buddhs,[3] and Parsis, are, and ever have been, the victims of "the Myth of Indianism." That is the myth which teaches that India is, "the country of India," i.e., the exclusive domain of Caste Hindooism and Caste Hindoos; and which has been built up by the Caste Hindoos, buttressed by the British, and, thanks to our own folly, believed by the world.

PAST RECORD OF THE MYTH

False in its origin and foul in its teachings, this myth, from its very beginning, has wrought havoc and ruin to the cause of human freedom in the world. Throughout the ages it has compromised the status of Asia,

---

[1] India. Dinia is an anagram of India coined by Rahmat Alī on the basis of Arabic *din* "faith, religion." Thus Dinia is the land of religions, while India is the land of the Hindus.

[2] The real word is *acchūt*, meaning "untouchable." Rahmat Alī changed the word into Akhoots—by stretching Arabic grammar, it comes nearer *akhuwwat*, Arabic for "brotherhood."

[3] The Urdu word for Buddhists.

distorted the history of Dinia, and degraded our peoples who have had the misfortune to live and to die in its sphere of domination.

Indeed, such is its evil spirit that, though left stripped of every excuse for its mischievous activity since 711, yet, throughout the last thirteen centuries of its vogue, it has mentally enslaved and socially enchained, nationally "minoritized" and territorially disinherited, us all. Not only that. It has frustrated our spiritual missions and perverted our civilizations, caged us in India, and made India herself a country of doom for all—the Indian as well as the non-Indian nations.

PRESENT ROLE OF THE MYTH

Nor has it stopped there. On the contrary, thanks to its priests and parasites, it has remained as active as ever and is now busily engaged in sabotaging the revival and recognition of us all as nations.

That is the cynical role which it is playing at present through its first believers, the Caste Hindoos, and its latest beneficiaries, the British imperialists, who, in spite of their other differences, are cooperating with one another to canonize it anew and to preach its fatal cult with a view to perpetuating its strangle-hold on us all in the continent of Dinia.

Why are they doing that?

The Caste Hindoos, who are more numerous than all our nations combined, are doing it because to them the existence of the myth gives an opportunity first of keeping us mixed with themselves, then of disintegrating us as nations, and finally of absorbing us into their Indian nation. The British are doing it because to them, as an imperial power, the existence of the myth gives an opportunity first of keeping us and the Caste Hindoos intermingled, then of exploiting our conflict, resulting from that intermingling, to strengthen their hold on India, and finally of justifying before the world, by citing the record of that conflict, their imperial rule over all the nations in India.

So it is to maintain their respective positions of sublordship and overlordship that both the Caste Hindoos and the British imperialists are hymning the myth and hypnotizing us—the non-Indian nations—into accepting its teachings and, thereby, committing national self-immolation and submitting to the Indo-British Condominium.

To rationalize—and to realize—their aims, they are using two main arguments. First, that the unity of "the country of India" is too natural to permit of its partition into separate homelands for all the Indian and the non-Indian nations. Secondly, that the constitutional principle of "one country, one nation" is so decisive as to reduce even one hundred and ten million Muslims, sixty million Akhoots, forty million Dravidians, seven million Christians, and six million Sikhs, to the position of mere sub-nations and satellites of the Indian nation, and thereby to disqualify each one of us from claiming the status of distinct sovereign nations in our own homelands, i.e., the areas to which we are individually entitled in proportion to our populations in the "country of India."

It is obvious that both these arguments are pure cant and casuistry. For the assumption of the unity of the so-called "country of India" is contradicted by the facts of its geography and history; and the application to its case of the constitutional principle of "one country, one nation" is disputed by all the canons of international law.

MIGHT WITH METHOD

The truth is that, in their heart of hearts, both the British imperialists and the Caste Hindoos know this. Yet, in utter disregard of that knowledge, they assume the unity of India, invoke the principle of "one country, one nation," and enforce both—the mythical unity and the constitutional principle.

What does all this mean?

It means might with method; in other words, a firm stand by the Anglo-Hindoo Entente for their own present and future purposes; and a final warning to us, the non-Indian nations, that, in the name of the myth, they won't let us be sovereign nations in separate homelands in the continent of Dinia, but will hold us down as the sub-nations and satellites of the India nation in "the country of India."

OUR CHOICE: MYTH-DESTRUCTION OR SELF-DESTRUCTION

False but final, that is their position. What is ours? It can only be summed up as a choice between life and death; that is to say, between myth-destruction and self-destruction. For it is sun-clear that if we do not destroy the myth, the myth will certainly destroy us.

It is, therefore, time for us all to realize the fatefulness of our position, and, in that realization, make our choice.

As we do that, we must remember that, for each one of us, everything is at stake; and that, to save everything, this is our last and our best opportunity. For now, as never before, the myth is not only discredited but also damned; and its supporters, though materially powerful, are morally powerless. They are aware both of the weakness of their case and of the strength of ours. So, if now we all challenge the myth and give it a smashing blow, it will die a deserved death, and we shall all be free. But if we dilly-dally and miss this opportunity, the Indo-British Entente will reimpose it upon us in all its tyranny. In that case, everything will be lost, and we shall all be the slaves of the Indian nation, perhaps for centuries, perhaps forever. . . .

THE WRITING ON THE WALL

Let them [the other minority communities] make no mistake about it. In the country of India—as for the Muslims, so for them—the fate of national subordination is inescapable. They cannot dodge it; they cannot defy it; they cannot defeat it. The reason is that, even if they achieve the recognition of their distinct nationhoods in the country of India, they can never be sovereign nations in separate homelands. On the contrary, they will ever be the sub-nations and satellites of the Indian nation in, at best, the renamed regions of India—which is, and ever will be, another name for the Hindoo lands.

MUHAMMAD ALĪ JINNĀH AND THE FOUNDING OF PAKISTAN

The founder of Pakistan, Muhammad Alī Jinnāh, was born at Karachi in the year 1876. His father was a merchant of modest means, yet affluent enough to send his son to England for training as a barrister. The house where Muhammad Alī Jinnāh was born, and which is now maintained as a museum by the government of Pakistan, evinces middle-class respectability without much comfort or any trace of luxury. In England Jinnāh was attracted by the political views of the British liberals and he saw an Indian Parsi, Dādābhāi Naoroji, elected to the British Parliament from Central Finsbury, reflecting the growing strength of British liberalism.

Shortly after returning to India in 1896, Jinnāh moved to Bombay, which, being a much larger city, promised greater opportunities to the young barrister. The first three years were years of grim struggle, after which the tide began to turn. Through his ability, integrity, and hard work, Jinnāh ultimately found himself one of the best-known lawyers in the subcontinent. He had devoted himself to his profession to the exclusion of other interests; but having made his mark and ensured his financial independence, Jinnāh's thoughts turned in the direction of politics. His earlier contacts with British liberalism had created an interest in public affairs which now asserted itself. He joined the Indian National Congress and simultaneously took up a secretaryship to Dādābhāi Naoroji, through which he served his apprenticeship in Indian politics. In 1909 the Bombay Muslim constituency elected him to the imperial Legislative Council of the government of India, where his ability and independence soon won him recognition. He came into contact with the able Mahārāshtrian leader, Gokhale, and a warm friendship grew up between the two men. In Gokhale he found the kind of Hindu patriot who, he thought, had the same approach to Indian politics as himself; Gokhale, for his part, considered Jinnāh to be a potential ambassador of Hindu-Muslim unity.

In 1913, while the two friends were in England for a holiday, Jinnāh was persuaded by Muhammad Alī, editor of the *Comrade,* to join the Muslim League. He did this on the assurance that the aims of the League were now similar to those of the Congress, and that his membership in the League would not imply disloyalty to "the larger national cause to which his life was dedicated." A few months later he led a delegation to England to put the views of the Indian National Congress regarding the Council of India Bill before the Secretary of State for India. Consideration of the bill was postponed, however, because the First World War broke out in August, 1914. Still Jinnāh continued to work for a Hindu-Muslim understanding and brought about the Lucknow Pact between the Congress and the League in 1916, by which the Congress accepted the principle of separate electorates for the Muslims. In 1917 Montagu, the Secretary of State for India, went to the subcontinent to assess the situation regarding a further installment of self-rule. His description of Jinnāh is interesting:

They were followed by Jinnāh, young, perfectly mannered, impressive looking, armed to the teeth with dialectics. . . . I was rather tired and I funked him.

Chelmsford tried to argue with him, and was tied up into knots. Jinnāh is a very clever man, and it is, of course, an outrage that such a man should have no chance of running the affairs of his own country.[1]

The end of the First World War saw the rise of Gāndhi as the leader of the national movement. Jinnāh, however, had no use for the new techniques of civil disobedience and noncooperation; nor had he much liking for the Khilāfat Movement. This movement reflected, indeed, a romanticism in politics upon which the Muslims had fed so long that they had lost a sense of realities. Their attitude towards political problems was seldom based upon a clear appreciation of all the factors involved. The unrealistic aims of this movement, the unqualified acceptance of Gāndhi's leadership, the confidence that withdrawal of the British would automatically solve the Hindu-Muslim problem, and unbounded faith in the willingness and power of the Congress Hindu leaders to settle Hindu-Muslim differences were all manifestations of this romanticism. When the spell was broken by the inauguration of the Shuddhi and Sangathan Movements and the unwillingness or inability of the Congress Hindu leaders to curb such extremism, the Muslims' disappointment was extreme. Especially after the death of Muhammad Alī in 1930 it was felt that new policies and new leadership were needed.

Nevertheless, Jinnāh's emergence as the leader could not have been foretold at that time, since he had none of the qualities the Muslims had been accustomed to look for in a leader. Jinnāh was a realist who never permitted his vision to be obscured by emotionalism. Though an ardent Muslim, he did not wear his religion in his buttonhole, whereas the Muslim masses were steeped in sentimentalism and religiosity. Jinnāh was aristocratic by temperament and Western in outlook; the masses distrusted Westernized leaders who lived in a style so different from their own. He was a statesman and a true leader who spoke simply and to the point; the masses wanted a demagogue. Jinnāh did not offer a ready-made solution to the problems confronting his people. He was a cautious man and given to feeling his ground before saying a word, to weighing the pros and cons of a policy before recommending it to any-one. The only qualities in him which could be appreciated at first sight were his independence, courage, integrity, ability, and perseverance. Moreover, his strict sense of discipline, which reconciled him to the loss

[1] Edwin S. Montagu. *An Indian Diary*, p. 57 f.

of politically important allies rather than tolerate indiscipline, did nothing to enhance his popularity.

Still Jinnāh could see that the Muslims needed policies which would safeguard their position. His faith in the old liberal leaders of Indian nationalism was yielding to doubt over the newer forces which had made their appearance. The older liberal leaders had been able to keep the ideals of nationalism clearly defined; now mass feelings were so aroused that agreement on well-defined aims would be impossible. In the beginning Jinnāh worked tirelessly to forge some agreement with the Congress. There still seemed some hope of re-establishing a *modus vivendi,* if the Muslim position were sufficiently understood by the Congress. This hope declined, however, when the Congress in the 1937 elections was able to win so overwhelmingly in provinces possessing Hindu majorities that it did not need the support of any other community to form a government. The Congress decided to form exclusively Congress ministries. Legally the position taken by the Congress was unassailable; but to the Muslims it indicated that the Congress would care little for their cooperation in the hour of its final triumph. Inevitably the two communities began to act upon their deep-rooted instincts and move away from each other. The search for safeguards and formulas proved vain and the emotions of the two peoples asserted themselves with such force that all were helpless in their grip.

Jinnāh had wanted to be the architect of Hindu-Muslim unity. With his usual perseverance, he continued his pursuit of this aim until it became clear that such efforts were doomed to fail. In the fall of 1939 he told a small delegation of Muslim students from Cambridge, who were advocates of Pakistan, "I am getting more and more convinced that you are right in spite of myself." Yet once he became convinced, no obstacle could stand in his way. The Muslim masses of India gave him such support and loyalty as they had given no one before in their history, acclaiming him as their Qaid-i-azam—"the supreme leader." Under his command they marched forward to establish Pakistan as a fact—a country with a population of more than seventy-six million people, which had been dismissed less than two decades before as a fantasy unworthy of consideration.

In 1948, when the cortege of his funeral emerged from the gates of his palace, hundreds of thousands of people who had been waiting, grief-

stricken, shouted spontaneously in unison: *"Qaid-i-azam zindah bād!"*—
"Long live our supreme leader!" Today, too, a grateful people still honors
him as the father of their nation.

MUHAMMAD ALĪ JINNĀH
An International Problem

The selection is taken from Jinnāh's presidential address to the Muslim League
session at Lahore in March, 1940, which marked the adoption by the League
of the principle of a separate Muslim state.
[From Jinnāh, *Some Recent Speeches and Writings*, I, 174–80]

The British government and Parliament, and more so the British nation, have been for many decades past brought up and nurtured with
settled notions about India's future, based on developments in their own
country which has built up the British constitution, functioning now
through the Houses of Parliament and the system of cabinet. Their concept of party government functioning on political planes has become the
ideal with them as the best form of government for every country, and
the one-sided and powerful propaganda, which naturally appeals to the
British, has led them into a serious blunder, in producing the constitution envisaged in the Government of India Act of 1935. We find that
the most leading statesmen of Great Britain, saturated with these notions,
have in their pronouncements seriously asserted and expressed a hope that
the passage of time will harmonize the inconsistent elements of India.

A leading journal like the London *Times,* commenting on the Government of India Act of 1935, wrote: "Undoubtedly the differences between the Hindus and Muslims are not of religion in the strict sense
of the word but also of law and culture, that they may be said, indeed,
to represent two entirely distinct and separate civilizations. However, in
the course of time, the superstition will die out and India will be molded
into a single nation." So, according to the London *Times,* the only difficulties are superstitions. These fundamental and deep-rooted differences,
spiritual, economic, cultural, social, and political, have been euphemized
as mere "superstitions." But surely it is a flagrant disregard of the past
history of the subcontinent of India as well as the fundamental Islamic
conception of society vis-à-vis that of Hinduism to characterize them as

mere "superstitions." Notwithstanding a thousand years of close contact, nationalities, which are as divergent today as ever, cannot at any time be expected to transform themselves into one nation merely by means of subjecting them to a democratic constitution and holding them forcibly together by unnatural and artificial methods of British parliamentary statute. What the unitary government of India for one hundred fifty years had failed to achieve cannot be realized by the imposition of a central federal government. It is inconceivable that the fiat or the writ of a government so constituted can ever command a willing and loyal obedience throughout the subcontinent by various nationalities except by means of armed force behind it.

The problem in India is not of an intercommunal character but manifestly of an international one, and it must be treated as such. So long as this basic and fundamental truth is not realized, any constitution that may be built will result in disaster and will prove destructive and harmful not only to the Mussalmans but to the British and Hindus also. If the British government are really in earnest and sincere to secure [the] peace and happiness of the people of this subcontinent, the only course open to us all is to allow the major nations separate homelands by dividing India into "autonomous national states." There is no reason why these states should be antagonistic to each other. On the other hand, the rivalry and the natural desire and efforts on the part of one to dominate the social order and establish political supremacy over the other in the government of the country will disappear. It will lead more towards natural good will by international pacts between them, and they can live in complete harmony with their neighbors. This will lead further to a friendly settlement all the more easily with regard to minorities by reciprocal arrangements and adjustments between Muslim India and Hindu India, which will far more adequately and effectively safeguard the rights and interests of Muslims and various other minorities.

It is extremely difficult to appreciate why our Hindu friends fail to understand the real nature of Islam and Hinduism. They are not religions in the strict sense of the word, but are, in fact, different and distinct social orders, and it is a dream that the Hindus and Muslims can ever evolve a common nationality, and this misconception of one Indian nation has gone far beyond the limits and is the cause of most of your troubles and will lead India to destruction if we fail to revise our

[284]

notions in time. The Hindus and Muslims belong to two different religious philosophies, social customs, literatures. They neither intermarry nor interdine together and, indeed, they belong to two different civilizations which are based mainly on conflicting ideas and conceptions. Their aspects on life and of life are different. It is quite clear that Hindus and Mussalmans derive their inspiration from different sources of history. They have different epics, different heroes, and different episodes. Very often the hero of one is a foe of the other and, likewise, their victories and defeats overlap. To yoke together two such nations under a single state, one as a numerical minority and the other as a majority, must lead to growing discontent and final destruction of any fabric that may be so built up for the government of such a state.

History has presented to us many examples, such as the union of Great Britain and Ireland, Czechoslovakia, and Poland. History has also shown us many geographical tracts, much smaller than the subcontinent of India, which otherwise might have been called one country, but which have been divided into as many states as there are nations inhabiting them. [The] Balkan Peninsula comprises as many as seven or eight sovereign states. Likewise, the Portuguese and the Spanish stand divided in the Iberian Peninsula. Whereas under the plea of the unity of India and one nation, which does not exist, it is sought to pursue here the line of one central government, we know that the history of the last twelve hundred years has failed to achieve unity and has witnessed, during the ages, India always divided into Hindu India and Muslim India. The present artificial unity of India dates back only to the British conquest and is maintained by the British bayonet, but termination of the British regime, which is implicit in the recent declaration of His Majesty's government, will be the herald of the entire break-up with worse disaster than has ever taken place during the last one thousand years under Muslims. Surely that is not the legacy which Britain would bequeath to India after one hundred fifty years of her rule, nor would Hindu and Muslim India risk such a sure catastrophe.

Muslim India cannot accept any constitution which must necessarily result in a Hindu majority government. Hindus and Muslims brought together under a democratic system forced upon the minorities can only mean Hindu rāj [rule]. Democracy of the kind with which the Congress High Command is enamored would mean the complete destruction of what is most precious in Islam. We have had ample experience of the working of the provincial constitutions during the last two and a half years and any repetition of such a government must lead to civil war and raising of private armies as recommended by Mr. Gāndhi to [the] Hindus of Sukkur when he said that they must defend themselves violently or nonviolently, blow for blow, and if they could not, they must emigrate.

Mussalmans are not a minority as it is commonly known and understood. One has only got to look round. Even today, according to the British map of India, four out of eleven provinces, where the Muslims dominate more or less, are functioning notwithstanding the decision of the Hindu Congress High Command to noncooperate and prepare for civil disobedience. Mussalmans are a nation according to any definition of a nation, and they must have their homelands, their territory, and their state. We wish to live in peace and harmony with our neighbors as a free and independent people. We wish our people to develop to the fullest our spiritual, cultural, economic, social, and political life in a way that we think best and in consonance with our own ideals and according to the genius of our people. Honesty demands and the vital interests of millions of our people impose a sacred duty upon us to find an honorable and peaceful solution, which would be just and fair to all. But at the same time we cannot be moved or diverted from our purpose and objective by threats or intimidations. We must be prepared to face all difficulties and consequences, make all the sacrifices that may be required of us to achieve the goal we have set in front of us.

The Aims of Pakistan

These excerpts from Jinnāh's speeches, made after the adoption by the Muslim League of the principle of a separate state, suggest the type of political program he hoped the Muslims would pursue. Despite his opposition to majority rule by the Hindus over Muslims, he hoped the latter would adopt for themselves the ideals of liberal and social democracy.

[From Jinnāh, *Some Recent Speeches and Writings,* I, 519–21, 560–62]

The progress that Mussalmans, as a nation, have made, during these three years, is a remarkable fact. Never before in the history of the world has a nation rallied around a common platform and a common ideal in such a short time as the Muslims have done in this vast subcontinent. Never before has a nation, miscalled a minority, asserted itself so quickly, and so effectively. Never before has the mental outlook of a nation been unified so suddenly. Never before has the solidarity of millions of population been established and demonstrated in so limited a time and under such peculiar circumstances as are prevalent in India. Three years ago Pakistan was a resolution. Today it is an article of faith, a matter of life and death with Muslim India. . . .

We have created a solidarity of opinion, a union of mind and thought. Let us concentrate on the uplift of our people for their educational, political, economic, social and moral well-being. Let us cooperate with and give all help to our leaders to work for our collective good. Let us make our organization stronger and put it on a thorough[ly] efficient footing. In all this, the final sanction and censure rests with and upon the verdict of our people. We, the Muslims, must rely mainly upon our own inherent qualities, our own natural potentialities, our own internal solidarity and our own united will to face the future.

I particularly appeal to our intelligentsia and Muslim students to come forward and rise to the occasion. Train yourselves, equip yourselves for the task that lies before us. The final victory depends upon you and is within our grasp. You have performed wonders in the past. You are still capable of repeating the history. You are not lacking in the great qualities and virtues in comparison with the other nations. Only you have to be fully conscious of that fact and act with courage, faith and unity, [pp. 519–21]

. . . .

You will elect your representatives to the constitution-making body. You may not know your power, you may not know how to use it. This would be your fault. But I am sure that democracy is in our blood. It is in our marrows. Only centuries of adverse circumstances have made the circulation of that blood cold. It has got frozen and your arteries have not been functioning. But, thank God, the blood is circulating again, thanks to the Muslim League efforts. It will be a people's government. Here I should like to give a warning to the landlords and capitalists who have flourished at our expense by a system which is so vicious, which is so wicked and which makes them so selfish that it is difficult to reason with them. [Tremendous applause.] The exploitation of the masses has gone into their blood. They have forgotten the lessons of Islam. Greed and selfishness have made these people subordinate others to their interests in order to fatten themselves. It is true we are not in power today. You go anywhere to the countryside. I have visited villages. There are mil lions and millions of our people who hardly get one meal a day. Is this civilization? Is this the aim of Pakistan? [Cries of no, no.] Do you visualize that millions have been exploited and cannot get one meal a day? If that is the idea of Pakistan I would not have it. [Cheers.] If they are wise they will have to adjust themselves to the new modern conditions of life. If they don't, God help them. [Hear, hear, renewed cheers and applause.] Therefore let us have faith in ourselves. Let us not falter or hesitate. That is our goal. We are going to achieve it. [Cheers.] The constitution of Pakistan can only be framed by the Millat [the Muslim community or nation] and the people. Prepare yourselves and see that you frame a constitution which is to your heart's desire. There is a lot of misunderstanding. A lot of mischief is created. Is it going to be an Islamic government? Is it not begging the question? Is it not a question of passing a vote of censure on yourself? The constitution and the government will be what the people will decide. The only question is that of minorities.

The minorities are entitled to get a definite assurance and ask: "Where do we stand in the Pakistan that you visualize?" That is an issue of giving a definite and clear assurance to the minorities. We have done it. We have passed a resolution that the minorities must be protected and safeguarded to the fullest extent and as I said before any civilized government will do it and ought to do it. So far as we are concerned our own history, our Prophet have given the clearest proof that non-Muslims have been treated not only justly and fairly but generously. [pp. 560–62]

PAKISTAN'S COURSE IN THE MODERN WORLD

Pakistan, emerging so suddenly as a nation, was immediately faced with grave problems affecting not only its future but also the fundamental basis of the state. What would be its relationship to the rest of the world, and especially to its neighbors? How far should the government go toward assuming the responsibilities of a welfare state, or toward adopting the political institutions of the democratic West? Above all, what would be the status of the Islamic religion, which had been such a crucial factor in the determination of Indian Muslims to found a separate state?

This last question, of course, was the subject of the most intense controversy. There were few Muslims, it is true, who advocated a completely secular state. Most people agreed that Islam should hold a place of special importance in the life of the nation. Nevertheless, there was much difference of opinion as to what its precise role should be. Some held that the principles of Islam should be applied in strict accordance with the precedents established in earlier tradition; others that there should be enough flexibility in their application to allow for the needs of contemporary society. Naturally enough this controversy soon focused on the problem of adopting a constitution. The main exponents of the conservative point of view were the ulama, or recognized theologians of Islam; representatives of the more liberal and progressive approach included a majority of the political leaders of Pakistan, including its first prime minister, Liāquat Alī Khān.

LIĀQUAT ALĪ KHĀN: ARCHITECT OF PAKISTAN

The credit for creating a government in Pakistan out of the chaos which followed Partition goes mainly to Liāquat Alī Khān (1895–1951). Jinnāh was the founder of Pakistan, Liāquat its chief architect.

Born to a rich and noble family which had extensive landed property in the Punjab and the United Provinces, Liāquat was educated at Alīgarh and Oxford and, having been called to the bar from the Inner Temple, he entered politics as a Muslim Leaguer. He was a member of the United Provinces Legislative Council from 1926 to 1940, when he was elected to the central legislature. From 1936 to 1947 he was the general secretary of the Muslim League and Jinnāh's right-hand man. On the establishment of Pakistan in August, 1947, he became its first prime minister until his death in 1951. Despite his wealthy origins and success in public life, Liāquat died a poor man.

During Liāquat's tenure, the reputation of Pakistan as a progressive and stable state increased steadily. A powerful speaker, whose addresses thrilled and inspired the masses, Liāquat still was no demagogue but a coolheaded statesman dedicated to the service of his country. Though he fully shared his people's love for Islam, there was no narrowness or bigotry in his soul; he judged issues on their merits and combined breadth of outlook with regard for detail. When finally struck down by the bullets of an assassin, the only words he muttered were the Muslim formula of faith and the prayer, "May God protect Pakistan."

LIĀQUAT ALĪ KHĀN
Pakistan As an Islamic State

The Objectives Resolution was adopted by the Constituent Assembly of Pakistan on March 7, 1949, after a debate lasting for six days. It has since been incorporated into the constitution of Pakistan. Liāquat Alī Khān's speech moving the Objectives Resolution represents the ideas of the liberal wing of Muslim opinion which has since been dominant in the government of Pakistan notwithstanding several changes in its composition.

[From *The Constituent Assembly of Pakistan Debates,* Vol. V, No. 1, pp. 1–7]

Sir, I beg to move the following Objectives Resolution embodying the main principles on which the constitution of Pakistan is to be based:

"In the name of Allāh, the Beneficent, the Merciful;

WHEREAS sovereignty over the entire universe belongs to God Almighty alone and the authority which He has delegated to the State of Pakistan through its people for being exercised within the limits prescribed by Him is a sacred trust;

This Constituent Assembly representing the people of Pakistan resolves to frame a constitution for the sovereign independent State of Pakistan;

WHEREIN the State shall exercise its powers and authority through the chosen representatives of the people;

WHEREIN the principles of democracy, freedom, equality, tolerance, and social justice, as enunciated by Islam, shall be fully observed;

WHEREIN the Muslims shall be enabled to order their lives in the individual and collective spheres in accord with the teachings and requirements of Islam as set out in the Holy Qur'ān and the Sunna; [1]

WHEREIN adequate provision shall be made for the minorities freely to profess and practice their religions and develop their cultures;

[1] The customs and sayings of the Holy Prophet.

WHEREBY the territories now included in or in accession with Pakistan and such other territories as may hereafter be included in or accede to Pakistan shall form a Federation wherein the units will be autonomous with such boundaries and limitations on their powers and authority as may be prescribed;

WHEREIN shall be guaranteed fundamental rights including equality of status, of opportunity, and before law, social, economic, and political justice and freedom of thought, expression, belief, faith, worship and association, subject to law and public morality.

WHEREIN adequate provision shall be made to safeguard the legitimate interests of minorities and backward and depressed classes;

WHEREIN the independence of the judiciary shall be fully secured;

WHEREIN the integrity of the territories of the Federation, its independence and all its rights including its sovereign rights on land, sea and air shall be safeguarded;

So that the people of Pakistan may prosper and attain their rightful and honored place amongst the nations of the world and make their full contribution towards international peace and progress and happiness of humanity."

Sir, I consider this to be a most important occasion in the life of this country, next in importance only to the achievement of independence, because by achieving independence we only won an opportunity of building up a country and its polity in accordance with our ideals. I would like to remind the House that the Father of the Nation, Qaid-i-azam, gave expression to his feelings on this matter on many an occasion, and his views were endorsed by the nation in unmistakable terms. Pakistan was founded because the Muslims of this subcontinent wanted to build up their lives in accordance with the teachings and traditions of Islam, because they wanted to demonstrate to the world that Islam provides a panacea to the many diseases which have crept into the life of humanity today. It is universally recognized that the source of these evils is that humanity has not been able to keep pace with its material development, that the Frankenstein monster which human genius has produced in the form of scientific inventions, now threatens to destroy not only the fabric of human society but its material environ-ment as well, the very habitat in which it dwells. It is universally recog-nized that if man had not chosen to ignore the spiritual values of life and if his faith in God had not been weakened, this scientific development would not have endangered his very existence. It is God-consciousness alone which can save humanity, which means that all power that humanity possesses must be used in accordance with ethical standards which have been laid down by inspired teachers known to us as the great Prophets of different religions. We, as Pakistanis, are not ashamed of the fact that we are overwhelmingly Muslims and we believe that it is by adhering to our faith and ideals that we can make a genuine contribution to the welfare of the world. Therefore, Sir, you would notice that the Preamble of the Resolution deals with a frank and unequivocal recognition of the fact that all authority must be subservient to God. It is quite true that this is in direct contradiction to the Machiavellian ideas regarding a polity where spiritual and ethical values should play no part in the governance of the people and, therefore, it is also perhaps a little out of fashion to remind ourselves of the fact that the State should be an instrument of beneficence and not of evil. But we, the people of Pakistan, have the courage to believe firmly that all authority should be exercised in accordance with the standards laid down by Islam so that it may not be misused. All authority is a sacred trust, entrusted to us by God for the purpose of being exercised in the service of man, so that it does not become an agency for tyranny or selfishness. I would, however, point out that this is not a resuscitation of the dead theory of divine right of kings or rulers, because, in accordance with the spirit of Islam, the Preamble fully recognizes the truth that authority has been delegated to the people, and to none else, and that it is for the people to decide who will exercise that authority.

For this reason it has been made clear in the Resolution that the State shall exercise all its powers and authority through the chosen representatives of the people. This is the very essence of democracy, because the people have been recognized as the recipients of all authority and it is in them that the power to wield it has been vested.

Sir, I just now said that the people are the real recipients of power. This naturally eliminates any danger of the establishment of a theocracy. It is true that in its literal sense, theocracy means the Government of God; in this sense, however, it is patent that the entire universe is a theocracy, for is there any corner in the entire creation where His authority does not exist? But in the technical sense, theocracy has come to mean a government by ordained priests, who wield authority as being specially appointed by those who claim to derive their rights from their sacerdotal position. I cannot overemphasize the fact that such an idea is absolutely foreign to Islam. Islam does not recognize either priesthood or any sacerdotal authority; and, therefore, the question of a theocracy simply does not arise in Islam. If there are any who still use the word theocracy in the same breath as the polity of Pakistan, they are either laboring under a grave misapprehension, or indulging in mischievous propaganda.

You would notice, Sir, that the Objectives Resolution lays emphasis on the principles of democracy, freedom, equality, tolerance, and social justice, and further defines them by saying that these principles should be observed in the constitution as they have been enunciated by Islam. It has been necessary to qualify these terms because they are generally used in a loose sense. For instance, the Western Powers and Soviet Russia alike claim that their systems are based upon democracy, and, yet, it is common knowledge that their polities are inherently different. . . . When we use the word democracy in the Islamic sense, it pervades all aspects of our life; it relates to our system of government and to our society with equal validity, because one of the greatest contributions of Islam has been the idea of the equality of all men. Islam recognizes no distinctions based upon race, color, or birth. Even in the days of its decadence, Islamic society has been remarkably free from the prejudices which vitiated human relations in many other parts of the world. Similarly, we have a great record in tolerance, for under no system of government, even in the Middle Ages, have the minorities received the same consideration and freedom as they did in Muslim countries. When Christian dissentients and Muslims were being tortured and driven out of their homes, when they were being hunted as animals and burnt as criminals—even criminals have never been burnt in Islamic society— Islam provided a haven for all who were persecuted and who fled from tyranny. It is a well-known fact of history that, when anti-Semitism turned the Jews out of many a European country, it was the Ottoman empire which gave them shelter. The greatest proof of the tolerance of Muslim peoples lies in the fact that there is no Muslim country where strong minorities do not exist, and where they have not been able to preserve their religion and culture. Most of all, in this subcontinent of India, where the Muslims wielded unlimited authority, the rights of non-Muslims were cherished and protected. I may point out, Sir, that it was under Muslim patronage that many an indigenous language developed in India. My friends from Bengal would remember that it was under the encouragement of Muslim rulers that the first translations of the Hindu scriptures were made from Sanskrit into Bengali. It is this tolerance which is envisaged by Islam, wherein a minority does not live on sufferance, but is respected and given every opportunity to develop its own thought and culture, so that it may contribute to the greater glory of the entire nation. In the matter of social justice as well, Sir, I would point out that Islam has a distinct contribution to make. Islam envisages a society in which social justice means neither charity nor regimentation. Islamic social justice is based upon fundamental laws and concepts which guarantee to man a life free from want and rich in freedom. It is for this reason that the principles of democracy, freedom, equality, tolerance, and social justice have been further defined by giving to them a meaning which, in our view, is deeper and wider than the usual connotation of these words.

The next clause of the Resolution lays down that Muslims shall be enabled to order their lives in the individual and collective spheres in accord with the teachings and requirements of Islam as set out in the Holy Qur'ān and the Sunna. It is quite obvious that no non-Muslim should have any objection if the Muslims are enabled to order their lives in accordance with the dictates of their religion. You would also notice, Sir, that the State is not to play the part of a neutral observer, wherein the Muslims may be merely free to profess and practice their religion, because such an attitude on the part of the State would be the very negation of the ideals which prompted the demand of Pakistan, and it is these ideals which should be the cornerstone of the State which we want to build. The State will create such conditions as are conducive to the building up of a truly Islamic society, which means that the State will have to play a positive part in this effort. You would remember, Sir, that the Qaid-i-azam and other leaders of the Muslim league always made unequivocal declarations that the Muslim demand for Pakistan was based upon the fact that the Muslims had a way of life and a code of conduct. They also reiterated the fact that Islam is not merely a relationship between the individual and his God, which should not, in any way, affect the working of the State. Indeed, Islam lays down specific directions for social behavior, and seeks to guide society in its attitude towards the problems which confront it from day to day. Islam is not just a matter of private beliefs and conduct. It expects its followers to build up a society for the purpose of good life—as the Greeks would have called it, with this difference, that Islamic "good life" is essentially based upon spiritual values. For the purpose of emphasizing these values and to give them validity, it will be necessary for the State to direct and guide the activities of the Muslims in such a manner as to bring about a new social order based upon the essential principles of Islam, including the principles of democracy, freedom, tolerance, and social justice. These I mention merely by way of illustration; because they do not exhaust the teachings of Islam as embodied in the Qu'rān and the Sunna. There can be no Muslim who does not believe that the word of God and the life of the Prophet are the basic sources of his inspiration. In these there is no difference of opinion amongst the Muslims and there is no sect in Islam which does not believe in their validity. Therefore, there should be no misconception in the mind of any sect which may be in a minority in Pakistan about the intentions of the State. The State will seek to create an Islamic society free from dissensions, but this does not mean that it would curb the freedom of any section of the Muslims in the matter of their beliefs. No sect, whether the majority or a minority, will be permitted to dictate to the others and, in their own internal matters and sectional beliefs, all sects shall be given the fullest possible latitude and freedom. Actually we hope that the various sects will act in accordance with the desire of the Prophet who said that the differences of opinion amongst his followers are a blessing. It is for us to make our differences a source of strength to Islam and Pakistan, not to exploit them for narrow interests which will weaken both Pakistan and Islam. Differences of opinion very often lead to cogent thinking and progress, but this happens only when they are not permitted to obscure our vision of the real goal, which is the service of Islam and the furtherance of its objects. It is, therefore, clear that this clause seeks to give the Muslims the opportunity that they have been seeking, throughout these long decades of decadence and subjection, of finding freedom to set up a polity, which may prove to be a laboratory for the purpose of demonstrating to the world that Islam is not only a progressive force in the world, but it also provides remedies for many of the ills from which humanity has been suffering.

Pakistan's Mission in Asia

In 1950, when an honorary degree was conferred on Liāquat Alī Khān by the University of Kansas City (Mo.), he delivered an address, "Pakistan, the Heart of Asia," from which are taken these excerpts, expressing his conviction that Pakistan stands as a bastion of religious and democratic ideals amidst the political and social upheavals shaking all of Asia.

[From Liāquat Alī Khan, *Pakistan, the Heart of Asia*, pp. 55–61]

Pakistan is a new state; or to be more exact, a new democracy. As a democracy it is not yet three years old. There was a time when your country, where the traditions of civil liberty, freedom, and democracy have now taken such firm root, was a new and young democracy and the memory of your struggle for independence was yet fresh in the minds of men. If you can, in your imagination, reconstruct those times for a little while, you will in many ways be reading the history of Pakistan and of the first three years of its new life.

Till three years ago, Pakistan was only an ideal and a longing. In the vast subcontinent where present-day Bhārat [India] and Pakistan were situated and where the British held sway, there lived a hundred million Muslims who for centuries had made this part of the world their homeland. They lived, side by side, with three hundred million others—mostly Hindus who had come to this continent in an earlier era. As the day of freedom for these four hundred million people drew near, it became increasingly obvious that at the end of the British rule the one hundred million Muslims would have to live their new life as a perpetual political minority. Long experience and the history of several centuries had taught them that under a dominating majority of three to one, freedom from British rule would mean to the Muslims not freedom but merely a change of masters. . . .

We believed then [before Partition] and we believe now that the demand of the Muslims in British India to have a separate state of their own was, both on human and geopolitical grounds, a very reasonable demand. To millions of Muslims it meant the only opportunity for genuine freedom and genuine self-government. To millions of Hindus it gave the same opportunity for developing their own culture, untrammeled by the constant discontent of a large and unmanageable minority. From the point of view of world peace the creation of two independent and comparatively homogeneous states instead of a single uneasy and un-wieldy state with great strains and stresses within the body politic was the greatest contribution that could be made towards the creation of a stable new Asia. Peace-loving men and women who today lament the strained relations between Pakistan and Bhārat—and none laments them more than we do—should at least have this consolation that had Pakistan not been separated from the rest of British India, far more serious and dangerous cracks would have appeared in that subcontinent resulting in untold upheavals. Potentially, therefore, the creation of Pakistan has by itself dissolved what would have been a perpetual danger zone in Asia.

But it has done more than that. Cast your mind on all the coun-tries of Asia one after another. Almost everywhere you will see intense nationalism, great backwardness, impatience with colonial rule, and, in some, a greater or lesser degree of democratic rule. But in many of them you will also see internal strains, moral doubts, ideological conflicts, waverings, hesitations, and confusions. Halting democracies and ideologi-cal confusions create great anxieties for the governments in Asia, for the peoples of Asia and for peace-loving and world-minded people anywhere. In the midst of these Pakistan stands unified. It stands unified because its people are free from mental confusions which elsewhere create disruption and cast menacing shadows on the future. They have chosen for them-selves the part chalked out for them by their simple, practical, clear-cut beliefs and decisions. Foremost amongst those beliefs are the belief in the supreme sovereignty of God, belief in the equality of men, belief in democracy and the right of the people to be governed by their own freely chosen representatives, belief in individual destiny, in the funda-mental freedoms of every single man and woman, in the right of every individual to the fruits of his own honest effort, belief in the sanctity of human life and human liberty, belief in the sanctity of the home, belief in universal peace but an equally strong belief in resisting aggression, tyranny, and exploitation. We did not have to acquire or inculcate these beliefs after the foundation of our new state. On the contrary, we founded a new state because we wanted to practice these beliefs without being inhibited by the contiguity, and without being thwarted by the domination, of other conflicting ways of life. For us to be undemocratic, or to ignore individual rights whether of property, belief or expression, or to bend our knee to aggression, is to destroy completely the very ideals which inspired us in our demand for Pakistan.

This intensity of purpose and this firm faith have, during the last three years, been demonstrated in ways which surprised our critics and our friends, and in some ways went beyond our own expectations. When British India was partitioned we, the Pakistanis, were asked to set up a new state of eighty million people within a period of two months. We had no capital and no flag. Our administrative machinery had to be built up from scratch. We were allotted an army, but its personnel was dispersed far and wide and could not come together for months. We had no military equipment. Our share of the military equipment of British India which was allotted to us on paper remains largely undelivered even today when three years have elapsed. Being a backward people we had no industry, no engineers, and practically no traders. Within a few months of independence seven million homeless refugees driven out of India came over to us in a miserable plight to seek shelter. Had it not been for the unity of our people we might have floundered. But today after three years we are stronger than before. And in spite of some very anxious moments when our international rights and our freedom seemed to be in jeopardy, we are still free.

What are the demands that our freedom makes on us? Our first duty is to ourselves. I do not say this in any spirit of selfishness or chauvinism. A free people must maintain their own freedom first. Otherwise they disgrace the fair name of free men and women all over the world. But the maintenance of freedom requires constant vigilance. "Liberty does not descend upon a people; a people must raise themselves to it. It is a fruit that must be earned before it can be enjoyed." That freedom means freedom only from foreign domination is an outworn idea. It is not merely governments that should be free but the people themselves who should be free; and no freedom has any real value for the common man or woman unless it also means freedom from want, freedom from disease, freedom from ignorance. This is the main task which confronts us if we are to take our rightful place in the modern world. We cannot hold the clock back and therefore it is *we* who must

go forward at a double pace, bending all our resources and all our energies to this great purpose. Students of history are aware that during
the last two or three centuries of foreign domination our people have not
kept pace with the march of civilization. It was during these centuries that
Western civilization, of which you are the proud torch-bearers, discovered
a use for science, which, though not new, was so fast in tempo and so
vast in its magnitude that it gave civilization a new orientation altogether. This was the phase that for various reasons our people missed. The
result is that today we find multitudes emerging as large, free nations in
Asia with their material and mental resources utterly undeveloped and
with their standards of living so low that the world conscience should
not be content to leave them stagnant. Our ancient steadfast faith which
is such a source of strength to us on the ideological front in these modern
uneasy times must be wedded to the pioneering virility of modern tech-
nology. This is the synthesis we must achieve and achieve quickly, not
merely for the sake of progress but for the sake of world peace itself.

For I sincerely believe that war and peace and progress and prosperity
are all indivisible today. The innumerable millions of Asia, heirs to ancient cultures and ancient civilizations, have, after centuries of suppression, entered upon a new and dynamic phase of nationalism. Most of
them were accustomed to looking at the West from the position of subject peoples and could see little beyond the less attractive side of what
to them was Western civilization. Their newly won freedom has, however, corrected their vision and they are better able to see both the
Western world and their own surroundings in their true perspective.
While on the one hand they are filled with admiration at the sight of
the progress and the advancement of civilization in such great countries
as the United States of America, they are more impatient than ever before with their own misery and backwardness and are keenly searching
the horizons for the signs of a bright day. They are acutely aware of
the great contrast between their own standard of living and the standards
of living in the Western world. This disequilibrium is in many ways most
disquieting and has in it the seeds of unpredictable upheavals. For the
sake of world peace, for the sake of world civilization, Asia must be
made stable but it cannot be made stable unless discontent is removed
and the germs of disruption are killed by better and cleaner living which
means no more and no less than enabling the peoples of Asia to enjoy

the fullest advantages of freedom and democracy. In this situation, we consider the role of Pakistan to be that of a stabilizing factor in a backward and discontented part of the world. We hope to be able to play this role successfully by our strong faith in God, in democracy and in our own unity, by the resources of our lands and waters and by our will to work. On these points Pakistan stands firm.

What, however, is the role of the Western world in this situation? It is to demonstrate that true democracy is international in its very conception and does not shirk its responsibility for the maintenance of world peace; that it discharges this responsibility by defying not only this or that particular aggressor, but aggression everywhere; and that it has a constructive and not merely a defiant outlook. We conceive the role of the Western world to be the enlightened one of sharing its great fund of knowledge, skill, and experience with those who were denied their opportunities but who constitute a major part of the world's population and without whose progress, the world will limp along only on one leg, if at all. I have met many liberal-minded and thoughtful men in your country to whom these are the only aims worth pursuing in the domain of international affairs today. I am certain therefore that the vast majority of your people regard the emergence of the democracy of Pakistan, its progress, and future development, as of great importance in Asia for they are convinced that Pakistan's strength will be a happy augury for peace.

THE CONSERVATIVE STAND

The most powerful conservative force in Pakistan today is represented by the ulamā, or theologians of Islam, who have fought for an Islamic constitution and for a legal system adhering strictly to traditional Islamic law. One of the chief spokesmen for this point of view has been Syed Abū'l-A'lā Maudoodī (1903–   ), himself a journalist rather than a theologian. Known for the clarity and elegance of his style in Urdu, Maudoodī devoted himself to the study of Islamics and won respect for his opinions even in the most learned circles. In 1929 he published *Holy War in Islam* (*al-jihād fī-'l-Islām*), and in 1932 started *Exegesis of the Qur'ān* (*Tarjumān-u'l-Qur'ān*), a monthly devoted to the discussion of Islamic subjects. This journal had a deep influence upon contemporary Muslim thought. Maudoodī's main thesis was that the Muslims, to be effective in the pursuit of their ideals, must have only one loyalty—their Faith. He criticized those theologians who had thrown in their lot with the Indian National Congress; but such popularity as this brought him waned considerably when he took an unsympathetic attitude toward the movement for Pakistan. Maudoodī transferred his headquarters to Pathankot in East Punjab and established a center there which prospered until Partition. Then, as the result of disturbances, he and his colleagues had to flee for their lives to Pakistan, where he became a staunch supporter of the new state.

Maudoodī had organized a movement called the Islamic Association (Jamāat-i-Islāmi) to spread among Muslims his ideas regarding the renaissance of true Islam. In Pakistan this body has since come into frequent conflict with the government because of its politics. It has consistently agitated for the enactment of an Islamic constitution. Maudoodī's ideas are more fundamentalist than those of the Muslim League and other Muslim political parties. His party has occasionally won isolated seats in provincial elections, but this does not represent its real strength, as it has many cells of workers in all schools and colleges, factories, government offices, and many townships and villages. The party undertakes relief and medical work in poorer or calamity-stricken areas. Most of this work is financed through the sale of party literature, especially the writings of Maudoodī himself, which reach a wide audience.

SYED ABŪ'L-A'LĀ MAUDOODĪ

Islamic Law and Constitution
[From Maudoodī, *Islamic Law and Constitution*, p. 14 ff.]

Commencing with stagnation in the domains of knowledge and learning, research and discovery, and thought and culture, it [the degeneration of the Muslims] finally culminated in our political breakdown, making many a Muslim country the slave of non-Muslim imperialist powers. Political slavery gave birth to an inferiority complex and the resultant intellectual serfdom, which eventually swept the entire Muslim world off its feet, so much so that even those Muslim countries which were able to retain their political freedom could not escape its evil influences. The ultimate consequence of this evil situation was that when Muslims woke up again to the call of progress, they were incapable of looking at things

[301]

except through the colored glasses of Western thought. Nothing which was not Western could inspire confidence in them. Indeed, the adoption of Western culture and civilization and aping the West even in the most personal things became their craze. Eventually, they succumbed totally to the slavery of the West.

This trend towards Westernism was also the result of the disappointment which came from the side of the Muslim religious leaders. Being themselves the victims of the widespread degeneration that had engulfed the entire Muslim world, they were incapable of initiating any constructive movement or taking any revolutionary step which could combat the evils afflicting Muslim society. Quite naturally, this disappointment turned the discontented Muslims towards that system of life which had the glamour of being successful in the modern world. Thus they adopted modern thought and the new culture of the West and blindly aped Western morals and manners. Slowly but surely the religious leaders were pushed into the background and were replaced, as regards power and control over the people, by men bereft of all knowledge of their religion and imbued only with the spirit of modern thought and Western ideals. That is why we find that many a Muslim country has, in the recent past, either completely abrogated the Islamic law or confined its operation to the domain of purely personal matters—a position conferred on the non-Muslims in a truly Islamic state.

In all Muslim countries suffering from foreign domination, the leadership of political and cultural movements fell into the hands of those who were shorn of all Islamic background. They adopted the creed of "Nationalism," directed their efforts towards the cause of *national* independence and prosperity along secular lines, and tried to copy step by step the advanced nations of our age. So, if these gentlemen are vexed with the demand for Islamic constitution and Islamic laws, it is just natural for them. It is also natural for them to sidetrack or suppress the issue, as they are ignorant even of the A B C of the Islamic Sharī'a. Their education and intellectual development has alienated them so completely from the spirit and the structure of Islamic ideology that it is at least for the moment impossible for them to understand such demands.

As regards the Muslim religious leadership, it fares in no way better, because our religious institutions are tied up to the intellectual atmosphere of eight centuries ago, as a consequence of which they have not been able to produce such leaders of Islamic thought and action as could be capable of administering the affairs of a modern state in the light of Islamic principles. This is, indeed, a very real obstacle facing the Islamic countries in their march towards the goal of Islamic revolution.

This is the situation obtaining throughout the Muslim world and impeding the path of the establishment of Islamic constitution. The case of Pakistan is not, however, the same as that of other Muslim countries, certain similarities of situation notwithstanding. This is so because it has been achieved exclusively with the object of becoming the home land of Islam. For the last ten years, we have been ceaselessly fighting for the recognition of the fact that we are a separate nation by virtue of our adherence to Islam. We have been proclaiming from house-tops that we have a distinct culture of our own, and that we possess a world view, an outlook on life, and a code of living fundamentally different from those of non-Muslims. We have all along been demanding a separate homeland for the purpose of translating into practice the ideals envisaged by Islam, and, at last, after a long and arduous struggle, in which we sustained a heavy loss of life and property and suffered deep humiliation in respect of the honor and chastity of a large number of our womenfolk, we have succeeded in attaining our cherished goal—this country of Pakistan. If, now, after all these precious sacrifices, we fail to achieve the real and ultimate objective of making Islam a practical, constitutional reality which inspired us to fight for Pakistan, our entire struggle becomes futile and all our sacrifices meaningless.

Indeed, if a secular and Godless, instead of Islamic, constitution was to be introduced and if the British Criminal Procedure Code had to be enforced instead of the Islamic Shari'a what was the sense in all this struggle for a separate Muslim homeland? We could have had it without that. Similarly, if we simply intended to implement any socialist program, we could have achieved it in collaboration with the Communist and Socialist parties of India without plunging the nation into this great blood-bath and mighty ordeal.

The fact is that we are already committed before God and man and at the altar of History about the promulgation of Islamic constitution and no going back on our words is possible. Whatever the hurdles and however great they are, we have to continue our march towards our goal of a full-fledged Islamic state in Pakistan.

[303]

The Islamic Law and Modern Needs
[From Maudoodī, *Islamic Law and Constitution*, p. 38 ff.]

The first objection that is raised is that because the Islamic laws were framed thirteen centuries ago in the light of the requirements of a primitive society, they cannot be of any use for a modern state of our days.

I doubt very much whether people who take this stand are conversant even with the elementary knowledge of the Islamic law. In all probability, they have heard from somewhere that the fundamentals of the Islamic law were enunciated more than thirteen hundred years ago, and they have assumed that this law has remained static since then and has failed to respond to the requirements of changing conditions of human life. On this misconception they have further assumed that the Islamic law will be unsuited to the needs of the present-day society and will clog the wheels of progress. These critics fail to realize, however, that the laws propounded thirteen and a half centuries ago, did not remain in a vacuum; they formed part and parcel of the life of Muslim society and brought into being a *state* which was run in the light of these laws. This naturally provided an opportunity of evolution to Islamic law from the earliest days, as it had to be applied to day-to-day matters through the process of *Ta'wīl, Qiyās, Ijtihād,* and *Istihsān.*[1]

Very soon after its inception, Islam began to hold sway over nearly half the civilized world stretching from the Pacific to the Atlantic and, during the following twelve hundred years, the Islamic Law continued to administer the affairs of all Muslim states. This process of the evolution of Islamic law, therefore, did not stop for a moment up to the beginning of the nineteenth century, because it had to meet the challenge of the ever-changing circumstances and face countless problems confronting different countries in different stages of history. Even in our Indo-Pakistan subcontinent, the Islamic civil and penal codes were in vogue up to the beginning of the nineteenth century.

Thus, it is only for the last one hundred years that the Islamic law remained inoperative and suffered stagnation. But, firstly, this period

---

[1] *Ta'wīl* is the process of enlarging the applicability of a text by finding analogous situations; *qiyās* is to determine how one should act in the spirit of Islam, if there is no clear injunction available; *ijtihād* is the application of human reason in the interpretation of the meaning of a text; *istihsān* is to find the best procedure in the light of the teachings of Islam.

does not form a big gap and we can easily make up for the loss with some amount of strenuous effort; secondly, we possess full records of the development of our jurisprudence, century by century, and there can be absolutely no ground for frustration or despondency, and our path of legal progress is thus already illumined.

Once we have grasped the fundamental principles and the basic facts concerning the evolution of the Islamic system of law, we cannot remain in doubt that this law shall be as responsive to the urges of a progressive society in the present and the future as it has been in the past. Only those who suffer from ignorance can fall a prey to such nonsense, while those who have a grasp of Islam and the Islamic law are aware of its potentialities of progress, and those who possess even a cursory knowledge of the history of its development can never suspect it of being an antiquated or stagnant system of life which cannot keep pace with the march of history.

Gradual Reform

[From Maudoodī, *Islamic Law and Constitution,* p. 47 ff.]

If we really wish to see our Islamic ideals translated into reality, we should not overlook the natural law that all stable changes in the collective life of a people come about gradually. The more sudden a change, the more shortlived it is. For a permanent change it is necessary that it should be free from extremist bias and unbalanced approach.

The best example of this gradual change is the revolution brought about by the Holy Prophet (peace be on him) in Arabia. One who is acquainted even superficially with the history of the Prophet's achievements knows that he did not enforce the entire body of Islamic laws with one stroke. Instead, the society was prepared gradually for their enforcement. The Prophet (peace be on him) uprooted the practices of the "Age of Ignorance" one by one and substituted for them new, moderate principles of human conduct. He started his efforts for reformation by inculcating belief in the fundamentals of Islam, namely, the unity of God, the Life Hereafter and the Institution of Prophethood and by inducing the people to live a life of righteousness and piety. Those who accepted this message were trained by him to believe in and practice the Islamic Way of Life. When this was achieved to a considerable degree, the Prophet went a step further and established an Islamic State in Medina with the sole object of making the social life of the country conform to the Islamic pattern. . . .

Coming to our own times and our own country, Pakistan, if we wish to promulgate Islamic Law here, it would mean nothing less than the demolition of the entire structure built by your British masters and the erection of a new one in its place. It is obvious that this cannot be achieved by just an official proclamation or a parliamentary bill, because it is a stupendous task and demands a good deal of hard and systematic work on the basis of an all-embracing program. For instance, we need a thorough reorientation of our educational system. At present, we find two kinds of educational institutions running simultaneously in our country, namely, the old, religious "madrasahs" and the modern, secular universities and colleges. None of them can produce people needed to run a modern Islamic State. The old-fashioned schools are steeped in conservatism to such an extent that they have lost all touch with the modern world. Their education has been disconnected from the practical problems of life and has thus become barren and lifeless. It cannot, therefore, produce people who might be able to serve, for instance, as judges and magistrates of a progressive modern state. As for our modern, secular institutions, they produce people who are ignorant of even a rudimentary knowledge of Islam and its laws. Moreover, we can hardly find such persons among those whose mentality has not been affected by the poisonous content and the thoroughly materialistic bias of modern, secular education.

There is yet another difficulty. The Islamic law has not been in force for the last century or so. Consequently our legal code has become stagnant and has lagged behind the march of time, while our urgent need is to bring it abreast of the latest developments of the modern age. Obviously, this would require a considerable amount of hard work.

There is, however, an even bigger hurdle. Living as slaves of an alien power and deprived of the Islamic influence for a long time, the pattern of our moral, cultural, social, economic and political life has undergone a radical change, and is today far removed from Islamic ideals. Under such circumstances it cannot be fruitful, even if it were possible, to change the legal structure of the country all at once, because then the general pattern of life and the legal structure will be poles apart, and the legal change will have to suffer the fate of a sapling planted in an uncongenial soil and facing hostile weather. It is, therefore, inevitable that the required reform should be gradual and the changes in the laws should be effected in such a manner as to balance favorably the change in the moral, educational, social, cultural and political life of the nation.

The Sources of Islamic Law

Maudoodī holds that the Islamic law is not static, but he concedes that it will have to be redefined if it has to become the fundamental law of Pakistan.
[From Maudoodī, *Islamic Law and Constitution,* p. 99 f.]

We should first clearly understand the nature of the problem that confronts us. When we say that this country should have an Islamic constitution, we do not mean that we possess a constitution of the Islamic state in a written form and that the only thing that is required to be done is to enforce it. The core of the problem is that we want an unwritten constitution to be transformed into a written one. What we term as Islamic constitution is really an unwritten constitution drawn from certain specific sources, and it is from this that we have to evolve a written constitution in keeping with the present-day requirements of our country.

An unwritten constitution is nothing unique or strange for the world. Indeed, up to the end of the eighteenth century, the structure of government throughout the world rested on unwritten constitutions; and even today the British government is functioning without a written constitution. As for a written constitution, even this great government, if it desires to have one, will inescapably have to take recourse to the various sources of its unwritten constitution to collect its material therefrom and then codify it article-wise. Our own need at the present moment is almost of the same kind.

There are four sources of the unwritten Islamic constitution:

1. *The Qur'ān* is the first and primary source, containing as it does all the fundamental directives and instructions from God. These directives and injunctions cover the entire gamut of man's existence. Herein are to be found not only directives relating to individual conduct but also principles regulating all the aspects of the social and cultural life of man.

[307]

It has also been clearly shown therein as to whether and why Muslims should endeavor to create and establish a state of their own.

2. *The Sunna* is the second source. It shows the way how, in accordance with the Qur'anic directives, the Prophet (peace be on him) translated into practical life the ideological spirit of Islam and developed it into a positive social order, finally elevating it to a full-fledged state. These things we can know from the Sunna and Sunna alone, thereby also learning how to ascertain the precise sense, purport and meaning of the Qur'anic directives. In other words the Sunna is the practical application of Qur'anic principles to mankind's social existence and we can, therefore, obtain the greatest possible number of invaluable precedents relating to Islamic constitution from this very important source.

3. *The Conventions of Khilāfat-i-Rāshidah* [1] form the third source. After the passing away of the Holy Prophet, the Righteous Caliphs managed the Islamic state in the best Islamic traditions, and books of Hadīth, History, and Biography are replete with glittering precedents of that golden era. It has been accepted in Islam from the very beginning that interpretations of the Qur'ān and the Sunna having the unanimous approval of all the Companions (technically known as ijmā') and the decisions of the Caliphs relating to constitutional and judicial problems accepted by the Companions should be binding on all and for all time. In other words, such interpretations and such decisions have to be accepted *in toto,* as the consensus of the Companions on any matter is tantamount to an authoritative exposition of the law. Wherever they have differed, it is but too evident there that two or even more interpretations were actually probable and one may be preferred to the other on the basis of sound reasoning. In cases of general consensus, however, the decision is inescapably the only logical one and has to be accepted as the only authoritative rule. As all the Companions were direct disciples of the Holy Prophet, trained by him personally, their general consensus in matters of interpretations and decisions was bound to be free from even the most trifling chance of error.

4. *The Rulings of Great Jurists* comprise the fourth source. These are the decisions of top-ranking jurists in regard to various constitutional problems of their times. They may not be of eternal validity, yet it cannot

[1] *Khilāfat-i-Rāshidah,* the period of the rule of the first four caliphs after the death of the Prophet, also known as the Republic, which lasted for thirty years.

[308]

be gainsaid that they contain fundamentals of the best guidance for a proper understanding of the Islamic constitution.

For writing down the constitution of an Islamic state, we will have to collect relevant material from all these sources, in the same way as the people of England, were they inclined to reduce their constitution to writing, would have to refer to their Common Law decisions and conventions and note down all the inferences therefrom and from judgments of their courts relating to constitutional problems.

THE ULAMĀ

A convention of learned theologians, representing all schools of Islamic thought, was held January 21–24, 1951. It unanimously recommended that the following principles be incorporated in the constitution of an Islamic state. Though their point of view has not met with general acceptance, it is significant as the expression of the most conservative force in present-day Pakistan.

Basic Principles of an Islamic State

The Constitution of an Islamic state should comprehend the following basic principles:

1. Ultimate Sovereignty over all Nature and all Law shall be affirmed in *Allāh,* the Lord of the universe, alone.

2. The law of the land shall be based on the Qur'ān and the Sunna, and no law shall be passed nor any administrative order issued, in contravention of the Qur'ān and the Sunna. *Explanatory Note:* If there be any laws in force in the country which are in conflict with the Qur'ān or the Sunna, it would be necessary to lay down (in the Constitution) that such laws shall be gradually, within a specified period, amended in conformity with the Islamic Law or repealed.

3. The State shall be based not on geographical, racial, linguistic or any other materialistic concepts, but on those principles and ideals which form the life-blood of Islamic ideology.

4. It shall be incumbent upon the State to uphold the Right (*Marūf*) and to suppress the Wrong (*Munkar*) as presented in the Qur'ān and

the Sunna, to take all measures necessary for the revival and advancement of the cultural pattern of Islam, and to make provision for Islamic education in accordance with the requirements of the various recognized schools of thought.

5. It shall be incumbent upon the State to strengthen the bonds of unity and brotherhood among all the Muslims of the world and to inhibit among the Muslim citizens of the State the growth of all prejudicial tendencies based on distinctions of race or language or territory or any other materialistic consideration so as to preserve and strengthen the unity of the *Millat-al-Islamiah*.[1]

6. It shall be the responsibility of the government to guarantee the provision of basic human necessities, i.e., food, clothing, housing, medical relief, and education to all citizens who might temporarily or permanently be incapable of earning their livelihood due to unemployment, sickness, or other reason, and to make no distinction of religion or race in that regard.

CITIZEN'S RIGHTS

7. The citizens shall be entitled to all the rights conferred upon them by the Islamic law, i.e., they shall be assured, within the limits of the law, of full security of life, property and honor, freedom of religion and belief, freedom of worship, freedom of person, freedom of expression, freedom of movement, freedom of association, freedom of occupation, equality of opportunity, and the right to benefit from public services.

8. No citizen shall, at any time, be deprived of these rights, except under the law, and none shall be awarded any punishment on any charge without being given full opportunity of defense and without the decision of a court of law.

9. The recognized Muslim schools of thought shall have, within the limits of the law, complete religious freedom. They shall have the right to impart religious instruction to their adherents and the freedom to propagate their views. Matters coming under the purview of Personal Law shall be administered in accordance with their respective codes of jurisprudence (*fiqh*), and it will be desirable to make provision for the administration of such matters by their respective judges (*qādīs*).

10. The non-Muslim citizens of the State shall have, within the limits

[1] The Muslim community.

of the law, complete freedom of religion and worship, mode of life, culture and religious education. They shall be entitled to have all their matters concerning Personal Law administered in accordance with their own religious code, usages, and customs.

11. All obligations assumed by the State, within the limits of the Sharī'a, towards the non-Muslim citizens shall be fully honored. They shall be entitled equally with the Muslim citizens to the rights of citizenship as enunciated in paragraph 7 above.

GOVERNANCE OF THE STATE

12. The Head of the State shall always be a male Muslim in whose piety, learning, and soundness of judgment the people or their elected representatives have full confidence.

13. The responsibility for the administration of the State shall primarily vest in the Head of the State, although he may delegate any part of his powers to any individual or body.

14. The function of the Head of the State shall not be autocratic but consultative (*Shura'i*), i.e., he will discharge his duties in consultation with persons holding responsible positions in the Government and with the elected representatives of the people.

15. The Head of the State shall have no right to suspend the Constitution wholly or partly or to run the administration in any other way but on a consultative basis.

16. The body empowered to elect the Head of the State shall also have the power to remove him by a majority of vote.

17. In respect of civic rights, the Head of the State shall be on the level of equality with other Muslims and shall not be above the law.

18. All citizens, whether members of the Government and officials or private persons, shall be subject to the same laws and the jurisdiction of the same courts.

19. The judiciary shall be separate from and independent of the executive, so that it may not be influenced by the executive in the discharge of its duties.

20. The propagation and publicity of such views and ideologies as are calculated to undermine the basic principles and ideals on which the Islamic State rests, shall be prohibited.

21. The various zones or regions of the country shall be considered

administrative units of a single state. They shall not be racial, linguistic, or tribal units but only administrative areas which may be given such powers under the supremacy of the Center as may be necessary for administrative convenience. They shall not have the right to secede.

22. No interpretation of the Constitution which is in conflict with the provisions of the Qur'ān or the Sunna shall be valid.

THE LIBERAL APPROACH

An influential school of thought in Pakistan which differs from the orthodox ulamā believes in a more radical interpretation of the principles contained in the Qur'ān and the traditions of the Prophet. That is, it does not contest the orthodox belief in the validity of the basic principles of Islam, nor does it reject all earlier thinking concerning them, but it insists that the interpretation of these principles should be freed from the shackles of inherited opinion and should make allowance for the changed needs of the times. The difference between the conservative and liberal approaches is thus not one of principle but of degree.

The selections included here are from the speeches and writings of Ishtiāq Husain Qureshī, who has compiled this section of our readings on the rise and growth of Pakistani nationalism. Qureshī was born in India in 1903 and completed his education at the University of Delhi and at Cambridge, where he was a member of Rahmat Alī's group. Even as a student he took part in the noncooperation and Khilāfat movements, and subsequently became a member of the District Congress Committee of Etah and of the Provincial Khilāfat Committee of the United Provinces. As a result of his efforts in behalf of the Muslim League on the eve of Partition, he was elected to the Constituent Assembly of India on the Muslim League ticket and later to the Constituent Assembly for Pakistan, of which he remained a member until its dissolution in 1954. Appointed to the government of Pakistan in early 1949, Qureshī rose from deputy minister to minister with full cabinet rank (1951–1954). The author of numerous works on Indo-Muslim institutions and culture, he has held the chairs of History and Political Science in the Universities of Delhi and Lahore, and more recently has come to the United States as visiting professor at Columbia University.

ISHTIĀQ HUSAIN QURESHĪ
The Basic Principles of an Islamic Polity

[From All-Pakistan Political Science Conference, *Proceedings*, 1950, Presidential address of Session III, pp. 1–5]

The constitution of a country must reflect the ideals on which its people want to base their political life. In Pakistan these ideals have never been debatable or ambiguous and have now been clearly set forth in the Objectives Resolution passed by the Assembly, with which all of you are familiar. The most outstanding feature of the Objectives Resolution is that the constitution of Pakistan shall be based on the ideals of Islam. The implementation of this decision, I would point out, requires the utmost circumspection and is beset with formidable difficulties. Broadly speaking, we are fully familiar with the ideology of Islam, but we have failed to keep abreast of the progress made by the world in the development of political institutions and the social fabric alike. We have now been suddenly faced with the great task of applying our ideology to modern needs. . . . If Islam were simply a code of certain rigid laws or even legal concepts, it would, perhaps, have been easy enough to apply them to such spheres of political life as were covered by it. But Islam is a dynamic force, a concept of life not of law, a guidance for the springs of thought and action and not a static code of action. In other words, Islam is a live and dynamic ideology and not a dead unprogressive and static collection of injunctions and prohibitions. It requires a new interpretation at every stage of our development and cannot be content merely with precedents and past usage. Islam does not discard precedents and traditions, but it lays emphasis upon the progressive unfolding of the creative instincts of mankind in accordance with the eternal principles defined by revelation. Islam limits the field of human deliberation within the precincts of moral and spiritual righteousness, but within these limitations it gives the human spirit the fullest freedom to find new methods of fulfillment in creative effort. If this analysis of the spirit of Islam is correct, you would understand what a difficult task we have set ourselves in this twentieth century by proclaiming to the world that our constitution will be based upon Islamic principles, because these principles have to be interpreted in accordance with all that is best and profound in human thought today.

At every step, however, we may be pulled by conflicting forces. On the one hand, we have a group of persons who seem to think that it is no longer possible to go beyond the institutions or even the procedure adopted in the early days of Islam when conditions were entirely different. These persons would want us to reproduce a society which no longer exists and a polity which was suited to that society. They would make us believe that all that was done at that time was the final interpretation of Islam and [that] it is not possible for the human intellect to deviate from it in any detail. This position is fallacious as I will try to show very shortly. If we were told to follow the principles which guided the creators of the Republic after the death of the Prophet, there could have been no difference of opinion with them. But when for every action or institution we are expected to find a precedent, we are being asked to act in a most un-Islamic manner, We must distinguish from the principle and the methods of its expression, from the spirit and the form which the action to fulfill it had to take in those circumstances. To give you a parallel, whereas a person who says that the Hāj [pilgrimage to Mecca] is a religious obligation is speaking the truth, he would not be in his senses if he insisted that the journey must be made on camels and not by any modern vehicle of transport. A constitution, I must emphasize, is only an instrument, a vehicle for achieving certain ends. It should be such as can serve those ends, it is true, but it should not be considered to be the end in itself. . . .

The moral concepts of our people are based upon the teachings of our religion. If, therefore, the polity of Pakistan is to be based upon a firm foundation of a righteous ideology, there is no motive force, but that of Islam which can act as the basis. To ask an overwhelmingly Muslim people to discard its innermost convictions in framing its constitution is to ask it to commit suicide. Therefore, there should be no doubt in the mind of any Pakistani, whether a Muslim or a non-Muslim, that the only enduring polity which can ensure justice and fairplay to all and which can make a contribution to the welfare of . . . humanity can be one which is based upon the principles of Islam. For the sake of a handful of persons who may have come to disbelieve either in Islam itself or in its dynamic possibilities this essential need cannot be overlooked.

[314]

Thus the only rational conclusion which emerges is that the Constituent Assembly was right in setting for itself the ideal of Islam as the main objective to be achieved in its constitution; but this ideal should be given a rational, dynamic interpretation. It is in this matter of interpretation, as I said before, that our main difficulties lie. For one thing, the critics of my views may ask me how we can distinguish the essence from the form. In other words, how far is it possible to define the principles which should actuate an Islamic polity, and how far can we go in discarding precedents without injuring the principles? Fortunately, so far as I can see, this question was answered for us in a most miraculous manner by the Prophet himself. Some time before his death, in his last Hāj, the fulfillment of his mission was proclaimed by revelation in the verse which heralded the completion of the faith for the Muslims. At that time it was realized by the Prophet as well as his companions that his mission having been fulfilled, his life in this world was also to come to an end; and yet he did not define any political institutions or lay down any definitive forms of government for his people. This I take to mean that having, by his teachings and through revelation, given to his people an ideology, he abstained from laying down any hard and fast rules for organizing the governmental or administrative machinery of his people. A complete code of principles was now in the hands of the community, but it was not fettered by any rigid rules in the matter of applying those principles to the needs of government. The foundations of the polity were laid in the Qur'ān and the teachings of the Prophet, the edifice was to be built in accordance with the needs of the successive generations by the creative spirit of the Muslim peoples guided by the teachings of Islam. Is this action of the great Exemplar not a clear guidance for us? Does it not show us that for guidance in the matter of framing a constitution for Pakistan we should turn to the principles contained in the teachings of the Qur'ān and the Prophet and should look upon precedents only as an ephemeral interpretation of those principles?

So far as constitutional matters, as apart from moral behavior and rules of conduct in certain circumstances, are concerned, we find two principles clearly narrated in the Qur'ān. The first principle is that the Muslims should obey God, His Prophet, and those who from amongst themselves are put in authority over them; the other principle, repeated at various places, is that Muslims should cooperate in righteousness and justice, but never in unrighteousness and injustice. These are important constitutional principles which form the basic principle of good government. The first verse properly interpreted means that a Muslim's first duty is to God and he should do nothing which comes into conflict with that duty. He should not, whatever be the cost, compromise his allegiance to the clear injunctions of the Qur'ān and the teachings of the Prophet by obeying any un-Islamic orders of the State. In other words, a really Islamic government can never ask its people to carry out an un-Islamic policy or to follow an order which is in clear contravention of Islam. And this is further strengthened by the second verse which I have quoted. The basis of human action should be moral and not merely political. There should be no divorce between fundamental morality and political activity. This refers to states and individuals alike. A Muslim state should so frame its policies that it does not become an engine of oppression at home or a supporter of injustice abroad. The individual should refrain from any activity which is unrighteous, unjust, or immoral. He must refuse to subordinate his moral principles to other considerations. This view carried to its logical interpretation confers the right of disobedience on the individual; but then he should be quite clear in his mind that he is in the right. If he is in doubt, he must obey the government so that the bonds of discipline and unity are not broken asunder. Thus by a two-fold emphasis upon righteousness, Islam attempts to build up a righteous polity, but, having provided that, it expects complete discipline. Where it is absolutely clear that on obeying an order a man is likely to contravene an injunction of God, he must disobey, but in all other circumstances, he must abide by the dictates of the government.

It should, however, be emphasized that the right of disobedience is to be used only in extreme circumstances. It is even possible to hold that this right does not exist. Having laid down a severe moral code for the State, it may be argued, Islam does not envisage any circumstances in which it can palpably deviate from the right path. The order to obedience is positive, the right of disobedience can only be inferred. Actually if the state is effectively prevented from disobeying the injunctions of Islam, the right of disobedience would automatically disappear. But has Islam provided effective safeguards against the deviation of the state from the right path? Legally it could have been laid down that a body of jurists would have the authority to declare any action of the government illegal, which ruling would be binding. But no such authority was ever set up nor envisaged, for the simple reason that Islam does not invest any body of jurists or lawyers with political power. This is in keeping with its refusal to set up a priestly class. Islam is a religion without any priests; it is a Faith, not a church, it trusts its followers and does not seek to set up human guardians over their conscience.

This is in accordance with the great political sagacity which the liberal creed of Islam has displayed in other fields. A state will remain Muslim to the extent and for the time that its people are Muslim. An Islamic state cannot be forced upon an un-Islamic people. Islam, therefore, concentrates on the necessity of making the people true Muslims and for this purpose has laid it down that there should always be a group of persons among the believers, who by their precept and example, hold aloft the torch of true Islam and preach righteousness and true belief, but these persons have not been given any political power, because Islam does not believe in compulsion which defeats its own purpose. The true safeguard against the state deviating from the path of truth is, therefore, an effective machinery for the dissemination of true knowledge so that the mass of the people may abide by the ideals of Islam. Having provided that, Islam trusts the people to run the government in accordance with the tenets of the Faith.

The government has, therefore, to be organized on a basis which makes it possible that all decisions should be the results of mutual consultation. This brings me to the third fundamental principle which has been clearly defined in the Qur'ān. Muslims are expected to order their affairs by mutual consultation, which is the basis of democracy. It is inherent in the idea of consultation that the majority view shall prevail and personal opinions shall be subordinated to discipline and requirements of unity.

Sovereignty in a Truly Islamic State

This excerpt from Qureshi's presidential address before the second all-Pakistan Political Science Conference, 1951, is directed against the claims of the ulamā to be the sole authoritative interpreters of Islamic law, Shar' (Sharī'a). The author's faith in democracy has been shared by most leading politicians in Pakistan.

[From the second All-Pakistan Political Science Conference, *Proceedings*, 1951, Presidential address of Session I, pp. 2–8]

The political sovereign in Pakistan, like any other country, are the people. This does not come into conflict with the idea of the sovereignty of God. God is sovereign in the universe and His will cannot be challenged by anyone. In that sense God is sovereign in every country, Muslim or non-Muslim. He is equally sovereign in those socialist countries where His authority is challenged and His existence denied as He is in countries where people prostrate themselves before Him five times a day in recognition of the fact that He is the sole arbiter of their fates, their Creator and Master. But when we are talking of the real sovereign this idea does not remain relevant. In spite of the sovereignty of God there have been states, nations, and communities which have denied His existence. It is not inconceivable, howsoever improbable it may be, that the people of Pakistan may cease to believe in God. It is in the very nature of the freedom given by his Creator to man that he should be free to act in accordance with his beliefs and convictions. If the people of Pakistan— God forbid—stray from the path of the Truth, the sovereignty of God will not cease, but the authority of the people will direct the life in the country in entirely different channels. In a worldly sense, therefore, the people of Pakistan possess at present the final authority even to decide whether they shall be Muslims or not. It is, therefore, obvious that the people of Pakistan are as sovereign as the people of any other country because they can, if they so desire, make any decisions, for better, for worse.

The concept of legal sovereignty has been strong in the annals of Islam. Looking at the past, the Muslims have recognized the sovereignty of the law. No authority has been permitted to stand between the law and its majesty. The law of Islam—the *Shar'*—has been considered to be the final legal authority in all Muslim countries. The highest executive in the land—the caliph, for that matter, the Prophet himself—was not considered higher than the law. The law equally applied to everyone because the Islamic conception of law is different from the Western conception. In the West, the law is the will of the sovereign. In Islamic countries the law is the will of God. In this sense we might say that Islam recognizes the sovereignty of God and, therefore, in a limited sense a Muslim state is a theocratic state. But the terms "theocracy" as well as the sovereignty of God have been misapplied in many communities and, therefore, they are not applicable to an Islamic state. Theocracy in the West is a kingdom of God where authority vests in specially ordained priests who exercise it on behalf of God. This is not the conception of Islam. Islam has no priest-hood and, therefore, no special agents of God to administer the law which expresses His will.

It would be of some interest to us to analyze the position as envisaged by Islam and to remove the pitfalls which exist for the unwary in this quest. Islam envisages a Muslim people guided by the teachings of Islam in ordering its affairs. This community, for the purposes of convenience, elected, in the earlier days, a high executive, called the caliph, to carry on the business of the State on its behalf. This executive of the State, the caliph and later the sultan, was only an agent to carry out the will of the people and the people being Muslims naturally demanded that their af-fairs should be conducted in accordance with their beliefs and convictions. The *Shar'* included within its fold three main principles, two immutable and one mutable. The immutable principles are the Qur'ān and the authentic Hadīth of the Prophet; the latter, according to the Muslims is not so much an enlargement as an interpretation of the principles enun-ciated in the revelation. The mutable factor is the interpretation of these principles which has been arrived at by the application of human reason to apply them to the changing needs of humanity in different conditions. It is wrong, therefore, to say that the *Shar'* is entirely immutable. The first two principles of it certainly are immutable, but, as I have pointed out, the third principle which is so necessary for the application of Islamic principles to our own lives must necessarily be progressive. In the body of Islamic law known to us today there is considerable contribution of this third principle and it needs reconsideration for being applied in circum-stances which have so considerably altered.

The recognition of the legal sovereignty of a code of law has certain implications: one of these is that the courts would directly administer it without the interference of the legislature or the executive authority. This method was followed during the Middle Ages in all Islamic countries. But today there are very few countries where this conception prevails. Those Muslim countries which had to give up this practice had certain valid reasons to do so. As I have pointed out earlier, the *Shar'*, as it exists today, has a considerable corpus of judge-made law. Unfortunately, the tendency amongst Muslim jurists has been, like other judges, of basing their interpretation on the past body of previous interpretations. This was healthy, because otherwise it would have been impossible to maintain a

[319]

continuity of tradition in the Muslim legal system. However, after a lapse of many centuries, with changing conditions, whereas the immutable principles upon which the *Shar'* is based continued to be valid, the line of reasoning which led to the interpretation of these eternal principles was not always in keeping with the progress that human knowledge had made. To leave the courts to decide what is in accordance with Islamic law, it is necessary to define Islamic law properly and to separate the grain from the husk. From such a complex mass it is not within the capacity of every lawyer or judge to extricate the basic principles, because this will in itself involve fresh interpretation. For the purposes of uniformity it is also necessary that a sound tradition should grow up and, if the judge-made law makes deviations either from the principles or the needs of the people, it should be possible to correct the mistakes through a different human agency.

This analysis brings us to the fundamental considerations which hold today in determining the legal sovereign in our new constitution. Should we accept the *Shar'* as it stands today without any reinterpretation or reorientation? Should we have a legislature and what part has the legislature to play if the sovereignty of the *Shar'* is accepted? Would it be wise to put any limitations on the power of the legislature which may be enforced constitutionally? And, lastly, what would be the relationship between the legal sovereign that we may choose to accept and the political sovereign, on one hand, and the real sovereign, on the other? . . .

It has been recognized in all Muslim countries that in many respects the mutable part of the *Shar'* requires considerable overhauling and the immutable bases need a new interpretation. This feeling has been shared by some of the leading theologians of the Muslim world. Therefore, it would not be in keeping with the progressive tendencies of Islam to recognize the *Shar'* in its present form as the legal sovereign. It may be argued that there is no difficulty in accepting the Qur'ān and the Sunna as the legal sovereign; but until a new interpretation is accepted by the people, the difference in interpretation will create not only difficulties but discord as well. How the interpretation should be revised and made acceptable to the people is quite a different problem. It will require considerable research, careful thinking and propagation amongst the people. If the work is left entirely to the courts, it is obvious that the interpretation will be only legalistic and not necessarily wise or sound; besides, to make it universally acceptable it is necessary in this twentieth century that every interpretation should be put in the public forum so that the combined judgment of the people may accept the one which it finds the most rational. It is a well-known principle of legislation that a law should conform to the moral conscience of the people, otherwise it will fail in its application. The moral conscience of the people can be swayed in favor or against an interpretation only with the help of public discussion. Treated as the close preserve of a few lawyers, theologians, jurists, or judges, the law would gradually find itself in disharmony with public sentiment. Our present attitude towards the dictates of the *Shar'* will completely illustrate my point. Our theologians, learned in the traditions of the Islamic legal system, have kept the torch burning, but have failed to spread its light among the people, because they have not trusted the people. They have considered the interpretation of the principles of Islam as their close preserve and by not taking the people into their confidence have created a wide gulf between their own views and the outlook of the intelligent sections of the nation. In every Muslim country, therefore, there has come into existence a wide gulf between the ulamā of the orthodox schools and the intelligentsia. This has done a great harm to Islam, because, as the result of this division, Islam has ceased to play that vital role in the life of the people which was its due. The intensity of these antagonisms varies from country to country and even in the same country from class to class but it does exist everywhere, yielding a most pernicious crop of laxity and indifference. But it is a disease which must be rooted out from the body politic of Islam.

It is obvious that the only place where discussions can take place in connection with the reinterpretation and reorientation of the *Shar'* is the legislature, because as the supreme representative of the people, the legislature alone can speak for them and accept on their behalf what seems rational and proper out of the mass of argument and commentary putting forward different points of view. Another happy result of these discussions will be that every problem shall come into the public forum and will be discussed from a million platforms; and, as problems are discussed they will sink into the subconscious mind of the people and ultimately become a part of their convictions. Thus interpretation and conviction will go hand in hand. It has been suggested by some that the constitution should provide for a body of learned theologians and jurists to veto any legislation that they consider to be against the *Shar'*. This would be a most retrograde step, because then the responsibility of understanding and interpreting Islam will be limited to a few persons rather than the entire nation. All the difficulties which would arise if the courts are left with the interpretation of the Qur'ān and the Sunna will be accentuated if a body like this is set up to control the activities of the legislature. Instead of harmony it would create resentment and even rebellion.

It has been argued that none except those who are deeply steeped in legal knowledge and theology have the capacity to interpret the Qur'ān. This is true in a limited sense; when it comes to the application of a law to a case with legal nicety, the layman is at a grave disadvantage. The comprehensive principles and their broad application to the life of the community is not so technically legal. Only a lawyer can be a judge; but a legislator need not be a trained lawyer. The legislator accepts principles which are given a legal garb by experts and a judge-made law grows up around that legislation. It is, therefore, a mistake to think that only the ulamā are capable of legislating in accordance with the principles enunciated in the Qur'ān and the Sunna. The last of the Prophets was born amongst a backward and uneducated people; he did not limit his mission to trained jurists and lawyers. It is quite likely that the legislature may make mistakes, but these mistakes will be rectified in course of time. On the other hand if the interpretation of Islamic principles is to be based entirely upon authoritative rulings of judges and jurists, their mistakes would take long to rectify, for then the entire approach would be authoritative and not persuasive. For achieving a quick rectification of mistakes, the legislature will have to be left unhampered and it would be unwise to put any limitations on its authority.

This does not mean that our experts in Islamic learning and law will have no influence. Their learning and piety will add authority to their opinion. There is, however, much difference between the authority which the opinion of an expert possesses and the legal sanction behind it. Once the opinions of a small body of experts begin to be vested with the authority of the law, the freedom of the mass of the people to choose from amongst the interpretations vanishes. Besides, persuasion and discussion are at a discount; they gradually disappear. There is a danger of the emergence of a class or a set of persons vested with sacerdotal authority. Islam does not tolerate the growth of a priesthood, nor does it encourage the division of the people into a clergy and the laity. Indeed no particular class has been given any authority to interpret the principles of Islam. The reason for this attitude is that the growth of a class vested with any sacerdotal authority or religious sanctity discourages the mass of the people from acquiring the true knowledge of the Faith. Real knowledge becomes the monopoly of the few and creates indifference among the rest. Sometimes it even engenders hostility. Although the history of the ulamā of Islam has been remarkably free from a class consciousness based upon selfish motives, yet there are many instances in which certain sections of the ulamā have exploited their position to the detriment of the *millat* [the Muslim community or nation]. Islam envisages the Muslims as a secular society believing in the principles of Islam and, therefore, acting upon its precepts. It trusts the mass of the Muslims to do their duty. It does provide for discipline and goes even to the extent of punishing the black sheep, but so far as the Muslims as a community are concerned, they have been entrusted, and no one else, to organize themselves into an instrument for practicing and propagating, by precept and example, the message that was delivered to our Prophet in its final form. There is a tradition of the Prophet which says that there shall be no consensus on an error amongst his people. This is not only a prophecy but is also the embodiment of the trust that Islam places in its followers. If the mass of the people are Muslims and their faith is sound, they will instinctively accept the correct interpretation. If they do not accept the correct interpretation and wilfully persist in error, it is obvious that no authority can put them right. The Muslim people, therefore, are the sole authority, guided, of course, by the advice of the experts to decide which interpretation they would follow. The advice, however, has no binding authority. To leave the legislature unhampered, therefore, will be in keeping with the spirit of Islam.

By adopting this attitude Islam has acted in accordance with human nature. All philosophies and religions can thrive only on conviction and a voluntary surrender of the human will to their precepts. No conviction or religion can be forced upon a people. Attempts to do so result either in failure or in disasters. From the point of view of political philosophy, this attitude of Islam is not only correct but the very essence of wisdom. From the analysis of the theory of sovereignty which I have given in the beginning it would be obvious that Islam seeks to establish a complete harmony among the real sovereign, the political sovereign, and the legal sovereign. The legal sovereign shall be the Muslim law; but its definition shall be in the hands of a legislature representing the people which will, by deliberation and discussion, decide how to apply the principles of Islam to the needs of the community in varying circumstances. If the people of Pakistan are overwhelmingly Muslims and their representatives in the legislature represent their opinions and views, it is obvious that they will be honest guardians of the teachings of Islam. The political sovereign shall be the people who will elect and dismiss their legislatures and their governments. We have accepted this principle in our Objectives Resolution wherein we have recognized that the people are the vehicle of the authority delegated by God to the state of Pakistan. The real sovereign will be basically the principles of Islam, which influence the public mind only if the problems are brought into the public forum and discussed at full length. If we want that Islam should be the real sovereign in Pakistan we will have to strengthen the Islamic elements in the education of our children and our people. And one of the methods of education is that the problems facing the community shall be discussed openly, permitting all those who have something to say to participate in the discussion.

CHAPTER XXVII

SIX PATHS TO
INDIA'S FUTURE

The intellectual climate of India has usually allowed a great variety of ideas to flourish and coexist with one another. The modern period of Indian thought reveals this luxuriant tendency as much as do the classical and medieval periods, with one significant difference. Whereas the speculations of the literate class (both Hindu and Muslim) had traditionally centered in religion, by the time the British withdrew from the subcontinent educated Indians and Pakistanis were primarily concerned with urgent economic and political problems.

This remarkable transformation of values had of course by no means permeated the entire society in the space of a century and a half. Hundreds of millions of peasant- and artisan-villagers in South Asia continue to abide by the rules and precepts laid down centuries ago in their sacred books, and the thought of changing their traditional way of life would seem to them as fantastic and dangerous as travel to other solar systems may seem to the average Westerner today. Genuine Hindu saints, such as Rāmana Maharshi in South India, continue to appear, and pilgrimages to holy places have actually increased with the advent of modern transportation. Even among the educated and Westernized fraction of the population there is no lack of interest in religious speculation and no dearth of writing on religious subjects.

Nevertheless, now that independent India has become a part of the modern world, the pull of the tide is today strongly secular, drawing men's minds toward the practical tasks involved in creating a better social order. Many prescriptions are being offered as to the best means of achieving this goal, some old and some new. The moderate program of social reform and gradual political change initiated by Rāmmohun Roy could be said to be the dominant philosophy of the Congress Party which governs India today. Meanwhile, Gāndhi's more radical social gospel is still being preached by his disciple Vinobā Bhāve, under whom the *bhūdān* (land-gift) movement has reached astounding proportions.

As these older traditions, including the Hindu nationalism of the Extremists, have continued into independent India, so younger ones have emerged in recent decades, each proclaiming a different path to a better future. The seed-time of these philosophies, interestingly enough, was the Gāndhian era, when many of the younger leaders brought to the fore by the intensification of the nationalist movement found the Mahātmā's ideas medieval, much as they admired him personally. Inevitably their minds reached out for more modern ideas to Europe, where many had lived as students. Ideologies such as Fascism, Socialism, and Communism seemed to answer India's needs in two ways. Not only did the collectivist spirit common to them all promise to heal the psychological and economic gap between the tiny educated elite and the impoverished mass of the population, but British Socialists, German and Italian Fascists, and Russian Communists provided moral support (and in some instances material assistance) to the independence movement.

In this concluding chapter of our survey of more than three thousand years of Indian thought, the doctrines of six contrasting schools—not of metaphysics but of political philosophy—are presented by authoritative spokesmen. Hindu nationalism in its most virulent form, dictatorial National Socialism, liberal Democratic Socialism, revolutionary International Communism, evolutionary National Communism, and Gāndhian decentralism—all vie with one another for control of men's minds in independent India. Which school, if any, will win out will perhaps in the long run prove less important than the fact that all together have been slowly but surely acting to leaven the dough of age-old custom and belief with the bitter yeast of politics.

V. D. SĀVARKAR: HINDU NATIONALIST

Unaffected by the new political ideas that came into India after the First World War, but exacerbated by the rise of Muslim nationalism, the tradition of extremist Hindu nationalism has been carried forward into the post-independence period by a group of zealots deeply imbued with its

[326]

ideology. Its most outstanding proponent and theoretician in recent decades has been Vinayak Damodar Sāvarkar. Born in 1883, and a Chitpāvan brāhman like his fellow-Mahārāshtrians Rānade, Gokhale and Tilak, Sāvarkar was the second son of a landowner known for both his Sanskrit scholarship and his Western-style education. Two incidents from his youth presaged his lifelong antipathy to those he considered Hinduism's foes. At the age of ten, hearing of bloody Hindu-Muslim riots in the United Provinces, he led a gang of his schoolmates in a stone-throwing attack on the village mosque. At sixteen, his anger at the hanging of two Mahārāshtrian terrorists made him vow to devote his life to driving the British out of India.

On entering Fergusson College at Poona, Sāvarkar quickly organized a patriotic society among his fellow-students. Through poems, articles, and speeches he reminded them of India's glorious past and the need to regain her freedom. In 1905 he arranged for a huge bonfire of foreign cloth and persuaded Tilak to speak to the crowd gathered around it. For this he was rusticated from his college, but with Tilak's help secured from an Indian patriot in London a scholarship to study there, on the under-standing that he would never enter government service.

From 1906 to 1910, in the guise of a student of law, the young Sāvarkar bearded the British lion in its den. His "New India" group learned the art of bomb-making from a Russian revolutionary in Paris, and planned the assassination of the hated Lord Curzon. One member of the group electrified London when he shot and killed an important official of the India Office and then went proudly to the gallows. Sāvarkar himself was arrested a few months later, but by this time he had already published his nationalistic interpretation of the 1857–58 Mutiny and Rebellion, entitling it *The First Indian War of Independence of 1857*.

When the ship carrying him back to India for trial stopped at Marseilles, Sāvarkar created an international incident by swimming ashore and claiming asylum on French soil. The Hague International Tribunal ultimately judged his recapture by the British authorities irregular but justifiable, but by this time he had already been twice sentenced to life-imprisonment. In 1911 Sāvarkar was transported to the Andaman Islands (India's "Devil's Island" in the tropical Bay of Bengal) where he found his elder brother, a renowned terrorist, already there before him.

[327]

Agitation in India secured his release from confinement in 1924, but until 1937 his movements were restricted and he was forbidden to take part in politics. Nehru, Bose, and Roy all sent him congratulatory messages on his final return to the political arena, and the Hindu Mahāsabhā (Great Assembly of Hindus, founded in 1919 and the largest Hindu communal party), elected him as their president for seven consecutive years, until failing health forced him to resign.

Intending to unite and strengthen all Hindudom, Sāvarkar advocated the removal of inter-caste barriers, the entry of untouchables into orthodox temples, and the reconversion of Hindus who had become Muslims or Christians. During the Second World War he propagated the slogan: "Hinduize all politics and militarize Hindudom," and urged Hindus to enlist in the armed forces in order to learn the arts of war.

Sāvarkar and Gāndhi had disagreed from the time of their discussions in London in 1909 (which may have helped to provoke the latter to write his famous *Hind Swarāj*). Sāvarkar now made no bones about his conviction that Gāndhi's doctrine of absolute nonviolence was "absolutely sinful." [1] As the fateful hour of independence from British rule drew near, Sāvarkar and the Mahāsabhā strenuously opposed the Muslim League's demand for Pakistan. Gāndhi's apparent vacillation on this issue and his post-Partition fasts for the protection of India's Muslims and for good-will toward Pakistan infuriated many Hindu nationalists. Early in 1948 one of them, to avenge what he felt was Gāndhi's betrayal of the Hindu cause, felled him with three pistol shots.

The assassin, N. V. Godse, although no longer a member of the Mahāsabhā, was still known as a devoted lieutenant of Sāvarkar, who consequently had to stand trial with him. Acquitted because of lack of evidence linking him to the crime itself, but too ill to lead an active life, Sāvarkar retired to his home in Bombay. The ideology he helped to shape continues to animate the Hindu nationalist organizations, which in addition to the Hindu Mahāsabhā now include the Rāshtriya Swayamsevak Sangh (National Self-Service Organization), the Jan Sangh (People's Party), and Rām Rājya Parishad (Followers of the Divine Kingdom). Although greatly overshadowed by the Congress Party, their appeal to both patriotic and religious sentiment gives them a potentially strong position in India politics.

[1] Dhananjay Keer, *Savarkar and His Times,* p. 219.

VINAYAK SĀVARKAR
The Glories of the Hindu Nation

Deprived of writing materials during his days of imprisonment, Sāvarkar scratched on the whitewashed walls of his cell and then committed to memory the notes for his treatise on *Hindutva* ("Hindu-ness"). In the final portion of this work, published in 1924, he exultantly cited the geographical, racial, cultural, numerical, and religious ways in which the Hindu nation is superior to all other polities.

[From Sāvarkar, *Hindutva*, pp. 108–16]

So far we have not allowed any considerations of utility to prejudice our inquiry. But having come to its end it will not be out of place to see how far the attributes, which we found to be the essentials of *Hindutva,* contribute towards [the] strength, cohesion, and progress of our people. Do these essentials constitute a foundation so broad, so deep, so strong, that basing upon it the Hindu people can build a future which can face and repel the attacks of all the adverse winds that blow; or does the Hindu race stand on feet of clay?

Some of the ancient nations raised huge walls so as to convert a whole country into a fortified castle. Today their walls are trodden to dust or are but scarcely discernible by a few scattered mounds here and there; while the people they were meant to protect are not discernible at all! Our ancient neighbors, the Chinese, labored from generation to generation and raised a rampart, embracing the limits of an empire—so wide, so high, so strong—a wonder of human world. That too, as all human wonders must, sank under its own weight. But behold the ramparts of Nature! Have they not, these Himalayas, been standing there as one whose desires are satisfied—so they seemed to the Vedic bard—so they seem to us today. These are *our* ramparts that have converted this vast continent into a cosy castle.

You take up buckets and fill your trenches with water and call it [a] moat. Behold, Varuna [1] himself, with his one hand pushing continents aside, fills the gap by pouring seas on seas with the other! This Indian ocean, with its bays and gulfs, is *our* moat.

These are our frontier lines bringing within our reach the advantages of an inland as well as an insular country.

[1] God of the Waters.

She is the richly endowed daughter of God—this our Motherland. Her rivers are deep and perennial. Her land is yielding to the plow and her fields are loaded with golden harvests. Her necessaries of life are few and a genial nature yields them all almost for the asking. Rich in her fauna, rich in her flora, she knows she owes it all to the immediate source of light and heat—the sun. She covets not the icy lands; blessed be they and their frozen latitudes. If heat is at times "enervating" here, cold is at times benumbing there. If cold induces manual labor, heat removes much of its very necessity. She takes more delight in quenched thirst than in the parched throat. Those who have not, let them delight in exerting to have. But those who have—may be allowed to derive pleasure from the very fact of having. Father Thames is free to work at feverish speed, wrapped in his icy sheets. She loves to visit her ghats and watch her boats gliding down the Ganges, on her moonlit waters. With the plow, the peacocks, the lotus, the elephant, and the *Gītā,* she is willing to forego, if that must be, whatever advantage the colder latitudes enjoy. She knows she cannot have all her own way. Her gardens are green and shady, her granaries well stocked, her waters crystal, her flowers scented, her fruits juicy, and her herbs healing. Her brush is dipped in the colors of dawn and her flute resonant with the music of Gokul.[2] Verily Hind is the richly endowed daughter of God.

Neither the English nor the French—with the exception of [the] Chinese and perhaps the Americans, no people are gifted with a land that can equal in natural strength and richness the land of *Sindhustān.*[3] A country, a common home, is the first important essential of stable strong nationality; and as of all countries in the world our country can hardly be surpassed by any in its capacity to afford a soil so specially fitted for the growth of a great nation; we Hindus, whose very first article of faith is the love we bear to the common Fatherland, have in that love the strongest talismanic tie that can bind close and keep a nation firm and enthuse and enable it to accomplish things greater than ever.

The second essential of *Hindutva* puts the estimate of our latent powers of national cohesion and greatness yet higher. No country in the world, with the exception of China again, is peopled by a race so homogeneous,

---

[2] The village near Mathura where Krishna is said to have spent his boyhood.

[3] "Land of the Rivers." *Sindhu* (river) is presumably the earlier form from which *Hindu* derives.

yet so ancient and yet so strong both numerically and vitally. The Americans too, whom we found equally fortunate with us so far as the gift of an excellent geographical basis of nationality is concerned, are decidedly left behind. Mohamedans are no race nor are the Christians. They are a religious unit, yet neither a racial nor a national one. But we Hindus, if possible, are all the three put together and live under our ancient and common roof. The numerical strength of our race is an asset that cannot be too highly prized.

And culture? The English and the Americans feel they are kith and kin because they possess a Shakespeare in common. But not only a Kalidas or a Bhas, but Oh Hindus! ye possess a Ramayan and a Mahabharat in common—and the Vedas! One of the national songs the American children are taught to sing attempts to rouse their sense of eternal self-importance by pointing out to the hundred years twice told that stand behind their history. The Hindu counts his years not by centuries but by cycles—the *Yug* and the *Kalpa* [4]—and amazed asks: "O Lord of the line of Raghu [Rama], where has the kingdom of Ayodhya gone? O Lord of the line of Yadu [Krishna], where has Mathura gone!!" He does not attempt to rouse the sense of self-importance so much as the sense of proportion, which is Truth. And that has perhaps made him last longer than Ramses and Nebuchadnezzar. If a people that had no past have no future, then a people that had produced an unending galaxy of heroes and heroworshipers and who are conscious of having faught [fought] with and vanquished the forces whose might struck Greece and Rome, the Pharaohs and the Incas, dead, have in their history a guarantee of their future greatness more assuring than any other people on earth yet possess.

But besides culture the tie of common holyland has at times proved stronger than the chains of a Motherland. Look at the Mohamedans. Mecca to them is a sterner reality than Delhi or Agra. Some of them do not make any secret of being bound to sacrifice all India if that be to the glory of Islam or [if it] could save the city of their prophet. Look at the Jews. Neither centuries of prosperity nor sense of gratitude for the shelter they found can make them more attached or even equally attached to the several countries they inhabit. Their love is, and must necessarily be, divided between the land of their birth and the land of their prophets.

[4] The age and the eon.

If the Zionists' dreams are ever realized—if Palestine becomes a Jewish state and it will gladden us almost as much as our Jewish friends—they, like the Mohamedans, would naturally set the interests of their holyland above those of their Motherlands in America and Europe, and, in case of war between their adopted country and the Jewish state, would naturally sympathize with the latter, if indeed they do not bodily go over to it. History is too full of examples of such desertions to cite particulars. The Crusades again, attest to the wonderful influence that a common holyland exercises over peoples widely separated in race, nationality, and language, to bind and hold them together.

The ideal conditions, therefore, under which a nation can attain perfect solidarity and cohesion would, other things being equal, be found in the case of those people who inhabit the land they adore, the land of whose forefathers is also the land of their Gods and Angels, of Seers and Prophets; the scenes of whose history are also the scenes of their mythology.

The Hindus are about the only people who are blessed with these ideal conditions that are at the same time incentive to national solidarity, cohesion, and greatness. Not even the Chinese are blessed thus. Only Arabia and Palestine—if ever the Jews can succeed in founding their state there —can be said to possess this unique advantage. But Arabia is incomparably poorer in the natural, cultural, historical, and numerical essentials of a great people; and even if the dreams of the Zionists are ever realized into a Palestine state still they too must be equally lacking in these.

England, France, Germany, Italy, Turkey proper, Persia, Japan, Afganistan, [the] Egypt of today (for the old descendants of "Punto" and their Egypt is dead long since)—and other African states, Mexico, Peru, Chilly [Chile] (not to mention states and nations lesser than all these)— though racially more or less homogeneous, are yet less advantageously situated than we are in geographical, cultural, historical, and numerical essentials, besides lacking the unique gift of a sanctified Motherland. Of the remaining nations Russia in Europe, and the United States in America, though geographically equally well-gifted with us, are yet poorer, in almost every other requisite of nationality. China alone of the present comity of nations is almost as richly gifted with the geographical, racial, cultural, and numerical essentials as the Hindus are. Only in the possession of a common, a sacred, and a perfect language, the Sanskrit, and

[332]

a sanctified Motherland, we are so far [as] the essentials that contribute to national solidarity are concerned more fortunate.

Thus the actual essentials of *Hindutva* are, as this running sketch reveals, also the ideal essentials of nationality. If we would we can build on this foundation of *Hindutva,* a future greater than what any other people on earth can dream of—greater even than our own past; provided we are able to utilize our opportunities! For let our people remember that great combinations are the order of the day. The leagues of nations, the alliances of powers, Pan-Islamism, Pan-Slavism, Pan-Ethiopism—all little beings are seeking to get themselves incorporated into greater wholes, so as to be better fitted for the struggle for existence and power. Those who are not naturally and historically blessed with numerical or geographical or racial advantages are seeking to share them with others. Woe to those who have them already as their birthright and know them not; or worse, despise them! The nations of the world are desperately trying to find a place in this or that combination for aggression:—can any one of you, Oh Hindus! whether Jain or Samāji [5] or Sanātani [6] or Sīkh or any other subsection, afford to cut yourselves off or fall out and destroy the ancient, the natural, and the organic combination that already exists? —a combination that is bound not by any scraps of paper nor by the ties of exigencies alone, but by the ties of blood and birth and culture? Strengthen them if you can; pull down the barriers that have survived their utility, of castes and customs, of sects and sections. What of interdining? But intermarriages between provinces and provinces, castes and castes, be encouraged where they do not exist. But where they already exist as between the Sīkhs and Sanātanies, Jains and Vaishnavas, Lingayats [7] and Non-Lingayats—suicidal be the hand that tries to cut the nuptial tie. Let the minorities remember they would be cutting the very branch on which they stand. Strengthen every tie that binds you to the main organism, whether of blood or language or common festivals and feasts or culture love you bear to the common Motherland. Let this ancient and noble stream of Hindu blood flow from vein to vein . . . till at last the Hindu people get fused and welded into an indivisible whole, till our race gets consolidated and strong and sharp as steel.

Just cast a glance at the past, then at the present: Pan-Islamism in Asia,

---

[5] A member of the Brāhmo, Prārthanā, or Ārya Samājes.   [6] Orthodox Hindu.
[7] A Hindu sect devoted exclusively to the worship of Shiva.

the political leagues in Europe, the Pan-Ethiopic movement in Africa and America—and then see, Oh Hindus, if your future is not entirely bound up with the future of India and the future of India is bound up, in the last resort, with Hindu strength. We are trying our best, as we ought to do, to develop the consciousness of and a sense of attachment to the greater whole, whereby Hindus, Mohamedans, Parsis, Christians, and Jews, would feel as Indians first and every other thing afterwards. But whatever progress India may have made to that goal one thing remains almost axiomatically true—not only in India but everywhere in the world —that a nation requires a foundation to stand upon and the essence of the life of a nation is the life of that portion of its citizens whose interests and history and aspirations are most closely bound up with the land and who thus provide the real foundation to the structure of their national state. Take the case of Turkey. The young Turks after the revolution had to open their parliament and military institutions to Armenians and Christians on a nonreligious and secular basis. But when the war with Servia came the Christians and Armenians first wavered and then many a regiment consisting of them went bodily over to the Servians, who politically and racially and religiously were more closely bound up with them. Take the case of America. When the German war broke out she suddenly had to face the danger of desertions of her German citizens; while the Negro citizens there sympathize more with their brethren in Africa than with their white countrymen. The American state, in the last resort, must stand or fall with the fortunes of its Anglo-Saxon constituents. So with the Hindus, they being the people, whose past, present, and future are most closely bound with the soil of Hindusthan as *Pitṛbhū,*[8] as *Puṇyabhū,*[9] they constitute the foundation, the bedrock, the reserved forces of the Indian state. Therefore even from the point of Indian nationality, must ye, Oh Hindus, consolidate and strengthen Hindu nationality: not to give wanton offense to any of our non-Hindu compatriots, in fact to any one in the world but in just and urgent self-defense of our race and land; to render it impossible for others to betray her or to subject her to unprovoked attacks by any of those "Pan-isms" that are struggling forth from continent to continent. As long as other communities in India or in the world are not respectively planning India first or Mankind first, but all are busy in organizing offensive and defensive alliances and com-

[8] Ancestral land.   [9] Holy land.

binations on entirely narrow racial or religious or national basis, so long, at least so long, Oh Hindus, strengthen if you can those subtle bonds that like nerve-threads bind you in One Organic Social Being. Those of you who in a suicidal fit try to cut off the most vital of those ties and dare to disown the name Hindu will find to their cost that in doing so they have cut themselves off from the very source of our racial life and strength.

The presence of only a few of these essentials of nationality which we have found to constitute *Hindutva* enabled little nations like Spain or Portugal to get themselves lionized in the world. But when all of those ideal conditions obtain here what is there in the human world that the Hindus cannot accomplish?

Thirty crores of people, with India for their basis of operation, for their Fatherland and for their Holyland, with such a history behind them, bound together by ties of a common blood and common culture can dictate their terms to the whole world. A day will come when mankind will have to face the force.

Equally certain it is that whenever the Hindus come to hold such a position whence they could dictate terms to the whole world—those terms cannot be very different from the terms which [the] *Gītā* dictates or the Buddha lays down. A Hindu is most intensely so, when he ceases to be a Hindu; and with a Kabir claims the whole earth for a Benares . . . or with a Tukaram exclaims: "My country? Oh brothers, the limits of the Universe—there the frontiers of my country lie."

SUBHĀS CHANDRA BOSE: NATIONAL SOCIALIST LEADER

"The earliest recollection I have of myself is that I used to feel like a thoroughly insignificant being."[1] So wrote the man who rose to become one of the most controversial figures in modern Indian politics. The sixth son and ninth child of a successful Bengali lawyer in Orissa, Subhās Chandra Bose (1897–1945) showed from his youth a burning desire to excel. Throughout his scholastic career he generally stood at the top of his class. His primary education was gained at a Baptist mission school,

[1] *Netaji's Life and Writings, Part One, An Indian Pilgrim; Or, Autobiography of Subhas Chandra Bose, 1897–1920*, p. 3.

but his parents insisted on his studying Sanskrit at the same time. At the age of fifteen Subhās discovered in the writings of Swāmī Vivekānanda the ideals of self-purification and social service. Soon afterward, as a student at Presidency College of the University of Calcutta, he became a great admirer of Aurobindo Ghose's mystic nationalism.

Subhās grew to manhood during the First World War, and found military life so appealing that he joined the Calcutta University unit of the India Defense Force. After finishing his B.A. in 1919, he was sent by his father to Cambridge to prepare for the Indian Civil Service. He succeeded in passing the rigorous I.C.S. examination, but a few months later resigned from the Service and returned to India to join the noncooperation movement, which was then at its height.

Subhās Chandra Bose's career both paralleled and rivaled that of his contemporary, Jawaharlāl Nehru. Each got his start under the wing of an outstanding Congress statesman—Bose under the Bengali lawyer Chittaranjan Dās, and Nehru under his father, Motilāl Nehru, who was a very close friend of Dās. Both Subhās and Jawaharlāl agitated for Congress to adopt the goal of complete independence (as opposed to dominion status) in the late 1920s; both were interested in spreading socialist ideas and in bringing the youth of the country into the nationalist movement. With his emergence as the spokesman for Bengal in the 1930s, however, Bose grew increasingly impatient with Gāndhi's leadership and his favoritism toward Nehru. Finally, in 1939, he openly disobeyed Gāndhi by running for a second term as Congress president and proposing a renewal of civil disobedience under his own direction. Although re-elected, Bose was so hampered by Gāndhi's noncooperation with his program that he resigned within a few months and founded his own leftist party, the Forward Bloc.

In 1941, making a dramatic escape from police surveillance after his release from jail for the eleventh time, Bose traveled via Afghānistān and Russia to Germany. Fascism had long attracted him and during his visits to Europe in the 1930s he had met Mussolini several times. He now called on Hitler and secured his backing in forming an Indian National Army, to be made up of captured Indian soldiers and officers. In 1943 a German submarine took him to Indonesia, whence he flew to Japan. General Tojo welcomed his collaboration and soon he was back in Southeast Asia organizing his Indian National Army there. As a military venture the I.N.A. had no effect, but it did create in the British grave doubts about the loyalty of their Indian troops, upon whom their rule in India ultimately depended.

Bose seems to have pictured himself as a sort of Indian Führer, and his troops and admirers addressed him as Netājī—"the leader." Rumors that he is still alive persist in India despite the attested fact that he died after a plane crash on Taiwan in 1945. Had he lived, there is little doubt that he would have greatly complicated the political negotiations of the post-war period. Bose owed his personal popularity in large part to the continuing appeal of quasi-religious nationalism, but he added to the Extremist tradition the glamor of military discipline under a colorful leader. His death and the failure of Fascism abroad brought to a sudden close this brief period of Indian interest in National Socialist ideology.

SUBHĀS CHANDRA BOSE
A Philosophy of Activism

Speaking to a conference of students in the 1920s, Bose attacked the theories of both Gāndhi and Aurobindo for their passive and antimodern tendencies. Stressing the importance of sound leadership, he called for an optimistic and combative outlook on life.

[From *Netaji Speaks to the Nation*, pp. 44–47]

As I look around me today, I am struck by two movements or two schools of thought about which, however small and insignificant I may be, it is my duty to speak out openly and fearlessly. I am referring to the two schools of thought, which have their centers at Sabarmati and Pondichéry. I am not considering the fundamental philosophy underlying those two schools of thought. This is not the time for metaphysical speculation. I shall talk to you today as [a] pragmatist, as one who will judge the intrinsic value of a school of thought [not] from a metaphysical point of view, but from experience of its actual effects and consequences.

The actual effect of the propaganda carried on by the Pondichéry school or thought is to create a feeling and an impression that there is nothing higher or nobler than peaceful contemplation, that Yoga means Pranayama and Dhyana, that while action may be tolerated as good, this propaganda has led many a man to forget that spiritual progress under the present-day conditions is possible only by ceaseless and unselfish action,

[337]

that the best way to conquer nature is to fight her, and that it is weakness to seek refuge in contemplation when we are hemmed in on all sides by dangers and difficulties.

It is the passivism, not philosophic but actual, inculcated by these schools of thought against which I protest. In this holy land of ours, Ashramas [1] are not new institutions and ascetics and Yogis are not novel phenomena. They have held and they will continue to hold an honored place in society. But it is not their lead we shall have to follow if we are to create a new India at once free, happy, and great.

Friends, you will pardon me if in a fit of outspokenness I have trod on your sentiments. As I have just said I do not for one moment consider the fundamental philosophy underlying the two schools of thought but the actual consequences from a pragmatic point of view. In India we want today a philosophy of activism. We must be inspired by robust optimism. We have to live in the present and to adapt ourselves to modern conditions. We can no longer live in an isolated corner of the world. When India is free, she will have to fight her modern enemies with modern methods, both in the economic and in the political spheres. The days of the bullock-cart are gone and are gone for ever. Free India must prepare herself for any eventuality as long as the whole world does not accept wholeheartedly the policy of disarmament.

I am not one of those who in their zeal for modernism forget the glories of the past. We must take our stand on our past. India has a culture of her own which she must continue to develop along her own distinctive channels. In philosophy, literature, art, science, we have something new to give to the world which the world eagerly awaits. In a word, we must arrive at a synthesis. Some of our best thinkers and workers are already . . . engaged in the important task. We must resist the cry of "Back to the Vedas" on the one side, and on the other the meaningless craze for fashion and change of modern Europe. It is difficult to restrict a living movement within proper bound[s], but I believe that if the pioneers and leaders of the movement are on the right track, things will take their proper shape in due time.

A Synthesis Between Communism and Fascism

Writing in 1934, Bose stated his ambition of creating in India a synthesis of the new totalitarian ideologies of Europe. In passing he repudiated the hope of

[1] Religious communities or hermitages.

preserving parliamentary democracy to which Nehru, despite his sympathies for the Communist ideal, has continued to cling.

[From Bose, *The Indian Struggle, 1920–1934*, pp. 345–47]

A question which is on everybody's lips in Europe is: "What is the future of Communism in India?" In this connection it is worth while quoting the expressed opinion of Pandit Jawaharlāl Nehru, whose popularity in India today is, according to the [present] writer, second only to that of Mahatma Gandhi. In a press statement issued on December 18, 1933, he said: "I do believe that fundamentally the choice before the world today is one between some form of Communism and some form of Fascism, and I am all for the former, that is Communism. I dislike Fascism intensely and indeed I do not think it is anything more than a crude and brutal effort of the present capitalist order to preserve itself at any cost. There is no middle road between Fascism and Communism. One has to choose between the two and I choose the Communist ideal. In regard to the methods and approach to this ideal, I may not agree with everything that the orthodox Communists have done. I think that these methods will have to adapt themselves to changing conditions and may vary in different countries. But I do think that the basic ideology of Communism and its scientific interpretation of history is sound."

The view expressed here is, according to the [present] writer, fundamentally wrong. Unless we are at the end of the process of evolution or unless we deny evolution altogether, there is no reason to hold that our choice is restricted to two alternatives. Whether one believes in the Hegelian or in the Bergsonian or any other theory of evolution—in no case need we think that creation is at an end. Considering everything, one is inclined to hold that the next phase in world-history will produce a synthesis between Communism and Fascism. And will it be a surprise if that synthesis is produced in India? The view has been expressed in the Introduction that in spite of India's geographical isolation, the Indian awakening is organically connected with the march of progress in other parts of the world and facts and figures have been mentioned to substantiate that view. Consequently, there need be no surprise if an experiment, of importance to the whole world, is made in India—especially when we have seen with our own eyes that another experiment (that of Mahatma Gandhi) made in India has roused profound interest all over the world.

In spite of the antithesis between Communism and Fascism, there are certain traits common to both. Both Communism and Fascism believe in the supremacy of the State over the individual. Both denounce parliamentarian democracy. Both believe in party rule. Both believe in the dictatorship of the party and in the ruthless suppression of all dissenting minorities. Both believe in a planned industrial reorganization of the country. These common traits will form the basis of the new synthesis. That synthesis is called by the writer "Samyavada"—an Indian word, which means literally "the doctrine of synthesis or equality." It will be India's task to work out this synthesis.

Proclamation of the Provisional Government of Azād Hind [1]

Bose's career came to a climax on October 21, 1943, when he proclaimed from Singapore the establishment of a provisional government of Free India, with himself as "Head of State, Prime Minister and Minister for War, Minister for Foreign Affairs and Supreme Commander of the Indian National Army." [2] His proclamation on that occasion set forth the program and claims of the I.N.A.

[From *Netaji Speaks to the Nation*, pp. 315–18]

Having goaded Indians to desperation by its hypocrisy, and having driven them to starvation and death by plunder and loot, British rule in India has forfeited the good will of the Indian people altogether, and is now living a precarious existence. It needs but a flame to destroy the last vestige of that unhappy rule. To light that flame is the task of India's Army of Liberation. Assured of the enthusiastic support of the civil population at home and also of a large section of Britain's Indian Army, and backed by gallant and invincible allies abroad, relying in the first instance on its own strength, India's Army of Liberation is confident of fulfilling its historic role.

Now that the dawn of freedom is at hand, it is the duty of the people to set up [a] provisional government of their own, and launch the last struggle under the banner of that government. But with all the Indian leaders in prison and the people at home totally disarmed—it is not possible to set up a provisional government within India or to launch an armed struggle under the aegis of that government. It is, therefore, the duty of the Indian Independence League in East Asia, supported by all patriotic Indians at home and abroad, to undertake this task—the task

[1] Free India.   [2] *Netaji Speaks to the Nation*, p. 318.

of setting up a provisional government of Azad Hind (Free India), and of conducting the last fight for freedom, with the help of the Army of Liberation (that is, the Azad Hind Fauj or the Indian National Army) organized by the League.

Having been constituted as the Provisional Government of Azad Hind by the Indian Independence League in East Asia, we enter upon our duties with a full sense of the responsibility that has devolved on us. We pray that Providence may bless our work and our struggle for emancipation of our Motherland, and our comrades in arms for the cause of her freedom, for her welfare and her exaltation among the nations of the world.

The provisional government is entitled to and hereby claims the allegiance of every Indian. It guarantees religious liberty, as well as equal rights and equal opportunities to all its citizens. It declares its firm resolve to pursue the happiness and prosperity of the whole nation and of all its parts, cherishing all the children of the nation equally and transcending all the differences cunningly fostered by an alien government in the past.

In the name of God, in the name of by-gone generations, who have welded the Indian people into one nation, and in the name of the dead heroes who have bequeathed to us a tradition of heroism and self-sacrifice, we call upon the Indian people to rally round our banner, and to strike for India's freedom. We call upon them to launch the final struggle against the British and all their allies in India, and to prosecute the struggle with valor and perseverance and with full faith in final victory —until the enemy is expelled from Indian soil, and the Indian people are once again a free nation.

JAWAHARLĀL NEHRU: DEMOCRATIC SOCIALIST

Descended from a proud line of Kashmiri brāhmans, Jawaharlāl Nehru was born in 1889 in Allahabad, where the Ganges and Jumna rivers converge. His ancestors had settled in Delhi and served at the court of the Mughal emperors, but his father, Motilāl Nehru, had moved on to Allahabad to become a successful and wealthy lawyer at the high court there. As Jawaharlāl wrote of his childhood, "An only son of prosperous parents is apt to be spoilt, especially so in India."[1] The apple of his father's eye, he studied at home under a series of English governesses and tutors. When he was fifteen, his father sent him to Harrow; at seventeen he entered Cambridge University; and at twenty he went down to London to take his law degree at the Inns of Court, where Gāndhi had studied some two decades earlier. After seven formative years in England, Jawaharlāl returned to India in 1912 to practice law with his father.

Motilāl Nehru possessed a powerful personality and a patrician bearing, and his son admired him tremendously. Jawaharlāl would no doubt have been drawn to politics of his own accord, but his father's position as leading Moderate in the Indian National Congress made the attraction an irresistible one. He joined the Congress and began to speak at its sessions, but it was not until 1920, when Gāndhi launched his great non-cooperation movement against British rule, that Jawaharlāl found full expression for his energies. He made tours in remote village areas (discovering the hard lot of the peasantry), organized volunteer workers, and delivered speeches to large patriotic gatherings. "I experienced [then] the thrill of mass-feeling, the power of influencing the mass,"[2] he tells us, and this power has been one of the keys to his success as a national leader. The climax of his activities came when, for the first of many times in his career, he went gladly to jail as a political prisoner.

Jawaharlāl was disappointed by Gāndhi's sudden suspension of the movement in 1922 after an outbreak of violence, and in the following years he felt himself groping for a clearer analysis of and a more predictable solution to India's problems than those provided by the Mahātmā's intuitive and moralistic mind. A trip to Europe for his wife's health in 1926–27 gave him a new perspective on the conflict between Indian nationalism and British rule. Conversations with Socialists and Communists in Europe—especially at the Congress of the League of Oppressed Peoples at Brussels—convinced him that the principal international conflict was between capitalist imperialism and anticapitalist socialism. A week's visit to Moscow, where he talked with M. N. Roy, impressed him with the achievements of the Soviet system, and with the common interest of Russia and India in opposing British imperialism.[3]

---

[1] Jawaharlāl Nehru: *An Autobiography*, p. 1.   [2] *Ibid.*, p. 77.
[3] Jawaharlāl Nehru: *Soviet Russia, Some Random Sketches and Impressions.*

Back in India once more, Jawaharlāl threw himself with renewed vigor into the national struggle, for he now saw it as part of a world wide movement to liberate mankind from every kind of oppression and exploitation. He demanded that the Congress declare its ultimate goal to be, not dominion status (as his father wished), but complete independence. Jawaharlāl was supported by Subhās Chandra Bose and others, and Gāndhi wisely yielded to their demand in order to keep the nationalist movement from splitting into Moderate and Extremist wings, as it had in 1907. Gāndhi went on to persuade the Congress to accept Jawaharlāl as its president on the eve of the second nation-wide campaign of civil disobedience, which lasted from 1930 to 1934.

From this time onward Jawaharlāl came increasingly to be regarded as Gāndhi's heir-apparent. Devotion to the cause of Indian freedom, and compassion for the lot of their nation's poor, created between the two men an indissoluble bond. In their attitudes toward other questions, however, Nehru and Gāndhi were poles apart. Religion held no meaning for Nehru, while for his guru it was all-important. Gāndhi held nonviolence and simple living to be ends in themselves, but Nehru considered them merely as practical expedients in the political struggle. Gāndhi's ideal India was a decentralized family of self-sufficient villages; Nehru's ideal India was a centralized modern state with a planned industrial economy. Despite their intellectual differences, however, Nehru found in Gāndhi a faithful friend and a wise counsellor. At one time he telegraphed him, "I feel lost in a strange country where you are the only familiar landmark . . . ,"[4] and after Gāndhi's assassination he mourned, "the light has gone out of our lives and there is darkness everywhere."[5]

India has been fortunate in having Jawaharlāl Nehru as her Prime Minister since receiving independence in 1947, for he has provided the dynamic leadership necessary to preserve national unity and accelerate economic progress. His sponsorship of a "third force" of neutralist nations and his role as mediator between the Western democracies and the Communist powers have enhanced India's position in world affairs. If he has tended, in his public statements, to be more critical of the West than of the Communist powers, it should be remembered that he is

[4] Anup Singh, *Nehru, the Rising Star of India*, p. 143.
[5] *Independence and After. A Collection of the More Important Speeches of Jawaharlal Nehru from September 1946 to May 1949*, p. 17.

still a convinced Socialist. At the same time, his commitment to uphold parliamentary government and to defend civil liberties constitutes, during his lifetime, one of the strongest bulwarks of democracy in India.

JAWAHARLĀL NEHRU
Communalism—A Reactionary Creed

Nehru abhorred the political groups who based their power on the membership of a particular religious community—whether Hindu, Muslim, or Sikh. His determination to make independent India a secular state shows clearly in this attack on communalism in an article written in the 1930s. He later used these same arguments in opposing Jinnāh's demand for a separate Muslim state.
[From Nehru, *Recent Essays and Writings,* pp. 76–77]

Communalism is essentially a hunt for favors from a third party—the ruling power. The communalist can only think in terms of a continuation of foreign domination and he tries to make the best of it for his own particular group. Delete the foreign power and communal arguments and demands fall to the ground. Both the foreign power and the communalists, as representing some upper class groups, want no essential change of the political and economic structure; both are interested in the preservation and augmentation of their vested interests. Because of this, both cannot tackle the real economic problems which confront the country, for a solution of these would upset the present social structure and divest the vested interests. For both, this ostrich-like policy of ignoring real issues is bound to end in disaster. Facts and economic forces are more powerful than governments and empires and can only be ignored at peril.

Communalism thus becomes another name for political and social reaction and the British government, being the citadel of this reaction in India, naturally throws its sheltering wings over a useful ally. Many a false trail is drawn to confuse the issue; we are told of Islamic culture and Hindu culture, of religion and old custom, of ancient glories and the like. But behind all this lies political and social reaction, the communalism must therefore be fought on all fronts and given no quarter. Because the inward nature of communalism has not been sufficiently realized, it has often sailed under false colors and taken in many an unwary person. It is an undoubted fact that many a Congressman has almost unconsciously partly succumbed to it and tried to reconcile his nationalism with this narrow and reactionary creed. A real appreciation of its true nature would demonstrate that there can be no common ground between the two. They belong to different species. It is time that Congressmen and others who have flirted with Hindu or Muslim or Sikh or any other communalism should understand this position and make their choice. No one can have it both ways, and the choice lies between political and social progress and stark reaction. An association with any form of communalism means the strengthening of the forces of reaction and of British imperialism in India; it means opposition to social and economic change and a toleration of the present terrible distress of our people; it means a blind ignoring of world forces and events.

The World-View of a Socialist

In his presidential address of 1936, Nehru frankly declared to the Congress his faith in Socialism. Both the international situation and the domestic problems of India seemed to him to prove the superiority of Socialism as a political creed. At the same time, Nehru emphasized the importance of civil liberties and of persuasion rather than coercion, but paid scant heed to the fact that these democratic values scarcely existed in the state he took as his model, Soviet Russia.

[From *Important Speeches of Jawaharlal Nehru*, pp. 4–6, 8, 12–14]

During the troubled aftermath of the Great War came revolutionary changes in Europe and Asia, and the intensification of the struggle for social freedom in Europe, and a new aggressive nationalism in the countries of Asia. There were ups and downs, and sometimes it appeared as if the revolutionary urge had exhausted itself and things were settling down. But economic and political conditions were such that there could be no settling down, the existing structure could no longer cope with these new conditions, and all its efforts to do so were vain and fruitless. Everywhere conflicts grew and a great depression overwhelmed the world and there was a progressive deterioration, everywhere except in the wide-flung Soviet territories of the U.S.S.R., where, in marked contrast with the rest of the world, astonishing progress was made in every direction. Two rival economic and political systems faced each other in the world and, though they tolerated each other for a while, there was an inherent antagonism between them, and they played for mastery on the stage of the world. One of them was the capitalist order which had inevitably developed into vast imperialisms, which, having swallowed the colonial world, were intent on eating each other up. Powerful still and fearful of war which might endanger their possessions, yet they came into inevitable conflict with each other and prepared feverishly for war. They were quite unable to solve the problems that threatened them and helplessly they submitted to slow decay. The other was the new socialist order of the U.S.S.R. which went from progress to progress, though often at terrible cost, and where the problems of the capitalist world had ceased to exist.

Capitalism, in its difficulties, took to Fascism with all its brutal suppression of what Western civilization had apparently stood for; it became, even in some of its homelands, what its imperialist counterpart had long been in the subject colonial countries. Fascism and imperialism thus stood out as the two faces of the [now] [1] decaying capitalism, and though they varied in different countries according to national characteristics and economic and political conditions, they represented the same forces of reaction and supported each other, and at the same time came into conflict with each other, for such conflict was inherent in their very nature. Socialism in the West and the rising nationalism of the eastern and other dependent countries opposed this combination of Fascism and imperialism. Nationalism in the East, it must be remembered, was essentially different from the new and terribly narrow nationalism of Fascist countries; the former was the historical urge to freedom, the latter the last refuge of reaction.

Thus we see the world divided up into two vast groups today—the imperialist and Fascist on one side, the Socialist and nationalist on the other. There is some overlapping of the two and the line between them is difficult to draw, for there is mutual conflict between the fascist and imperialist powers, and the nationalism of subject countries has sometimes a tendency to Fascism. But the main division holds and if we keep it in mind, it will be easier for us to understand world conditions and our own place in them.

Where do we stand then, we who labor for a free India? Inevitably we take our stand with progressive forces of the world which are ranged against Fascism and imperialism. We have to deal with one imperialism

[1] The original has "new." [Ed.]

in particular, the oldest and the most far-reaching of the modern world, but powerful as it is, it is but one aspect of world-imperialism, and that is the final argument for Indian independence and for the severance of our connection with the British empire. Between Indian nationalism, Indian freedom, and British imperialism there can be no common ground, and if we remain within the imperialist fold, whatever our name or status, whatever outward semblance of political power we might have, we remain cribbed and confined and allied to and dominated by the reactionary forces and the great financial vested interests of the capitalist world. The exploitation of our masses will still continue and all the vital social problems that face us will remain unsolved. Even real political freedom will be out of our reach, much more so than radical social changes. . . .

But of one thing I must say a few words for to me it is one of the most vital things that I value. That is the tremendous deprivation of civil liberties in India. A government that has to rely on the Criminal Law Amendment Act and similar laws, that suppresses the press and literature, that bans hundreds of organizations, that keeps people in prison without trial, and that does so many other things that are happening in India today, is a government that has ceased to have even a shadow of a justification for its existence. I can never adjust myself to those conditions, I find them intolerable. And yet I find many of my own countrymen complacent about them, some even supporting them, some, who have made the practice of sitting on a fence into a fine art, being neutral when such questions are discussed. And I have wondered what there was in common between them and me and those who think like I do. We in the Congress welcome all cooperation in the struggle for Indian freedom; our doors are ever open to all who stand for that freedom and are against imperialism. But they are not open to the allies [of] [2] imperialism and the supporters of repression and those who stand by the British government in its suppression of civil liberty. We belong to opposite camps. . . .

Perhaps you have wondered at the way I have dealt at some length with the background of international affairs and not touched so far the immediate problems that fill your minds. You may have grown impatient. But I am convinced that the only right way of looking at our own problem is to see them in their proper place in a world setting. I am

[2] The original has "to" here. [Ed.]

convinced that there is intimate connection between world events and our national problem is but a part of the world problem of capitalist-imperialism. To look at each event apart from the others and without understanding the connection between them must lead us to the formation of erratic and erroneous views. Look at the vast panorama of world change today, where mighty forces are at grips with each other and dreadful war darkens the horizon. Subject peoples struggling for freedom and imperialism crushing them down; exploited classes facing their exploiters and seeking freedom and equality. Italian imperialism bombing and killing the brave Ethiopians; Japanese imperialism continuing in aggression in North China and Mongolia; British imperialism piously objecting to other countries misbehaving, yet carrying on in much the same way in India and the Frontier; and behind it all a decaying economic order which intensifies all these conflicts. Can we not see an organic connection in all these various phenomena? Let us try to develop the historic sense so that we can view current events in proper perspective and understand their real significance. Only then can we appreciate the march of history and keep step with it.

I realize that in this address I am going a little beyond the usual beat of the Congress president. But I do not want you to have me under any false pretenses and we must have perfect frankness with each other. Most of you must know my views on social and economic matters, for I have often given expression to them. Yet you chose me as president. I do not take that choice to mean an endorsement by you all, or by a majority, of those views, but I take it that this does mean that those views are spreading in India and that most of you will be indulgent in considering them at least.

I am convinced that the only key to the solution of the world's problems and of India's problems lies in Socialism, and when I use this word I do so not in a vague humanitarian way but in the scientific economic sense. Socialism is, however, something even more than an economic doctrine; it is a philosophy of life and as such also it appeals to me. I see no way of ending the poverty, the vast unemployment, the degradation, and the subjection of the Indian people except through Socialism. That involves vast and revolutionary changes in our political and social structure, the ending of vested interests in land and industry, as well as the feudal and autocratic Indian states system. That means the ending of private property, except in a restricted sense, and the replacement of the present profit system by a higher ideal of cooperative service. It means ultimately a change in our instincts, habits and desires. In short, it means a new civilization, radically different from the present capitalist order. Some glimpse we can have of this new civilization in the territories of the U.S.S.R. Much has happened there which has pained me greatly and with which I disagree, but I look upon that great and fascinating unfolding of a new order and a new civilization as the most promising feature of our dismal age. If the future is full of hope it is largely because of Soviet Russia and what it has done, and I am convinced that, if some world catastrophe does not intervene, this new civilization will spread to other lands and put an end to the wars and conflicts which capitalism feeds.

I do not know how or when this new order will come to India. I imagine that every country will fashion it after its own way and fit it in with its national genius. But the essential basis of that order must remain and be a link in the world order that will emerge out of the present chaos.

Socialism is thus for me not merely an economic doctrine which I favor, it is a vital creed which I hold with all my head and heart. I work for Indian independence because the nationalist in me cannot tolerate an alien domination; I work for it even more because for me it is the inevitable step to social and economic change. I should like the Congress to become a socialist organization and to join hands with the other forces that in the world are working for the new civilization. But I realize that the majority in the Congress, as it is constituted today, may not be prepared to go thus far. We are a nationalist organization and we think and work on the nationalist plan. It is evident enough now that this is too narrow even for the limited objective of political independence and so we talk of the masses and their economic needs. But still most of us hesitate, because of our nationalist backgrounds, to take a step which might frighten away some vested interests. Most of those interests are already ranged against us and we can expect little from them except opposition even in the political struggle.

Much as I wish for the advancement of Socialism in this country, I have no desire to force the issue on the Congress and thereby create difficulties in the way of our struggle for independence. I shall cooperate gladly and with all the strength in me with all those who work for independence even though they do not agree with the socialist solution. But I shall do so stating my position frankly and hoping in course of time to convert the Congress and the country to it, for only thus can I see it achieving independence.

On the Threshold of a New Era

More than most modern Indians, Nehru possessed and cultivated a deep aware-ness of his country's past. This sense of history stands out in his speech to the Constituent Assembly in 1946 as it prepared to adopt its basic "Declaration of Objectives." It is important to note, however, that the three examples which he cited as models of constituent assemblies are all taken not from Indian but from Western history.

[From Nehru, *Independence and After*, pp. 346–48]

As I stand here, Sir, I feel the weight of all manner of things crowding upon me. We are at the end of an era and possibly very soon we shall embark upon a new age; and my mind goes back to the great past of India, to the 5,000 years of India's history, from the very dawn of that history which might be considered almost the dawn of human history, till today. All that past crowds upon me and exhilarates me and, at the same time, somewhat oppresses me. Am I worthy of that past? When I think also of the future, the greater future I hope, standing on this sword's edge of the present between the mighty past and the mightier future, I tremble a little and feel overwhelmed by this mighty task. We have come here at a strange moment in India's history. I do not know, but I do feel, that there is some magic in this moment of transition from the old to the new, something of that magic which one sees when the night turns into day and even though the day may be a cloudy one, it is day after all, for when the clouds move away, we can see the sun again. Because of all this I find a little difficulty in addressing this House and putting all my ideas before it and I feel also that in this long succes-sion of thousands of years, I see the mighty figures that have come and gone and I see also the long succession of our comrades who have labored for the freedom of India. And now we stand on the verge of this passing age, trying, laboring, to usher in the new. I am sure the House will feel the solemnity of this moment and will endeavor to treat this Resolution which it is my proud privilege to place before it in a correspondingly solemn manner. I believe there are a large number of amendments coming before the House. I have not seen most of them. It is open to the House, to any member of this House, to move any amendment and it is for the House to accept it or reject it, but I would, with all respect, suggest that this is not the moment for us to be technical and legal about small matters when we have big things to face, big things to say and big things to do, and, therefore, I hope that the House will consider this Resolution in a broadminded manner and not lose itself in wordy quarrels and squabbles.

I think also of the various constituent assemblies that have gone before and of what took place at the making of the great American nation when the fathers of that nation met and fashioned a constitution which has stood the test for so many years, more than a century and a half, and of the great nation that has resulted, which has been built up on the basis of that constitution. My mind goes back to that mighty revolution which took place also over one hundred fifty years ago and the constituent assembly that met in that gracious and lovely city of Paris which has fought so many battles for freedom. My mind goes back to the difficulties that that constituent assembly had to face from the king and other authorities, and still it continued. The House will remember that when these difficulties came and even the room for a meeting was denied to that constituent assembly, they betook themselves to an open tennis court and met there and took the oath, which is called the Oath of the Tennis Court. They continued meeting in spite of kings, in spite of the others, and did not disperse till they had finished the task they had undertaken. Well, I trust that it is in that solemn spirit that we too are meeting here and that we too whether we meet in this chamber or in other chambers, or in the fields or in the market place, will go on meeting and continue our work till we have finished it.

Then my mind goes back to a more recent revolution which gave rise to a new type of state, the revolution that took place in Russia and out of which has arisen the Union of the Soviet Socialist Republics, another mighty country which is playing a tremendous part in the world, not only a mighty country, but for us in India, a neighboring country.

So our mind goes back to these great examples and we seek to learn from their success and to avoid their failures. Perhaps we may not be able to avoid failures, because some measure of failure is inherent in human effort. Nevertheless, we shall advance, I am certain, in spite of obstructions and difficulties, and achieve and realize the dream that we have dreamt so long.

India's Role in World Affairs

In contrast to the theory of Keshub, Vivekānanda, Tagore, and others to whom India was important in the world mainly for her "spirituality," Nehru saw India as an emerging "giant" of world affairs, able to stand on an equal footing with any other nation.

[From Nehru, *Independence and After*, pp. 231–33]

One of the major questions of the day is the readjustment of the relations between Asia and Europe. When we talk of Asia, remember that India, not because of any ambition of hers, but because of the force of circumstances, because of geography, because of history and because of so many other things, inevitably has to play a very important part in Asia. And not only that; India becomes a kind of meeting ground for various trends and forces and a meeting ground between what might roughly be called the East and the West.

Look at the map. If you have to consider any question affecting the Middle East, India inevitably comes into the picture. If you have to consider any question concerning Southeast Asia, you cannot do so without India. So also with the Far East. While the Middle East may not be directly connected with Southeast Asia, both are connected with India. Even if you think in terms of regional organizations in Asia, you have to keep in touch with the other regions. And whatever regions you may have in mind, the importance of India cannot be ignored.

One of the major questions of the day is the readjustment of the relations between Asia and Europe. In the past, especially by virtue of her economic and political domination, the West ignored Asia, or at any rate did not give her the weight that was due to her. Asia was really given a back seat and one unfortunate result of it was that even the statesmen did not recognize the changes that were taking place. There is, I believe, a considerable recognition of these changes now, but it is not enough yet. Even in the Councils of the United Nations, the problems of Asia, the outlook of Asia, the approach of Asia have failed to evoke the enthusiasm they should. There are many ways of distinguishing between what may be called the approach of Asia and the approach of Europe. Asia today is primarily concerned with what may be called the immediate human problems. In each country of Asia—under-developed countries more or less—the main problem is the problem of food, of clothing, of education, of health. We are concerned with these problems. We are not directly concerned with problems of power politics. Some of us, in our minds, may perhaps think of that.

Europe, on the other hand, is also concerned with these problems, no doubt, in the devastated regions. Europe has a legacy of conflicts of power, and of problems which come from the possession of power. They have the fear of losing that power and the fear of some one else getting greater power and attacking one country or the other. So that the European approach is a legacy of the past conflicts of Europe.

I do not mean to say that we in Asia are in any way superior, ethically or morally, to the people of Europe. In some ways I imagine that we are worse. There is, however, a legacy of conflict in Europe. In Asia, at the present moment at least, there is no such legacy. The countries of Asia may have their quarrels with their neighbors here and there, but there is no basic legacy of conflict such as the countries of Europe possess. That is a very great advantage of Asia and it would be folly in the extreme for the countries of Asia, for India, to be dragged in the wake of the conflicts in Europe. We might note that the world progressively tends to become one—one in peace, and it is likely to be one, in a sense of war. No man can say that any country can remain apart when there is a major conflagration. But still one can direct one's policy towards avoiding this conflict and being entangled in it.

So the point I wish the House to remember is this: first of all, the emergence of India in world affairs is something of major consequence in world history. We who happen to be in the government of India or in this House are men of relatively small stature. But it has been given to us to work at a time when India is growing into a great giant again. So, because of that, in spite of our own smallness, we have to work for great causes and perhaps elevate ourselves in the process.

M. N. ROY: FROM INTERNATIONAL
COMMUNIST TO RADICAL HUMANIST

Perhaps the most potent of the political ideologies which entered India in the twentieth century arrived not from Western Europe but via Russia —a country with which Indians had previously had very little direct contact. Vladimir I. Lenin had long seen the nationalist movements in Asia as useful adjuncts to the revolution he expected to sweep Europe. Immediately on seizing power in Russia in 1917, his Bolshevik Party championed the right of colonial peoples to complete independence of foreign rule. Although British vigilance prevented Communist literature from entering the Indian empire openly and in quantity, the news that Bolshevik Russia stood ready to help their cause gave new hope to the numerous Indians in exile all over the world.

One of these was Narendranāth Bhattāchārya (1887–1954), who had slipped out of India in 1915 to make contact in Java with German agents bringing arms for an Indian insurrection. This plot having failed, he continued eastward to the United States and settled in Mexico under the name of Mānabendra Nāth Roy. When news of the Bolshevik Revolution reached him, he first helped found the Mexican Communist Party and then hurried to Moscow. There he made such a favorable impression on Lenin that he was put on the Executive Committee of the newly founded Communist International. For a time Roy was busy in Tashkent, Central Asia, training for revolutionary work Indians who had come to Russia via Afghanistan. His career as an international Communist leader extended through the 1920s, but after his unsuccessful mission to China in 1927 and the victory of Stalin over Trotsky he fell from favor and left Russia for Germany.

Severing his connection with the Comintern in 1929, Roy returned incognito to India, but was arrested by the British authorities and imprisoned for six years. On his release he attempted to organize a non-Stalinist Marxist party within the Indian National Congress. During the Second World War he opposed Gāndhi and Nehru, whom he called the tools of Indian Fascism, and supported the Allied cause. After independence he abandoned Marxism and sought in the rational and secular humanism of Europe the basis for a new social order.

Notwithstanding his disillusionment with Communism, M. N. Roy remained an internationalist to the end of his life, and the Radical Humanist group which he founded has ties with similar groups in the Western world. Significantly, he also retained from his Communist period a belief in materialism and a deep suspicion of the religious outlook on life, which has played such a dominant role throughout the history of Indian culture. It was precisely what others considered "changeless" in India that he wanted most to change.

MĀNABENDRA NĀTH ROY
The Anti-Imperialist Struggle in India

Roy's article with this title, written in 1924, is a typical expression of his hopes for an Indian revolution, whose momentum was to come from the hitherto unorganized energies of the workers and peasants.

[From M. N. Roy, "Anti-Imperialist Struggle in India," in *The Communist International*, No. 6 (1924), pp. 83, 92–93]

Slowly but surely British domination in India is being undermined. It is true that this historic process is not so speedy as many expected or even prophesied. Nevertheless, the process is going on unceasingly. The depression that followed the sudden collapse of the great noncooperation movement lasted rather long, only to be enlivened, not by an intensified revolutionary activity, but by a concerted effort on the part of the bourgeoisie to challenge the absolute position of imperialism on constitutional lines. The development of this new stage has been during the last twelve months. It has culminated in a political deadlock which has not only non-plussed the nationalist bourgeoisie, but has also placed the British government in a somewhat uncomfortable position. Some decisive action must be taken from one side or the other to break this deadlock. For the nationalists, it is necessary either to compromise with imperialism or to go a few steps further towards revolution. Imperialism, on the other hand, is faced with the alternatives: to placate the nationalist bourgeoisie with concessions or to adopt openly the policy of blood and iron.

It is obvious what should be the nature of our activities. While supporting the nationalist bourgeoisie in every act of resistance to imperialism, we should mobilize the revolutionary mass energy which the nationalist bourgeoisie is afraid of touching. The rapid crystallization of bourgeois nationalism around a reformist program has left the field clear. For the first time in the history of the Indian national movement, there will come into existence a political party demanding separation from the empire. Nationalist elements, which up till now followed the bourgeoisie, will enter this party; because the program of reformism advocated by the bourgeoisie neglects their interests altogether. To aid the organization of this party of revolutionary nationalism is our immediate task. The objective situation is quite ripe, although there are enormous subjective difficulties. The masses are very restive. The peasantry is a veritable inflammable material, while the city proletariat demonstrates its revolutionary zeal whenever there is an opportunity. The process of uniting all these revolutionary elements into an anti-imperialist army is going on steadily. The collapse of bourgeois nationalism, as expressed by the present Parliamentary deadlock, will only accentuate this process. The people will see that the reformist program of the bourgeoisie does not lead anywhere. The center of gravity of the nationalist movement will be shifted back to its proper place—namely, mass action. As soon as the rank and file of the nationalist forces are freed from the reformist leadership of the bourgeoisie, they will begin to follow the standard of revolution, because in that case, they will be convinced that the anti-imperialist struggle cannot be conducted successfully in a different way. There is every indication that things are moving in that direction, and that the next stage of the Indian movement will be a great advance towards revolution.

Revolution—Necessary and Inevitable

Belief in the inevitability of the proletarian revolution being a central tenet in the Communist faith, M. N. Roy declared himself simply a servant of this historical process. Not he, but the British were to blame for refusing to cooperate with the inevitable, he asserted in the statement he intended (but was not allowed) to make at his trial for conspiracy in 1931.

[From M. N. Roy, *I Accuse*, pp. 26–27, 28–29]

The evidence proves that I pointed out the inevitability of a revolutionary change in the social and political conditions of India and that the welfare of the toiling masses was dependent upon the revolution. I have been working for the welfare of the Indian masses and have urged the elimination of all obstacles in the way to that goal. I tried to organize a working class party because it is necessary for the liberation of the masses from political slavery, economic exploitation, and social degradation. The party is a historic necessity and has a historically revolutionary mission. It is neither a conspiracy nor a weapon in any conspiracy. The British king, as well as any other power that stands in the way of the progress and prosperity of the Indian masses, must go.

Of course, our attempt to organize a party of the workers and peasants would be a quixotic venture had the condition of the masses been really what the public prosecutor imagines it to be. In his opening address he told the assessors that the Indian peasants were happy in their misery and that I was trying to disturb their happiness for some sinister purpose of mine. I have already given a few facts and figures to show that "happy peasants" live only in the imagination of the public prosecutor, unless the gentleman would venture to advance a theory that the less one eats and the more one toils the happier he is.

In reality, the government is against the most harmless economic program, for its enforcement would mean loss to imperialism and its Indian allies, the princes, big landlords, and capitalists. Therefore, the realization of the program will necessarily mean violation of the laws of the imperialist government. The function of the laws is to hold the masses on the starvation level so that foreign imperialism and its native allies can grow rich, and to suppress the attempts of the masses to rise above the present conditions.

I have not preached violent revolution. I have maintained that revolution is a historic necessity. From time to time, surging forces of social progress reach the period of a violent outburst. This is caused by the resistance of the old to the new. An impending revolution produces its pioneers who force events and herald the maturing of the conflict. The task of the revolutionary vanguard is to expedite the historical process caused by objective necessity. They consciously organize the forces of the revolution and lead them to victory. I have acted as a pioneer of the Indian revolution; but the revolution itself is not my invention. It grows out of the historical conditions of the country. I have simply been one who perceived it earlier than others.

[357]

I do not make a secret of my determination of helping the organization of the great revolution which must take place in order to open up before the Indian masses the road to liberty, progress, and prosperity. The impending revolution is an historic necessity. Conditions for it are maturing rapidly. Colonial exploitation of the country creates those conditions. So, I am not responsible for the revolution, nor is the Communist International. Imperialism is responsible for it. My punishment, therefore, will not stop the revolution. Imperialism has created its own grave-digger, namely, the forces of national revolution. These will continue operating till their historic task is accomplished. No law, however ruthless may be the sanction behind it, can suppress them.

India's Message to the World

In one of his most pungent essays, M. N. Roy sought to debunk the popular notion that Indian spirituality in general, and Gāndhism in particular, held an important message for the world. On the contrary, he argued, it was only by following the philosophy of materialism (to which classical Indian thought had also given expression) that modern civilization could go forward.

[From M. N. Roy, *India's Message* (*Fragments of a Prisoner's Diary*, II), pp. 190–91, 209–11, 217–18]

The "decline of the West" being in reality only the decline of capitalism, the crisis of Western civilization means only disintegration of the bourgeois social order. In that context, India's "spiritual mission" appears to be a mission with a mundane purpose, namely, to salvage a social system based upon the love of lucre and lust for power. It is not suggested that the believers in India's spiritual mission are all conscious of its reactionary implication. Probably very few of them are. Most of them may be credited with a sincere antipathy for capitalism. But antipathy does not necessarily give birth to a desire to go farther than capitalism. It indicates an attachment to pre-capitalist social conditions, which are idealized. Objectively, it is therefore the token of a reactionary social outlook. Indian spiritualism is not different from the Western kind. The merit of a philosophy is to be judged by its historical role and social significance. The sincerity or otherwise of its protagonists is altogether beside the point.

The preachers of India's "world mission" nevertheless take their stand on the dogmatic assertion that Indian philosophy is different from Western idealism. The basic principles of idealist philosophy, together with the survey of its medieval and pre-Christian background, prove that this assertion is utterly groundless. While the emotional aspect of Indian speculation is well matched, if not surpassed, by Christian mysticism, intellectually it can hardly claim superiority to Western idealism, either modern or ancient. As regards transcendental fantasies, the Western mind has been no less fertile. The great Sage of Athens, the seers of Alexandria, the saints of early Christianity, the monks of the Middle Ages—that is a record which can proudly meet any competition. On the question of moral doctrines, Christianity stands unbeaten on the solid ground of the Jewish, Socratic, and Stoic traditions. Should the modern West be accused of not having lived up to those noble principles, could India conscientiously be absolved of a similar charge? The claim that the Indian people as a whole are morally less corrupt, emotionally purer, idealistically less worldly, in short, spiritually more elevated, than the bulk of the Western society, is based upon a wanton disregard for reality. . . .

The most commonly agreed form of India's world message is Gandhism. Not only does it dominate the nationalist ideology: it has found some echo outside of India. It is as the moralizing mysticism of Gandhi that Indian thought makes any appeal to the Western mind. Therefore, an analysis of Gandhism will give a correct idea of the real nature of India's message to the world.

But Gandhism is not a coordinated system of thought. There is little of philosophy in it. In the midst of a mass of platitudes and hopeless self-contradictions, it harps on one constant note—a conception of morality based upon dogmatic faith. But what Gandhi preaches is primarily a religion: the faith in God is the only reliable guide in life. The fact that even in the twentieth century India is swayed by the naive doctrines of Gandhi speaks for the cultural backwardness of the masses of her people. The subtlety of the Hindu philosophy is not the measure of the intellectual level of the Indian people as a whole. It was the brain-child of a pampered intellectual elite sharing power and privileges with the temporal ruling class. It still remains confined to the comparatively small circle of intellectuals who try to put on a thin veneer of modernism, and represents nothing more than a nostalgia. The popularity of Gandhi and the uncritical acceptance of his antics as the highest of human wisdom knock the bottom off the doctrine that the Indian people as a whole are morally and spiritually superior to the Western. The fact is that the great bulk of the Indian people are steeped in religious superstitions. Otherwise, Gandhism would have no social background and [would] disappear before long. They have neither any understanding of philosophical problems nor are they concerned with metaphysical speculations in preference to material questions. As normal human beings, they are engrossed with the problems of worldly life, and being culturally backward, necessarily think in terms of religion, conceive their earthly ideals, their egoistic aspirations, in religious forms. Faith is the mainstay of their existence, prejudice the trusted guide of life, and superstition their only philosophy.

Gandhism is the ideological reflex of this social background. It sways the mass mind, not as a moral philosophy, but as a religion. It is neither a philosopher nor a moralist who has become the idol of the Indian people. The masses pay their homage to a Mahātmā—a source of revealed wisdom and agency of supernatural power. The social basis of Gandhism is cultural-backwardness; its intellectual mainstay, superstition. . . .

The Gandhist utopia thus is a static society—a state of absolute social stagnation. It is an utopia because it can never be realized. Absolute stagnation is identical with death. To begin with, all resistance to the established order must cease. That would offer absolute guarantee to the *status quo*. The ruling classes would refrain from using force simply because it would not be necessary. Their power and privilege, being completely undisputed, would require no active defense. But this idyllic picture can be drawn only by the cold hand of death. Life expresses itself as a movement—individually, in space, and collectively, in time. And movement implies overwhelming of obstacles on the way. Disappearance of all resistance to the established order would mean extinction of social life. Perfect peace reigns only in the grave.

Neither the preachers nor the proselytes of Gandhism, however, would have the consistency of carrying their cult to the nihilistic extreme. There would be a certain macabre majesty in such a boldness. But with all the absoluteness of its standards, Gandhism remains on the ground of the relative. After all, it prescribes a practical cure for the evils of the world. Philosophically, it is pragmatic. And the remedy suggested is the reactionary program of forcibly keeping society in a relatively static condition. Gandhism offers this program because it is the quintessence of an ideology which developed on the background of a static society.

But India's spiritual message, while still finding an echo in the ruins of the native society, can have no standing appeal to the world of modern civilization. There, the society is armed with potentialities which preclude its falling into a state of stagnation. Modern civilization is a dynamic process. It must go forward. Not only the masses, but even the capitalist rulers of the West must reject the ideology of social stagnation. And precisely in this dynamic nature of the civilization, developed under its aegis, does the nemesis of capitalism lie. It cannot carry civilization farther, nor can it hold it back in a static state permanently as a guarantee for its continued existence. The perspective, therefore, is an advance of modern civilization over the boundaries of capitalism. The materialist philosophy throws a flood of light on that perspective of the future of mankind. India's spiritual message, on the contrary, would teach the West to turn back upon the goal within reach, and relapse into medieval barbarism.

Radical Humanism

In August, 1947, M. N. Roy presented a summary of his new political ideals, which were founded, not on dogma or Machiavellianism, but on human reason and morality.
[From M. N. Roy, *New Humanism: A Manifesto,* pp. 34–47]

The question of all questions is: Can politics be rationalized? An affirmative answer to this controversial question would not take us very far unless rationalism was differentiated from the metaphysical concept of reason. To replace the teleology of Marxist materialism by an appeal to the mystical category of reason would not be an advance.

The cognate question is about the relation of politics and morality: Must revolutionary political practice be guided by the Jesuitic dictum —the end justifies the means? The final sanction of revolution being its moral appeal—the appeal for social justice—logically, the answer to the latter question must be in the negative. It is very doubtful if a moral object can ever be attained by immoral means. In critical moments, when larger issues are involved and greater things are at stake, some temporary compromise in behavior may be permissible. But when practices repugnant to ethical principles and traditional human values are stabilized as the permanent features of the revolutionary regime, the means defeat the end. Therefore Communist political practice has not taken the world, not even the working class, anywhere near a new order of freedom and social justice. On the contrary, it has plunged the army of revolution— proletarian as well as nonproletarian—in an intellectual confusion, spiritual chaos, emotional frustration, and a general demoralization.

To overcome this crisis, the fighters for a new world order must turn to the traditions of Humanism and moral Radicalism. The inspiration for a new philosophy of revolution must be drawn from those sources. The nineteenth-century Radicals, actuated by the humanist principle of individualism, realized the possibility of a secular rationalism and a rationalist ethics. They applied to the study of man and society the principles and methods of the physical sciences. Positive knowledge of nature—living as well as inanimate—being so much greater today than a hundred years ago, the Radical scientific approach to the problem of man's life and interrelations is bound to be more successful. Today we can begin with the conviction that it is long since man emerged from the jungle of "pre-history," that social relations can be rationally harmonized, and that therefore appreciation of moral values can be reconciled with efforts for replacing the corrupt and corrosive *status quo* by a new order of democratic freedom. A moral order will result from a rationally organized society, because, viewed in the context of his rise out of the background of a harmonious physical universe, man is essentially rational and therefore moral. Morality emanates from the rational desire for harmonious and mutually beneficial social relations.

Man did not appear on the earth out of nowhere. He rose out of the background of the physical universe, through the long process of biological evolution. The umbilical cord was never broken: man, with his mind, intelligence, will, remains an integral part of the physical universe. The latter is a cosmos—a law-governed system. Therefore, man's being and becoming, his emotions, will, ideas are also determined: man is essentially rational. The reason in man is an echo of the harmony of the universe. Morality must be referred back to man's innate rationality. Only then, man can be moral, spontaneously and voluntarily. Reason is only sanction for morality, which is an appeal to conscience, and conscience, in its turn, is the instinctive awareness of, and reaction to, environments. In the last analysis, conscience is nothing mystic or mysterious. It is a biological function, as such mechanistic, on the level of consciousness. The innate rationality of man is the only guarantee of a harmonious order, which will also be a moral order, because morality is a rational function. Therefore, the purpose of all social endeavor should be to make man increasingly conscious of his innate rationality.

Any effort for a reorganization of society must begin from the unit of society—from the root, so to say. Such an effort to develop a new philosophy of revolution, on the basis of the entire stock of human heritage, and then to elaborate the theory and formulate the principles of the practice of political action and economic reconstruction, therefore, can be called Radicalism.

Radicalism thinks in terms neither of nation nor of class; its concern is man; it conceives freedom as freedom of the individual. Therefore, it can also be called New Humanism, new, because it is Humanism enriched, reinforced and elaborated by scientific knowledge and social experience gained during the centuries of modern civilization.

Humanism is cosmopolitan. It does not run after the utopia of internationalism, which presupposes the existence of autonomous national states. The one makes of the other a pious desire or wishful thinking. A cosmopolitan commonwealth of free men and women is a possibility. It will be a spiritual community, not limited by the boundaries of national states— capitalist, fascist, communist or of any other kind—which will gradually disappear under the impact of cosmopolitan Humanism. That is the Radical perspective of the future of mankind.

THE APPEALS OF "NATIONAL" COMMUNISM

Imitation being the truest form of flattery, Western Europe and America might take pride in the fact that India's educated elite now desire ardently to rid their society of ancient inequalities, to build a modern, industrial economy, and to make India a strong national state. When a young nation comes to be dominated by such desires, but finds that it has been left far behind in the race for modernity, it commonly reacts by making desperate attempts to "catch up" with the rest of the world. The success of similar endeavors by other late-comer nations is bound to make a deep impression on the most recent entrant in the race. Some fifty years ago, India was thrilled by Japan's victory over Tsarist Russia. Today, a large percentage of the Indian intelligentsia look to Soviet Russia and Communist China as models for their own country's future development.

This frame of mind, compounded as it is of nationalistic strivings and of admiration for the achievements of Communist states, might aptly be termed "National" Communism. While not committing itself to the international conspiracy in which M. N. Roy played so conspicuous a part, National Communism promises to strengthen and modernize politically independent but economically underdeveloped countries through the Communist program of accelerated industrialization and social reorganization. National Communism diverges from Democratic Socialism, with which it otherwise has much in common, at the point where this increasing acceleration involves the sacrifice of parliamentary democracy and civil liberties.

The sheer magnitude of India's population, now over the 450,000,000 mark, seems to render irrelevant the experience of countries like the United States, where an abundance of land and mineral resources have been exploited by a fairly small population during several centuries of undisturbed isolation. Indian free enterprise, faced with much more urgent problems and equipped with much scantier resources, lacks the capacity to undertake the large-scale development projects required by the situation, and is in any case less public-spirited and more monopolistic than its American counterpart. Foreign aid is gratefully accepted, but a deep-seated prejudice exists in India against capitalists in general and Western capitalists in particular.

Prime Minister Nehru, in articulating these suspicions, once explained them as a product of persisting attachment to the classical hierarchy of occupations. Of the traditional culture of India he wrote: "it is fighting silently and desperately against a new and all-powerful opponent—the *bania*[1] civilization of the capitalist West. It will succumb to this newcomer, for the West brings science, and science brings food for the hungry millions. But the West also brings an antidote to the evils of this cutthroat civilization—the principles of socialism, of cooperation, and service to the community for the common good. This is not so unlike the old

[1] Merchant.

[364]

Brahman ideal of service, but it means the brahmanization (not in the religious sense, of course) of all classes and groups and the abolition of class distinctions." [2] Thus capitalism has been associated with the tradition of the vaishyas, the lowest of the three "twice-born" castes, and Socialism or Communism with the more prestigious brāhman tradition.

As with the people of every nation, Indians tend to see the outside world as it is reflected in the mirror of their own preconceptions. Many find this stereotype of idealistic socialism opposing materialistic capitalism helpful in interpreting the "cold war" between Soviet Russia and the United States of America. China, by entering the Communist camp, both increased its prestige and lent it a pan-Asian tinge—until her troops invaded India in 1962. Another source of sympathy for Russia and China is the absence of marked racial discrimination in these countries. Finally, there is the simple fact that in modern times Indians have become much better acquainted through reading and travel with Western Europe and North America than with these giant neighboring countries. Just as familiarity may breed contempt, so distance (in this case not so much geographical as psychological) may lend enchantment.

Prime Minister Nehru's policy of friendship with Soviet Russia and the People's Republic of China has made it possible for the Communist Party of India to appeal to nationalist sentiment by loudly championing India's present role in world affairs. In domestic policies however, the Communists have emerged as the strongest opposition party to the Congress government. The effectiveness of their National Communist program was demonstrated in the 1957 general elections, when they unexpectedly won a sufficiently large plurality in the Kerala legislature to assume parliamentary control of that state.

On the purely personal level, the combination of nationalist and Communist ideals appeals to many Westernized intellectuals who would like to improve the hard lot of the common people. Accustomed to middle-class standards of morality and material well-being, they often feel keenly the gap between their lives and those of the un-Westernized, uneducated, and impoverished peasants and urban laborers. Doctrines which emphasize solidarity between the educated elite and "the masses" alleviate the feelings of guilt created by the alienation of the former from the latter. They also promise full employment and the hope of transforming village

[2] *Jawaharlal Nehru, An Autobiography,* p. 432.

India (where 85 percent of her population lives) in the image of the Westernized city-dwellers rather than, as Gāndhi proposed, remaking the Westernized minority in the image of the peasant majority.

To illustrate some of the appeals of National Communism two writers have been chosen, neither a Communist Party member, but each in substantial agreement with one or more aspects of the National Communist line. J. C. Kumarappa, an Indian Christian, took his M.A. in economics at Columbia University, and on his return to India became a leading exponent of Gāndhian economic theory, and head of Gāndhi's village hand-industry program. Although he does not subscribe to their emphasis on rapid industrialization, he does accept the National Communist diagnosis of the world situation and sees "American machinations" as a great danger to his country.

Romesh Thapar expresses a more comprehensive and optimistic outlook, for he expects the gradual emergence of a socialist order throughout the world. Thapar edited the Communist Party's weekly organ from 1949 to 1951 (a period when most of its leaders were in hiding or in prison), and was secretary to the Indian delegation at the Warsaw Peace Congress of 1950. His writings, although sometimes critical of the Party, seem to have a degree of influence on its policy. This fact in itself is symptomatic of the importance the Party attaches to winning the minds of the Indian intelligentsia as a whole—a task in which to date it has had surprising success.

J. C. KUMARAPPA
The American Plot Against India

In 1952 a book entitled *American Shadow Over India* appeared which construed as subversive to India American activities in India in such varied fields as trade, investments, economic aid, intelligence activities, propaganda, Christian missions, motion pictures, and books. The selection which follows is J. C. Kumarappa's foreword to this book.

[From L. Natarajan, *American Shadow Over India,* pp. xi–xiii]

In centuries past every nation was at liberty to express its way of life and thought and its national culture. From time to time this freedom was interfered with by neighboring chieftains who descended on prosperous people for the loot they could get. Their followers stayed behind, in some cases to found dynasties of their own.

Since the Industrial Revolution these personal ambitions have given way to organized exploitation of the weak. This is done by holding down the unwary in groups, in geographical units, or as whole nations. The methods adopted have been termed variously according to their nature, but in effect they were all the same. It was to secure raw materials or labor for large-scale mechanized industries. This was a development over individual slavery, serfdom or feudalism.

Britain came to India with a feudal background and hence her relations with her colonies were characterized by a socio-economic order which took the form of political imperialism. This carried with it certain duties towards the subject nations even though exploitation was the ultimate purpose. This method laid the responsibility for good government on the so-called "Metropolitan Country."

A little later in the field came the Americans. They appeared on the scene with a tradition of slavery. Hence their mode of control of "undeveloped" countries took on a different color from the British one. They are following a financial imperialism which is practically irresponsible for the welfare of those who come under its grip.

Further, at this time, there is an attempt to gather together the nations of the world under two prevailing ideologies of either private enterprise or for social justice. In this struggle for proselytes the world is being divided into two competing groups. The U.S.A. stands for private enterprise based on private property leading to private profit while the U.S.S.R. advocates social justice based on the fundamental equality of man and the need therefore for equality in opportunities of life.

These two camps are splitting the world into two blocs. Russia is going about her work in a missionary spirit by practicing what she preaches and demonstrating her theories by experiments and thus strives to gather adherents by convincing the neighbors.

The U.S.A. is proceeding on various plans to entrap the nations by guile, by compulsion, by coercion and financial entanglements. These methods are not calculated to liberate its victims but to carry on its nefarious purpose like the spider. The webs are woven so well and close that the victim hardly realizes what is happening and all its struggles only make the end come sooner.

Unfortunately, people are far too busy today to halt and take note of what is taking place round them. The hurry and flurry of life hardly leave them any leisure to stand up and look at their surroundings and appraise the situation. Advantage is taken of this pressure of life to hasten the end.

For over a century and a half, the U.S.A. has been spreading her financial nets the world over. India was somewhat in a protected position because of British vested interests and jealousies. Of late, this protective fencing has been disbanded and India presents an open field of ruthless exploitation. It is sad that this should happen under the leadership of a patriot of the order of Nehru. The wiles of the Americans, who go about their work with the aid of modern psychology, are a little too much for the straightforward, simple, trusting statesman.

It is, therefore, all the more necessary for the man in the street to be well-informed of what is going on to entrap him. Hence it is a boon to India that full information should be made available in a small compass, without much argumentation, with proper references and documentation. This little book is a mine of such information. The author has laid us under a deep debt for the pains he has taken to glean valuable material and place it at our disposal in so lucid a fashion. He traces the American machinations to get India within its financial web for over a century. It is a fascinating story and we may well be warned by the danger. If we do not avail ourselves of the timely warning we shall, before long, be overtaken by the tragedy that has befallen Korea.[1] May we awake and beware before it is too late.

ROMESH THAPAR
India's Socialist Future

In the concluding chapter of his *India in Transition*, Romesh Thapar pictures Socialism (using the word as Communists do to denote the intermediate stage between capitalism and pure Communism) established throughout the world. He implies by his criticism of "the evils of Stalinist practice" that he expects the new world order to be based on democratic values.

[From Romesh Thapar, *India in Transition,* pp. 259–64]

Each land and people has its prophets and visionaries. Learning from the past and the present, they project that experience into the future to understand the processes which will mold events yet unrecorded.

---

[1] Kumarappa accepts the Communist allegation that South Korea, encouraged by the U.S.A., was responsible for starting the Korean War.

India is a rewarding field for such study and speculation. Perhaps no other people in the world have found themselves in so interesting a situation; the more so when it is compared with the immediate perspectives before those powers who are today making world events.

In the U.S.A., the enlightened may feel the torture of the McCarthy witch-hunts, the democratic-minded mass may be tormented by the international dealings of the State Department, but they are now beginning to locate the cause of these aberrations. If prosperity dulls their senses, makes them impotent to counter policies which can only spell ruin in the final accounting, the wide-awake among them do know that, sooner or later, the truth will out. Each day the blinkers are being lifted. Cold war policies are boomeranging on those who initiated them. It is the climate in which the thought of a Franklin Delano Roosevelt, steeled and sharpened, will again rise triumphant.

Great Britain, corrupted and corroded by centuries of international swindling, bungles along at the bidding of her master across the Atlantic. Her empire dwindles, and sometimes a morsel, here and there, is digested by the senior partner in "Imperialism Limited." The theme of democracy at home and brutal autocracy abroad no longer inspires. The British people must return to their island home. Then they will learn to live on soil that is their own.

For France, the transformation has already begun. Today, in Africa, we are witnessing her last frenzied attempts to retain the trappings of a "big power." But the working people of that gifted land now realize that these trappings are but chains holding back the fulfillment of many dreams. The cobwebs are being removed. A new, strong voice is heard proclaiming the path to real and lasting greatness.

Germany and Japan, conserving the industrial strength of giants, have healed the wounds caused by their costly military ventures. Their domestic problems are many, but the solutions lie within their grasp. Significantly, these arsenals of the West and the East now depend for their progress on peace. Their future is not clouded by stratagems of empire, only by the logic of international tension and foreign intervention.

China, now risen again, is a great source of hope. These ancient people have battled against immense odds and now they work with a single resolve to turn a vast country into a modern, industrialized nation. By 1962, they will have outstripped the rest of Asia in economic development. They are able to do so, for they have found the weapons to triumph over man-made tragedy and disaster. No obstacles, no errors, can halt their advance.

Even more decisive will be the advance of the Soviet peoples—that is, when they have purged their society of the evils of Stalinist practice. This practice has distorted their life and the life of those allied to them in Eastern Europe. It will take time and courage to overcome the distortions. The task is immense; the trials, too.

Free India, born in this crucial period of transition and beginning a delayed journey into a future that is often the past of many advanced peoples, feels the impact of all this emotion and experience. There was a time when, on the banks of the Indus and its tributaries, she led the advance of civilization. Today, she learns, and while she emulates, creatively develops the experience of other peoples.

This process her prophets and visionaries interpret according to their respective attitudes. We must look for the most intelligent and consistent interpretation.

The transition which India is making is from the age of cow-dung to the age of the atom. Naturally, in the course of it, many values and traditions, concepts and practices, will experience a violent shaking. But, if experience is of any use, the transition will be made rapidly and without the degree of sacrifice which other nations had to undergo. True, this generation is condemned to hard labor, but at least it knows that the effort is linked to the creation of a society which will be very different from the familiar capitalist jungle. This is the dominant fact of our time, a fact that will condition attitudes and action.

Today, there may be serious linguistic tensions in the land. Tomorrow, there may be cleavages between the North and South. The day after, a series of international intrigues may be launched against the freedom and sovereignty of the land. Even more critical events are possible, but the confusion and uncertainty will pass as surely as the day follows night. We live in an age where science and scientific planning are steadily overcoming traditional anarchy in every field.

We have seen how the policies of India, both foreign and domestic, during the first decade of her independent nationhood have been molded by the facts of our era. The formative process will proceed with greater vigor and momentum as the field of economic and political controversy narrows. Such a narrowing is most visible in the former colonial world, where the philosophy of dog-eat-dog no longer makes sense and there is no large and established group to propagate it effectively. Moreover, should such an attempt be made, the technological advance of the socialist world and its ability to aid Asia and Africa will very soon destroy the possibility of such a philosophy becoming popular. India is striking out on a path which has been cleared by the processes of historical experience made available to her by her own past and the past of other lands.

India's progress to Socialism, the ordered and equitable way of life, can be peaceful and sustained. In many ways the foundations are being laid with each day that passes. On one side socialistic measures are being extended, and on the other a growing mass consolidation creates the sanction for their wider application and implementation. If a tiny minority attempts to place hindrances in the way, it can only succeed in causing a temporary dislocation. If this same minority seeks to make the dislocation permanent, it will realize to its cost that the determination of the people can not be tampered with for long.

In many respects India will also lead experiment into the mysteries of this new transition to socialism, for she is ahead of others who, like her, are also advancing in the same direction—Indonesia, Burma, Egypt, and such newly risen nations. It is certain that developments unique in political and economic science will take place. They will require profound and creative understanding, for they will be inexplicable in terms of the usual yardsticks. Those who doubt this should remember that the first years of freedom of countries like India, Indonesia, Burma, and Egypt have provided many such revealing examples.

India, in common with other lands, will feel the glow of new experience, the tensions of new problems, and the elation of finding new solutions. She does not have to go through the harrowing experiences of early industrial revolutions. She need not repeat the errors made by others. She can look forward to substantial, lightning advances, for she has begun her journey into the atomic age, made possible by the achievements of world science.

To realize what this means, one has only to consider how the discovery of fire, of the wheel, of a new metal, dramatically changed the story of mankind. How much more decisive will be the impact of atomic energy and its uses. For the first time, science offers us unlimited energy to transform the deserts, the mountains, and the oceans; it is energy which has lain hidden for centuries in tiny drops of water. The boundaries of endeavor are now vastly extended. Even the planets in space and beyond are within reach.

What all this means is too early to say. One conclusion is inescapable. It has become a crucial duty to guard and protect the possibilities of such development. Only scientific social organization can do this. How is it to be achieved without sacrificing the great achievements of mankind? This is the central task of political, economic, social, and cultural leadership.

History shows that as our forefathers gained control over mighty nature, they also, strangely enough, lost control over their own relations with one another. They became helpless victims of vast, overwhelming, and often intangible forces which dragged them into bloody conflicts, class struggles, racial and communal strife, and international war.

But history will also record the dominant fact of today—that the greatest effort of man, of all men, is the effort to save the world of the mid-twentieth century from atomic destruction.

Is it possible then that, learning from this living experience, he will succeed in mastering by reason, and hence peacefully, other forces in society which have hitherto kept him poor, hungry, and ignorant?

The answer lies with us. We can set our world on fire or build on it as we have never built before.

VINOBĀ BHĀVE: GANDHIAN DECENTRALIST

During his lifetime, Gāndhi emphasized that his twin principles of truth and nonviolence could solve a wide variety of human problems. Since the achievement of political independence, some of the social and economic implications of these principles are being worked out by a small group of devoted disciples. The leader of this growing band is the Mahārāshtrian brāhman Vinobā Bhāve—often referred to as Āchārya, "the teacher" or "preceptor."

Vinobā was born in 1895 and spent part of his youth in the pilgrimage town of Wai, at the headwaters of the Kistna River. His mother was a pious and generous woman; his father was a textile expert who wanted his sons to go to England for their higher education. Showing an early inclination toward an ascetic life in his late 'teens, Vinobā gave up his studies, burned his all-important school certificates, and set off for holy Banaras. Reading a newspaper version of a public lecture by Gāndhi (then fresh from South Africa) he felt so drawn by the latter's combined moral and political program that he joined his ashram at Sabarmati, near Ahmedabad.

Vinoba distinguished himself by his austerity and reliability, and Gāndhi sent him in 1921 to Wardha, in central India, to open a new ashram there. At the start of the 1940 civil disobedience movement, Gāndhi chose Vinobā to be the first satyāgrahi (practitioner of *satyā-graha* [1]) to court arrest. During the ensuing years of imprisonment, Vinobā, already a master of Sanskrit, set himself to learning Arabic and the four Dravidian languages of South India. After Gāndhi's assassination, Vinobā was generally looked to as the Mahātmā's heir and successor in the realm of nonviolent theory and practice.

It was in 1951, while walking through the disturbed areas of Hyderabad State, that Vinobā hit upon an alternative to the terrorizing and looting of wealthy landlords which Communist leaders were inciting in this part of India. Placing the emphasis on voluntary donations, he begged land from those who had more than they needed in order to give it to those who had none. His new method of distributing wealth had an immediate practical appeal to the embattled large landholders of Hyderabad. Those in the many other provinces which he has since toured on foot have also responded on ethical and religious grounds. By April 1957 over four million acres—including 2,500 villages—had been donated to the *bhūdān* (land-gift) movement. Few donations have been made since that date, and in 1963 three fifths of the usable land remained undistributed.

The philosophy behind the *bhūdān* mission is essentially that of Gāndhi, for Vinobā, like his guru before him, seeks a society ruled by love instead of coercion, and envisions an India composed of a network of self-sufficient village communities. Although agreeing with the Communists in desiring the ultimate "withering away" of the state, his program of radical decentralization contrasts sharply with their clear intention to centralize both economic and political power in the hands of a single, monolithic party.

[1] See p. 249.

VINOBĀ BHĀVE

Communism and Sarvodaya

The word *sarvodaya*—"the welfare of all"— was coined by Gāndhi to denote the full range of his attempts at social and rural uplift. In a speech to Gandhian workers in Kerala in 1957, Vinobā compared the aims and methods of *sarvodaya* with those of Communism and found them in substantial agreement. These remarks, which show Vinobā's indifference to parliamentary government, as well as his waving aside of all differences with the Communists except their espousal of violent means, have since caused no little consternation among the advocates of parliamentary democracy in India.

[From "Acharya Vinoba Bhave, Concluding Address," *A.I.C.C. Economic Review,* May 25, 1957, pp. 31–32]

Many people feel that the Communists are a destructive force. No doubt we have differences of opinion on many points. Communism by itself is not destructive. By itself Communism is an ideology worth consideration. The Communist ideology has something in it which was not in the world before it. I do not want to go into details. I have written a brief introduction on Communism. In that I have called Marx a *Mahamuni* (great sage). By reading the works of *Mahamuni* Marx, innumerable people in the world have changed their views. What is, however, amazing is the fact that even when the heart of the Communists has been converted by Marx, they do not themselves believe in change of heart. It is clear that we differ from them. I told them that "My friends, you yourselves are an example of change of heart. Then how can you say that change of heart is not possible?" So far as the Communists' objective is concerned, I regard it as a good thing. The main point is how that objective is to be achieved.

No Communist, in the final analysis, believes that man is not essentially good. They accept that after a certain stage, the State will disappear. I say that a person who has this conviction undoubtedly entertains in himself a faith in human nature. In the absence of such faith, nobody can believe that State will finally wither away.

Some people say that in *Satya Yuga* [the golden age] the State was not necessary and there really was no State at that time. There are others who say that there never was a *Satya Yuga* in human history but it will come at some subsequent date. So those who believe that there was a *Satya Yuga* are *Puranavadis* (who believe in *Puranas*). Those who believe that *Satya*

Yuga will come at a later stage are the Communists. And so these *Purana-vadis* and Communists are both *Satya Yugavadis.*[1] One says that there had been a *Satya Yuga* and the other says that a *Satya Yuga* will come. What do we say? We say that neither the past nor the future is in our hands. We have only the present in our hands and we want to bring *Satya Yuga* in the present. That is the only difference. The *Puranist* is a past-*Satya-Yugavadi* and the Communist is a future *Satya-Yugavadi.* But the Sarvodayite is a present *Satya Yugakari.*[2] Please note that I have not used the word *Vadi* but *Kari.* Now for us both these can have sympathy. Many Jan Sangh people met me and said: "Why do you talk of *Ahimsa* in this *Kali yuga;* you cannot practice *Ahimsa* work in *Kaliyuga.*" These *Puranists* believe that nonviolence obtained in *Satya Yuga* and they believe that it cannot work today. So they oppose it.

Communists also oppose it sometimes and say that we are Utopians. They say that today, if it is necessary, we should be prepared to take to violence, but ultimately, of course, we will have nonviolence. In other words, for the ultimate establishment of nonviolence, they want that today we must have the courage to take to violence. But I believe that today if the heart is bent upon violence and if after this you expect that nonviolence will appear at a certain stage in the future, the possibilities are that it will never come. These are some of the basic differences. There are, however, no differences in so far as the conception of *Satya Yuga* is concerned. There are hardly any differences about the concept of an ideal society. I do not want to go into minute details. The picture of heaven which the *Puranists* present before us and the dream of heaven which the Communists place are hardly different. And we ask the *Puranists:* "Your picture of heaven is undoubtedly attractive, but will you tell us—which is the ladder for ascending to that place?" We also ask the Communists: "Your dream of heaven also appeals to us, but which is the ladder for reaching there?" The Communists reply that today we will have to be prepared for the fullest violence. And so, in effect, one says that we will achieve heaven after our death and the other says that we will achieve it after killing others. Both these concepts become difficult to digest.

Now they also find difficulty with us. They say that you give very good sermons, but then are you the only ones who have sermonised like this? There have been innumerable saints and you have read all their works and

[1] Believers in golden age-ism.   [2] One who realizes the golden age in practice.

you repeat the same things. But can you hope to succeed where Christ and Buddha failed to succeed? Is there any dearth of teaching regarding non-violence in the Bible? I have heard that the Bible has been translated into 1,000 languages of the world, and at present it is being translated into many other languages. And when soldiers die in the battle field, they have a Bible in the pocket. Nevertheless, violence continues. These followers of the Bible take the name of God, read the Bible every Sunday and forget it for the remaining six days of the week? And so they ask us: what special thing can be achieved through these sermons? "Do you really believe that we can bring about a transformation through such sermons? If you do this well and good. But we do not have faith in it."

Thus, in effect, their difficulty with regard to us is that even though they like our idea, they cannot accept it. But why should we enter into controversies? We have to understand that if we sincerely believe that our ideas have in themselves the seeds for creating a new power in the world, then we have actually to create that power. When without any previous knowledge I had the great experience at the village of Pochampalli [3] for the whole night I meditated on the event. I wondered whether it had the hand of God behind it. Now along with my faith in God, I also have a little faith in mathematics. I made a rapid calculation. I understood that the problem will be solved only when we can get 5 crore acres of land as donation. But then this huge figure created doubts and fears in my mind. It appeared almost impossible to believe that we will get 5 crore acres of land, and so when I became doubtful I thought of the Communists. They were also doing some work in that area. And then I thought that if I cannot believe that we shall get enough land through love and persuasion, then there is no alternative for me but to have faith in the Communist ideology. If this work of nonviolence and Sarvodaya has no effect, then you will have to take to Communism. Such is the nearness between the two ideologies. I thought that the last two points in a circle are nearest to each other. And this nearness begins where the circle ends. In other words, that which is the farthest is the nearest. Communism believes in violence but there can be no doubt that it is generated by compassion. This is a strange paradox. There is inspiration from compassion but at the same time there is faith in violence. . . .

[3] The first voluntary gift of land for the landless was made in Hyderabad on April 18, 1951.

What do we find today? We see that some people who are always talking of peace in actual effect believe in *status quo*. They are afraid of a change in human society. As against this, people who want a social revolution do not want to confine themselves within the four walls of *Ahimsa*. They actually do not believe either in violence or in nonviolence. They are in a sense compassionate, and so the contradiction visible in a compassionate people taking to violence is nothing new and is not surprising. This contradiction has been there. But then they say where do you find a logic in life? Life is full of contradictions. Which place is there where contradiction is not to be seen? And so they say for once let us attack this contradiction, and keep aside your nonviolence for a time and accept violence. They say violence is after all as old as the world and has been coming down to us from ancient times, but, of course, ultimately we will have to bring about nonviolence.

In other words, they say that after one big spate of violence, we will establish nonviolence which will continue to the very end. And so their advice is that [you should] keep faith in nonviolence but have some weapons in your hands. And they ask: Have you no compassion for the poor? The poor are being crushed and oppressed and for their redemption get ready to commit some violence. If you do not agree to this violence, you in effect become incompetent. We have to answer this objection. It is said that those who stand for peace actually maintain the *status quo,* and the revolutionaries take to violence. But what are we? We are revolutionaries but we work peacefully. On us lies the responsibility to show to the world that any problem of this world can be solved through peace. I want to lay down before this gathering its responsibilities. The experience of the last six years has been the development of a great hope that we will be able to bring about a peaceful revolution. Thus, innumerable people who never believed that we can have a peaceful revolution have now developed a faith in these possibilities. I regard it as our great success which we never anticipated.

Renunciation As a Force for Social Good

The ancient ideal of the renunciation of worldly goods and concerns has found a new purposefulness in Vinobā's program. In addition to the giving of land to the landless, he has requested the giving of one-sixth of one's property and wealth for use by the community (*sampattidān*) and finally the giving of one's entire life for the service of the poor (*jīvandān*).

[From Ramabhai, *Vinoba and His Mission,* pp. 181, 182, 184]

We consider stealing to be a crime, but connive at those who encourage this antisocial activity by amassing heaps of money. In a story in a[n] Upanishad a king says: "In my kingdom, there is neither a thief nor a miser." As we know it is the miser who gives rise to the thief. We condemn the thieves to rot in the prisonhouse, but let their creators roam about in complete freedom. They even occupy seats of honor and respectability in the society. Is this justice? . . .

The highly expensive administrative and other departments of the government are known as "services." And there are services galore: Civil Service, Medical Service, Educational Service. The officials of the Civil Service are paid four figure salaries [in rupees per month], while their masters, the poor of the country, whom they profess to serve have to live on a pittance of annas eight [one-half rupee] a day. It is a tragic paradox that those who earn laks [hundreds of thousands] are called servants, while those who produce food for the nation are regarded as self-seekers working merely to feather their own nest. . . .

It is in order to put an end to this hypocrisy that I have put forward the idea of land being the common property of all. All that we have, our land and property and intelligence—everything has to be an offering to the society. . . .

Today he who earns money does also earn worry. Though he may make money, he loses something more precious than money, namely, the love of his fellow-men, the love of friends and neighbors. That is why even the moneyed are unhappy in the existing society. Both the rich and the poor are unhappy. The remedy is to change the order and place it on the secure basis of nonpossession. . . .

There is one thing which we will demonstrate through *Sampattidan*: that nonpossession is a force for social good. We have long known that nonpossession brings about individual purification. We have to realize that it can also serve as a powerful means of social wellbeing. We have to prove that it is not only spiritually efficacious but it can help us in constructing [a] better and richer worldly life. The Gandhi Memorial Fund collected ten crore rupees. But not even [a] hundred crores will suffice for all we want to do. The need of the hour is to mobilize all our wealth in every form and press it into the service of the society. The *Sampattidan* way will turn every house into a bank on which the society can draw freely for all its wants. And because what is offered will be used locally, it will make a very easily workable plan. It will directly lead to the building up of the collective strength of the people. It will unite them with one another and release tremendous energy for constructive effort. We know that [the] practice[s] of equality and renunciation are good, but we have to look at them afresh and see them as forces for promoting social welfare.

INDEX

Abū Tāleb Khān, 8-13, 188
Ahimsā, see Nonviolence
Alīgarh, 195, 217, 289
Al-jihād fī-'l-Islām: Holy War in Islam (Maudoodī), 300
Allahabad, 211, 341
All-India Liberal Federation, 123
All-India Muslim Conference, 215, 220n
All-India Muslim League, 196, 199, 211, 225, 276
Amīr Alī, 196
Ānandamaṭh: The Abbey of Bliss (Bankim), 157-65
Ārya Samāj (Society of the Aryas), 77, 196, 219
Asiatic Society (formerly Asiatick Society), 38
Assam, 196
Aurobindo, see Ghose, Aurobindo
Autobiography, An (Gāndhi), 271-72
Autobiography (Debendranāth) Tagore, 53-63
Azād Hind (Free India) provisional government of, 340-41

Banaras (Varanasi), 19
Bande Mātaram, 173, 217
Banerjea, Surendranāth, 110, 121-28
Banerjee, Kālī Chāran, 180
Baroda, 173, 217
Bengal, literature of, 233; influence in India, 121, 128, 155, 176-77; partition of, 154, 156, 173, 196; birthplace of Tagore, 230
Bepin Chandra Pāl, 181
Besant, Annie, 52
Bhagavad Gītā (Song of the Lord), renewed interest in, 51; Tilak's commentary on, 166-67, 171-72

Bhāve, Vinoba, 372 ff.
Bhūdan (Bhoodan, land-gift) movement, 326, 373, 377-79
Bombay, 128, 227, 280
Bose, Subhās Chandra, 335-41
Boycott, use of, 154, 175; see also Passive resistance
Brahmabāndhab Upādhyāy, 180-86
Brahmanism, 19
Brāhmo Samāj (Society of God), 20, 51, 57-59, 63-65, 181, 230
British East India Company, 1, 20, 32, 36

Calcutta, 2, 13, 19, 85, 128, 155, 180-81
Capitalism, 345-48, 358, 364; see also West, the
Castes: Ānanda Ranga Pillai on, 6-7; Keshub Chunder Sen on, 74-75; Vivekānanda on, 97-98; Rānade on, 135-36; Christianity and, 183; R. Tagore on, 233; see also Specific Castes, e.g., Brāhmanism
Catholicism, 180-84; see also Christianity
Chastity, Gāndhi on, 263-64
Chatterjee, Bankim Chandra, 155-65
Chaudhari Rahmat Alī, 275
Child marriage, 76, 82, 129, 136
China: Communist, 364, 365, 369-70
Chitpavin brāhman caste, 129
Christianity: influence on Muslim ideas, 1-2; Derozio's views of the West as convert to, 13-14; Rāmmohun Roy and, 20-28; efforts to check advance of, 51-52; Indianization of, 63-75; Dayānanda's debate on, 79-81, 82; Rāmakrishna on, 90; Brahmabandhab on Hinduism's contributions to, 182-83; Iqbāl on, 212; influence on Gāndhi, 248-49
Civil disobedience movement, 220, 249, 281, 373

[381]

Indian National Social Conference, 129-30
International relations, Nehru on, 352-53
Iqbāl, Muhammad, 197-216
Islam, 187-229; importance of study of history in, 205-6; attitude toward the West as expressed by Abū Tāleb, 8-13; influence of English education on, 36-38; Dayānanda Saraswati's debate on, 79-81; revival in, 187-229; see also Hindu-Muslim relations; Muslim; Pakistan
Islamic Association (Jamāat-i-Islāmī), 301
Islamic State, basic principles of, 190, 275, 309-12; see also Pakistan

Jamāat-i-Islāmī (Islamic Association), 301
Jana Gana Mana: The Mind of the Multitude of the People (Tagore), 235-36
Jan Sangh (People's League), 328
Jinnāh, Muhammad Alī, 199, 217, 272, 279-88
Jivandān, 378-79
Jones, Sir Willliam, 38-40

Keśari: The Lion (periodical), 165-66
Khilāfat movements, 216-29, 281, 312
Kumarappa, J. C., 366-68

Languages in India, 226-29
Liāquat Alī Khān, 289-300
Literature: Jones on oriental, 38-40; novels of B. C. Chatterjee, 155-56

Macauley, Thomas Babington, 36, 44-49, 110
Mahārāshtra, 129, 142, 165
Mahratta (periodical), 165-66
Maratha-Kunbi castes, 129
Marriage: European, 82; see also Child Marriage
Materialism, 11-13, 355-61
Maudoodī, Syed Abū'l-A'lā, 300-9
Moderates, 108-52, 167
Montagu, Edwin S., 280-81
Mughals, 1-2, 3, 108
Muhammad Alī, 216-29
Muhammad ibn Asad Jalāl ud-dīn al Dawwānī, 197
Muhammad Iqbāl, 197-216
Muslim League, 154, 217, 280-90 *passim*
Muslims, separate state for, 195-96, 211-16; see also Hindu-Muslim relations; Islam; Pakistan

Mutiny of 1857, 109, 165, 190
Mysteries of Selflessness (Iqbāl), 203-6
Mystical quietism, 197-98, 200, 202
Mysticism, Muslim, 208-9

Naoroji, Dādābhāi, 110, 111-21, 279, 280
Narendranāth Bhattāchārya (Mānabendra Nāth Roy), 354-63
Natal Indian Congress, 248
National Communism, 363-72
Nationalism, 18, 35, 36; Vivekānanda's contribution to, 100; Moderates and, 108-152, 167; Dādābhāi as architect of, 111-21; Extremists and, 153-86; Muslim, 188-95, 214; Iqbāl on, 208-9; Hindu, 214, 326-35; linguistic, 226-29; script and, 228-29; R. Tagore on, 234-38; Jinnāh's attitude toward, 282; Bose and, 337; Nehru on, 346; M. N. Roy on, 355-56
National Socialism, 326, 335-41
Nehru, Jawaharlāl, 336, 341-53, 365
Nehru, Motilāl, 220*n*, 336, 341-42
Newspapers, 19, 32-34
Noncooperation, 219, 270, 281, 312, 336, 342
Nonviolence: Muslims and, 219; Gāndhi and, 247, 249-51, 271; Bhāve on, 375-77; see also Passive resistance

Olcott, Colonel, 51-52

Pacifist anarchism, 248
Pakistan, 275-324; Iqbāl as spiritual founder of, 197-200; Jinnāh's campaign for, 217; derivation of word, 275; founding and future of, 275-324; Islam and, 289; Liāquat and, 290-300; constitution of, 309-17; see also Islamic State
Pan-Islamism, 203
Parsis ("Persians"), 112
Passive resistance, 174-76, 219, 251, 259-65, 337-38; see also Nonviolence
Patriotism, 214, 221-26; see also Nationalism
Pilgrimages, 325
Pillai, Ānanda Ranga, 3-8
Politics: and religion, 153-86; in Modern India, 325 ff.; see also Government; Nationalism
Prārthanā Samāj, 129
Precepts of Jesus, The (Rāmmohun Roy), 23-25
Predestination, doctrine of, 7

[382]